PERSON PERCEPTION AND STEREOTYPING

Person Perception and Stereotyping

ROBERT A. STEWART
GRAHAM E. POWELL
S. JANE CHETWYND
*Institute of Psychiatry,
University of London*

with a foreword by
PROFESSOR HANS J. EYSENCK

SAXON HOUSE

Published by Saxon House
Teakfield Limited,
Westmead, Farnborough, Hants., England.

British Library Cataloguing in Publication Data

Stewart, R A
Person perception and stereotyping.
1. Social perception 2. Stereotype (Psychology)
I. Title II. Powell, G E III. Chetwynd, S J
153.7'5 HM291

ISBN 0 566 00072 5

Typeset by Inforum Ltd., Portsmouth, Hants.
Printed in Great Britain by Biddles Ltd., Guildford, Surrey

Contents

Foreword

William James said once that habit is the flywheel that keeps society going; in the same way stereotypes may be said to keep our thinking going. No doubt we would like to think of ourselves as rational, reasoning human beings, examining every problem in terms of its cognitive content and acting accordingly, but this picture of unbiased, unprejudiced *homo sapiens* is unfortunately (or fortunately!) quite wrong. We all develop habits of thinking, called stereotypes, and approach questions and problems in terms of these "thought habits"; indeed, life could hardly go on if we had to take thought anew each time we were presented with a problem. Stereotyping has had a bad name in psychology, but it may be doubted if it deserves this bad name. Stereotyping is undesirable where it prevents necessary thought or change, but it is essential in much of our thinking as the flywheel that keeps us on an even keel.

This is the first book devoted to the experimental and theoretical examination of the concept. Wisely, the authors have chosen to look at stereotypes outside the usual field of racial or national prejudices; there are too many complications and biasing factors in this field to make experimentation easy. Instead, they have chosen to work with concepts related to body shape and physical attractiveness — issues much nearer to most people's interest, and much less coloured by ideological and political overtones. Even so, there are many problems of design and analysis, and these have been squarely faced, and appropriate decisions made which it would be difficult to fault. Many different studies and analyses are discussed in this book, all undertaken from a particular theoretical point of view; it may be said with certainty that the results will form the basis of much further work in this field.

Among the interesting features of the work reported is the fact that some of the studies were carried out in the U.S.A., others in the U.K. The possibility of looking at the results from a cross-cultural point of view is an exciting one, and again it is to be hoped that many other investigators will follow the authors of this book in undertaking such cross-cultural work. How, one wonders, would Indian or Chinese subjects react to the stimuli here presented, i.e. outline drawings of fat, thin and average women?

Among the interesting sidelines pursued by the authors are studies in stereotyping in children, and the relationship between stereotyping and personality. Both have given results of importance, and deserve to be followed up; hitherto children have been somewhat neglected in this type of work, as has the exciting topic of development over the years of stereotyped responses, and personality, although obviously of importance in the process of stereotyping, has also been rather neglected. Like most empirical studies, this one raises more problems and questions than it answers, but it does provide a clear methodology which is superior to that employed in many earlier studies, and which can be easily followed by future workers.

Altogether, this book presents us with a rather novel look at problems that have been with us for a long time; the extensive historical introduction enumerates many studies that have been done in this field. Combing experimental rigour with novelty, it is a welcome new arrival on the scene, and can as such be safely recommended to readers interested in individual differences, and their measurement, in personality, in concept formation, and in mental normality and abnormality.

Professor Hans J. Eysenck, Ph.D., D. Sc.
Institute of Psychiatry, University of London.
26th January, 1979.

1 Stereotyping, Person Perception and Cognition

Stereotyping is probably one of the most important, and at the same time, most abused concepts in the whole of psychology. Stereotyping is important because it is considered to be one of the main avenues for the expression of social and cultural attitudes, i.e. the products of socialisation. In a somewhat inconsistent manner, the abuse arises because none has seen fit to attempt a rigorous definition of the concept since it was first popularised by Lippman in 1922, allowing it to be employed in the most cavalier of fashions. Consequently, it is important at the outset to consider just what is a proper or at least working definition of stereotyping.

In approaching the problem of definition, it seems that few if any researchers have attempted to formulate a rigorous construct, possibly because the meaning of the term seems to be so simple and self evident. However, as we shall see below, the notion of stereotyping is neither simple nor self evident, and the assumption that it is (as manifested in the 'commonplace' definitions) has resulted in serious errors and logical inconsistencies. Consequently, we will contrast the traditional or commonplace definitions of stereotyping with that which we have derived in the course of carrying out our series of studies.

By way of background, this present work is a direct outgrowth of our involvement in several earlier studies (e.g. Kiker & Miller, 1967; Miller & Stewart, 1968) which indicated that a thorough and careful analysis of the data arising from stereotyping might yield results more meaningful and informative than had been hitherto anticipated. In particular, the early work of Miller and his colleagues (e.g. Miller, 1967, 1969; Miller et al., 1968) suggested that stereotyping studies are pertinent to the issues of personality, sex differences, self theory, social development and psychopathology, to mention only some of the more important possibilities. Accordingly, we have carried out five more or less independent investigations — three involving adult subjects and two based on adolescents — which have been analysed in detail and form the main part of the present book. We believe that the results from these studies fully bear out our expectations concerning the importance of stereotyping — that it is a psychological process of unique importance and a research technique of considerable scope and power.

Having said this, we can return to the more immediate problem of finding an adequate definition.

1.1. Definitions of stereotyping

1.1.1. The commonplace or traditional view of stereotyping

Following the publication of Lippman's (1922) book, *Public Opinion,* and the early studies of Katz & Braly (e.g. 1933), it has been customary to treat stereotyping as an atavistic mode of perception which is largely erroneous and unadaptive. Moreover, it has often been asserted that stereotyping is a characteristic of poor social and psychological adjustment (e.g. Perlmutter, 1956; Siegel, 1954). With connotations such as these, it is not surprising that the phenomenon of stereotyping has not been afforded the interest and detailed consideration which are required to get beyond its more superficial aspects.

We can now look at the particulars upon which this impression is based, and the simplistic definitions of stereotyping which it has given rise to. From the traditional vantage point (as discussed by Cauthen, Robinson & Krauss, 1971), stereotyping is conceived to be a form of categorising behaviour — in which a single characteristic or label serves to elicit a set of expectations or attributions which are (1) too simple to describe accurately the class of person in question (or any of its members) and, at the same time, are (2) too broadly generalised to individuals to have more than occasional validity. Additionally, it is sometimes assumed that stereotypes are (3) particularly rigid and resistant to change.

In such a context, the consensual endorsement of adjectives from a checklist has usually been taken as a straightforward method of uncovering and defining social or cultural stereotypes. This somewhat limited and negativistic conception of stereotyping, derived mainly from research concerned with ethnic stereotyping and prejudice, is discussed at length in the excellent review article by Cauthen et al. (1971).

1.1.2. Critique of the traditional conception of stereotyping

In spite of the quantity of research encouraged by the traditional view of stereotyping, there is now accumulating evidence which shows that this earlier conception is unjustifiably simple, thus masking the true complexity and importance of the process. In other words, stereotyping is not the simple 'logical error' that it was thought to be. Below, we shall comment briefly upon some of the considerations which have helped to maintain this limited view of stereotyping.

Testing procedures. In line with the belief that stereotyping is simple, many investigators have relied heavily upon simple testing procedures, i.e. using adjective checklists and simple ethnic or racial labels. As early as 1948, Eysenck & Crown had pointed out that this type of procedure was wholly inadequate, sometimes forcing or encouraging subjects to make responses which they would not otherwise make. Later studies (e.g. Aboud & Taylor, 1971; Bayton, McAlister & Hamer, 1956; La Gaipa, 1971; Rokeach, 1961; Rokeach, Smith & Evans, 1960; Triandis & Davis, 1965) have shown that the social class, educational attainment, and social role which are ascribed to a target do a great deal to modify or even obliterate any racial stereotype, indicating that judgements based on race in isolation are unrealistic. Indeed, Jenkins (1971), coming closer to the concern of the present book, found that extremes of body build were much more potent in altering impressions and expectations than was race — that it was, in America, far more undesirable to be obese than black.

The unsuitability of ethnic and racial material. Recognising that the balance of data regarding stereotyping has been derived from studies concerned with racial and ethnic differences, we must consider whether this type of material is capable of providing a representative picture of stereotyping. Notwithstanding the excellent and inventive work of some investigators, such as Gardner and his colleagues (e.g. Gardner, Kirby & Finlay, 1973; Gardner, Taylor & Feenstra, 1970), we think that the outlook for a theory of stereotyping based primarily on this domain is distinctly unpromising.

In the first place, ethnic differences are among the most evocative sentiments which one could undertake to study, and from this standpoint are unusually resistant to change and rational consideration. Secondly, the material is often remote — with the subjects having little or no opportunity for firsthand experience with the class of target persons whom they are called upon to judge, such as Turkish or Russian nationals. In marked contrast, our own data show stereotyping to be unexpectedly well articulated, with small differences in body build or manner of dress creating quite large and systematic changes in impression.

The limitations of consensus as a test of stereotyping. In the majority of studies by others, the finding of consensual attributions by the subjects has been taken as the sole and sufficient criterion of stereotyping, conveying the misleading impression that consensus is an intrinsic feature of stereotyping. Taking a critical look at this position, Secord and Backman (1964, p. 70) have shown that there are classes of stereotypes which do not involve consensus — as when an individual holds a strongly cherished belief which is at variance with that of the reference group — but may none the less be of considerable importance (when held by a powerful politician, for example). Accordingly, Secord and Backman have suggested that one should be careful to distinguish between social stereotypes, which are evidenced by consensus, and personal stereotypes, which represent personalised beliefs of a more or less idiosyncratic nature. Taking Secord and Backman's point one step forward, it should be obvious that tests of stereotyping which rely on consensus cannot serve to document personal stereotyping, and must therefore present a biased or incomplete description of stereotyping and its consequences.

Irrespective of the fact that few, if any, other researchers have considered the clear distinction between social and personal stereotyping put forward by Secord and Backman, we have found it to be of the greatest importance, with personal stereotyping often being far more psychologically significant than social stereotyping. Indeed, when contrasted with personal stereotyping, measures of social stereotyping (i.e. of consensus) in many instances, yield totally false conclusions concerning the data at hand and their implications. Consequently, we devote the whole of Chapter 2 to a consideration of the distinction between social and personal stereotyping, and the methods for their objective measurement.

Having considered some of the more blatant shortcomings of the traditional conceptualisation of stereotyping, we can now attempt a formulation which will overcome some of these problems, and at the same time place stereotyping in its proper psychological and cognitive perspective.

1.2 Stereotyping in a contemporary context — a constructive redefinition

In view of Lippman's (1922) well-reasoned argument that stereotyping is a necessary requirement in cognition—because 'the real environment is altogether too big, too complex, and too fleeting for direct acquaintance' (p. 18) — it is remarkable just how few investigators have concerned themselved with the necessary, beneficial or adaptive aspects of stereotyping. To give some idea of the magnitude of this problem, Luce (1956; Berlyne, 1960) has suggested that the human ear or eye are capable of receiving, respectively, 10,000 and 4 million 'bits' of of information per second, but that the person (the central nervous system) is not capable of utilising more than about 50 'bits' of information per second. Hence well over 99 per cent of the information contained in the stimuli reaching the eye or ear does not enter directly into cognition. The practical side of this issue is well illustrated when one recalls the rather severe limitations associated with span of apprehension (Miller, 1956; Woodworth & Schlosberg, 1954, pp. 90-105) and the closely related problem of digit span (Doppelt & Wallace, 1955; Maher, 1957).

In the light of this material, we would, along with Lippman, stress that stereotyping is one of the processes which assists in reducing or editing sensory input into meaningful wholes. In this guise, it is possible to view stereotyping as a rough equivalent of the notion of perceptual schemata which has been developed and elaborated by Bartlett (1932) and others (e.g. Oldfield & Zangwill, 1943). This similarity is important because much of the interesting research and methodology which has arisen in the context of perceptual schemata (e.g. Frith, 1971, 1974a, b; Hess & Pick, 1974; Kagan, Henker, Hen-tov, Levine & Lewis, 1966; Kolers, 1968; Lewis, 1966; Neisser, 1967) has a direct relevance to stereotyping and the development of new research strategies in this area.

Environmental complexity is not, however, the only condition which occasions stereotyping for, as we have already seen, the notion of stereotyping has also been applied to circumstances where the stimulus input is relatively meagre, as in the case of ethnic labels or target persons which are defined in terms of body build. Consequently, stereotyping should not be viewed as a process restricted solely to identification and simplification, but in addition as one involving 'construction', where, for example, the attributions and expectations elicited go well beyond the information which is available from the stimulus itself. This constructive aspect is particularly evident when dealing with simple stimuli, but is probably no less important in the stereotyping of complex events and stimuli (Allport & Postman, 1958).

A third type of input condition might also be noted, for it can be suggested that stereotyping also occurs whenever the available information is ambiguous, incomplete, conflicting, equivocal or inconsistent in nature. Here, then, we have the start of an alternative basis for explaining the function of stereotyping, which places it in a much more central context than is usually attempted.

1.2.1 Stereotyping as a central process in cognition

While noting that the present position has been partly anticipated by others (e.g. Miller et al., 1968, p. 359), it seems in order to posit that stereotyping is an outgrowth of (or identical with) the human ability to formulate definite plans and expectations from information which is characterised by a moderate to high degree of uncertainty or unreliability. Irrespective of the complexities which enter into this process, which are well illustrated in various papers (e.g. Feather, 1967; Kagan, 1965; Sieber & Lanzetta, 1964, 1966), it is clear that it is involved in a very large percentage of behaviour, embracing both the trivial and the significant. Indeed, it is probably safe to say that virtually all behaviour originates from premises which to a greater or smaller extent are unreliable — Lippman alludes to these points, but tends to stress their potential for creating problems rather than their central position in facilitating behaviour.

Consistent with the present position, it is becoming increasingly clear that uncertainty and unpredictability result in states of marked disequilibrium and discomfort, which in turn alter both behaviour and perception (e.g. Ball & Vogler, 1971; Belanger & Sattler, 1967; Cohen, Stotland & Wolfe, 1955). These considerations are important because they demonstrate that there are dynamic factors which motivate persons towards closure and the resolution of ambiguity, indicating that stereotyping and related processes are active in nature rather than passive.

1.2.2 The diversity of stereotyping

Equating stereotyping with those cognitive processes responsible for resolving and mediating uncertainty raises some rather interesting theoretical possibilities, allowing us to entertain the notion that shape constancy, size constancy, and form perception are forms of stereotyping. This idea may not be so far fetched as it first appears, noting that Vernon (1955) has already suggested that the constancy phenomena are based on perceptual schemata, a concept which we feel is closely related to that of stereotyping.

Returning to the more immediate implications of stereotyping, it seems worthwhile to point out that this concept has been usefully applied to situations other than those involving the simple attribution of traits to target persons. First, there is clear but limited evidence (Allport & Postman,1958; Lippman, 1922, p. 83; Loftus & Palmer, 1974) that stereotyping is as influential in the interpretation and recall of events as it as in other more static instances. Allport & Postman (1958, pp. 63-4) have introduced the notion of the Embedding Process in explaining the alterations and additions which they encountered in recall, but an examination of this concept shows it to be very close to that of stereotyping, if not identical. Moreover, it is not unreasonable to suppose that the ability to stereotype events is a direct consequence of the ease with which observers can attribute typically human motives, characteristics and activities to animated geometric figures (Bassili, 1976; Heider & Simmel, 1944; Johansson, 1973; Michotte, 1950; Shor, 1957), which may represent the limiting case for this type of cognitive processing.

A second area — that of relationships between persons — also occasions a good deal of stereotyping, with the best documented evidence being perhaps that derived from studies of social schemata. In respect to the relationship between stereotyping and social schemata, Kuethe (1962a, p. 31) acknowledges that the 'Unit forming principles in social perception can be regarded as social schemas or response sets to the extent that they function to structure ambiguous situations involving human objects'. Since it is one of our main contentions that stereotyping serves primarily to reduce ambiguity in cognition, it is clear that Kuethe's conception of social schema and ours of stereotyping, while differing in degree of generality, are to be regarded as being more or less synonymous.

Turning briefly to some typical results, it has been shown that the 'relationships' between various classes of persons — such as superiors and subordinates, and men, women and children — are subject to stereotyping and display a significant degree of cultural conditioning (e.g. Kuethe, 1962a, b; Little, 1968). When, for example, confronted with sets of felt figures there is a marked tendency for the judges to place the 'child' closer to the female figure than to the male figure, or in other cases to construct opposite sexed pairings rather than like sexed pairings. Going beyond these initial findings, Little (1968) was able to demonstrate that the emotional tone of an encounter interacts with the characteristics with which the figures have been imbued, such as age, sex and status, in determining the resultant stereotype or schema. Many of the current and more important papers concerning schemata can be found in some of the more recent papers by Tolor (e.g. 1975).

As it stands, the observation by Little (1968) and others (e.g. Guardo & Meisels, 1971; Spinetta, Riger & Karon, 1974) — that stereotypes are capable of being systematically adjusted in accordance with the prevailing circumstances — is probably one of the most important single contributions of this literature to the understanding of stereotyping. The outstanding importance of these observations does, of course, stem from the fact that they contradict the notion that stereotypes are inherently rigid. It is worth noting that the factors which alter stereotypes can be either situational, such as the 'mood' which is assumed to be present (Little, 1968), or as a result of judges' own experiences (e.g. Spinetta et al, 1974), recent or otherwise (e.g. Miller et al., 1971).

Turning to a more delimited, but equally important area, several papers have indicated that stereotyping and stereotypes may exert a strong and pervasive influence on attitudes and beliefs concerning children (Faggot, 1973a, b), and in a more explicit manner, in beliefs about child rearing practices (Shoben, 1949, pp. 119-21; Zuckerman, Ribback, Monashkin & Norton, 1958). Since certain data (Powell & Stewart, 1978) show that some children find it particularly difficult to modify or divest themselves of attitudes and beliefs established in childhood, this would seem to be a class of stereotype which is of marked practical as well as theoretical significance.

Since it is not our intention to survey all the possible areas where stereotyping may be of interest, we will conclude this discussion by considering conceptual stereotypes. Conceptual stereotyping can be said to occur when two concepts which have markedly different implications are treated as being synonymous, with it being expected that one of the concepts will be grossly distorted by simplification. Our own data (see Section 5.8.1) show, for example, that male subjects tend to equate desirability as a Wife with maximal Physical Attractiveness ($r = 0.86$), indicating among other things that many of the more varied aspects of being a wife have been disregarded or displaced by the notion of attractiveness. Conceptual stereotyping is earmarked by various signs, such as large intercorrelations (say $\pm$ 0.7 or greater) between concepts which are not logically identical or by the finding of a solitary and exhaustively large factor loading for some particular concept. Examples of both will be found in some of the various studies which follow in the later chapters.

Futhermore, because of their abstract nature, conceptual stereotypes may not be so open to inspection and correction as are attributions to persons who differ in race or sex, which are open to more immediate confirmation or disconfirmation through social interaction. But, lest we be too quick to pass judgement, it is necessary to recognise that this may be a part of the mechanism which allows us to create an efficient coding of concepts, such as managing the 18,000 or so English terms which Allport and Odbert (1936; Guilford, 1959, pp. 92-3) thought to be necessary for describing persons in the course of everyday parlance.

Having illustrated the range and diversity of possible instances of stereotyping, it is hoped that this brief section will serve to establish an openmindedness towards stereotyping which will encourage others to seek out circumstances where they are operative but as yet unrecognised, in both their beneficial or desultory aspects.

1.2.3 Stereotyping as a basis for behaviour

It is not uncommon for investigators of widely differing viewpoints (e.g. Berlyne, 1960; Diamond, Balvin & Diamond, 1963; Luria, 1932) to agree that behavioural responses are, in most circumstances, fluid and emitted without signs of conflict — that behaviour, once initiated, tends to proceed freely to its goal. For example, Diamond et al. (1963), stress that the massive development of the inhibitory capacity of the central nervous system has arisen in part to ensure that responding will be integrated and reasonably free from disabling conflicts.

This aspect of motor behaviour and overt responding is important to the present discussion because it carries certain implications for the cognitive antecedents of behaviour, namely that the cognitive determinants which instigate and moderate behaviour must themselves be relatively few in number if conflict is to be avoided or kept within reasonable bounds.

We raise this largely hypothetical matter here, because it is in good agreement with the material on stereotyping and person perception which are to be presented in the sections and chapters which follow, with the agreement arising irrespective of whether we are considering our own data or those of others.

1.3 Person perception and stereotyping

Having established a conceptual framework for stereotyping (with operational definitions being taken up in Chapter 2), we can now turn our attention to the topic of person perception, and trace those portions of it which are relevant to the present discussion. It will be necessary, however, to retreat slightly — going back to the original aims and definitions of person perception research — in order to gain a clear perspective of the role of stereotyping in person perception.

1.3.1 The traditional view of person perception: origin and aspirations

While it is true to say that there have almost always been a few psychologists interested in studying the way in which persons come to learn about others and evaluate them (e.g. Adams, 1927; Newcomb,

1931; Thorndike, 1920), it is usually accepted that the speciality which we recognise as person perception really took form during the late 1940s and early 1950s, and was shaped by the *zeitgeist* of those particular times. Two of the more important or prominent issues of that period were 'insight orientated psychotherapies' and 'social adjustment,' so it is not perhaps surprising that many of the earlier person perception studies focused on insight and empathy (e.g. Dymond, 1949), clinical perceptiveness (e.g. Luft, 1950), the accuracy of the perception of others (e.g. Cline, 1955; Taft, 1955), and the role of this supposed accuracy in interpersonal behaviour (e.g. Gage, 1953).

It is obvious that the investigators assumed that social perception could be thought of as veridical in nature, and accordingly that this ability played a central role in both everday social interactions and psychotherapy. Based on this assumption, attempts were made to isolate the variable of accuracy in person perception and to understand how and why it varied between different individuals. Below, where some of the older definitions of person perception are considered, it will be seen how this largely untested assumption became central to the whole notion and subsequently led to a great deal of disenchantment when found to be either nonexistent or inaccessible to direct experimental investigation.

1.3.2 Knowing others — definitions of person perception based on the premise of 'total accessibility'

R. Tagiuri (1969, pp. 395-6), in a revision of his 1954 paper (Bruner & Tagiuri, 1954), defines person perception in the following way:

> Person perception refers to the processes by which man comes to know and to think about other persons, their characteristics, qualities, and inner states ... The observations or inferences we make are principally about intentions, attitudes, emotions, ideas, abilities, purposes, traits, thoughts, perceptions, memories — events that are inside the person and strictly psychological.

Three important features emerge from this definition. First, it makes the implicit assumption that observers really are capable of achieving some certain and significant (i.e. useful) degree of global or overall accuracy in their evaluations of others. Second, this definition does, by default, place a disproportional stress on the covert nature of what is involved in person perception. And third, it is implied that observers are capable of processing an appreciable quantity of potentially heterogeneous information — say intentions, memories and abilities, for example — in a constructive or synthetic manner, such that they become instrumental. Not only is this last point at odds with our consideration of limitations in information load (see Section 1.2) and potential for conflict (see Section 1.2.3), but it also seems to be an exaggerated estimate of what we can usefully know about others. In this context, it has been shown that excessive information can actually be deleterious to the accurate perception of others, especially if the information is inappropriately weighted by the judges (e.g. Cronbach, 1955; Taft, 1959, p. 348).

1.3.3 The rise and fall of the traditional view of person perception

For whatever complex of reasons, the amount of research devoted to person perception increased dramatically in the 1950s, and at first appeared to be making real and constructive progress (e.g. Baker & Block, 1957; Crandall & Bellugi, 1954; Dymond, 1948, 1949, 1950; Estes, 1938; Tagiuri & Petrullo, 1958). On the basis of such studies, there were numerous claims — of the finding of generalised accuracy, of systematic differences between the abilities of various persons, of specific personality traits affecting performance, of which traits were most easily discerned, and so on — with some investigators (i.e. Lindgren & Robinson, 1953) being sufficiently optimistic as to attempt to use the then current techniques for the purposes of occupational selection.

However, this optimism was short lived since there appeared at almost the same time a series of papers (e.g. Bender & Hastorf, 1950; Crow & Hammond, 1957; Hastorf & Bender, 1952; Lindgren & Robinson, 1953), which raised grave doubts concerning the veracity of the presumably confirmatory studies, noting that they were contaminated by a variety of response biases. But the most damning of the critical papers were those of Cronbach and Gage (Cronbach, 1955, 1958; Gage & Cronbach, 1955), which indicated that virtually all the work until that time was invalidated by various statistical artifacts as well as the more straightforward response biases.

According to some (namely Cook & Smith, 1974; Vernon, 1964) the net result of these papers was to cause an almost complete cessation of interest in this global, validity orientated approach to person perception. Unfortunate as this was, it nevertheless transpires that the response biases in question are of particular interest because they correspond with several of the more commonplace and useful instances of stereotyping and, as such, figure prominently in our own work.

Before closing this section it seems appropriate to point out that the traditional view of person perception was bound to fail, irrespective of the criticisms of Gage and Cronbach, simply because the aims and assumptions were too ambitious and, in the absence of reliable experimental data, relied too strongly on a theoretical foundation which had not, itself, been subjected to a critical enough examination. This is not to say, however, that the study of accuracy is futile — with, for example, several studies (Cook & Smith, 1974; Estes, 1938; Eysenck & Eysenck, 1963) showing that the trait of extraversion can be perceived accurately by others — but rather that the study of accuracy requires realistic reconsideration. Here, in contrast to the older view which assumed that the majority of traits and other details are ultimately palpable or knowable, we are suggesting that there is a relatively small set of traits which can (or need to be) judged accurately, and differ from other less salient traits because they have easily observable behavioural manifestations (as eye contact in extraversion (Mobbs, 1968), for example) and because they play a central role (i.e. functional or instrumental) in some of the more significant social processes. In respect to this problem, we believe that the present book goes some way towards pointing up certain of these more salient traits and by implication the circumstances within which they function.

1.3.4 Self stereotypes or assumed similarity in person perception

While the 'self stereotype' or assumed similarity was one of the first biases to be noted (Bender & Hastorf, 1950), it has often been treated in isolation and thereby confounded with social stereotyping, making it difficult to assess the true impact of this type of stereotype. As its name implies, this stereotype arises when subjects ascribe traits to others in the same manner as they would ascribe them to themselves, making the implicit assumption that others are to a large degree similar to themselves. Bender and Hastorf (1950) found, for example, that the correlations between Self and Others ranged between 0.71 and 0.55 in the absence of any evidence of a true similarity. In the case of children, Mintz (1956) found that assumed similarity resulted in correlations of 0.34 (for boys) and 0.68 (for girls) when estimating the age of a female target person (namely Peter Pan).

Besides the studies already mentioned, there are numerous other sources (e.g. Alfert, 1958; Bender & Hastorf, 1953; Cronbach, 1955; Halpern, 1955; Stelmachers & McHugh, 1964; Suchman, 1956; Tagiuri, Blake & Bruner, 1953) which show that the assumed similarity stereotype exerts a strong and pervasive influence upon the judgements of others. But, as mentioned above, it is difficult to estimate the true impact of this bias because it is, in most instances, totally confounded with cultural stereotypes — this being the tendency for persons to perceive both themselves and others as behaving in accord with cultural norms and expectations. And while the precise nature of this confounding — between self and social stereotypes — will be illustrated more clearly in the following section, which deals specifically with cultural stereotypes, it is worth noting that the tendency to use targets which are neutral (i.e. typical of the norm) may exaggerate the apparent influence of self stereotypes and encourage their confounding with cultural stereotypes at the same time.

1.3.5 Cultural/social stereotypes as a bias in person perception

Along with the self stereotype, the cultural norm or social stereotype was correctly identified at an early date (e.g. Bender & Hastorf, 1950, p. 559) as being one of the more serious biases in person perception, but did not receive appreciably systematic treatment until considerably later (e.g. Cronbach, 1955; Lindgren & Robinson, 1953). This particular bias implies that judges possess generalised expectations about how others are motivated, behave, feel, etc., and apply these norms or stereotypes indiscriminately when called upon to judge others. In other words, some judges implicitly adopt cultural norms when predicting the behaviour of others. Thus if there is a norm for, say, politeness, then many or most judges will attribute a corresponding degree of politeness to all but the most exceptional target persons.

In considering the degree of influence of social stereotypes, Lindgren and Robinson (1953, pp. 174-5) found, when examining Dymond's (1949, 1950) 'test of insight and empathy', that it made little difference whether the subjects' attributions were compared with individual target persons or a stereotypic criterion based on cultural norms, and concluded that the subjects were, in fact, employing cultural stereotypes irrespective of the availability of actual persons to serve as referents. Turning to a somewhat more general case, we have also found these cultural or social stereotypes in our own work, with agreement of subjects with a stereotypic criterion fairly frequently resulting in correlations ranging between 0.6 and 0.8 or even larger in some instances. From these examples it would appear that social stereotypes, as embodiments of cultural norms, are among the more potent determinants of attribution in person perception.

Coming back to the problem of confounding between self stereotypes and social stereotypes (i.e. normative attributions), it is easy to see that a spuriously high relationship between Self and Others could arise if both these entities were, in fact, being judged or stereotyped according to cultural norms — which is to say that the systematic variation in Self ratings is derived from the same source, i.e. norms, as that of the systematic variation in the judgement of Others. In this case, it would be inappropriate to suggest that Self was 'projected' on to Others, but rather that the same cultural stereotypes were 'projected' on to both Self and Others. While some instances (Lindgren and Robinson, 1953), where subjects and targets are all relatively homogeneous, indicate that this confounding is quite serious — in so far that one cannot easily distinguish between the relative influences of assumed similarity and cultural norms — it is evident from our own work (where the judges, targets and trait vocabulary all show a reasonable degree of heterogeneity) that the self stereotypes and the social stereotypes each make independent contributions to the process of atribution, and accordingly should be considered as distinct psychological entities.

1.3.6 Stereotyping as the central process and major determinant in social perception

Recognising the main sources of 'bias' in person perception, a number of different procedures have been developed to control these and eliminate or minimise their influence (see Cronbach, 1955; Crow & Hammond, 1957; Gage, Leavitt & Stone, 1956; Hatch, 1962; Sechrest & Jackson, 1961). In spite of these efforts, it nonetheless remains true that the variance accounted for by the stereotypic components in person perception have continued to be persistently and embarrassingly large as compared with that due to accuracy. Indeed, some studies (e.g. Gage et al., 1956; Haire & Grunes, 1950; Jerdee, 1961) have concluded that there is little evidence of any predictive accuracy remaining after the stereotypic biases have been removed or controlled for.

This somewhat surprising outcome has given rise to an alternative position, namely that accuracy is achieved only when judges employ their stereotypic response predispositions — such as social desirability, cultural norms which assume normality, and assumed similarity — and eschew the more detailed or individualised information (Gage, 1952; Hastorf, Bender & Weintraub, 1955; Little & Schneidman, 1959; Stelmachers & McHugh, 1964). The notion that stereotyping is the focal or central process in the perception of others has gained considerable impetus from a variety of investigations (Cronbach, 1955; Clark, 1965; Crow, 1957; Giedt, 1955; Haire & Grunes, 1950; Hathaway, 1956; Lee &

Tucker, 1962; Mash & McElwee, 1974; Sarbin, 1942; Slovic, 1966; Soskin, 1954; Taft, 1959; Wiggins, Hoffman & Taber, 1969), which have shown that judges either become less accurate with increasing information, or that they tend to disregard most of the potentially useful information, relying instead upon two or at most three of the items available from the mass at hand.

Notwithstanding the overwhelming bulk of this evidence, some of the methodological problems require comment. One can, for instance, question the wisdom of using a target's questionnaire responses as the criterion against which accuracy is evaluated (see Cook (1971) for a fuller discussion), the limited motivation and commitment of the participating judges (Bender & Hastorf, 1950, pp. 559-60), and lastly, the artificiality of the majority of procedures (e.g. Rodin, 1972). On the other hand, some of the studies (e.g. Sechrest & Jackson, 1961) have avoided or minimised many of these pitfalls, and still show accuracy to be relatively meagre except for that due to stereotyping. Consequently, it seems reasonable to conclude that the above studies, irrespective of their various shortcomings, indicate correctly that global accuracy does, indeed, depend primarily upon the operation of several different classes of stereotyping rather than some elusive form of 'personal sensitivity'. (The reader is reminded that this does not preclude the possibility of finding highly specific instances of accuracy, such as the ability to evaluate extraversion (Section 1.3.3), which do not depend upon gross stereotyping or crude response predispositions.)

A more serious shortcoming arises, however, from the way in which these studies have treated the concept of stereotyping. Considering that stereotyping was shown at a fairly early date to be the most important process in person perception, it seems extraordinary that most of the studies, with few exceptions (e.g. Alfert, 1958), concentrated their efforts on controlling or eliminating these influences, with little or no thought of taking up the investigation of stereotyping *per se*. This facile treatment of stereotyping, which was in all probability encouraged by its 'bad reputation', is a consequence of serious misconceptions on the part of the investigators. They treat the various stereotypes as though each represented only a single entity (or at best manifested itself in only two or three variations), and by implication suggest that stereotypes are fixed or rigid. In other words, the traditional view of stereotyping was transferred to the context of person perception with little or no modification. In the section which follows, we shall consider some alternative conceptions of the role of stereotyping in person perception, noting in advance that these lead to greater flexibility than had been anticipated in the preceding papers.

1.3.7 A model of person perception based on a multiplicity of stereotypes — apparent continuity through taxonomic sortings

While agreeing with their colleagues that person perception consists mainly of stereotyping, Sarbin, Taft & Bailey (1960; Taft, 1966) elaborated on this notion by suggesting that a certain degree of accuracy could be achieved through the use of 'taxonomic sortings' of persons into one or more of a large number of stereotypic categories. When the resulting categories are simple, broad and readily observable, this process clearly resembles traditional stereotyping, but when the categories are complex, narrow and covert, the process comes closer to or resembles that of insightful accuracy or empathy, while still being incontrovertibly based on stereotyping.

In essence, this point of view differs from its predecessors in two principal respects. First, it is assumed that there is a larger rather than smaller number of stereotypic categories available to the observers and judges, and second, that a target person can be a member of more than one of the available categories simultaneously. By these means it is possible for stereotyping to give the impression of flexibility and thus account adequately for those instances where differential accuracy or 'insight' were found to occur. It should be carefully noted, however, that the proposition put forward by Sarbin and his colleagues does not assume or suggest that the stereotypic categories are themselves flexible or adjustable, but rather that they give the appearance of flexibility through increased differentiation.

Irrespective of the theoretical advantages of this position — such as the simplicity of subsuming most of person perception under stereotyping — its application to the study of person perception has not greatly altered the type of results usually obtained, e.g. of relatively gross stereotyping accompanied by a small amount of so-called 'insight' or differential accuracy.

We have laid considerable stress upon this point of view because of its seemingly close affinity with the model of person perception and stereotyping which we favour. But as will be seen, there are some important differences between the position espoused by Sarbin et al. (1960) and that adopted by ourselves.

1.4 Person perception — a synthesis of complementary processes

Having looked at various facets of both stereotyping and person perception — and having seen the traditional conception of person perception virtually demolished towards the end of the late 1950s — we are now in a position to reconsider the whole question, and in light of later data from ourselves and others, to put forward some constructive suggestions. Accordingly, this section will begin with a reconsideration of accuracy in perceiving others and with some of the implications of this particular problem.

1.4.1 Accuracy: an empirical re-analysis stressing the need for limited but reliable 'knowledge of others'

In the course of this review it has become evident that the earlier conceptions of person perception — as exemplified by the definition appearing in Section 1.3.2 — have proved to be unsatisfactory for a variety of reasons. Among these, the main failing may well be the unwarranted assumption that valid inferences can be drawn about numerous aspects of others which are unobservable and only weakly, if ever, manifested intelligibly in overt behaviour. One may, for example, confuse level of intelligence with, say, verbal fluency and accent (Thorndike, 1920). Also, the amount of detailed information which an observer was expected to acquire about others — covering attitudes and memories as well as a variable number of traits and abilities — is totally unrealistic and in clear conflict with our earlier discussion of cognitive and sensory limitations. Indeed, it has been stressed at various points above that too much information may be more deleterious to the understanding of others than too little information, at least as assessed in the traditional manner.

One of the more serious consequences of this approach was to direct attention towards more high-level or abstract instances of performance, such as requiring predictions of the 'values' of target persons or the way in which they would endorse particular items in personality questionnaires, and away from more immediate aspects of the targets, such as requiring predictions of the 'values' of target persons or the way in which they would endorse particular items in personality clear evidence that these more mundane aspects of target persons can and are perceived accurately (or at least in the manner which the target wishes to convey) and, taken in conjunction with other information, such as age, sex and occupation, form a basis for social interaction. We will look briefly at some of these more palpable cues and their roles in accuracy and in the moderating of social interactions.

Physical attractiveness. There is accumulating evidence (discussed at length in Chapter 4) that a person's own level of physical attractiveness is accurately perceived by others, and in turn plays an important part in determining how these others will respond. To consider only two examples, it has been shown that attractiveness is instrumental in the selection of dating and marriage partners (e.g. Miller & Rivenbark, 1970; Murstein, 1972; Walster, Aronson, Abrahams & Rottman, 1966) and again, in moderating the evaluation of actual academic performance (e.g. Landy & Sigall, 1974; Lerner, 1965) and overall expectations of educational potential (e.g. Clifford & Walster, 1973).

Occupation. While this quality cannot always be immediately ascertained, it can sometimes be inferred roughly from dress — as say working class versus professional — and frequently arises during conversation. Moreover, occupation is almost always called for on forms and applications, irrespective of their purpose. Many studies (e.g. Sarbin & Berdie, 1940) indicate that occupation, whether known or inferred, provides a good deal of information about those persons who pursue them, i.e. about their values, abilities, etc.

With regard to evaluation, it has long been known that occupations differ widely in prestige or social desirability (e.g. NORC, 1947; Sharma & Sinha, 1968) and create differing stereotypes concerning those who engage in them (e.g. Braun, 1962; Grunes, 1957). On the other hand, it is important to recognise that the stereotypes attributed to particular occupations may alter systematically according to the perspectives of the judges — whether pro-worker, pro-management, etc. Outside this personal subjectivity, it remains to be determined how social desirability, specific job requirements (e.g. strength versus intelligence) and stereotypes are combined in arriving at impressions and evaluations.

Normality and deviancy. Irrespective of the fact that some psychiatric patients do, with certain exceptions (Klett, 1957; Klett & Tamkin, 1957), fill in personality questionnaires according to a 'normality stereotype', there are other circumstances which show how some aspects of deviancy are registered by others. In the case of more seriously disturbed persons, close acquaintances (Kennard, 1974) and psychiatrists (Wahler, 1958) are both able to recognise certain characteristics, such as lowered self-esteem, inability to communicate adequately, being frightening to others, etc., which set the patients apart from nonpatients. Noting that both these studies could be confounded by 'psychiatric stereotypes', it is probably more useful to consider how persons with elevated psychiatric scales on the MMPI (but who are normal and functional in all other senses) are perceived by others who have no knowledge of their test scores. Under these conditions, Black (1956a, pp. 165-7) found that subjects with marked *Sc* scores (indicative of schizophrenia or a schizoid personality) were rated as more Apathetic and Worldly than low scorers by a group of persons who had lived with the subjects over a long period of time.

Turning to delinquency, there is some limited evidence (Powell, 1977; West & Farrington, 1973, pp. 98-108) that teachers and peers are able to predict in advance which children and adolescents will later become either delinquents or behaviour problems. In what may be a partial explanation, Cowie, Cowie & Slater (1968, p.64) have pointed out that delinquent girls (and men — see Kurtzberg et al, 1968) suffer from a number of physical stigmata, including dysplastic physiques, extremes of weight and evidence of childhood neglect. Nor should one overlook the significance of self-induced stigmata such as tattooing (Cowie et al., 1968; Measey, 1972; Taylor, 1968), as a useful sign for predicting delinquency. This is especially true among girls, with Taylor finding that among the 67 girls he examined, those with the most tattoos were the most disturbed.

Because of the varied nature of these studies, it is not entirely clear just how the observers arrive at their valid perceptions of deviancy and delinquency, except perhaps in the case of tattooing. Our own work, however, indicates that manner of dress is, at least for adolescents, one of the more potent cues for discriminating between conforming persons and those who are less constrained or, indeed, delinquent.

Extraversion. We have already noted that extraversion is a trait which can be accurately perceived (Cook & Smith, 1974; Estes, 1938; Eysenck & Eysenck, 1963), and suggested that some nonverbal cues, such as eye contact (Mobbs, 1968), might be involved in this process. Black (1956a, pp. 167-8), in considering the *Ma* scale of the MMPI (which is closely allied with extraversion), found that judges characterised those with low scores as being Quiet, while those with high scores were described as being more likely to Show Off and Boast or be Infantile and Disruptive than persons with more moderate scores, thus indicating some of the behaviours which may be used to infer extraversion in others.

In common with the other accurately perceived traits, the best available evidence indicates that extraversion is also perceived as ranging along a dimension or continuum. Cook and Smith (1974) have shown that targets can be rank ordered with respect to degree of extraversion and, as is pointed out by Woodworth and Schlosberg (1954, pp. 260-1), rank orderings directly imply scales and scalability for the attribute under consideration.

Manner of dress. The influence of clothes is reviewed in Section 7.3.1, but it is worth while to point out here that manner of dress has a marked influence in moderating behaviour by allowing one to infer, with varying degrees of accuracy, social class, occupation and income, propensity for deviancy and delinquency, and in a more general sense, life style and values, as in the case of 'Bohemian' dress. Dress has been little studied, but there seems to be every reason to assume that the inferences drawn from it can be valid, at least when the persons in question are dressed in their habitual manner.

We introduce the variable of dress here because, as with the previously considered classes of cues or traits, it also rests upon a dimensional foundation. Gibbins (1969) has shown, for example, that women's clothes are scaled along three dimensions — Evaluation (including 'Fashionability'), Socialisation (corresponding roughly with our Conforming/Deviant dimension), and lastly, a minor dimension reflecting degree of formality. In a slightly later study, Sailor (1971) also found a factor of fashionability among her subjects. And finally, our own data (in Chapter 7) show that the implications of dress are clearly dimensional in nature, with the dimensions being perhaps better delineated because of the wide range of dress employed.

Miscellaneous cues. Clearly, there are numerous additional cues and qualities, such as Age (e.g. Tipton & Browning, 1972) and Masculinity/Femininity (e.g. Faust, 1960; Mussen & Jones, 1958), which can also be gauged with relatively good accuracy, and in turn yield plausible and sometimes valid inferences. Again these qualities are intrinsically scalable, but there is as yet insufficient data to warrant a full scale discussion at this time.

Recapitulation. The various classes of cues which have been considered here — Attractiveness, Age, etc. — all share several common features, such as perceptual immediacy and salience in social interactions and, depending upon circumstances, are capable of being accurately perceived and supporting valid conclusions. It is also possible to draw inferences from these cues but the veracity of the inferences will be strongly influenced by their level of abstraction, generality, etc. And with a few exceptions, such as the physical implications of age differences, it is expected that the 'meaning' of these qualities are determined largely by cultural considerations. However, and as we have been at pains to point out, the single most important attribute common to this set of cues is the fact that all of them represent qualities which are scalable rather than qualities which are amenable only to discrete categories or typing, as in male/female dichotomies, for example. Bearing this last point in mind, we are now better equipped to take up the problems of synthesis and integration, and observation and inference as they occur in person perception.

1.4.2 The structural aspects of person perception: Evaluation, Potency, Activity, Control, Age, etc.

In the previous section we identified several commonplace variables, such as physical attractiveness, age and manner of dress, which can be perceived accurately. In order to understand the relationship between these somewhat heterogeneous variables — and in a broader sense, to lay the groundwork for a revised theory of stereotyping — we will consider some additional studies and their implications for a structural model of person perception.

It is now widely known (e.g. Hamilton & Huffman, 1971; Miller et al., 1968; Pyron, 1965; Warr & Knapper, 1968) that experimental circumstances can be arranged — by employing the semantic differential — so that differences between target persons are expressed largely in terms of Evaluation (E), Potency (P), Activity (A) and Control (C). In this context, E corresponds with a 'good-bad' dimension, P to a dimension rather like 'strong-weak'; A is represented by scales such as 'quick-slow' or 'active-passive', while C is characterised by terms like 'deliberate-impulsive' (Gitin, 1970; Osgood, 1966; Osgood, Suci & Tannenbaum, 1957).

As might be anticipated from the specialised 'demand characteristics' surrounding social perception, EPAC structures frequently show alterations and adaptations not often found in the more generalised context of semantic meaning. In some instances (Abelson & Surmat, 1962; Kirby & Gardner, 1972), portions of the EPAC structure, such as P, are absent or do not emerge as solitary entities (i.e. are decomposed into one or more of the remaining components), while in other studies the degree of independence between the factors of EPAC is lower than is anticipated from studies which are entirely semantic in context (e.g. Friendly & Glucksberg, 1970; Hayes & Sievers, 1972; Kirby & Gardner, 1972; Kubiniec & Farr, 1971; Manis, 1959; Rosenberg et al., 1968). Moreover, it has been observed (Rosenberg & Olshan, 1970) that the usual order of salience is sometimes altered, with A (or a combination of A and P) being more influential than E, with this finding being especially common when the objects under consideration are fairly esoteric in nature (Gitin, 1970; Osgood, Ware & Morris, 1961; Tanaka & Osgood, 1965).

Irrespective of these variations from the expected, the bulk of evidence examined here does suggest that a somewhat modified and better elaborated version of the EPAC dimensions can be expected to figure importantly in most structural models of person perception and stereotyping, noting in advance that social interaction may require a different EPAC structure than that derived from the perception of objects and other passive entities.

A tentative indication of this expanded EPAC structure is provided by Rosenberg and Olshan (1970) in their highly informative re-examination of Peabody's (1970) work and theory. An adaptation of one of their more important summary tables — representing an orthogonal factor analysis of the ratings of 60 traits on nine scales — is shown here in Table 1.1, and indicates, among other things, that descriptive scales (which include complex entities such as Extraversion) can be used to describe adequately a cognitive or trait space, either alone or in conjunction with the more usual semantic differential scales.

In considering some of the more particular aspects of these data, Rosenberg and Olshan make several comments which are pertinent here. First, they note that nine different scales are more than are required to interpret a three-dimensional space but go on to point out that the 'redundancy' of descriptive terms may be of assistance by providing additional 'insights' into the nature of the trait spaces in question. The existence of this redundancy also points up the possible arbitrariness of any one particular interpretation. Second, the Table shows three relatively distinct subsets of loadings, each of which corresponds reasonably well to one of the connotative dimensions from the semantic differential — Potency, Evaluation, and Activity (or Control, as will be considered below) — and at the same time delimits the descriptive dimensions as well. This clustering also provides a provisional indication of the relationship between descriptive and connotative scales. Finally, they observe that the subsets of loadings are surprisingly distinct, and in spite of a few exceptions (e.g. Active-passive), provide a particularly clearcut structure.

The data adapted from Rosenberg and Olshan also serve as a clear illustration of some of the variations which arise as one moves from a semantic to a social context. First, the usual EPAC is disturbed, with P being considerably more prominent than E in this case. Second, the Activity scale, rather than showing a single large loading, is almost evenly divided between the dimensions of A and P. Last, and probably most important, the factor labelled as Activity by Rosenberg and Olshan could, in light of the marked loadings of Extraversion and Impulsiveness, and the modest loading of Active-passive, be equally appropriately designated as Control. As we mentioned earlier, Control tends to gain in importance in social perception, sometimes to the detriment of either A or P in the process. Irrespective of these variations, it is clear that the EPAC structure (and its descriptive analogues) retains a central place in social perception; accordingly we will take a closer look at the constituent components of EPAC and their analogues below.

Evaluation. Many of the studies included in our brief review are consistent with Rosenberg and Olshan, showing that E is much more broadly constituted in person perception than in semantic studies. By way of illustration, Kirby and Gardner (1972) were able to show that E and Social Desirability were virtually tautological ($r = 0.98$) for 208 words frequently used as descriptions in person perception. Other variables which find expression in terms of E are 'Intellectual

Table 1.1

Factor Analysis of Nine Semantic/Descriptive Scales When Employed in a Social Context[1]

Property/Scale		Factor	
	Potency	Evaluation	Activity
Hard-Soft	.93	—.06	.05
Dominant-Submissive	.84	.06	.42
Decided-Undecided	.83	.30	.07
Good-Bad	.00	.97	.03
Intellectual Good-Bad	—.03	.96	.15
Social Good-Bad	.31	.81	.04
Active-Passive	.58	.07	.69
Introverted-Extraverted	.00	—.06	—.86
Impulsive-Inhibited	.12	.08	.90
% total variance	42.0	24.9	17.3

1. Adapted from Rosenberg & Olshan (1970).

Desirability' (Rosenberg, et al., 1968; Rosenberg & Jones, 1972), certain qualitative aspects of social interaction (e.g. Levy & Dugan, 1960; Rosenberg et al., 1968; Wish et al., 1976), Occupational Prestige (e.g. Hanno & Jones, 1973; Himmelfarb & Senn, 1969; Kuusinen, 1969; NORC, 1947; Triandis & Fishbein, 1963; Tzeng, 1975), and Physical Attractiveness (see Chapters 3 and 4). The Evaluative dimension can become a remarkably polyglot construct in social perception.

Potency and activity. P and A are discussed together here because it is usual for both to be less distinct than E, and in the present context, for them to show some loss of definition in social perception. A and P are sometimes found, for example, to merge into a single dimension — of 'Dynamism' (e.g. Gitin, 1970; Hamilton & Huffman, 1971; Kirby & Gardner, 1972; Levin, 1965; Triandis & Osgood, 1958) — or that some of the more characteristic scales, such as Strong-Weak (P) or Fast-Slow (A), may yield their largest loadings on E rather than P or A (Grey, 1973; Hamilton & Huffman, 1971).

Turning first to P, there is gradually accumulating evidence that this dimension is one of the primary vehicles for the attribution of Masculinity/Femininity in social perception (e.g. Reece, 1964; Rosenberg & Jones, 1972; Rosnow, Wainer & Arms, 1969; Sappenfield, Kaplan & Balogh, 1966). As one might anticipate, adjectives such as Hard, Assertive and Gruff are associated with Masculinity, while their opposites are perceived as being related more closely to Femininity. This relationship is particularly well illustrated by Jenkins (1971) who, while investigating the influence of race and body build upon impression, found that Masculinity had its largest loadings on the dimension of Potency in four of her six sets of data.

At present the situation with Activity seems to be much more complicated than that surrounding P. First, a number of studies (e.g. Friendly & Glucksberg, 1970; Frijda & Philipszoon, 1963; Grey, 1973; Kuusinen, 1969; Rosenberg & Olshan, 1970) have provided data which suggest that the traits usually associated with A merge in various proportions with other traits to form, in social perception, a dimension which could be better described as one of Control (Gitin, 1970; Osgood, 1955, 1966). On the other hand, a second set of studies (e.g. Grey, 1973; Hallworth, 1965; Hebron, 1968; Mulaik, 1964; Norman, 1963; Peterson, 1965; Rosenberg & Olshan, 1970) indicate a clear linkage between A and extraversion in social perception. This distinction may, however, prove to be largely artificial since there is mounting evidence that extraversion is involved with two distinct aspects of behaviour, one being greater social involvement and the other being greater impulsiveness or diminished control (e.g. Carrigan, 1960; Eaves & Eysenck, 1975; Sparrow & Ross, 1964).

The dimension of control. While C is relatively obscure in semantic studies *per se* and therefore receives little mention in that quarter, it appears, in contrast, to be one of the most characteristic and easily identified dimensions in social perception. To put this matter in perspective, more than one half of the papers dealing with cognitive structures in social perception reviewed by us provided some evidence for a dimension of Control, with these ranging from tentative suggestions (e.g. Pyron, 1965; Wiggins et al., 1969) to the isolation of a fully developed or self evident factor (e.g. Gitin, 1970; Levy & Dugan, 1960).

Again, however, there are complications, with those papers which yield a reasonably well elaborated dimension of Control showing that the notion of C can be represented in two rather distinctly different ways, one ostensibly relating to Social Control or Socialisation, while the other is nearer to an expression of a Primary Personality Trait or Temperament. Socialisation is represented by terms such as Immoral, Untrustworthy (Kuusinen, 1969, p. 185), Irritable, Dishonest (Rosenberg et al., 1968, p. 290), or Fighting and Arguing (Powell, Stewart & Tutton, 1973; or in Figure 8.1) whereas personality or temperament is characterised by Immature, Impulsive (Gitin, 1970, p. 274), Uncontrolled or Warm (Frijda & Philipszoon, 1963, p. 46) versus Calm and Self Disciplined (Hanno & Jones, 1973, p. 371).

Before turning to the dimension of Extraversion it will simplify matters to point out that the temperamental component of C, which is evidenced by traits such as Immature, Impulsive, Active, etc., corresponds with one of the commonly recognised aspects of Extraversion. Unfortunately we have no ready explanation as to why the social and impulsive facets of Extraversion should become isolated from one another in social perception.

Social Activity as an expression of extraversion. Extraversion is of particular importance because (as mentioned earlier) it is one of the few personality traits which can be assessed in others with any real degree of accuracy (Cook & Smith, 1974; Eysenck & Eysenck, 1963; Sappenfield, 1969). In light of these findings, it is not at all surprising that a corresponding dimension, being roughly the equivalent of Social

Activity (SA), should emerge from numerous studies of social perception.

From a qualitative standpoint the traits which characteristically show larger loadings on SA are Friendly, Cooperative (Wish et al., 1976), Popular and Social (Rosenberg et al., 1968). In certain of the more detailed treatments, SA demonstrates a clear association with Evaluation (Frijada & Philipszoon, 1963; Gitin, 1970; Hayes & Sievers, 1972; Kuusinen, 1969; Levy & Dugan, 1960) accompanied by the occasional intrusion of items more representative of Activity than E (e.g. Grey, 1973; Tzeng, 1975). Other data (e.g. Friendly & Glucksberg, 1970), including some of our own (see Figures 8.1 & 8.2), cannot be related directly to this scheme because of an insufficiency of Evaluative scales, but even here inspection still suggests that the observed SA dimensions carry a connotation of E — an observation which is all the more important for showing that SA items can coalesce into a factor in the absence of support from traditional E-type scales.

Summary and conclusions. As is well known in this area of research, the interpretations derived from factor analyses and other types of multidimensional procedures almost always suffer from a certain degree of subjectivity and arbitrariness since there are generally a few loadings

Table 1.2

A summary of the Connotative and Descriptive Dimensions most frequently obtained from Studies of Social Perception

Connotative Dimensions	Examples of Scales[1]	Connotative Features	
		Primary	Secondary
Evaluation (E)	Good-Bad		
Potency (P)	Weak-Strong		
Activity (A)	Quick-Slow		
Control (C)	Deliberate-Impulsive		
Descriptive Dimensions			
Masculine/Feminine (M/F)	Tough-Tender	P	
Social Control (SC)	Honest-Dishonest	C	E
Temperamental Control (TC)	Restrained-Rash	C	
Social Activity (SA)	Social-Solitary	E	A

1. A more extensive sample of Scales is presented in Table 1.3.

(or equivalent measurers), which fail to conform to the otherwise simple patterning of results. Accordingly, our interpretations of some of the above data are open to alternative suggestions but, as it stands, there appears to be (as shown in Table 1.2) four connotative dimensions and four descriptive dimensions which are more or less well confirmed in social perception. It should not be concluded however that eight cognitive dimensions are required, since we have seen that certain of the connotative and descriptive dimensions tend to merge or parallel one another. On the other hand, the exact relationship between these dimensions, and even their generality, is to a certain extent questionable because of the marked differences between the studies from which they were derived. Later research may show that some of the present designations for the descriptive scales can be improved upon, or indeed that new dimensions may be required or unearthed, but we will treat these eight dimensions as being sufficient for the moment.

In considering Table 1.2, it should be recognised that either set of dimensions, EPAC or their more descriptive counterparts, can serve with comparable efficiency in partitioning the cognitive spaces involved in social perception, but the descriptive dimensions may have a certain advantage with respect to clarity of interpretation, implications, etc. (e.g. Friendly & Glucksberg, 1970; Kuusinen, 1969; Rosenberg et al., 1968; Tzeng, 1975; Wish et al., 1976). Thus, while there is a certain elegance and universality in representations based on EPAC, it may, as noted by Rosenberg and Olshan (1970), be more psychologically meaningful to employ traits which result in descriptive dimensions.

The finding that either of two sets of relatively prosaic dimensions are adequate to account for a preponderance of variance in social perception accords well with the notion that the structure underlying person perception must, because of marked limitations in information capacity, itself be simple (see Sections 1.3.2 and 1.2). Nor is the support limited to the material at hand, since various investigators, in seeking to identify the more important implicit or explicit dimensions of personality, have found that four or five factors are generally sufficient for their purposes (D'andrade, 1965; Eysenck, 1953, 1967; Grey, 1973; Norman, 1963; Passini & Norman, 1966). Finally, even investigators who employ or study the Repertory Grid and related techniques — where tests are improvised to match the idiosyncratic demands of the testees — have found that two or three dimensions are usually adequate for describing the testee's 'personal meaning space' (Ryle, 1975, p. 35; Slater, 1976). Thus the notion that the structure underlying person perception is necessarily simple finds support from data which are far removed from stereotyping *per se*.

Turning to the last of the major issues, these data provide substantial evidence for the idea that person perception is based on a structure of graded or continuous dimensions rather than a complex set of discrete taxonomic categories as proposed by Sarbin et al. (1960 — see Section 1.3.7 above). But as this is one of the central themes of the following section, the discussion is best continued below.

1.5 Person perception and stereotyping — a provisional model

Having examined the various studies presented so far, it is now possible to consider a provisional model for stereotyping based on a limited number of continuous dimensions. Because of the intimate relationship between person perception and stereotyping (see Section 1.3.4 to 1.3.7), it appears likely that a similar model also applies to nonsituational instances of person perception, as when judgements about targets are derived in the absence of a situation or context. This qualification arises because some situations, especially if culturally defined, may, by decreasing uncertainty, enhance the accuracy of certain classes of perceptions, such as those involving motives, goals and emotions.

1.5.1 Stereotyping as a compound process: recognition and judgement

Before turning to structure *per se*, it needs to be stressed (as the traditional conception fails to do) that stereotyping is composed of two distinctive, time ordered phases: perception or recognition, followed by judgement or evaluation which, depending upon circumstances, may instigate overt behaviour. As pointed out by Frith and Lillie (1972), the failure to be cognisant of this distinction can lead to a good deal of unnecessary confusion. Anomalous stereotyping can, for example, result from an incorrect identification of the available cues or, following a correct recognition, because the judge in question regards certain targets in an eccentric manner (Miller et al., 1971).

The perceptual phase probably corresponds most closely with those processes treated under the rubric of perceptual schemata (see Section 1.2.2), whereby frequently recurring perceptual configurations are recognised or identified in accordance with cultural (Bagby, 1957; Engel, 1956; Hastorf & Myro, 1959) or personal considerations (Lo Sciuto & Hartley, 1963; Moore, 1966; Reitz & Jackson, 1964). This aspect of stereotyping has been largely ignored or minimised through the use of stimuli or targets which are artificially simple and therefore readily identifiable.

The relative obscurity of the recognition phase of stereotyping should not, however, be taken as implying that this is an unimportant aspect of the total process. Frith (1971, 1974a, b), for example, has provided data which suggest that stereotyping may exhibit the often denied property of flexibility or adaptability even in the process of recognition. Our own experience casts an interesting light on this aspect of stereotyping, namely that targets which are difficult to discriminate from one another in sequential presentations (e.g. Targets 5 and 6) nevertheless yield stereotypes which are reliably different in some important respects. Since the data which might prove to be relevant here are scattered throughout a wide domain — including perceptual schemata, short term memory, sensory processing, learning, etc. — we have not attempted to undertake a systematic review at this time, but rather have concentrated on the second stage of stereotyping — judgement and cognitive structure.

1.5.2 The fallacy of 'immutable categories' — an empirical disconfirmation

Even before the outset of our studies, there was accumulating evidence suggesting that stereotypes did not represent immutable categories but rather that they were remarkably plastic, responding in a most sensitive manner to a wide variety of secondary alterations to target persons (e.g. Bayton et al., 1956; La Gaipa, 1971), as discussed in Sections 1.1.2 and 1.2.2. Taken in conjunction with the widely replicated finding that three or four dimensions are adequate to 'explain' our judgements of Others (see Section 1.4), the notion of fixed categories as the basis of stereotyping becomes even more remote. Indeed, even the two instances mentioned in the section above are inconsistent with the idea of rigidity in stereotyping.

Looking more directly at the opposite side of the proposition — that stereotypes do represent fixed categories — we were more than a little surprised to find no indication that this often mentioned notion had ever been subjected to an experimental test. It is true that some targets have evoked a good deal of consensus and extreme responding, but this stands more as an indication of a poor or unrealistic experimental design and and inappropriate interpretation than it does for evidence of rigid stereotyping (Brigham, 1971; Eysenck & Crown, 1948). Such considerations have led us to conclude that there is no intrinsic merit to a conception of stereotyping based on categories — that categories are a fiction created by unjustified experimental conditionals. In other words, the impression created by strangers or other targets is not determined solely by some central trait such as race, but rather is modified by, say, body build, age, sex, manner of dress, etc., and in some circumstances traits which were presumed in advance to be central have been found to pale into insignificance (e.g. Jenkins, 1971).

1.5.3 Stereotyping and trait inference: a synthesis of pragmatic cues and abstract dimensions

By virtue of the material reviewed in Sections 1.3 and 1.4, it is now possible to propose a provisional model which accounts for many of the more common aspects of stereotyping and person perception. The model comprises three more or less distinct components — i.e. the Cognitive Space involved in stereotyping as well as the organisation of its Inputs and Outputs — each of which will be taken up in turn below.

Input — the transition from pragmatic cues to abstract meaning. As was discussed at length in Section 1.4.1, there are certain types of cues, adducible either from physical considerations (e.g. age, gender, attractiveness, attire) or social interaction (e.g. occupation, extraversion, social class), which can be related to a set of abstract dimensions, such as Social Desirability, Social Activity, Evaluation, Masculinity/Femininity, Potency, Social Control, etc., with a reasonable degree of accuracy. Essentially, a complex stimulus, consisting of many parts, is translated into a single abstract rating which can be used to effect meaningful comparisons between entities, which (or who) differ from one another in ways which are subjective or difficult to quantify. Thus a complex physical or behavioural reality is translated into a simple psychological rating which represents the entity as a whole.

In actuality, however, this process is somewhat more complex, with most of the cues in person perception being multivariate rather than univariate, i.e. requiring more than one rating for a definition of their 'meaning'. Thus, while social desirability may be the single most salient judgemental distinction between occupations, it is still necessary to recognise that they differ in Activity and Potency as well.

Some consideration should be given to the origins of the abstract ratings, for it is usually assumed that they are derived mainly from the cultural milieu. While there is a good deal of truth in this proposition — of culture being the single most important systematic influence on the derivation of abstract ratings — there is now accumulating evidence that this point of view is in itself far too limited (Blumberg, De Soto & Kuethe, 1966; Secord & Backman, 1964, p. 70). We have been able to show, for instance, that personal factors are equal to or stronger than cultural influences in stereotyping (see Chapters 2 and 3).

It is also important to bear in mind that there is no need for the abstract ratings to be a source of direct associations (i.e. as in rote learning); they merely serve as coordinates for locating target persons in a suitable portion of a judge's cognitive or trait space. By way of illustration, we have found that the type of target person corresponding to the 'maternal image' remains constant for subjects between the ages of eight and sixteen, in spite of marked changes in the attributions and expectations accorded to this role (Powell, Stewart & Tutton, 1974). The need for an indirect form of trait attribution will become self evident in the sections which follow.

Cognitive Integration — the infrastructure of trait inference and stereotyping. In Section 1.4.2 it was suggested that an exclusively social context occasioned a decomposition of the familiar semantic factors (EPAC) into four closely related descriptive dimensions — Social Activity (SA), Masculinity/Femininity (M/F), Social Control (SC) and Temperamental Control (TC) — which are particularly well suited to describing the trait space involved in person perception and stereotyping. For convenience, these latter four dimensions are presented in Table 1.3, accompanied by some of their characteristic scales.

In selecting the characteristic scales, the emphasis has been largely heuristic, i.e. to illustrate the range of behaviours embraced by these dimensions. It can be seen, for example, that Immoral and Quarrelsome share a common quality of nonconformity while relating to distinctly different behaviours. Against this background it should not be automatically assumed that the present scales are necessarily optimum for research purposes.

Turning to the potential factors, it depends very much upon the experimental conditions — e.g. the range of items composing the trait vocabulary, the qualities communicated by the targets, the heterogeneity of the sample of subjects — as to which particular dimensions will emerge and in what order of importance. In this respect, it is fully possible that a mixture of both semantic and descriptive dimensions might be obtained, although it is unlikely that the total set, however constituted, would exceed four in number. While we have never employed a trait vocabulary suitable for verifying the factor of

Temperamental Control, our own data have confirmed the remaining three dimensions — SC and M/F in Chapters 3 and 5, and SC and SA in Chapters 7 and 8. Irrespective of this partial confirmation, it is worth noting that we have not obtained more than two of the expected dimensions in any one investigation, possibly because of our somewhat specialised targets and trait vocabularies.

Having established a likely set of components for structuring or partitioning the cognitive space involved in social perception and

Table 1.3

Descriptive Factors likely to appear in Social Perception accompanied by a Sample of Traits which are frequently found to load on them

I. Social Activity/Social Involvement	
Popular[2]	Unpopular
Attractive[1,2]	Unattractive
Colourful	Colourless
Friendly	Unfriendly
II. Masculinity-Femininity/Potency	
Masculine	Feminine
Successful[1]	Unsuccessful
Rugged	Delicate
Leader[1]	Follower
III. Social Control/Deviancy	
Dishonest[2]	Honest
Immoral[1,2]	Moral
Quarrelsome[2]	Peaceful
Sensual[2]	Modest
IV. Temperamental Control	
Excitable	Calm
Impulsive	Deliberate
Energetic	Unenergetic
Talkative	Quiet

1. Terms or near-equivalents employed by us in Chapters 3 and 5.
2. Terms or near-equivalents employed by us in Chapters 7 and 8.

stereotyping, we can now look more specifically at their role in mediating the attribution of traits. As mentioned in the previous section, it is hypothesised that pragmatic cues, such as body build and dress, typically give rise to one or two abstract ratings which serve, in turn, to locate corresponding 'points' on whichever of the cognitive dimensions that are relevant to the circumstances. Thus, impressions derived from manner of dress and body build can yield ratings which serve to 'fix' a target person at particular points on the dimensions of, say, Social Control (e.g. according to formality of dress) and Social Involvement (e.g. according to 'attractiveness' of body build). It is important to note that the abstract ratings and their corresponding 'points' on the cognitive dimensions do not, themselves, determine the specific trait inferences, but rather they serve as coordinates for locating the target in the appropriate portion of the cognitive space — it is the traits occupying this region of cognitive space that determine which inferences will be accorded to the target.

We have illustrated this process graphically in Figure 1.1, which portrays a simulated trait space (a more generalised version of that obtained in Chapter 8) containing the coordinates of three fictitious female targets, differing from one another in manner of dress and degree of attractiveness: I. markedly attractive, but somewhat provocative in dress; II. slightly less attractive, but austere in dress; and III. unattractive and, in addition, dressed in a dishevelled manner. Since it is assumed that the traits become less characteristic with increasing distance from the target, the following patterns of attributions are obtained:

I. Dates Frequently, Popular, Sensual, Enjoys Parties, Keeps Irregular Hours, Nonconforming and Immoral.

II. Enjoys Parties, Sophisticated, Mature, Studious, Popular, Conforming and Dates Frequently.

III. Unpopular, Undesirable Companions, Quarrelsome, Steals, Nonconforming, Lonely and Aggressive.

The axes in this case are Social Activity and Social Control or Conformity, and it is evident from this example just how a system of dimensions can provide for a high degree of flexibility, as has been shown to be necessary in stereotyping (see Sections 1.1.2 and 1.5.2).

Notwithstanding its homiletic value, the representation put forward in Figure 1.1 is inaccurate on two counts. First, the trait space portrayed in Figure 1.1 should, in light of the availability of 18,000 terms for describing others (Allport & Odbert, 1936), be much more densely populated than is shown. The importance of this point will become more evident in the section dealing with Output, below.

The second inaccuracy stems from the failure of Figure 1.1 to take into

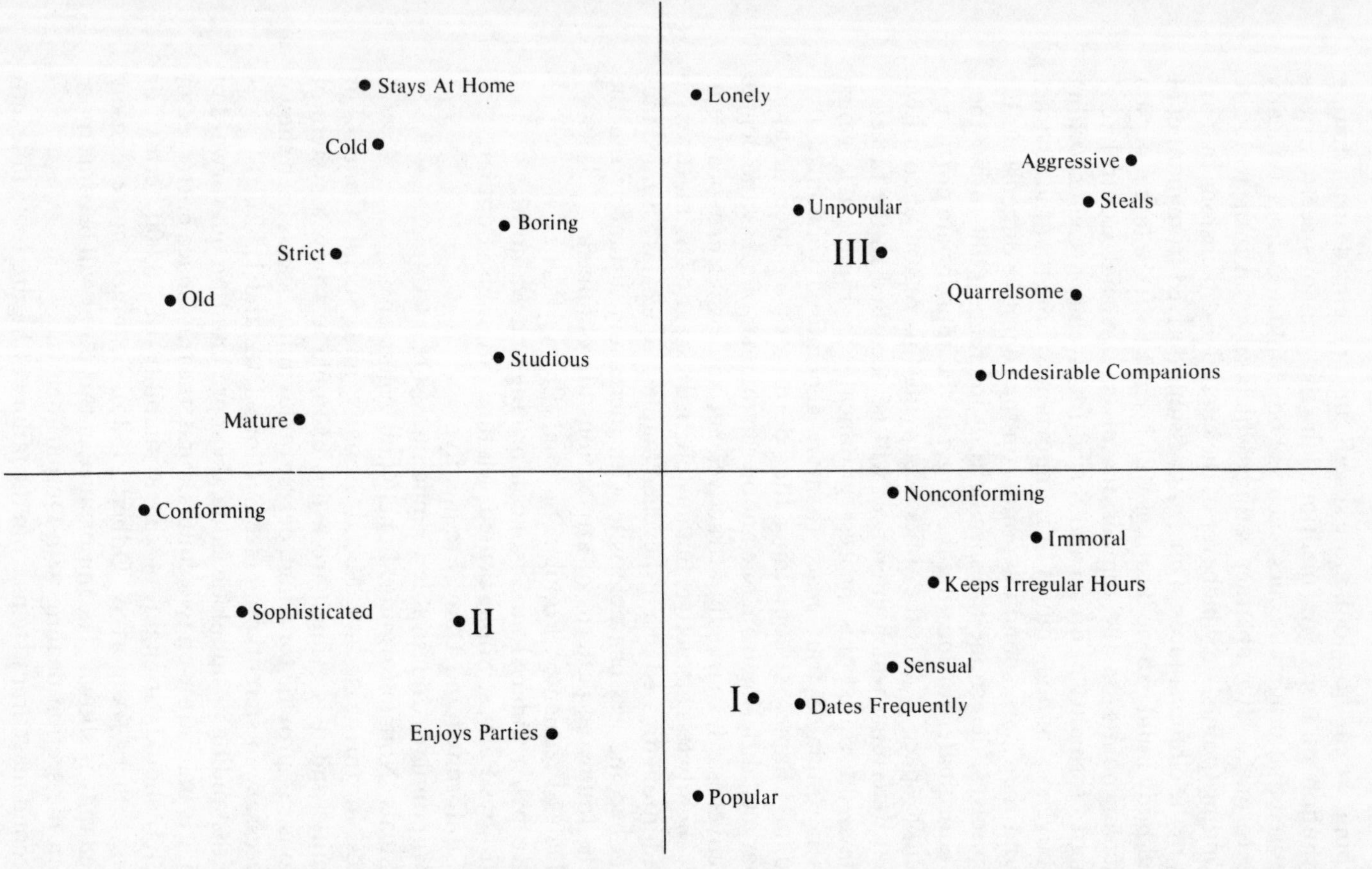

Figure 1.1 Hypothetical two-dimensional trait space based on *Conformity/Nonconformity* and *Introversion/Extraversion* (see Chapter 8). The coordinates of three fictitious target persons (I, II and III) are included in order to illustrate the way in which traits may be attributed to strangers.

account the ever-present possibility of inconsistency among the pragmatic cues. By way of illustration, it is possible that two cues, say occupation and physical attractiveness, will yield two abstract ratings of the same general type, i.e., two ratings of Social Desirability or Social Involvement, which are not consistent with one another, as in the case of an '*attractive* charwoman.' While many proposals have been put forward as a solution to this type of problem — including the use of averages, weighted averages, algebraic summations, discounting, and various forms of resolution based on balance and congruence (e.g., Hendrick, 1968; Kaplan, 1973; Warr & Smith, 1970) — none have proved to be universally satisfactory. Consequently, we must await further developments before this feature can be adequately expressed in the present model. This omission is of no great consequence to our own studies however, because the simplicity of our target persons largely precludes such conflicts (N.B., simple stimuli could be constructed in such a manner as to elicit conflict, if so desired).

In closing this section, it should be noted that the papers by Kuusinen
1968; Kaplan, 1973; Warr & Smith, 1970) — none have proved to be universally satisfactory. Consequently, we must await further
perception, were especially encouraging to the present point of view. In addition, the particular form of trait inference structure adopted here has been strongly influenced by the more generally cognitive models advanced by Slater (1969, 1972, 1976) and his colleagues (e.g. Ryle, 1975) in their investigations concerning the repertory grid and related techniques.

Output — trait attributions and their implications for stereotyping. Culminating in our discussion of Figure 1.1, it was argued that certain basic or pragmatic cues serve as a means for relating target persons to corresponding or equivalent points within a two or three dimensional trait space. Moving to the next stage, we proposed that it was the nature or constitution of the surrounding trait space which serves as the basis for trait attribution — with the traits most proximal to the target being considered as most characteristic and becoming less so with increasing distances. It is noteworthy that this proposal accords well with most available data, and at the same time deals with the problem of evaluating never before encountered targets more easily than can explanations based on direct association.

From a phenomenological standpoint, the process just described is rather like that of 'free association' — whereby one can derive many expectations, valid or otherwise, about persons with whom they are unacquainted, even from brief encounters. This quality, because it allows one to behave with certainty in uncertain situations, is of course one of the central features of stereotyping (see Section 1.2.1). The impression of certainty or 'knowing' is encouraged by several factors inherent within the present model. First, the density of traits within the trait space alluded to in the previous section ensures a ready supply of interchangeable descriptive terms, allowing functionally similar descriptions (i.e. of comparable targets) to provide the impression of differences which are more illusory than real. Second, and more important, a relatively small shift in any one coordinate may yield changes in impression and trait attribution which are quite marked (see Section 3.5.2). Provided with only these two mechanisms — and a few observables, such as posture, hair colour, gender, tone and quality of voice, etc. — it is undoubtedly easy to maintain the illusion of the 'insightful perception of Others' or a supposed awareness of 'real differences', which served as the starting point of so many unsuccessful studies of person perception (see Section 1.3.1). Here we find ourselves in agreement with Sarbin et al. (1960), who long ago pointed out that stereotyping was the basis of person perception, differing from them primarily in the way in which we conceptualise the notion of stereotyping.

The preceding discussion does, of course, raise questions of validity — can traits attributed in a stereotypic manner be in any sense valid? As has been pointed out in so many papers, there is no simple answer to the question of validity, but with respect to the model which we have proposed, and the actuarial quality of stereotyping, it seems more appropriate to compare the responses of the judges with the norms of the groups which the targets represent, rather than to the real (or reported) behaviour of the individual targets themselves. This approach to validity is in keeping with Sarbin et al. (1960) and others (Borke & Fiske, 1957; Gage, 1952; Soskin, 1959; Stelmachers & McHugh, 1964), who hold that stereotypic inputs, such as age, sex and occupation, provide additional accuracy by locating targets within particular groups which have norms that differ somewhat from the population at large. Unfortunately, there are not, as yet, many papers dealing with the acquisition of norms by groups with special or qualified interests (e.g. Faggot, 1973a, b; Lindzey, 1965).

The Attribution of Traits from Traits — an alternative mode of inference. The present discussion would be incomplete if we neglected to mention that some aspects of the trait inference model considered here are reversible — that traits can serve to infer other traits (e.g. Asch, 1946; Wiggins et al., 1969) or, indeed, to identify race (e.g. Gardner, Kirby & Findlay, 1973; Meenes, 1942) and other pragmatic qualities. In one study by Asch, subjects were asked to describe a target who was characterised as being 'energetic, assured, talkative, cold (or warm), ironical, inquisitive and persuasive', and some subjects even went so far as to provide physical descriptions. Irrespective of this apparent success, it is clear from these and other studies (see Sections 1.3.2 and 1.3.6) that too much information — i.e. being provided with too many traits — can interfere with this process (e.g. Gardner et al., 1973), and in some instances lead subjects to disregard all but two or three of the available cues in framing their inferences and predictions (e.g. Wiggins et al., 1969). Asch found, for example, that his subjects placed a disproportionately great emphasis on the trait of Warmth (or Coldness) in forming their impressions, giving rise to his now well known 'central trait' theory.

In looking at the inefficiency of inferences based on traits (or the identification of persons from trait descriptions), a number of problems come to mind. First, it may be unaccustomed or unnatural (Rodin, 1972) to approach the problem of inference or identification from this direction, a situation which is made all the more difficult because of the generality and ambiguity of traits. Second, it is easy for the number of traits supplied to exceed that which can be efficiently processed as an 'information load'. Third, there is some evidence (Powell, Stewart & Tutton, 1974) that trait spaces are less consistent from person to person than are ratings of pragmatic cues, suggesting that inferences based on trait descriptions will be less consensual than those based on pragmatic cues (N.B., certain aspects of this problem are treated in Chapter 2).

As pointed out by Rodin, these considerations are, because of the large number of studies which take trait descriptions as their starting point, of considerable importance. Against this background, it seems reasonable to suggest that a greater emphasis on pragmatic cues or methods of description embracing a greater degree of behavioural specificity (Rodin, 1972) might lead to more rapid advances in this area of research.

Status of the Present Model. Earlier, we laid stress upon the provisional nature of the proposed model, suggesting that various alterations and additions were to be expected. It can be pointed out, for example, that even now it is not certain whether the proposed descriptive dimensions (see *Cognitive Integration*) are best represented by an orthogonal or oblique structure. The fact that Evaluation appears to be strongly represented in several of the descriptive factors does, however, tend to favour the oblique notion — possibly reflecting a general inability to view social behaviour in a totally dispassionate manner. In a similar vein, it remains to be determined if the descriptive dimensions suggested here will, ultimately, prove to be the most useful ones. Furthermore, it is obvious that additional work will be required to ascertain which are the most informative items for inclusion in later trait vocabularies.

Unless someone should propose an entirely different method of cognitive integration, it is evident that many of the existing problems are largely technical, and can be resolved on the basis of additional research. In view of past failures, however, it seems obvious that future studies — irrespective of which theory or aspect of person perception they are concerned with — must employ a much broader sampling of traits and target persons if they hope to yield results which bear any resemblance to social reality. On the other hand, it is possible that we should be a bit circumspect in sampling subjects until the influences of sex differences, social class, and other 'special interests' are more fully appreciated.

Irrespective of this provisional status, it is believed that the present approach is capable of providing insights which would not be as readily obtained by other means. In our adolescent studies, for example, we get a clear indication of the relationship of sexual attitudes and activities to other aspects of social behaviour — how sexual attitudes relate to popularity, delinquency, etc. The same data also allow one to see quite clearly the attitudes and expectations which peers hold about the more adventurous or deviant members of their social group (see Chapters 7 and 8). As pointed out elsewhere (Powell, 1977, p. 43), the absence of apparently 'right' or 'wrong' answers in a stereotyping task precludes the operation of those response biases which are peculiar to psychological testing (i.e. responding so as to impress the examiner), while at the same time allowing full scope to naturally occurring biases such as the well known 'halo effect'. The absence of some of the more pernicious forms of response bias is a marked advantage when dealing with sensitive material, such as sexual attitudes in adolescent subjects. Accordingly, we are awaiting future developments with considerable optimism.

2 Culture, consensus and the individual — Some fundamental considerations in the measurement and implications of stereotyping

Irrespective of whether stereotyping is considered a constructive or reductive phenomenon (see Section 1.2), certain difficulties arise when one attempts to formulate a practical method od investigating stereotyping on the basis of consensus alone. Below, we shall consider the origins and shortcomings of consensual definitions of stereotyping, and propose a broader, alternative conceptualisation. We will reaffirm the importance of consensus in social behaviour but at the same time demonstrate that stereotyping can be independent of consensus.

2.1 Consensus as stereotyping — the perpetration of a 'logical error'

When the concept of stereotyping was in its infancy, the investigators, in failing to recognise the generality and utility of the process. seized upon its apparent weaknesses, such as presumed rigidity and fallibility in areas such as prejudice and race relations. Because of this emphasis on culture and group relations, there seems to have arisen the almost tacit assumption that stereotyping must involve or be expressed through consensus, and consensus alone, with little or no attempt to derive alternative conceptualisations. For reasons which are difficult to ascertain, this 'simple minded' conception of stereotyping has not only persevered — almost without examination — but has, indeed, flourished.

Turning to the study of body build, it is immediately apparent from an examination of the pre-1969 literature (listed on p. 61), that virtually all the previous investigators have equated stereotyping with consensus and thus implicitly shifted their universe of discourse from stereotyping *per se* to that of social stereotyping — thus giving rise to a self imposed restriction which is uncalled for (i.e. arbitrary and artificial) and severely limiting in its nature. In this respect, it will be recalled that the presence of consensus in trait attribution was considered to be required evidence for the existence of a (social) stereotype.

In contrast to this point of view, however, both Secord and Backman (1964, p. 71) and Kendall (1948, p. 89), in a more theoretical vein, have pointed up either alternative conceptualisations or methodological problems which should have cast doubts concerning the basic veracity of the consensual model. As we have pointed out elsewhere (Stewart, Powell & Tutton, 1974, P. 867), these critical comments and observations seem, however, to have gone largely unheeded or unnoticed.

2.2 Personal stereotypes, social stereotypes and consensus

In the first instance, Secord and Backman have suggested that persons might hold personal stereotypes (i.e. strongly held, but unverified or subjective beliefs) which are not necessarily in agreement with the majority view. To illustrate this point, they note that several attributes (e.g. low eyebrows, stubbornness and patience) were not thought by either the majority of the judges (i.e. 70 to 80 per cent) nor the experimenters themselves to be particularly characteristic of Negroes, but were held by a small proportion of the subjects (i.e. 13 to 23 per cent) to be very characteristic of Negroes (see Secord & Backman, 1964, Table 2-2, p. 71). Secord and Backman go on to summarise as follows, 'Thus, with considerable justification, we may speak of a personal stereotype as characterising a single individual's opinions and a social stereotype as representing the consensus of the majority of a given population of judges.' Implying that if one finds consensus among stereotypes, this simply indicates that some widespread cultural experience or expectation is operating to bring initially diverse opinions (i.e. personal stereotypes) into line with one another — a process which has been well documented in our developmental chapters (see Chapters 7 and 8). It will also be recalled that the individual nature of stereotyping was stressed, both implicitly and explicitly, throughout the whole of our introductory chapter. In this respect, it might be said that stereotypes may be collective, but that stereotyping is always an individual matter.

While Secord and Backman's approach to stereotyping is fundamentally sound in theory, it does present some rather thorny methodological problems. One can ask, for example, if the small proportion of extreme endorsements (i.e. personal stereotypes or opinions) are, in fact, reliable. Or, to consider only two alternative possibilities, can they be a product of either disinterested or erroneous responding? In this context, social stereotyping — where consensus on, say, the physical traits ascribed to Negroes may run as high as 90 to 96 per cent (Secord & Backman, 1964, p. 71) — has a very strong edge in regard to face validity; where errors and other sources of unreliability can bring about what appear to be 'personal stereotypes', but only responding which is both accurate and reliable can be responsible for the occurrence of consensus and social stereotypes. Viewed from this standpoint, social stereotypes represent very powerful tools and, as a consequence, are not going to be lightly or quickly dismissed by the apparently much more ephemeral personal stereotype.

What appears to be required, then, is an approach which will place personal stereotypes on a theoretical and methodological foundation which is just as reliable and relevant as that upon which social stereotyping is based. This is a problem for which we can provide an at least partial or provisional answer, as will be discussed at a slightly later point in the present chapter (see Section 2.3).

Before passing on to the second issue to arise out of the current conceptualisation of social stereotypes, it may be appropriate to pause here to consider why it is even necessary to introduce the notion of personal stereotypes or to go beyond the mere positing of their existence. After all, stereotyping theory and research have, to all appearances, been proceeding smoothly without the additional complication of this somewhat problematical concept. Below, we shall therefore attempt to present a case of the need for personal stereotypes, by showing that they are necessary to resolve certain ambiguities which arise in the course of research and theory.

In one of our earlier studies (Miller et al., 1969, 1971), whose data were in fact undergoing analysis in late 1967, it was found that subjects who scored high on the schizophrenia scale of MMPI were in general less concordant in stereotyping than were other groups of subjects, who appeared to be comparable in all other respects except personality. Under these conditions one might, in unwarranted haste and expedience, be tempted to conclude that 'schizophrenics' simply cannot, for whatever reasons, stereotype correctly. There is in this respect abundant evidence that hospitalised schizophrenics, both chronic and acute, suffer from a number of deficits, in both the perceptual (e.g. Niebuhr & Cohen, 1956) and cognitive spheres (e.g. DeWolfe, 1971; Kates & Kates, 1964), which lead to anomalous perceptual functioning, and could be the cause of the type of 'degraded' performance observed here and in closely related studies (Frith & Lillie, 1972), where schizophrenics have been shown to be unreliable.

However, the following points cannot be emphasised too strongly: our subjects were not hospitalised schizophrenics, nor to the best of our knowledge had they ever been diagnosed as schizophrenic, nor did we have any information to suggest that they in any way functioned any less adequately than their fellow subjects in the remaining experimental groups. Indeed, it has been shown by Black (1956a, b) and others

(Hovey, 1956) that persons with markedly elevated schizophrenia scores on the MMPI may, in fact, function perfectly adequately in demanding tasks such as the pursuit of a university degree or a career in nursing. On this basis, then, it must be concluded that there is absolutely no justification for invoking the 'schizophrenic deficit' hypothesis as the sole explanation for the results obtained by Miller and his colleagues. This being the case, what then are some of the alternative explanations which may be plausibly advanced?

One might argue, in the first instance, that the so-called schizophrenic subjects do, in fact, stereotype to the same extent as their more concordant counterparts — a statement or condition which (see Sections 2.2.1 and 2.3) can be validated (or infirmed) on the basis of measures of individual consistency (Stewart, Powell & Tutton, 1974, pp. 867-9). In this eventuality, it would be necessary to conclude that the failure to reach expected levels of concordance arose not from any disability but from the heterogeneity of the stereotypes held by the quasi schizophrenic subjects — that for reasons unknown to us, the social processes which normally guide personal stereotypes towards more culturally defined patterns have been ineffectual here. Or, to put it slightly differently, the personal stereotypes which most likely originate during childhood in the context of the immediate family are resistant to subsequent external and extra-familial cultural influences, and so never become social stereotypes.

This argument is, of course, only a conjecture (Miller's data being inadequate to resolve the matter either way), but in terms of weight of fact there is probably as much direct evidence for the 'personal stereotype' explanation as there is for the 'schizophrenic deficit' hypothesis.

The object of this hypothetical exercise is to point out that it is impossible to draw any conclusions from variations in consensus or concordance in the absence of data concerning personal stereotypes or some other index, which indicates the extent to which individual responding is consistent. One needs only to review the 'comments' and 'replies' which have arisen from Bannister's work on schizophrenic thought disorder to be reminded of the salience of this cautionary point (e.g. Bannister, 1972; Frith & Lillie, 1972; Williams, 1971).

Next, we shall examine Kendall's discussion of confounding in the measurement of consensus — a discussion which, in passing, tends to reinforce the notion of the importance of personal stereotypes, and at the same time introduces a new, but related, class of stereotype — that of multiple stereotypes, or more accurately, multiple social stereotypes.

2.2.1 *Multiple stereotypes: further limitations on consensus and its implications*

Kendall (1948, p. 89), in considering some of the ways in which the coefficient of concordance (W, see *Appendix* III) could be confounded, pointed out the theoretical likelihood of a third class of stereotype: the multiple social stereotype, or in short multiple stereotypes. Kendall pointed out that the failure to obtain a significant W was not sufficient evidence to conclude that the data from which the suspect W was derived, were, in fact, randomly distributed themselves.

To illustrate this issue more clearly, Kendall presented a set of

Table 2.1

Fictitious Data representing the Hypothetical Ranking of Three Target Persons by ten Judges when evaluating a Trait, such as Alcoholic, which may elicit Contradictory Social Stereotypes
(1 = Most Alcoholic, 3 = Least Alcoholic)

	Target Persons		
	Obese	Normal	Thin
Judges (1st Subset)			
2	1	2	3
3	1	2	3
5	1	2	3
8	1	2	3
9	1	2	3
Sums (1st Subset)	5	10	15
W (1st Subset) = 1.0			
Judges (2nd Subset)			
1	3	2	1
4	3	2	1
6	3	2	1
7	3	2	1
10	3	2	1
Sums (2nd Subset)	15	10	5
W (2nd Subset) = 1.0			
Sums (Total)	20	20	20
W (Total) = 0.0			

fictitious 'data' in an arrangement which is similar to that of Table 2.1. Basically, the data were (artificially) divided into two sections or subsets of subjects: within each of the two subsets, all the subjects showed perfect agreement with all other members of their particular subset; but when, in turn, the two subsets were themselves compared, it was found that there was perfect disagreement between them. And of course, the resulting coefficient of concordance (W), being computed across all the subjects rather than within subsets, was found to be zero. As Kendall was quick to point out, the implications of this zero order W are patently misleading. In the usual circumstances, it would be fair to conclude that there was very little relationship between the judgements of the various subjects, but in fact, in the present hypothetical example there is either perfect agreement or perfect disagreement between each of the judges. Obviously, as indicated by Kendall, it would not be correct to describe these data as being either independent or randomly distributed, and he goes on to suggest that data ought to be inspected for this type of anomaly before attempting to 'interpret' the implications of 'non-significant' Ws. We have illustrated a similar hypothetical situation in Table 2.1, but using fictitious 'data' which are more closely related to the emphasis of the present book, that of person perception rather than consensus.

Continuing in a similar hypothetical vein, it is reasonable to assume that data such as those in Table 2.1 could come about when attempting to stereotype a trait which has two distinctly different implications, each of which is represented by different target persons. Alcoholism is probably a good case in point: it is often assumed that excessive drinkers will, on account of what they drink, become more or less obese, but that they will become emaciated if they drink in such excess as to adversely affect their nutrition. In the case of this concept then, there is reason to expect some degree of competition between the moderately obese, the extremely obese and the thinnest target persons (i.e. Targets 1, 2, and 5, as presented in Appendix I) for nomination as the most Alcoholic. It can also be anticipated that the coefficient of concordance (W) will be somewhat attenuated, thus conveying an erroneous impression of the strength of stereotyping elicited by the trait Alcoholic. To illustrate the magnitude of this problem, we have seen one instance (that of Physical Attractiveness as discussed in Section 3.7) where the coefficients of concordance obtained for men ($W = 0.69$) and women ($W = 0.45$) differed by approximately 57 per cent (as zs), but were subsequently shown (i.e. when taking both personal and multiple stereotypes into account) to be based upon exactly the same degree of stereotyping.

It is probably worth while to point out that multiple stereotypes need not be contradictory in order to attenuate the coefficient of concordance — for example, the allocation of extreme nominations to two similar target persons will always yield a smaller W than does an allocation of extremes to one target only. In other words, W would be larger if, to use our example of confounding above, one of the obese physiques were to receive the majority of most Alcoholic nominations rather than their being divided between the two obese physiques. While this observation suggests, for the sake of statistical efficiency (Miller, 1967), that sets of target persons ought to be selected so that their members are maximally different, our own data (see Section 3.5.2) shows that this approach would (or does), in practice, lead to nonrepresentative results — that to maximise the differences between targets one would use Physiques 2, 4 and 5, but that to do so would be to ignore the fact that Physiques 1, 3 or 6 are in many instances ranked or rated as most (or least) typical or suiting of particular concepts (e.g. Attractive, Successful and Mother as presented in Tables 3.4 and 3.5). Since Gibrat (1966) has shown that reducing the number of targets to be evaluated, from say six to three, has an unpredictable effect on subsequent evaluations — that upon removing a target we cannot predict how subjects will redistribute their nominations within the remaining 'candidates' — it follows that we cannot generalise from larger sets of targets to smaller sets, and vice versa. In this respect, we are not especially satisfied with our own use of six targets, this being a number which was arrived at one the basis of availability of suitable targets rather than by design. Thus, while a total reliance upon a small set of targets might improve upon the statistical index of stereotyping, it does, at the same time, destroy any pretensions to generality.

2.2.2 Similarities and differences between personal stereotypes and multiple social stereotypes

We will preface this discussion by pointing out that there are important theoretical reasons for wanting to distinguish between personal stereotypes and multiple stereotypes. If it is found, for example, that stereotyping of, say, Mother is confounded by two antithetical social stereotypes, representing a positive image (embodying the traditional virtues of homemaking) and a negative image (stressing the restricting and unfulfilling demands of homemaking), then it might be suggested that an old norm was being supplanted by a new norm, that the role of Mother was in transition. There are, of course, other alternative explanations which may be less profound — e.g. younger subjects may view the maternal role in a different manner than do older subjects or subjects who are married and have children — but the finding of a clearcut multiple stereotype is probably, in many instances, a good indicator of a dislocation in the social structure which is of a fairly precise nature.

If, on the other hand, the stereotype of Mother was found to be confounded by personal stereotypes rather than multiple stereotypes, then the implications would be quite different. This outcome could come about if children based their parental role models on the behaviour of their respective parents and if there was a large variation in child rearing practices from family to family. Here, each subject would have a stereotype for the role of Mother, but one which was based specifically on their own mothers, and showing little generality from subject to subject.

From these hypothetical illustrations it should be obvious that it is desirable to be able to distinguish reliably between personal and multiple stereotypes, irrespective of the fact that both are subjective (i.e. a function of the subject). But, given the usual conditions surrounding psychological data — relatively small sample sizes, modest reliabilities and a certain amount of incorrect or indifferent responding — the fractionation of data into personal and multiple stereotypes proves to be a knotty problem. The problem itself is not made any the easier by the very real possibility that any set of data may contain responses which are based in varying proportions on both personal stereotypes and multiple stereotypes, and by the fact that we do not know in advance how many multiple stereotypes to anticipate.

A few general statements can now be made about subjective stereotypes. First, by subjective we mean relating to the subject or as a function of the subject and not, as is common in psychological parlance, as arbitrary or lacking in objectivity — it should be clear that subjective and consensual stereotypes do not, in general, differ from one another in degree of objectivity. To be more specific, a subjective stereotype follows directly from some definite aspect or experience of the subject — that two individuals stereotype Mother in different ways because one has had a kind mother while the other has had a harsh mother. Or, to cite another example, an instance of multiple stereotyping may arise for the concept of Wife, since men and women have learned different expectations for this role (see Chapter 6). It is important to note that if we asked certain specifically relevant questions of the subjects in either of the above examples it would have been possible to anticipate the occurrences of subjective stereotypes beforehand — clearly illustrating that subjective stereotypes are not arbitrary nor haphazard, but rather systematically determined with a fair degree of precision.

Second, we should like to reiterate the obvious, but important, fact that social stereotypes and multiple stereotypes are both based on consensus or agreement among personal stereotypes. From this standpoint, social and multiple stereotypes arise when social forces have been strong enough to shape existing personal stereotypes or create them anew. On the other hand, the finding of consensus of responding across subjects (i.e. social stereotyping), or within subsets of subjects (i.e. multiple stereotyping), does not in itself guarantee that subjects are responding according to the same rationale (i.e. would justify their responses with similar explanations). To be more specific one can, in the majority of instances, usually justify any particular nomination in a variety of ways. An obese female target may, for example, be nominated as Alcoholic because she is reported to be perceived as 'fat through drinking too much', or 'because she cannot control her appetites', or as 'drinking because she is fat and unpopular', and so on in almost unlimited variety.

Third, and returning to the comparison between personal and multiple stereotypes, it is always true, as pointed out so succinctly by Kendall (1948, p. 89), that subjective stereotypes (i.e. either personal or multiple) always reduce overall concordance, and tend to cause an under-estimation of the degree of stereotyping present in data so afflicted. Indeed, this suppression by subjective stereotypes can be so strong as to convey the entirely false impression that there is no stereotyping when there is, in fact, a very high level of stereotyping present. We will consider some specific, and particularly important, examples of this phenomenon after detailing one of the methods for measuring subjective stereotypes in the section below.

2.3 The Measurement of subjective stereotypes — those stereotypes which arise because of specific differences between individuals or between different classes of individuals.

In order to pursue this matter, it will be necessary to consider some alternative ways of defining or operationalising the concept of stereotyping — i.e. to consider alternatives which do not involve concordance or agreement between individuals. We suggested in an earlier paper (Stewart, Powell & Tutton, 1974, p. 867) that the assignment of similar or related traits, say for example Kind, Understanding and Reliable, to a particular target person by a given judge constitutes an instance of stereotyping, irrespective of how the other judges happen to evaluate this particular target; that the judge in question has formed a definite opinion (i.e. a personal stereotype) concerning this one particular target, notwithstanding that the other judges do not share this opinion. Here then, we seem to have data relating to consistency, which are amenable to analysis.

We have, in Table 2.2, illustrated how this type of stereotyping might arise in data from our own studies, but using a hypothetical example based on fictitious data purporting to relate to the concepts of Understanding and Reliable. For the sake of simplicity these data, as presented in Table 2.2, are only based on six subjects (S_1 through S_6) ranking each of six target persons (A to F) on two concepts, Reliable and Understanding.

Next, we will derive a statistical index which can serve to indicate the degree of personal stereotyping present in these or comparable data. To assess the consistency with which each subject, as an individual, applies these two concepts to the six targets, a Spearman *rho* (r_S) rank order correlation (Siegel, 1956) was computed for each subject's pair of rankings (e.g. between 3, 5, 4, 1, 6, 2 and 3, 5, 4, 1, 6, 2 in the case of S_1). All six individual correlations (r_Ss) are shown in the extreme right hand column of Table 2.2 — where by virtue of these being fictitious data, we have set all the correlations equal to unity (i.e. perfect or without inconsistencies). If these data are averaged, it yields a mean Spearman *rho* (*mean* r_S), which in this case is also equal to 1.0, and can serve in

Table 2.2

A Hypothetical Example of the Ranking by Six Subjects (S_1-S_6) of Six Target Persons (A-F) for Two Concepts (Reliable and Understanding) which show only Personnel Stereotypes

Judges	RELIABLE							UNDERSTANDING						r_S
	A	B	C	D	E	F		A	B	C	D	E	F	
S_1	3	5	4	1	6	2	—	3	5	4	1	6	2	1.0
S_2	1	3	2	5	4	6	—	1	3	2	5	4	6	1.0
S_3	4	6	5	2	1	3	—	4	6	5	2	1	3	1.0
S_4	5	1	6	3	2	4	—	5	1	6	3	2	4	1.0
S_5	6	2	1	4	3	5	—	6	2	1	4	3	5	1.0
S_6	2	4	3	6	5	1	—	2	4	3	6	5	1	1.0
Sums	21	21	21	21	21	21		21	21	21	21	21	21	

general as a measure of personal stereotyping with other sets of data. In other words, the *mean* r_S between closely related traits or concepts can serve in one sense to describe the degree of personal or subjective stereotyping which is present in the data or characteristic of the subjects as a whole. The mean Spearman *rho*, or *mean* r_S, is then the statistic which we shall use here and in later data to describe or index the degree of subjective stereotyping which is present (although with one slight technical modification — see Section 3.9.1).

Let us now turn to the assessment of social stereotyping. Agreement between judges can be measured by the coefficient of concordance (W), which is dependent upon differences between column sums (see Section 2.2.1). In fact, each of these 12 sums (6 per concept) is equal to 21. Therefore the targets have not been differentiated from one another. We can conclude, correctly in the present case, that there is no agreement between subjects. So, by virtue of artificial data, we have a set of scores which display perfect consistency within each and every subject (i.e. *mean* $r_S = 1.0$), but absolutely no generality across or between the various subjects (i.e. $W = 0.0$) — which is to say that perfect personal stereotyping was observed in the total absence of social stereotyping or any tendency towards consensus among the subjects.

The question is how the comparison between these two types of stereotype is to be carried out when dealing with real rather than fictional data — where the differences may not be so clearcut, and possibly requiring statistical evaluation rather than simple inspection. While there is some evidence (e.g. Haggard, 1958; Hartley, 1953) to suggest that W and *mean* r_S could be transformed to *z*s and compared in the usual manner (Edwards, 1950, p. 136; McNemar, 1969, pp. 157-8), this procedure raises a sufficient number of complications that we have chosen to eschew it. Rather, because the differences between personal stereotypes and social stereotypes have been found to be, in practice, reasonably large, we have chosen to base our arguments on inspection rather than become involved in a somewhat controversial statistical procedure. And while the hypothetical example shown above may seem to be a gross exaggeration (i.e. *mean* $r_S = 1.0$, $W = 0.0$), it can be pointed out that some data do show very high intercorrelations coupled with exceedingly low concordances. Consider, for example, a set of results arising from adolescent boys several years after we proposed the present analyses. For these boys, Like I Am and Like I Will Be correlated 0.65 (see Table 8.5), while the corresponding concordances (Ws in Table 7.3), were respectively 0.06 and 0.08, i.e. almost nonexistent, despite being based on the same scores from which the intercorrelation was derived.

If one is to employ the plan or model outlined in Table 2.2, it is first necessary to ensure in advance that two traits or concepts which are to be used are themselves related, either on the basis of prior research or by some other means, such as logic or semantics, so as to avoid capitalising on chance relationships in the data. In the US study, which was carried out in the absence of information concerning expected intercorrelations, the relationship between concepts was assured by the use of antonyms (synonyms could equally have been employed but it was felt that this might appear rather more artificial to the subjects) resulting in the inclusion of Like Least/Like Best, Young/Old, and Leader/Follower in the trait vocabulary. The use of Like I Am and Like I Will Be, mentioned above, is a stratagem similar to that of using antonyms or synonyms. Another approach, as yet unused by ourselves, would be to base the *mean* r_S statistic on the test and retest of a single concept, a procedure which has the advantage of involving only a single concept, and hence only a single coefficient of concordance.

Thus we have a method which is capable of measuring subjective stereotypes (i.e. those stereotypes which are personalised because of systematic differences between subjects). But this method is still unable to discriminate between multiple and personal stereotypes. It is necessary, therefore, to examine further the problem of distinguishing between personal and multiple stereotypes because of their differential implications for social theory, as was discussed in Section 2.2.2 above.

2.3.1 The disentanglement of personal and multiple stereotypes — some statistical considerations and implications

Having elaborated a method of measurement of subjective stereotypes, we can return to our discussion of the need to differentiate among the various types of subjective stereotypes. To recapitulate, the finding of a strong social stereotype is suggestive of an underlying social role concept which is stable, unitary and reasonably clearcut. In contrast, the finding of subjective stereotypes may be indicative of a fragmentation within cultural concepts — conditions which should be of signal importance to the social scientist.

It is possible that the observed fragmentation present in personal stereotypes is a function of their level of analysis; that subjective stereotypes arise more at the level of behavioural description than, say, at the level of broad definition. Here we are suggesting, for example, that the vast majority of subjects may agree that the conceptual Mother is expected to be Kind, but that they disagree on how this is to be translated into specific behaviours — that what some persons perceive as 'Kindness', others will perceive as 'Overprotection', etc.

Despite the appeal of the notion that subjective stereotyping is more likely to occur at some conceptual levels than others, this factor does not explain why some concepts are burdened with subjective stereotypes and others not — noting that the vast majority of concepts are equally well represented at each level. Furthermore, although we have suggested that subjective stereotyping occurs when the same concept title gives rise to divergently different sets of behavioural implications, it is equally logical for the same set of behaviours to give rise to two or more different concept titles — implying that a different type of subjective stereotyping may occur at the conceptual level rather than at the behavioural level. In other words, the qualities of being Clever, Bold and Successful may give rise to a different 'image' in a prison population than in a sample of college students. In consequence, it must be admitted that we do not know enough concerning the interaction of subjective factors with conceptual levels to make definitive statements or generalisations concerning the production of subjective stereotypes, either of the personal or multiple variety. Here, then, there seems to be an area ready for additional research and definition.

We shall initiate the discussion of how the two classes of subjective stereotype (personal and multiple) can be statistically discriminated by considering correlations. The crux of the following discussion hinges on the fact that multiple and personal stereotypes ought, in theory, to show differences in the distributions of individual correlations from which the mean intercorrelation between concepts is computed.

Case 1 — Subjectively stereotyped concepts versus nonstereotyped concepts (i.e. random responses) We begin with this case because it is quickly and easily dismissed, and because it serves to introduce the general approach. If we have data for two concepts, one which has been subjectively stereotyped (either multiple or personal), and the other which has been judged in a truly random manner, then it would be expected that the intercorrelation (as a *mean* r_S for example) would be zero, or within the null confidence interval of the statistic employed. In addition, if the individual correlations (r_Ss) for each subject were available, they would be expected to conform to the null case frequency distributions of r_S as were published by Olds (1938) — an 'example' of this type of distribution is shown in Figure 2.1, but as an 'idealised' normal curve for the sake of visual clarity. Here then, is an example

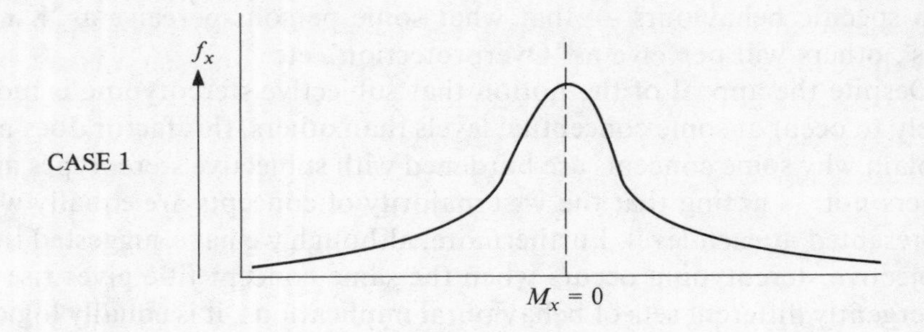

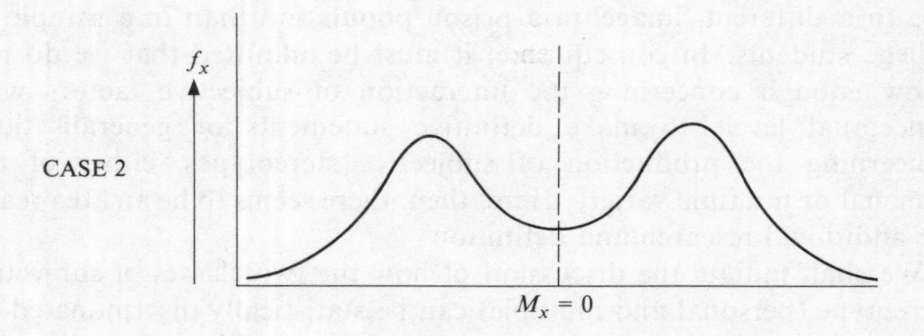

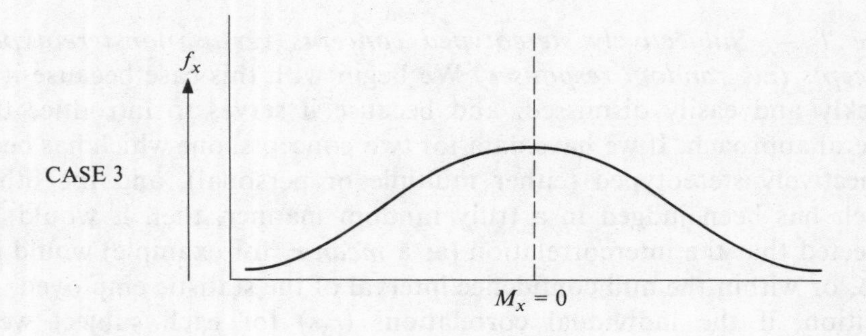

Figure 2.1 Intercorrelations with a mean of zero: Examples of certain of the distributions of constituent r_Ss which can be found to accompany this real or apparent lack of relationship.

where the mean correlation indicates that there is no association between the two concepts or stereotypes, and where the underlying distribution of individual correlations are also in accord with the conclusion based on the mean. Of course, the same outcome would obtain if a socially stereotyped concept were compared with a nonstereotyped concept. As the reader may have anticipated, there will be disagreement between the mean intercorrelations and the distributions of individual correlations (r_Ss) upon which they are based in the cases to be considered below.

Case 2 — A multiple stereotype in comparison with a strong social stereotype In this hypothetical example, we shall assume that we have correlated some concept, such as Attractive, which has a strong social stereotype with a multiple stereotyped concept such as Influential, which itself gives rise to two stereotypes, both of which are related to Attractiveness, but in a contradictory manner. Before turning to the statistical aspects, let us consider just how such (hypothetical) contradictory stereotypes might come about. In the first instance, a sizable proportion of the subjects may indicate by their rankings that attractive persons are influential, believing, for instance, that others are anxious to cooperate with and please attractive persons, and more especially if they are of the opposite sex. In the contradictory instance, an equal proportion of the judges may indicate that unattractive people are influential, believing for instance that they are rejected and therefore hostile and ready to assert themselves or, as an alternative, that unattractive persons have little prestige to lose and are thus more ready to assert themselves and their 'rights', having little fear of further censure for their 'awkward' behaviour.

Statistically speaking, the implications of this example are reasonably straightforward — considering the correlations between Attractive and Influential, one proportion of the subjects would show unexpectedly large positive correlations between the traits while an opposed proportion would show unexpectedly large negative correlations, the remainder of the subjects responding in either a neutral or random manner (N.B., random is not equivalent of neutral and vice versa). This state of affairs is depicted in Curve 2 of Figure 2.1, where the two peaks in the bimodal distribution represent the statistically unexpected incidence of extreme correlations (r_Ss) arising from contradictory stereotypes. The important feature to notice here is that the distribution is symmetrical — that in spite of the extreme differences between the distribution based on random responding (i.e. Curve 1) and the bimodal distribution based on multiple stereotyping, the mean correlation represented by Curve 2 is still zero. In other words, an unquestioned reliance on *mean* r_S as a measure of stereotyping would cause one to miss the difference between random data and data based on multiple stereotyping. Here, as one alternative (see Section 2.4.1. for others), an inspection of the distribution of r_Ss could serve to rule out the possibility that a nonsignificant mean intercorrelation is, in fact, disguising a multiple stereotype, as was suggested by Kendall (1948). But inspection is neither exact nor efficient, and we will have more to say on this matter when the variances associated with these various distributions are considered below.

Case 3 - The interaction between personal stereotypes and a related trait yielding a strong social stereotype As our point of departure here, we shall consider, in a hypothetical way, how the socially stereotyped trait of Attractiveness might interact with that of being Reserved or Reticent, which, for the sake of argument, is assumed to yield only personal stereotypes. By way of background, there are certain studies (e.g. Berscheid et al., 1971; Chaikin et al., 1974; Dermer & Thiel, 1975; Huston, 1973; Krebs & Adinolfi, 1975; Mills & Aronson, 1965; Murstein, 1972) which suggest that the 'social distance' between persons (i.e. their ease of mutual interaction) is, in part, a function of their relative standings with respect to physical attractiveness — that attractive persons interact freely, but are reticent when approached by unattractive persons, and vice versa. On the basis of this conjecture, it can be supposed that attractive subjects would tend to attribute Reticence or Reserve to Unattractive targets, unattractive subjects would attribute Reticence to Attractive targets, while subjects of more or less average attractiveness may not evidence any strong feelings in either direction. It is important to note here that, unlike multiple stereotyping, the precise degree of the relationship or association will be specifically moderated by the subject's own level of attractiveness, their attractiveness related experiences and their expectations — that the influence of personal stereotyping tends to be continuous, rather than discrete or modal, as in the case of multiple stereotyping.

Having established this background, we assume that the individual correlations between the rankings for Attractive and Reticent would follow a distribution something like that of Curve 3 in Figure 2.1 — with the frequency at the mean being depressed, and with the areas under the extremes being increased proportionally. The nature of this distortion is not unlike that found in the t distribution (relative to the normal distribution), but probably more extreme in the case of strong personal stereotyping. Again, the distribution, as idealised in Figure 2.1, is symmetrical, yielding a mean intercorrelation (*mean* r_S) of zero (which may be erroneously interpreted as implying a lack of relationship), but containing an unexpectedly large number of moderate to extreme correlations (r_Ss), both positive and negative.

We will examine further the implications of these distributions and their differences in the sections which follow, paying special regard to the ways in which one can discriminate between these three basic cases.

2.4 Inflated variances as an indication of subjective factors in stereotyping.

Returning to the three basic cases of interaction between stereotypes considered above, we will attempt to show how the variances of the samples of individual *rho*s can serve in these particular cases to indicate and test for the presence of subjective stereotyping, and possibly discriminate between multiple and personal stereotyping.

Distributions and samples of *rho*s, in common with most other statistics, can be characterised by either expected or observed means and variances. Since, as illustrated in Figure 2.1, we are dealing with idealised cases, we will continue with the simplifying assumption that the means of the distributions are all equal to zero. Thus in the following discussion we shall attend exclusively to the influence of the various types of stereotype on the observed distributions of *rho*s and how they depart from theoretical expectations of distributions of *rho*s.

Case 1, which compares stereotyped responses (either personal or social) with random responding, represents the base line with which the other distributions are compared. Because one set of data are random, Case 1 always yields, within the limits of sampling errors, the variance which is associated with samples of *rho* when the null hypothesis is in fact correct. When considering the variance (or standard deviation, S.D.) of a sample of *rho*s it is necessary to take into account the number of constituent observations or rankings which are embodied within each and all the *rho*s. Accordingly we have presented, in Table 2.3, the expected variances and S.D.s for samples of *rho*s ranging in size from three to seven observations per *rho*, given the condition that the size of *rho* is consistent within each sample. The comparable values for the somewhat more convenient Σd^2 statistic (which is an exact precursor of the more often used *rho* coefficient) are also presented in Table 2.3. These data, of course, represent the values which would be expected when the null hypothesis is in fact correct. The entries presented in Table

2.3 are based on the frequency distributions of Σd^2 found in Old's (1938) very useful paper.

Turning to our own data, which are based almost exclusively on *rhos* of size six, it is expected, when the concepts under consideration are uncorrelated and independent, that the variances of the *rhos* and Σd^2s will be, respectively, 0.200 and 245.0, with corresponding S.D.s of 0.477 and 15.65, departures from these values being due to sampling fluctuations. Below we shall consider some of the several ways in which variances can be used to shed light on the stereotyping process, illustrating the procedures with some examples from our own data.

2.4.1 The assessment of subjective stereotyping via the F *test — A procedure most suitable for use with large samples of* rhos.

Given that we have the variance of *rho* available as a population parameter, then the *F* test becomes one of the most straightforward methods of determining whether an observed sample of *rhos* is more variable than expected — that is, whether there are subjective processes at work or not. The *F* is especially appropriate to large samples, where visual inspection or nonparametric tests would be inapplicable or too laborious. On the other hand, the *F* test is relatively insensitive and so, for small samples, it is probably more desirable to carry out nonparametric tests, as described in the section below and at various other places (see Section 3.8.1).

To employ the *F* test, all that is required is to compute the variance of

Table 2.3

Variances and Standard Deviations (*SD*) expected for Samples of *Rhos* arising from various sizes of rankings when the Null Hypothesis is, in fact, correct

Number of Objects Ranked	Variance[a] of *Rhos*	*SD* of *Rhos*	Variance[b] of Σd^2s	*SD* of Σd^2s
N = 3	0.500	0.707	8.000	2.828
N = 4	0.333	0.577	33.333	5.773
N = 5	0.250	0.500	100.000	10.000
N = 6	0.200	0.447	245.000	15.652
N = 7	0.167	0.408	522.667	22.862

a. Additional values of S^2_{Rho} can be computed according to the following formula:

$$S^2_{Rho} = 1/(N-1)$$

b Additional values of $S^2_{\Sigma d^2}$ can be computed according to the following formula:

$$S^2_{\Sigma d^2} = (N^3-N)^2/36(N-1)$$

the observed *rhos* or Σd^2s (most easily acquired by the use of specially written but simple computer programmes) and to construct a simple F ratio using the observed variance as the numerator. The denominator is, of course, the appropriate population variance drawn from Table 2.3, and being a population parameter is assigned an infinite number of degrees of freedom. The degree of freedom for the numerator is the number of subjects (i.e. *rhos*) minus one. Using this approach, the resulting F ratio can be compared with conventional tables to ascertain whether the observed variance is greater than expected on the basis of chance, i.e. significant. We will illustrate this process immediately below with some data from the American study (see Chapter 3 for details).

For the sake of illustration we have selected two sets of intercorrelations — between Mother and Follower and between Sister and Alcoholic — from the male subjects' portion of the data arising from the US study. The data are summarised in Table 2.4, where it can be seen that neither correlation (mean *rho*) approaches significance. It can also be seen that with the exception of Sister ($W = 0.40$), all three remaining concepts are, as evidenced by the coefficient of concordance (W), only moderately or weakly socially stereotyped. Notwithstanding these broad similarities, it is evident that the sample of *rhos* arising from Alcoholic/Sister are more variable than expected (e.g. in the light of the non significant mean *rho*), while those associated with Mother/Follower ($s^2 = 249.6$) are almost exactly what one expects from uncorrelated data.

Given these results, one would suspect that there are subjective factors operating in the judgements of one or both of the concepts entering into

Table 2.4

Testing for Personal Stereotyping by means of a Simple F Ratio between Observed Variance and Expected Variance of the r_ss arising from the Intercorrelation of Two Traits[1]

Concepts Correlated							
1st	(W)		2nd	(W)	Mean *Rho*	Variance[2]	F ratio[3]
Alcoholic	(.14)	with	*Sister*	(.40)	0.02	471.0	1.92*
Mother	(.21)	with	*Follower*	(.22)	0.12	249.6	1.02

* p less than .01.
1. Details provided in text.
2. Divided by 245.0 to form F ratio.
3. DF = 24/Infinity.

the correlation between Alcoholic and Sister — that, across subjects, the concepts are uncorrelated but not independent of one another. As an alternative statement, it could be said that the two sets of rankings have arisen in a manner which precludes the finding of a correlation but at the same time violates expectations based on random assignment as well. On the other hand the relationship between Mother and Follower does seem to be minimal or truly absent.

Turning to potential explanations, it seems possible that the data for Alcoholic contain two more or less contradictory stereotypes — one tending in similarity towards that of Sister and one tending away from this concept — and nullifying one another in the computation of both W and mean *rho*. The means by which the variance comes to be inflated has been discused both generally (see Section 2.3) and in particular (see Case 2, p. 53) but basically the distribution of *rho* in question contains an unexpectedly large proportion of moderate to sizable *rho*s, both positive and negative. In addition, there may be some contradictory (i.e. subjective) stereotyping involved in the concept of Sister, but the reasonably high W of 0.40 suggests that it is of considerably less importance than that present in Alcoholic. Because a detailed, if hypothetical, discussion concerning the possible origins of one type of multiple stereotype has already been presented in Section 2.2.1 of this chapter, we will not repeat it here. To consider an alternative possibility, it may be that one image of the Alcoholic is that of Young, Slender, Immature (congruent with Sister), while another is Old, Fat and Worldly (incongruent with Sister), with these being the basis of the inflated variance noted above. And while we do not know which, if any, are the operative traits within these opposed descriptions, the data presented in Table 3.4 of Chapter 3 are reasonably consistent with this or other similar explanations.

Of course, the present findings are equally explained by positing the presence of a large number (i.e. approaching the number of subjects) of personal stereotypes in the data for Alcoholic — but in itself the F test does not, with the small sample of subjects employed, provide any simple means of discriminating between the explanations based on the alternatives of multiple or personal stereotyping. Assuming that the idealised distributions presented in Figure 2.1 are reasonably representative, then it would seem most likely that one would have to resort to visual inspection or one of the more exotic nonparametric tests, such as the Moses test of extreme reactions (Siegel, 1956, p. 145), in order to differentiate between personal or multiple stereotyping in a sample as small as this (i.e. $N = 25$).

Thus, while the F ratio seems to be a reasonably good device for detecting subjective processes in stereotyping, it does at the same time fail to provide much basis for explanation. Returning to Figure 2.1, it appears that multiple stereotypes will, in general, give rise to larger excesses of variance than will comparable conditions of personal stereotyping, suggesting that very large F ratios will be more indicative of multiple stereotypes than personal stereotyping, at least when considering samples ranging from moderate to large in size. Clearly, this is an area where some methodological or statistical innovations would be greatly appreciated. We will turn next to the use of nonparametric procedures in the evaluation of subjective factors in stereotyping.

2.4.2 The assessment of subjective stereotyping by nonparametric procedures — an alternative to the F *ratio which is more suitable to smaller samples.*

For small samples of subjects (i.e. less than 25 or 30) it is probably most efficient to use nonparametric or distribution free statistical procedures, such as the Kolmogorov-Smirnov one or two sample tests or the Wald-Wolfowits runs test (Siegel, 1956), to test for discrepancies between distributions of *rho*s. These or similar procedures can be used with larger samples, but as they usually involve sorting, ranking and counting, they may become rather tedious. Also, many nonparametric tests tend to become less powerful as the sample size is increased.

When selecting nonparametric tests the would-be investigator should keep in mind that various apparently similar procedures differ in their suitability to particular problems. It can be shown, for example, that the Mann-Whitney U statistic is influenced by every datum within the sample whereas the Kolmogorov-Smirnov tests are sensitive to local or circumscribed strictures or distortions of distribution and tend to be uninfluenced by the behaviour of data located in other portions of the sample. Consequently, the Mann-Whitney and Kolmogorov-Smirnov tests, when applied to the same data, can yield remarkably different levels of significance. The Wald-Wolfowitz runs test is, on the other hand, able to detect differences of any nature — in means, in medians, in variability or whatever — but is not particularly powerful as compared with more specific tests, such as the Mann-Whitney U test (which is concerned exclusively with central tendencies).

By reference to Figure 2.1 it can be seen that we are here primarily concerned with differences in distribution and/or variance. Accordingly, the Kolmogorov-Smirnov one sample test, which is sensitive to differences in distribution and variability as well as central tendencies, would appear to be a good candidate for this application. Given that the observed mean is equal to zero, a significant K-S one sample test would indicate that the observed data did not conform to the expected shape or variance associated with the null distributionof *rho*s. In this case one would be led to conclude that there were subjective factors at work in the data at hand, be these multiple or personal stereotyping.

In using the K-S one sample test it would, on the basis of the intrinsic symmetry of distributions of *rho*, seem reasonable to truncate both the observed distribution and the theoretical distribution, making the symmetrical *rho*s (e.g. +1 and -1, +.94 and -.94, etc.) equivalent with respect to frequency by combining the two comparable values into a single category or expected frequency. So far we have had little opportunity to employ this procedure, but it does seem to us to be one of the most efficient small sample methods available for testing for subjective stereotyping.

2.4.3 *The use of nonparametric tests in related applications, such as the comparison of mean* rhos *when both are significantly greater than zero.*

Notwithstanding that Hartley (1953; Bendig, 1956) has shown that z approximations hold for rank order correlations, there are still occasions where it is more desirable to use nonparametric techniques, especially as they seem to be more powerful when applied to small samples. The nonparametric techniques, such as the Friedman two way analysis of variance or the Kruskal-Wallis one way analysis of variance (Siegel, 1956), also represent clear alternatives when one needs to compare several small samples of subjects or different experimental conditions at the same time.

Since detailed discussions of these or similar procedures appear both here (e.g. Sections 3.6.3 and 3.8) as well as elsewhere (Miller et al., 1971; Stewart et al., 1973; Stewart et al., 1974) we will not elaborate upon them at this point.

3 The US Study: A Preliminary Investigation of 'Physiques' as True Social Stimuli

As a first step, we reviewed all of the available studies relating to the stereotyping of body build by adults — including Brodsky (1954), Dibiase & Hjelle (1968), Kiker & Miller (1967), Miller (1967, 1969), Miller et al. (1968), Miller & Stewart (1968), Miller et al. (1969), Sleet (1969), Strongman & Hart (1968) and Wells & Siegel (1961) — as well as several papers then in preparation (i.e. Jenkins, 1971; Miller et al., 1971) and the few papers dealing with the stereotyping of body build by children (reviewed in Chapter 7, below). In reading this unexpectedly small sample of papers, it was soon apparent that they shared many common faults and features.

First, most were concerned more with the implications of Sheldon's morphological theories rather than stereotyping *per se*. Second, and as might be anticipated from the preceding comment, all of the studies relied upon some measure of consensus as sole criterion for stereotyping, and with few exceptions (e.g. Miller et al., 1968) most failed to proceed beyond this level of analysis. Third, in many instances the data were obtained by the method of 'forced nominations', strongly criticised by Brigham (1971) and others (see Section 1.1.2 above), where the subjects are allowed to select only one target as 'most' (or 'least') suiting the trait in question. But even in those studies which did employ less restrictive procedures, such as ranking or grading, the number of targets (usually three, but occasionally four or five) and their nature (with extremes of endomorphy, mesomorphy and ectomorphy being the most commonly employed targets) were such as to abrogate any pretence to generality and the possibility of extrapolating to persons of more normal body forms (see Section 3.10 for an extended discussion of this problem). Fourth, all of the studies considered here, except for a small exploratory study by Miller & Stewart (1968), were concerned exclusively with male targets. Fifth, the majority of published papers suffered from excessive brevity and an insufficiently detailed ptresentation of results, greatly reducing their potential for developing additional hypotheses concerning the role of body build in impression formation or for building a more adequate conceptualisation of stereotyping.

As for results, all studies showed that differences in body build give rise to a wide variety of social stereotypes, with some achieving quite notable levels of consensus. In general, it was found that mesomorphs tended to create a positive impression, while the ectomorphs and endomorphs evoked images which were, respectively, more or much more negative than that of the mesomorph. For female target persons the roles of ectomorphy and mesomorphy in social image were, broadly speaking, reversed — with thinness being the valued characteristic. Unfortunately, a majority of the available papers failed to pursue further the underlying implications of these findings.

Going beyond these generalities, it is noteworthy that a few of the later studies (e.g. Jenkins, 1971; Kiker & Miller, 1967; Miller, 1967; Miller et al., 1968, 1969, 1971; Sleet, 1969) adopted broader perspectives and addressed themselves, directly or indirectly, to certain of the more important issues in stereotyping. Among the problems taken up were: the influence of Self and personality on stereotyping; alternative testing procedures (grading, ranking and paired comparisons); the application of more sophisticated analytical techniques (using coefficients of concordance, analyses of variance, and factor analyses); and optimising samples of targets (by employing as many as 11 targets, both mixed (e.g. 1-5-4) and singular (e.g. 1-1-7) somatotypes; while at least touching upon others, such as the functional basis of stereotyping, and the differences due to age and gender of subjects. As might be expected, such a small number of studies could not resolve these questions, but they did help to point up their relative importance and provided some useful indications as to how they might be approached in subsequent studies.

On the basis of these latter papers (and a few supplemental ones from other areas of stereotyping, e.g. Hamid (1968, 1969)), we have come to regard five features of stereotyping as being of key importance, these being: (1) an improved conceptualisation of stereotyping; (2) the relationship of personality to stereotyping, and vice versa; (3) sex differences and their implications for social processes; (4) an increased appreciation of the multidimensional nature of differences between targets, and in a related manner, the impact of minimal differences on impressions; and (5) the relationship between stereotyping and person perception. At a later date (i.e. while carrying out the English studies) it became apparent that the developmental features of stereotyping (treated in Chapters 7 and 8) should be added to this list of priorities. (Fortunately, each of these six topics has been treated in one or more of the five studies to be presented here.)

It follows that the purpose of the first study in this series — carried out in America and consequently referred to as the 'US study' — was to define better some of the problems listed above, and to explore further some of the more salient implications of the earlier studies. In this capacity, the US study should be considered as exploratory — useful in providing directionn for later investigations and clarifying methodological issues, but based on a sample of subjects ($N = 50$) too small to warrant broad generalisations.

3.1 Sex differences in stereotyping — implications for the US study

At the time of undertaking the US study we knew of three studies of stereotyping in which the data for men and women had been presented separately (i.e. Hamid, 1968; Kiker & Miller, 1967), and could thus be compared, or in which the performance of men and women had been explicitly compared within the study (i.e. Miller et al., 1968). Clearly, this is a meagre background out of which to attempt to construct meaningful hypotheses.

Turning first to the relevant studies of Kiker & Miller (1967) and Hamid (1968), we find a variety of indications of sex differences in stereotyping but very little consistency between or within them. It is the very lack of consistency which seems to be important — suggesting that if sex differences are to be found they will be specific to particular concepts and not generally evident across all traits. In other words, we are not arguing that women, relative to men, are in some sense less able or less willing to stereotype, but rather that differences between men and women will arise only in certain fairly specific instances of social stereotyping.

In a later study of body build stereotyping using semantic differentials (Miller et al., 1968) a sex difference approaching significance ($z = 1.24$, $p = 0.10$) was reported for data obtained by collapsing 198 scales — a surprisingly large difference considering that it was based on the summary of approximately 60,000 more or less hetereogeneous ratings. The authors, however, do not go into the nature of the sex difference which, being based on grading rather than ranking, may in fact be reflecting differences in biases or response tendencies rather than sex differences in stereotyping *per se* — a potential confusion which is not resolved by the limited amount of data presented in the publication. Still, the observed difference does tend to reinforce the notion that there are some sex differences involved in stereotyping — a consideration which has an even more will o' the wisp quality in person perception research (e.g. Tagiuri, 1969; Warr & Knapper, 1968, pp. 185-94; Westbrook, 1974).

Against this background of uncertainty and inconsistency we decided to approach the problem of sex differences from the broadest possible perspective — that is, by employing a wide ranging trait vocabulary in the hope that some of the items would tap or register sex differences (see Table 3.1 for a listing of the entire trait vocabulary). As an additional precaution we did, however, select several traits (i.e. Wife, Mother, Sister, and Homosexual) because they were directly relevant to sex roles, and might therefore be especially sensitive to sex differences, e.g. with men having, say, different role expectations than women.

3.2 Stereotyping as a true instance of person perception — the experimental implications

If one were to claim that the body of empirical data and methodology which we refer to as 'person perception' had achieved or even approached its ideal — namely to explain the processes by which we come to 'know' others and make valid inferences about them as individuals — then it would be patently misleading to even suggest that stereotyping represents a valid instance of person perception. But as we have seen in our preceding review (Sections 1.3.3 and 1.3.6 in particular), there is, as yet, very little accuracy or validity to be found in person perception.

Given this state of affairs, we would suggest that stereotyping ought to be included under this rubric, if it can be used to elicit the same classes of information and data. While this is not a particularly precise criterion, there does not appear to be any specific test which can serve to improve upon it. Indeed, even if one were to carry out a comparative experiment, involving both person perception (in a traditional form) and stereotyping, with the same subjects, the experimenter might, if the results differed, be hard pressed to decide which was the more valid set of data. Below, we shall consider briefly some of the implications and requirements of this position and its justification.

We can begin this discussion at the broadest level by reiterating that the most enduring and meaningful results from investigations of person perception centre, not on the correct or valid evaluation of target persons (i.e. the unachieved ideal), but rather on the cognitive organisation and processes which the subjects employ in arriving at a judgement. Here, of course, it is hopefully assumed that the same processes as are seen in the laboratory are operative in the world at large as well. Reflecting this altered emphasis, some of the main areas of activity in person perception research are trait integration and the synthesis of impression (e.g.

Anderson & Jacobsen, 1965; Warr, 1974), the nature of inferred personality structure (e.g. Norman, 1963), primacy, recency and extremity effects (e.g. Hendrick & Costantini, 1970; Warr & Jackson, 1975), the cognitive structure underlying social judgements (e.g. Bush, 1973; Frijda & Philipszoon, 1963; Rosenberg & Jones, 1972), and cultural influences (e.g. Little, 1968; Tzeng, 1975).

Returning to the problem at hand, we would argue that if studies conforming to the so called stereotyping paradigms (i.e. with targets of low information content) are able to provide meaningful answers to the problems set forth above, then there would be no legitimate obstacle to treating stereogtyping as a true instance of person perception.

Recognising that trait attribution has been the primary approach to the investigation of stereotyping, we will begin the present discussion by considering how this paradigm relates to the broader field of person perception. In even the earliest of studies (e.g. Katz & Braly, 1933) the central or most common procedure has been for subjects to indicate which particular items from a set of traits are (believed to be) characteristic of different target persons. Here, of course, the hypothetical target is usually characterised by one specific trait, such as 'obese', 'Jewish', 'Negro' or 'muscular', which is clear in intent, but possibly difficult to define. Under these circumstances, the main concern is the way in which the primary characteristic of the target influences or governs the attribution of the subsidiary or external traits (i.e. the trait vocabulary). Depending upon whether the target's defining trait is heavily biased by social attitudes (e.g. as in the case of ethnic groups) or is rather more neutral, subtle or nonspecific (i.e. as in the case of dress and body build where attitudes are less explicit and less well articulated), this two-trait stereotyping problem seems to be more or less similar to some of the less complex studies of 'inference rules' for traits in person perception (e.g. Bruner et al., 1958; Dustin & Baldwin, 1966; Hays, 1958; Rodin, 1972; Todd & Rappoport, 1964; Warr & Knapper, 1968, pp. 132-9; Warr & Smith, 1970) where, for example, it has been shown that *Intelligence* implies, among other things, *Independence*.

On the other hand, there are certain types of person perception problems — such as the way in which traits combine or interact to influence ratings of 'likeableness' (e.g. Anderson & Jacobson, 1965; Kaplan, 1971, 1973; Podell & Amster, 1966) — which have not been studied extensively with stereotyping methodologies. Jenkins (1971) did, however, present stereotypic targets who differed in both race and body build, and by this means was able to show that body build did, generally, have a greater influence on the judgements of a third variable, such as

Success for instance, than did ascribed race (i.e. Negro/White). Clearly then, as is the case of person perception, it is possible to carry out three trait (two coexisting within the target, one supplied), four trait (three coexisting within the target, one supplied), and even five trait (three within the target, two supplied) research within the context of stereotyping, as well as other types of multidimensional studies. Thus it appears quite feasible to design and carry out reasonably complex studies of trait integration in stereotyping.

There is, of course, another approach to the study of trait relationships, somewhat more abstract but equally applicable to both stereotyping and person perception, in which one simply computes the correlations between traits (i.e. as product moments or as mean *rhos*), while at the same time disregarding the mean attributions accruing to the various targets themselves. In this approach, the focus of interest is clearly upon the relations between traits, with the target person serving simply as the necessary vehicle or medium, and being thus ignored in the final analysis. It is assumed, however, when using this approach, that the targets are able to represent the traits in question — that, for example, the targets can be scaled or ranked according to, say, Kindness or Attractiveness. While this assumption is a prerequisite to the computation of meaningful correlations — the ease with which inanimate objects are personified (see Section 1.2.2) and the regularity with which inferred personalities are elicited from diverse stimuli — it seems to be a rather robust one.

The correlational approach described above is one of the most common in person perception (cf. Warr & Knapper, 1968, pp. 118-32) and is the one which we have used throughout most of our studies to compare and evaluate trait relationships. Here the evidence for a parallel between person perception and stereotyping requires that the trait intercorrelations generated by stereotyping are both reasonably large and at the same time sensible (i.e. reasonable in light of what is commonplace or is known from other studies). We have presented our obtained intercorrelations in various Tables (e.g. 3.10, 5.16, 5.17, 8.1 and 8.5) and from these it can be seen that the requirements of magnitude and reasonableness are well supported — that at this level of data analysis, stereotyping seems to be every bit as satisfactory or useful as are the more conventional studies based on person perception *per se*. To consider but one specific example, we find, in Table 5.17 (p.169), that male subjects, when considering female targets, perceive a strong relationship (mean *rho* = 0.86) between physical Attractiveness and the desirability or suitability of a target as a Wife — this being a relationship which has been found and confirmed in a fair number of more or less recent studies (e.g. Blood, 1956; Brislin & Lewis, 1968; Coombs & Kenkel, 1966; Hewitt, 1958; Murstein, 1972; Tesser & Brodie, 1971; Walster, Aronson, Abrahams & Rottman, 1966) using a variety of techniques. The consistency of this finding across various studies indicates that the results arising from the stereotyping study are valid.

In comparing stereotyping with the studies mentioned above, it should be noted that the stereotyping methodology is probably more efficient and less complex than many of the alternative methodologies and procedures which were employed (e.g. Murstein, 1972; Tesser & Brodie, 1971). Stereotyping has also proved more successful than many ordinary questionnaires (e.g. Hudson & Henze, 1969), in assessing the impact of attractiveness of liking and mate selection — subjects, in responding to questionnaires, seem to be unwilling to admit that they are influenced by something considered to be so superficial as physical attractiveness (Berscheid et al., 1971).

Besides supporting the notion that person perception and stereotyping are closely related, the finding of respectable intercorrelations also raises a second important point, namely that various stereotypes are not independent events but arise from an integrated, coherent and systematic cognitive structure, this being presumably the same structure which guides person perception as well. Previously, it could have been argued that each instance of stereotyping — often presumed to be irrational and contrary to logic — was a willy-nilly event, being guided by weak and capricious social learning or by impulse, guess and conjecture. In contrast to this point of view, the finding of reasonable intercorrelations implies that stereotyping is based on a cognitive structure which transcends the various concepts and groups of concepts, and 'fixes' them within a stable framework of relationships and reference points.

If it is the case that stereotyping taps the same cognitive structure as person perception, then it may be possible to resolve the resulting correlations by the same methods as are employed in person perception, such as factor analysis, cluster analysis (Everitt, 1974), or one of the various multidimensional scaling procedures (e.g. Coombs, 1964; Friendly & Glucksberg, 1970; Rosenberg et al., 1968), and thereby arrive at an approximation of the underlying cognitive structure. Here, we are suggesting that the analysis of a correlation matrix, or its equivalent, will show that the majority of variance can be attributed to three or four main influences or factors — and that factors derived from stereotyping will show a reasonable degree of similarity to those arising from various other sources.

Having discussed the relationship between trait inferences and stereotyping at some length, we will now turn to a second and somewhat less clear-cut issue in person perception; whether differences between judges, such as personality or gender, can be systematically related to differences in their social perceptions. These studies in the personalistic tradition are, in many instances, reflexive — that is, they aim to determine if differences in person perception are 'diagnostic' for certain personality variables, as well as to ascertain if these variables influence person perception *per se*. Here it should be immediately evident that if stereotyping does, in fact, tap the same cognitive functions as person perception, it can serve equally well to investigate these personalistic variables — that, for example, subjects who are cognitively complex in person perception ought to be found to be complex in stereotyping as well. While there is no direct evidence for this claim, it should be noted that at least two studies (Miller et al., 1971; Powell et al., 1974) have successfully investigated personalistic variables — age differences and differential psychopathology — by means of stereotyping. Again, this area of research would seem to be an important candidate for a systematic series of comparative studies.

As a final point, stereotyping, with its simple targets of low or controlled information content, may prove to be a more efficient method of studying the influence of personality and cognitive variables on social perception than are the conventional methods as embodied in person perception. Here we are assuming that the ease with which stereotypic targets can be constructed and defined (if that is not implicit within the construction) could serve as an aid to specific research endeavours. Scodel (1957), for example, found women who differed in breast development (i.e. size) to be difficult to equate on overall measures of attractiveness — a difficulty which could have been avoided had he used line drawings or their equivalents (e.g. Wiggins, Wiggins & Conger, 1968) rather than photographs of actual persons.

In any event, stereotyping, in spite of its previous history of unwarranted disuse and disrepute, seems to be a promising alternative — or primary procedure in its own right — for the study of various cognitive problems in the area of social perception.

3.3 Experimental treatment of certain basic aspects of stereotyping — personal stereotypes, fine discrimination in stereotyping, etc.

The US study was undertaken in the hope of shedding light on three issues which are more or less basic to stereotyping: (1) whether subjects make categorical responses (i.e. nondiscriminating judgements) towards stereotypic target persons who are qualitatively similar (e.g. moderately slender versus thin), or whether they make qualified discriminations according to the true differences between the targets (i.e. fine grained stereotypes); (2) to evaluate, in an experimental setting, the actual importance of the distinction between social stereotyping and personal stereotyping, as set forth in Chapter 2; (3) to investigate sex differences in stereotyping via the medium of personal stereotyping. We will discuss, briefly, each one of these topics in turn, so as to indicate its relationship to the US study as a whole, and at the same time, to indicate something of its broader backgound.

3.3.1 Stereotyping — fine grained or categorical?

Here we are addressing ourselves to the problem of ascertaining to what extent do variations in the degree of the stereotypic defining characteristic (e.g. skin colour, obesity, accent, etc.) alter impressions or stereotypes: are all obese persons perceived as being more or less alike; or does the impression alter according to how obese they are?

At least in the matter of race and ethnicity there has been a good bit of activity directed towards the problem of the interaction between combinations of stereotypic traits — e.g. race, sex and status (e.g. Aboud & Taylor, 1971), race and occupation (e.g. Feldman, 1972; La Gaipa, 1971) and race, occupation and social background (e.g. Feldman & Hilterman, 1975), but very much less work seems to have been directed towards the manipulation of surface cues, such as accent or skin colour, which indicate the degree of ethnic commitment or identification of an individual or the extent to which he is 'typical'. The absence of this type of research tends to perpetuate the notion, correct or not, that all classes of stereotyping are rigid.

Turning to stereotyping based on physique, it is somewhat disconcerting to see that this problem of discrimination between similar targets has been entirely ignored prior to our own work (e.g. Powell et al., 1974), nowithstanding that a fairly large proportion of the studies had the necessary data available. The finding of fine grained stereotypes would bind person perception and stereotyping just that much closer together — i.e. one expects fine discriminations in person perception.

3.3.2 Fine grained stereotypes — assumptions and method of measurement

If stereotyping is the crude and unsubtle process which some writers believe it to be, then it is expected that targets differing only slightly in body build will receive comparable or identical ratings on those traits whose evaluation is influenced by body build — that, for example, two obese targets will be rated as, say, equally lazy, irrespective of noticeable differences in their degree of obesity. In other words, target persons who show similarities in body build (or other respects) will, with regard to trait assignment, be treated as though belonging to the same category irrespective of a certain degree of obvious difference — with this unwarranted overinclusiveness being, as pointed out by many writers, the major hallmark and sin of stereotyping.

Second, the categorical point of view suggests that pairs of targets which have been constructed or selected so as to be similar ought, with respect to trait attribution, to show a closer correspondence to one another than with any of the unrelated targets. Here it is implied that similar targets should, at least on traits showing stereotyping, be expected to co-vary as a closely related pair, or that the mean rankings of similar targets should be clustered together, to the exclusion of less similar targets. The implications of these considerations are taken up in more detail in Section 3.10.3.

In contrast to the above, the fine grained point of view holds that there may be significant differences in the extent to which particular traits are ascribed to similar target persons — that subjects may be aware of the differences between the targets as well as their similarity. Here then, the differences between the categorical and fine grained points of view can be reduced to expectations about the mean ratings or rankings arising during the assessment of various traits — namely with significant differences supporting the fine grained position, and nonsignificant differences supporting the categorical position — which can be tested by various means, such as *t* tests, analyses of variance, or as an alternative, by selected nonparametric procedures.

3.3.3 Stereotyping — consensus versus consistency? — an experimental evaluation and comparison

Since the whole of Chapter 2 has been devoted to this complicated issue and its social ramifications, we shall reiterate only the most salient features here, and indicate at the same time how this problem was accommodated to the US study.

In the first place, we have argued, contrary to the majority of published studies, that consensus is not the most appropriate or fundamental means of defining stereotyping — that stereotyping can occur in many instances where consensus is not present.

As an alternative to social stereotyping, we have proposed that 'personal stereotypes', an entity which was first suggested by Secord & Backman (1964; Blumberg et al., 1966), should be considered as the most basic instance of stereotyping. At the outset of the US study, we knew virtually nothing of the properties or peculiarities of personal stereotypes, and therefore undertook the problem with a relatively conservative approach so as to ensure that our results, whatever they might be, would be suitable for unequivocal interpretation, i.e. without confounding. To be certain that some of the elements in our trait vocabulary would be closely related, and therefore capable of showing personal stereotyping, certain traits were selected to form antonymal pairs, e.g. Attractive/Unattractive, Leader/Follower and Old/Young.

With respect to a comparison of personal and social stereotypes, social stereotyping was to be assessed by computing a coefficient of concordance (*W*), individually, for each of the six terms. Personal stereotyping was to be quantified by computing a mean *rho* between the two terms constituting the antonymal pair — thus utilising exactly the same data as that upon which the *W*s are based, but in this case expressing within-subject consistency rather than between-subject consistency. In these circumstances, it would be concluded that personal stereotyping was present if the *rho* between, say, Old and Young, was appreciably larger than either of the *W*s arising individually from Young and Old — that personal consistency was greater than consistency between persons. Here it should be noted that the mean *rho* statistic reflects both social and personal stereotyping — that some of the association is due to social influence and some to personal or subjective influences.

Various aspects of the computation of mean *rho* are discussed in several places (i.e. Sections 2.3 and 3.9.1), all being more or less relevant to the problem at hand. *W*, the coefficient of concordance, is discussed primarily in *Appendix III*. The implications of differences between *W* and mean *rho* will be discussed when we take up the data relating to personal stereotyping as such (Section 3.7.2).

3.3.4 Sex differences in personal stereotyping — an additional consideration

Here, because of our use of antonyms in the experimental design, we have the opportunity not only to compare men and women on social stereotyping (i.e. differences in *W*s), but on personal stereotyping (i.e. differences in *rho*) as well. This is an important consideration because where women have been shown to have lower concordances (e.g. Hamid,

1968; Kiker & Miller, 1967), one is tempted to conclude that they stereotype less than men, whereas the lower concordances are really confounded on the issue of less stereotyping versus equal stereotyping but less concordance. To illustrate this issue, let us point out that women were less concordant in judging various styles of dress than were men (Hamid, 1968) — but does it, therefore, seem reasonable to conclude that women, relative to men, are less aware of dress, less interested in dress and its implications, less able to form opinions about style, etc? Indeed, from what we know of cultural patterns, it seems likely that the female subjects were, in fact, making finer discriminations, these somehow interfering with the process of formulating social stereotypes. Or, alternatively, that men, by their ability to ignore finer nuances, were able to construct such cognitive 'pigeon holes' as were required, and in such limited numbers as to allow social stereotyping to become evident. Indeed, we would argue that if the experimental conditions had been altered so as to take personal stereotyping into account, it would have been found that there was no difference between the sexes, or indeed that women, irrespective of their social stereotyping, may have been somewhat more consistent than men.

Because of this confounding between social stereotypes, personal stereotypes and nonstereotyping, we will take this opportunity to compare men and women on personal stereotyping as well as social stereotyping. The precise method and results are presented in Sections 3.7.1 and 3.7.2, but obviously will involve the comparisons of *rho*s arising from our three pairs of antonyms.

Table 3.1

Trait Vocabulary items employed in the US Study, with references to the Occurrence of their Equivalents in Earlier Studies

Items	Prior Studies	Items	Prior Studies
1. Like Best	3, 4, 5, 6, 8, 9	9. Homosexual	3, 4, 8
2. Like Least	3, 4, 5, 6, 8, 9	10. Alcoholic	1, 3, 6
3. Mother	6	11. Prostitute	6
4. Wife	Nil	12. Prudish	Nil
5. Sister	Nil	13. Young	9
6. Successful	3, 4, 5	14. Old	9
7. Leader	1, 2, 3, 7, 9	15. Self	7
8. Follower	1, 2, 3, 7, 9		

1 = Brodsky (1954), 2 = Dibiase & Hjelle (1968), 3 = Jenkins (1971), 4 = Kiker & Miller (1967), 5 = Miller et al. (1968), 6 = Miller & Stewart (1968), 7 = Miller et al. (1971), 8 = Sleet (1969), 9 = Wells & Siegel (1961).

3.4 The US study—procedural considerations

3.4.1 The subjects

The US study is based upon a sample of 50 student subjects (25 male) drawn from California State University at Los Angeles and Stanford University near San Francisco. By the use of two universities, it was hoped to increase the diversity of the subjects. The mean age for the males was 25.1 years and 23.8 years for the females.

3.4.2 The trait vocabulary — the concepts and qualities selected for the US study

Here, knowing in advance that we would be using female target persons, we had great latitude, and correspondingly few guidelines, due to the paucity of stereotyping studies using female targets, there being only one predecessor (i.e. Miller & Stewart, 1968) known to us.

The final trait vocabulary is listed in Table 3.1, along with an indication of the more important earlier studies (if any) in which the various traits have appeared. From Table 3.1 it can be seen that there is some precedent in the experimental literature (albeit most of the cited studies used male targets) for the majority of the items or their antonyms — the only exceptions being Wife, Sister and Prudish. Thus, in the case of twelve items from the trait vocabulary, we had information to suggest that they would yield reasonably strong social stereotypes, irrespective of how the four new items fared.

In brief, the previously used elements of the trait vocabulary were chosen because of (1) their general relevance in psychology (e.g. Like Best or Attractive); (2) an antonymal pairs (e.g. Old/Young) for the investigation of personal stereotyping, or (3) because of their specific relevance to the female sex roles (e.g. Mother). Moreover these items, because they had served successfully in earlier studies, seemed likely to yield useful information even if they failed in their specific tasks, i.e. to document personal stereotyping, etc.

Turning to the new items, Wife and Sister were included (along with Mother, Homosexual and Prostitute) because they embodied two of the most common sex typed roles, while Prudish was included because it represents an extreme in socialisation and is thus opposed to the more deviant traits (e.g. Homosexual, Alcoholic and Prostitute). Self was included in order to obtain an indication of the subject's own body build, and whether it was, or was thought to be, grossly deviant from the prevailing norm for his or her own group.

3.4.3 Origin and basic characteristics of the female target persons

The choice of female targets was extremely limited, and it was decided to continue with those used by Miller & Stewart (1968), which were derived from Sheldon's book (1940, 1963), *The Varieties of Human Physique* (Appendix 2, pp. 290-9). Indeed, we continued to use these targets, albeit with some significant modifications, in the later English studies as well.

Because of the redundancy present in the nine examples of female physique presented by Sheldon, we considered it feasible to utilise only six of these in our studies of stereotyping. These six targets are listed in Table 3.2 according to their somatotypes (i.e. their body builds as quantified by Sheldon in his three-digit method of classification) and estimated weights. It is especially important to note here that the numbers used to designate the targets (i.e. one to six) are used consistently to refer to the same target in both the US and English studies — that '2' refers to the most obese target in both the US and later studies.

In preparing the targets for the US study, exact photographic copies were made of the originals, while at the same time reducing the overall height or stature of the drawn figures from approximately 6 in. to a more

Table 3.2

Somatotypes and estimated weights of the six female physiques serving as targets in the US study

As Pairs	Stimulus[1] Number	Classification[2]	Somatotype	Weight[3]
Obese	1	Moderate Endomorph	6-3-2	133 lb
	2	Extreme Endomorph	7-3-1	164 lb
Muscular	3	Moderate Mesomorph	3-6-2	120 lb
	4	Extreme Mesomorph	1-7-1	123 lb
Thin	5	Extreme Ectomorph	1-2-7	80 lb
	6	Moderate Ectomorph	1-3-6	88 lb

1 These stimulus numbers have been used in a uniform manner throughout our studies, e.g. Target-1 or Physique-1 always indicating the moderate endomorph with the 6-3-2 somatotype.

2 Locations of the original drawings are noted in Table 6.3

3 The weights presented here have been estimated by the procedure outlined by Sheldon (1940, p. 265) for male somatotypes. The female equivalents were obtained from actuarial tables for the weights of males and females. A 'standard' height of 63 in. was adopted for these conversions.

convenient size of 2.5 in. for mounting on individual cards of 3 in. by 4 in. (H x W). As copied from the original, each card contained a frontal and profile view of a given target, the face of each representation (i.e. profile and full face) being masked prior to testing. The targets used in the US study are similar to those used in the later English studies (shown in Appendix I), but in spite of being drawn from the same source (e.g. Sheldon, 1940, 1963, Appendix 2) differ in a number of important ways. In the later studies the profile view was omitted (see Section 5.3.1 for the rationale), some details, such as fat folds and other marks, have been eliminated from the frontal views in an attempt to equate them for complexity of detail. The statures, which differ slightly in the originals, have been equalised, and last, the facial features have been removed photographically rather than by masking. Keeping these alterations in mind, the targets, as shown in Appendix I, convey a good likeness or impression of those used in the US study.

Briefly then, it can be seen, from Table 3.2 or graphically in Appendix I, that the US targets consisted of six physiques falling roughly into three pairs of similar body builds — two being obese (i.e. endomorphic), two being muscular (i.e. mesomorphic) and two being slender (i.e. ectomorphic). Each target person, represented in both frontal and profile views, was mounted on an individual card to facilitate its manipulation (i.e. ranking) during testing. According to Sheldon, the set of six targets spanned the whole range of physique, but there was no target of average body build available (i.e. not provided in Sheldon's set) — this being a lack which passed unnoticed by the subjects, but none the less limits the generality of the findings.

Thus equipped, we were prepared to undertake the testing of subjects.

3.4.4 Procedures and testing

Each subject was tested individually. It was explained to the subject that this was 'a test to determine if a person's body build influenced the impression which they made on another, to whom they were a stranger', and that this was a test of 'first impressions', these being impressions which might or might not change as one became acquainted with another person. The *S*s were required to arrange the stimulus cards side by side from most suiting to least suiting each trait.

During testing, the fifteen concepts were presented to each subject in a prearranged random order, with no two subjects ever receiving the concepts in the same order, i.e. randomised anew for each subject. For the sake of clarity, it was decided in advance of the study that several concepts required special instructions, so as to reduce ambiguity or, in other instances, to increase generality. Consequently, testing was interrupted at several points to give additional, concept-specific instructions.

In the case of Like Least and Like Best, the subject was instructed to use an aesthetic basis, as he believed others would rate the targets, and not to use his or her own preference in the sense of imputed personality — i.e. to judge their body build rather than their presumed personality or psychological attractiveness. These instructions were prompted by Sleet's (1969) data, in which it was observed that more concordance was afforded to physical attractiveness (Attractive Physique, $W = .74$) than to psychological compatibility (Best Liked, $W = .35$), with this discrepancy suggesting a potential source of confounding according to the subjects' variable or uncertain interpretation of the item.

On Successful, no specific type of success was suggested, and if the subject queried this item, the experimenter replied 'generally successful', without any further qualification. Because women can be successful in out-of-role circumstances, (e.g. as a successful career-woman) and/or in traditional in-role circumstances (e.g. happily married or as a good homemaker), we felt that it would be undesirable to 'lead' the subject by suggesting one or the other alternatives — that the problem of distinguishing between out-of-role success and traditional success could be taken up more profitably in other studies.

And lastly, on Wife, Mother, and Sister, the subject was asked to rank the targets 'as though selecting an actress for a role in a play or movie', and when ranking the targets, to try to disregard the physical appearance of any of their personal acquaintances or relatives (e.g. the subject's own mother) who would fulfil the role in question. In this instance it was hoped, by the use of these instructions, to obtain an indication of the generalised Mother concept (Secord & Jourard, 1956), Wife concept, etc., and to minimise the influence of personal stereotyping and other subjective influences.

3.5 Social stereotyping — analysis and results

Since consensus, in one form or another, is currently held, correctly or not, to be the most characteristic aspect of stereotyping, it is appropriate that we should begin the discussion of our results with this topic. Below, we shall consider various aspects of social stereotyping, including sex differences in consensus.

3.5.1 Consensus between judges — a general confirmation of the social stereotyping of females according to body build

Social stereotyping implies, among other things, agreement or consensus between subjects, and accordingly we first analysed our data by computing coefficients of concordance (*W*) for each of the fifteen traits. These *W*s are presented in Table 3.3, separately for males and females as independent groups, and again, for males and females as a combined group of 50 subjects.

In this context *W* represents the average correlation between all possible pairs of subjects (e.g. the mean of 300 correlations in the case of 25 subjects). In a more commonplace sense, *W* represents the correlation which one would expect if two subjects were chosen at random and a correlation computed between their rankings of targets for, say, Wife —

Table 3.3

Coefficients of Concordance (*W*s) obtained for Male and Female Subjects by the Method of Ranking in the US Study

	Men		Women		Total	
Concepts	*W*	*F*†	*W*	*F*†	*W*	*F*‡
1. Like Least	.69	53.4**	.45	19.6**	.57	65.0**
2. Like Best	.67	48.7**	.48	22.2**	.56	62.4**
3. Wife	.53	27.1**	.17	4.9**	.28	19.1**
4. Young	.48	22.2**	.41	16.7**	.44	38.5**
5. Successful	.47	21.3**	.50	24.0**	.48	45.2**
6. Sister	.40	16.0**	.45	19.6**	.42	35.5**
7. Leader	.40	16.0**	.41	16.7**	.38	30.0**
8. Old	.39	15.3**	.27	8.9**	.32	23.1**
9. Self	.32	11.3**	.34	12.4**	.31	22.0**
10. Follower	.22	6.8**	.34	12.4**	.26	17.2**
11. Mother	.21	6.4**	.23	7.2**	.20	12.3**
12. Prudish	.18	5.3**	.08	2.1	.13	7.3**
13. Homosexual	.16	4.6**	.03	0.7	.07	3.7*
14. Alcoholic	.14	3.9*	.03	0.7	.06	3.1*
15. Prostitute	.14	3.9*	.16	4.6**	.14	8.0**

† *F*s evaluated on 5/100 degrees of freedom.
‡ *F*s evaluated on 5/200 degrees of freedom.
* Significant at or beyond the .05 level.
** Significant at or beyond the .001 level.

that is, according to Table 3.3, we would expect the correlation between two randomly selected men to be about 0.53 on Wife. As a statistic, W ranges from 1.0 (e.g. perfect agreement) to 0.0 (i.e. total lack of agreement), with a large W implying that subjects use similar standards in arriving at their judgements, while a low W implies a divergence of standards. It needs to be carefully noted that consensus should not be construed as implying validity. The coefficient of concordance is discussed in detail in Appendix III and elsewhere (e.g. Maxwell, 1961; Siegel, 1956).

Turning to the data presented in Table 3.3, it can be seen that the vast majority of Ws, for both male and female subjects, are statistically significant, indicating that the degree of agreement between subjects is greater than one would expect on the basis of chance alone. Significance was evaluated by computing F equivalents (Maxwell, 1962, p. 120), this being the most general procedure available (i.e. adaptable to both small samples of subjects and to small set of targets).

The consensus implied by W is taken as evidence for the existence of social stereotypes, and in this capacity the present data go beyond those of Miller & Stewart (1968) by demonstrating that women, as well as men, hold social stereotypes concerning the implications of differences in the female physique.

Going beyond this broad generality, however, Table 3.3 yields two additional observations worthy of comment. First, by inspection it is apparent that the female subjects are generally less concordant than are the male subjects,with some of the discrepancies, such as that on Wife, being quite remarkable. Indeed, we shall show in Section 3.6 that some seven of these sex differences in social stereotyping are, in fact, statistically significant, begging for the moment the more complicated question of sex differences in personal stereotyping.

The second general feature which shows in Table 3.3 is the clear difference in concordances between the various elements of the trait vocabulary. Why, for instance, do male subjects show a marked difference in their social stereotyping of the concepts of Wife and Mother? As discussed in Section 2.2.2, investigations into these discrepancies, or indeed along these general lines, may prove valuable not only to stereotyping and person perception, but to the broader field of social psychology as well.

3.5.2 Social stereotypes in their qualitative aspects

In order to provide a detailed look at the qualitative implications of the various stereotypes, we must abandon the coefficient of concordance

Table 3.4
Mean Rank and Variance of the Six Physiques on Each Concept: Male Subjects*

Concepts		Physiques 1	2	3	4	5	6
Unattractive	Mean	2.4	1.2	3.8	3.4	4.3	5.8
	Variance	0.7	0.5	1.6	1.0	1.6	0.2
Attractive	Mean	4.6	5.6	3.1	3.7	2.8	1.2
	Variance	0.7	0.8	1.3	1.2	1.8	0.2
Wife	Mean	4.2	5.6	3.4	3.7	2.6	1.6
	Variance	1.3	0.7	2.3	1.6	1.8	0.9
Young	Mean	4.5	5.2	3.6	3.7	1.9	2.1
	Variance	0.8	1.6	1.4	1.5	3.1	1.0
Successful	Mean	4.2	5.5	2.6	3.4	3.5	1.8
	Variance	1.4	0.8	2.1	2.1	2.6	0.8
Sister	Mean	4.2	5.2	3.3	3.8	2.3	2.1
	Variance	1.5	1.8	1.5	1.1	3.2	1.9
Leader	Mean	4.2	5.4	2.6	2.8	3.7	2.3
	Variance	1.4	1.3	3.0	1.1	2.9	1.3
Old	Mean	2.6	1.9	3.8	3.3	4.6	4.9
	Variance	1.3	2.4	0.6	1.2	3.8	1.8
Self	Mean	3.5	5.5	3.0	3.0	3.5	2.5
	Variance	2.0	0.5	2.5	1.9	3.5	1.9
Follower	Mean	3.2	2.4	4.1	4.0	2.7	4.6
	Variance	1.9	2.4	2.6	2.4	3.3	1.8
Mother	Mean	2.5	3.6	2.8	3.2	4.8	4.0
	Variance	2.5	2.8	2.5	2.4	1.4	2.8
Prostitute	Mean	3.7	4.7	2.8	3.7	3.4	2.8
	Variance	2.7	3.2	1.9	2.1	3.4	2.3
Prudish	Mean	3.4	3.4	3.7	3.8	2.1	4.6
	Variance	1.5	3.3	2.2	1.6	3.3	3.0
Homosexual	Mean	3.8	3.8	2.6	3.1	3.0	4.7
	Variance	1.4	3.9	1.8	2.2	4.0	2.0
Alcoholic	Mean	3.6	3.8	3.3	3.9	2.2	4.2
	Variance	2.0	4.4	1.7	1.3	2.8	3.6

* The smaller the mean rank, the closer the relationship between the physique and the concept.

Table 3.5
Mean Rank and Variance of the Six Physiques on each Concept: Female Subjects*

Concepts		Physiques 1	2	3	4	5	6
Unattractive	Mean	2.8	1.6	3.8	3.3	4.3	5.2
	Variance	1.5	1.2	1.6	1.3	2.7	1.6
Attractive	Mean	4.2	5.4	3.8	3.4	2.7	1.6
	Variance	0.9	1.5	2.1	1.2	2.6	1.3
Wife	Mean	3.6	4.3	3.5	3.2	4.2	2.2
	Variance	1.9	3.6	2.3	1.8	3.0	2.5
Young	Mean	4.5	5.1	3.4	3.6	2.4	2.0
	Variance	0.8	1.6	1.1	1.3	4.8	1.2
Successful	Mean	4.2	5.6	2.5	3.4	3.6	1.8
	Variance	1.1	1.2	1.4	1.3	3.4	0.8
Sister	Mean	4.2	5.2	3.8	3.8	2.3	1.8
	Variance	0.6	1.8	2.2	1.5	2.6	1.3
Leader	Mean	4.1	5.1	2.0	2.6	4.4	2.9
	Variance	1.7	1.4	1.2	1.4	3.1	2.1
Old	Mean	2.5	2.4	3.9	3.3	4.1	4.9
	Variance	1.8	2.2	2.0	1.5	4.7	0.9
Self	Mean	4.1	5.3	3.2	3.4	2.8	2.2
	Variance	1.3	2.0	1.3	1.2	4.0	2.2
Follower	Mean	3.0	1.9	4.8	4.2	2.9	4.2
	Variance	2.0	1.9	1.1	1.6	3.2	2.3
Mother	Mean	2.5	4.0	3.2	3.4	5.0	2.8
	Variance	2.0	2.7	3.1	1.8	2.5	1.9
Prostitute	Mean	3.5	5.0	3.2	3.3	3.1	3.0
	Variance	1.9	2.4	2.6	1.9	3.2	3.5
Prudish	Mean	3.5	3.2	3.5	3.9	2.7	4.2
	Variance	1.8	3.5	2.9	2.1	3.9	2.5
Homosexual	Mean	3.4	4.0	3.1	3.1	3.6	3.7
	Variance	1.9	3.8	2.6	1.9	4.1	3.2
Alcoholic	Mean	3.2	3.7	3.8	3.5	3.0	3.7
	Variance	2.4	4.7	1.5	1.2	4.8	3.1

* The smaller the mean rank, the closer the relationship between the physique and the concept.

(W) in favour of the means and variances arising from the individual target persons. Here, in order to ascertain what type of target person is perceived as, say, Successful, it is necessary to refer to the individual means.

The means and variances arising from the US study are presented in Tables 3.4 and 3.5, separately for the male and female judges because of the very real possibility of sex differences. Here, as in all our tables, a lower mean ranking (or mean rating) implies a stronger relationship between the trait and target than does a higher mean. The variances have been included because they allow further statistical testing, and because they reflect, in a more immediate way, the certainty or consensus with which subjects have rated individual targets on particular traits. It can be seen, for example, in Table 3.4 that the male subjects perceived Target 5 and Target 6 as being almost equally Young, but that they were much more certain or consistent in their judgement of Target 6, who has much the smaller variance. The implications of these various differences in variance are discussed at length in Section 2.4.

One very much gets the impression that the six target persons each have reasonably distinct 'personalities' — that each possesses a cluster of related traits which would not be amiss in the description of actual persons. Here, one might characterise Target 6 as an 'attractive young woman who has an outgoing or forceful personality and realistic outlook', while Target 5 could be viewed as a 'retiring and slightly ineffectual young lady, who is attractive but excessively feminine or modest in outlook'. We will not carry these characterisations any further because their nature is expressly subjective — depending upon which traits are selected, how they are interpreted (i.e. in a broad or narrow sense), and how they are weighted in importance — but it is interesting to see just how much difference in overall impression can be produced by a relatively slight change in body build. These considerations are, of course, highly compatible with our view that stereotyping should be treated as a valid instance of person perception.

With respect to characterisation, it is noteworthy that Attractiveness is the trait which yields the highest degree of discrimination between the target persons (and consequently the greatest consensus as a stereotype) and thus, by implication, may be the most salient single element in the trait vocabulary. This consideration will figure importantly in later analyses and discussions.

3.5.3 Sex differences in the attribution of traits to individual targets

In this instance, sex differences were examined by computing t tests between the mean rankings arising from each of the 90 individual attributions of traits to targets — these data are presented in Table 3.6, where each entry represents a t based on 48 degrees of freedom. Since we had no specific hypotheses about differences in the evaluations arising from the two sexes, the resulting ts were evaluated against two tailed probabilities, a procedure which yielded only four significant differences.

Here, it is noteworthy that several of the significant and nearly significant differences originate with the two related concepts of Wife and Mother, this being a trend which continues in various aspects of the US data and reappears in the two later English studies presented in Chapter 5. In other words, men and women construe the roles of Wife and Mother differently when evaluating them on the basis of body build.

Table 3.6

A t Test Evaluation of Sex Differences in the Ranking of Physiques in the American Study*

Traits	Physiques					
	1	2	3	4	5	6
1. Unattractive	—1.08	—1.39	—0.11	0.53	0.10	1.94
2. Attractive	1.58	0.79	—1.84	1.04	0.29	—1.63
3. Wife	1.79	2.98††	—0.37	1.32	—3.76‡	—1.52
4. Young	0.15	0.11	0.63	0.36	—0.99	0.54
5. Successful	—0.13	—0.14	0.43	0.11	—0.25	0.00
6. Sister	0.00	0.11	—1.26	0.25	0.08	0.91
7. Leader	0.23	1.09	1.46	0.76	—1.39	—1.63
8. Old	0.22	—1.12	—0.37	—0.12	0.96	0.00
9. Self	—1.77	0.63	—0.51	—1.01	1.31	0.69
10. Follower	0.61	1.16	—1.86	—0.50	—0.39	1.00
11. Mother	0.00	—0.85	—0.85	—0.49	—0.41	2.67††
12. Prostitute	0.37	—0.68	—0.76	1.01	0.47	—0.42
13. Prudish	—0.22	0.38	0.35	—0.10	—1.05	0.68
14. Homosexual	1.10	—0.43	—1.33	0.00	—0.98	2.11†
15. Alcoholic	0.76	0.20	—1.34	1.15	—1.45	0.93

* Two-tailed t tests based on 48 degrees of freedom. A negative t indicates that the males thought the physique in question to be more closely related to the trait or concept than did the females.

† Significance level less than .05 on a two-tailed test.

†† Significance level less than .01 on a two-tailed test.

‡ Significance level less than .001 on a two-tailed test.

3.6 Sex differences in consensus and social stereotyping

Having treated the more straightforward aspects of the US data, we can now turn to some of the more specialised issues such as sex differences in social stereotyping, a comparison of social and personal stereotyping, and so on. It is convenient to carry on with sex differences as this issue tends to assert itself in each of the following sections. It is appropriate, therefore, that we begin with the most clearcut example — that of sex differences in consensus.

3.6.1 Résumé of the earlier data concerning sex differences

As is discussed in detail in Section 3.1, we were aware of only three studies (namely Hamid, 1968; Kiker & Miller, 1967; Miller et al., 1968) which either examined sex differences *per se* or presented the data for the two sexes separately in a context even remotely resembling those of the US study at the time of its undertaking. For various reasons, about the most that could be gained from an examination of these three studies was that there were occasional systematic differences between men and women in the consensus with which they could stereotype particular, possibly sex linked, traits and concepts.

Recognising that this was the only substantial data on hand, we decided, on this basis, that the best approach would be to include a somewhat disproportionately large number of sex typed items in our trait vocabulary and to investigate, specifically, the degree of consensus with which these were socially stereotyped by men and women respectively. The procedures, results and conclusions are as follows.

3.6.2 Statistical analysis of sex differences in social stereotyping: theoretical aspects

It was not known to us, at the time of first undertaking this analysis (i.e. in 1969), that there were, in fact, statistically appropriate methods of making direct comparisons between coefficients of concordance (see Appendix III). Therefore, we adopted the method developed by Miller and his colleagues (Miller et al., 1971), which in spite of being complicated, was known to function efficiently with small sample sizes.

First, it should be noted that Miller's procedure is based on what Kendall (1948, p. 87; Siegel, 1956, p. 238) referred to as the 'true ranking' — this being, in the present case, simply the rank ordering of the six targets according to their mean rankings. That is to say, that the target with the lowest mean rank receives a 'true ranking' of 1, the target with the second lowest mean rank receives a rank of 2, and so on until reaching the target with the highest mean rank which, in this particular case, receives a 'true rank' of 6. In looking at the mean rankings for Unattractiveness in Table 3.4, for example, it can be seen that Target 2, with a mean ranking of 1.2 (i.e. least Attractive), would receive a true rank of 1, while Target 6, with a mean of 5.8 (i.e. most Attractive), would receive a true rank of 6, and so on.

It is reasonable to assume that the individual rankings composing a set of concordant or consensual data will be reasonably similar to one another and to the 'true ranking'. In a set of discordant or nonconsensual data, on the other hand, it is more reasonable to expect that the individual rankings will be relatively unalike, both among themselves and with respect to the 'true ranking'.

Following this line of reasoning, the degree of consensus could be adequately indexed by computing a sum of squares for the differences between the 'true ranking' and each subject's individual ranking, resulting in one sum of squares (Σd^2) for each subject in the sample. Having computed such a set of sums of squares, it follows from our previous discussion that consensual data would yield sums of squares which were, on average, relatively small, while discordant data would yield, on average, a set of sums of squares which are, in comparison, relatively large. Now, if one did want to compare two sets of data to ascertain if they did differ in consensus, the two corresponding sets of sums of squares could be computed and then compared in any of several suitable nonparametric tests, such as the Mann-Whitney *U* test or the Kolmogorov-Smirnov two-sample test (Seigel, 1956). The use of nonparametric tests for comparing the samples of sums of squares may or may not be mandatory (see Appendix III), but is probably desirable when dealing with small samples.

Faced with the need to compare concordances, this is almost precisely what Miller et al. (1971, pp. 476-7) did, except for the use of a more elaborate nonparametric test (i.e. Kruskal-Wallis one-way analysis of variance) to accommodate to their more complex experimental design. Interestinly, an earlier study, by Eysenck, Granger & Brengelmann (1957, pp. 38-40), had also used a similar procedure — i.e. based on the Σd^2 statistic — but at the final stage had subjected their individual sums of squares to a conventional (i.e. parametric) one-way analysis of variance rather than to one of the distribution-free tests.

In approaching the problem of measurement via this type of logic, it is frequently overlooked that the first step — of computing a Σd^2 for each individual — is in essence tantamount to computing a Spearman rank order correlation (i.e. *rho*), requiring only the manipulation of a few constants to transform the Σd^2 into a proper *rho* (Siegel, 1956, p. 204). Returning, then, to the procedure employed by Miller et al., it can be seen from this new perspective that they did compute, in effect, a correlation between each subject's ranking and the 'true ranking' of his respective group. And in comparing groups one is asking, in reality, if the mean correlation of subjects to criterion (i.e. true ranking) is higher in one group than the other.

While this change in emphasis, from sums of squares to rank order correlation, may seem in itself trivial, it does confer one immediate advantage — it relates this apparently *ad hoc* procedure to a well established and developing psychometric tradition, that of the Average Rank Correlation (e.g. Lyerly. 1952; Taylor & Fong, 1963; Whitfield, 1954), which, in turn, relates the *ad hoc* procedure described here directly with the coefficient of concordance as developed by Kendall (1948; Siegel, 1956, pp. 229-38). These interrelationships, between Σd^2, mean *rho*, and the coefficient of concordance, are discussed in detail in Appendix III.

3.6.3. Analysis of sex differences in consensus in the US data: procedures and practical considerations

First, the mean rankings presented in Tables 3.4 and 3.5 were transformed into 'true rankings' according to the discussion presented above. Next, and treating each concept in order, a Spearman rank order correlation, or *rho*, was computed between each subject's ranking of targets and the 'true ranking' (i.e. criterion) of their respective sex group — resulting in 25 *rho*s for each sex group on each concept. Following this, the 50 *rho*s (1 per subject) for the concept in question were indexed by sex, ranked according to size, and then compared in a Mann-Whitney U test — this being a nonparametric test for comparing two independent samples, i.e. the nonparametric equivalent of the t test. This process was repeated 15 times, until a U statistic had been found for each element in the trait vocabulary.

In these circumstances the finding of a significant U indicates one or the other of the groups (i.e. sexes) is more consensual in its social stereotyping.

As a final comment, it should be pointed out that when employing nonparametric tests, it makes little or no difference whether the analyses are carried out on the *rho*s themselves, or upon their precursors, the Σd^2s, since they maintain the same ordinal relationship between one another (e.g. Olds, 1938).

3.6.4. *Sex differences in consensus — a confirmation*

The results from the 15 analyses described above are presented in Table 3.7, which includes the original *W*s for both sexes, the Mann-Whitney *U* statistic resulting from their comparison, and the level of significance of the sex difference, expressed by a *z* and its associated probability. In accordance with the findings of the previous studies — which have shown that men are, in general, slightly more concordant than women — the *p*s reported in Table 3.7 are one-tailed.

Turning to the data themselves, it can be seen that the male subjects were significantly more consistent in social stereotyping on six of the 15 concepts — Like Least, Like Best, Wife, Old, Homosexual and Alcoholic — with the sex difference on Wife being singularly disproportionate. In contrast, the female subjects were more consistent on only one concept — that of Self — which represents something of a paradox in that the male and females *W*s, as presented in Table 3.7, differ by very little. Because of the oddity of this finding concerning Self, we shall consider it separately below, after discussing the general implications of sex differences in social consensus.

Table 3.7

Results of *U* tests Comparing Sex Differences in Concordance (*W*)

Concepts	*W*-male	*W*-female	*U*	*z*	$p<$
1. Like Least	.69	.45	220	1.79	.05
2. Like Best	.67	.48	212	1.95	.05
3. Wife	.53	.17	135	3.44	.0005
4. Young	.48	.41	257	1.08	.20
5. Successful	.47	.50	304	0.16	.50
6. Sister	.40	.45	272	0.79	.30
7. Leader	.40	.41	303	0.18	.50
8. Old	.39	.27	208	2.03	.025
9. Self	.32	.34	168	2.80	.005
10. Follower	.22	.34	241	1.39	.10
11. Mother	.21	.23	276	0.71	.30
12. Prudish	.18	.08	245	1.31	.10
13. Homosexual	.16	.03	209	2.01	.025
14. Alcoholic	.14	.03	206	2.07	.025
15. Prostitute	.14	.16	279	.65	.30

3.6.5. *The interpretation of sex differences in social stereotyping — limitations of the findings and the need for further information*

To find that men and women differ in the concordance with which they formulate social stereotypes is not very useful unless it can be related to some specific process or rationale. Indeed, as will be seen, our discussion of specific sex differences in concordance can be carried out much more sensibly, and with less ambiguity, following the examination of sex differences in personal stereotyping — this being a factor which tends to rule out random responding as a basis for low concordances. Accordingly, we shall defer our particularised discussion of the individual sex differences arising in Table 3.7 until a more appropriate time.

However, an overview of Table 3.7 does yield two related generalities worth mentioning here. First, the observation of earlier studies, that men are slightly more concordant in stereotyping, receives some support. In averaging the *W*s (as *z*s) according to sex, we find that the male subjects, with a mean *W* of 0.38, are considerably more concordant than the females, who have an average *W* of just 0.28. Before making too much of this difference, however, it should be recognised that the relations between the sexes might be appreciably altered if a different or larger trait vocabulary were to be employed. Moreover, a good deal of the observed difference arises just from the discrepancy on the first three concepts — Like Least, Like Best and Wife.

This observation brings us to the second consideration, namely why should marked sex differences arise on a few specific concepts? That this is not an isolated instance can be easily verified by referring to Hamid's (1968) data, where it is seen, again, that men and women often achieve similar levels of concordance, but with women occasionally showing a marked lowering of consensus. The implications of this important feature will emerge more clearly after we have had the opportunity to examine some of the later data. But we can point out, in advance, that this pattern of exceptional discrepancies is an enduring sex linked phenomenon reflecting definite features of the cultural matrix.

Before concluding, we must turn our attention to the interesting and instructive anomaly arising out of the rating on Self, where a sharp sex difference is indicated by the *U* statistic, irrespective of the nearly equivalent *W*s of the two sexes. On the basis of the *W*s, males and females are seen to be equally concordant in judging their own body build against that of the six targets, and yet the *U* test indicates that the underlying distribution of *rho*s (between the individual judges and the criterion ranking of their respective groups) are markedly unalike ($U = 168$, $z = 2.80$, $p < .005$). Because of this discrepancy between the U and Ws, we undertook to inspect the two samples of *rho*s upon which the U test itself was based — and in doing this it was found that five of the female subjects perceived themselves as being markedly discrepant from the criterion ranking (i.e. 'true ranking') of their own group. In contrast, the remaining 20 female subjects showed good agreement between their self ratings and the criterion ranking, leaving the distribution of female *rho*s in a markedly bimodal condition, while the corresponding distribution of 25 male *rho*s was unremarkable. In removing the five most atypical subjects (i.e. those with the largest Σd^2s) from each group, the W for females increased to 0.73, while that for males rose only to 0.42. In passing, it should be noted that the W of 0.73 is the largest to be derived from any of the items in the trait vocabulary, suggesting that the 'self stereotype' might figure prominently in future studies.

By way of explanation, the five atypical females perceived themselves, in respect to their peers, as being relatively obese, but because of the rarity of this body build among female university students (Jenkins, 1971), the net effect of this was the degrading of their group's W, in much the manner described by Kendall (1948, p. 89; see Section 2.2.1). In other words, this small group of subjects tended to have strong negative intercorrelations with the remaining members of their group, and by this extremity, reduced the W in a disproportionate manner. Here, it is interesting that the U test, which is easily confounded by aberrant extreme scores, was able to pick up the discrepancy as well as it did — in circumstances such as these, the Kolmogorov-Smirnov two-sample test would, due to its equal weighting of all constituent data, be altogether more robust. In keeping with Kendall's caution concerning the interpretation of W, we would, in a like manner, suggest a visual inspection of the distributions of Σd^2 or, as an alternative, the use of two statistical tests which are sensitive to different aspects of the distributions under consideration.

3.7 Personal stereotyping — results and implications

Because many of the theoretical implications and some of the problems and methods of measurement have been discussed at length in other places, we will concentrate here on the data analysis *per se*, the results, and their more specific implications.

3.7.1 Statistical analysis and results

As will be recalled, we have suggested (Section 2.3), in brief, that the most fundamental instance of measurable stereotyping occurs when a judge is consistent in allocating traits to targets in a discriminating manner. As was pointed out, it is entirely possible that virtually perfect personal stereotyping could arise from data which are totally devoid of consensus or social stereotyping.

Given this background, it was decided that the average correlation (i.e. mean *rho*) between related traits — antonyms in the present case — would reflect the influence of both social and personal stereotyping, while the coefficient of concordance (*W*) is based on social stereotyping and social stereotyping alone. In view of these relationships, it seems reasonable to compare *W* and mean *rho* directly, to ascertain the relative contribution of social and personal stereotyping to total stereotyping — a comparison which is made possible by the availability of a procedure which allows *W* to be transformed to a mean *rho* equivalent (Siegel, 1956, pp. 229-32; Winer, 1962, p. 137).

Accordingly, we computed the *rho*s between our three pairs of

Table 3.8

Comparison of Indicators of Social Stereotyping (*W*) and Personal Stereotyping (*Rho*) for Three Pairs of Antonyms

	Antonyms	Individual *W*s*	Average *W*†	*Rho* between‡
I.	Like Least	.56		
	Like Best	.55	.56	.80
II.	Young	.43		
	Old	.31	.37	.59
III.	Leader	.37		
	Follower	.24	.31	.48

* Transformed to *r* in Winer's (1962) notation.
† Averaged as *z*s.
‡ All *rho*s shown to be significant ($p < .005$) elsewhere (Stewart et al., 1974, pp. 869-70).

specifically selected antonyms — Old/Young, Like Best/Like Least and Leader/Follower — which are presented in Table 3.8 so that they may be compared, by inspection, with the corresponding set of *W*s. As mentioned above, the *W*s presented in this Table have been transformed to their mean *rho* equivalents, thus reducing their value, as compared with Table 3.3, by 1 or 2 per cent — for the sake of clarity, however, we have continued to label them as '*W*s'. It will also be noted that we have omitted the negative signs from the correlations between antonyms.

As can be seen in Table 3.8, the average correlation between subjects (*W*) is invariably smaller than the average correlation between traits (*rho*), supporting our contention that personal stereotyping contributes significantly towards total stereotyping. Here it should be noted that both the *W*s and *rho*s are based on the entire sample of 50 subjects. For the reasons enumerated in Chapter 2 (p. 49), it was decided to rely on inspection, rather than statistical tests (Stewart et al., 1974, p. 870), in comparing *W*s with *rho*s. In fact the sheer difference in magnitude between the *W*s and *rho*s seem sufficient in its own right to obviate the need for formal significance testing.

3.7.2. Personal stereotyping — general implications

Undoubtedly, the most important aspect of this finding is to make suspect those definitions of stereotyping which rely on consensus — implying that social stereotyping is, indeed, a special case of stereotyping. Yet, while these results accord well with the notions of Kendall (1948) and Secord & Backman (1964) — all of whom advocated a certain shifting of focus from consensus towards the individual — this is not an unalloyed success, for now we are faced with the more awkward problem of having to deal with nomothetic and ideographic data simultaneously.

Inescapably, this change in emphasis in the method of defining stereotyping raises questions concerning the most appropriate means for measuring stereotyping. Except in the most unlikely case — where a single stereotype is shared by all the subjects — the coefficient of concordance (*W*) will, by confounding systematic individual differences, always underestimate the actual degree of stereotyping. By considering the data presented in Table 3.8 a bit further, the extent of this 'error' can be illustrated simply. Based on *W*, the variance explained (i.e. W^2 — recalling that *W* has been transformed to a mean *rho* equivalent) is, for the concept Like Least, estimated to be 31 per cent, while the estimate based on the corresponding antonymal intercorrelations (i.e. rho^2) is 64 per cent, or approximately twice as large. Continuing with Table 3.8, it can be seen that this 2:1 relationship — between total stereotyping and consensus — tends to hold for the remaining antonyms as well.

Looking ahead to our adolescent data in Chapters 7 and 8, we find (as has been noted in Section 2.3) even more serious distortions in the estimates of stereotyping based on *W*. Here, for example, the *W*s pertaining to Self and Future Self are found to attain values of only 0.07 approximately, while in complete contrast, the intercorrelation (mean *rho*) between Self and Future Self is seen to be a moderately respectable value of 0.65. In this case, the ratio of squares between *rho* and *W* is just slightly in excess of 80:1, rather than the 2:1 reported above. More important, however, is the fact that one measure (i.e. *W*) indicates a complete absence of stereotyping, while the other (i.e. *rho*) is indicating a quite reasonable level of stereotyping.

In one sense, these data cast grave doubts upon the ease and assurance with which *W*s of nonsignificant, small or even moderate magnitudes can be interpreted. While the finding of a large *W*, as in the case of Attractiveness, correctly implies the presence of a single social or cultural stereotype, the finding of a small *W* does not necessarily indicate that the converse is true. Among the several alternative possibilities arising from a small *W* are those of (1) random responding, (2) strongly personalised stereotyping, or most important here (3) that two or three more or less equally strong social stereotypes are nullifying one another in the data because they are contradictory. Thus, it may be patently incorrect to conclude that strong social or cultural forces are not at work simply because a small or nonsignificant *W* has been observed — that small *W*s are not, in themselves, sufficient evidence to reject the notions of stereotyping or social influence. We feel it necessary to stress this point because stereotyping is so closely identified with cultural influences and social learning, and the way in which their impact on behaviour is assessed and interpreted.

If, in spite of these difficulties, it is still decided to document or index social influences via *W*, it appears to be incumbent upon the investigator to demonstrate beforehand that the data in question are, in fact, suitable, and free from marked anomalies. At the very least, intercorrelations between traits should be computed, simply to see if they are consistent with the implications arising from the fallible *W*s. Before continuing, it is as well to point out that these suggestions for reducing ambiguity apply not only to *W* but to some of the more common place tests to be discussed below as well.

However, to enlarge upon this criticism, the coefficient of concordance is not the only commonly used statistical procedure which is open to the type of confounding considered above. Indeed, any statistical procedure which is applied in a trait by trait manner (i.e. analysing traits in isolation from one another) or is based on mean scores or is primarily concerned with differences between mean scores, is highly likely to obscure the degree of between trait consistency which may exist, unsuspected, at the level of the individual subjects and thereby underestimate the extent of structuring present in the data as a whole.

Turning to practicalities, many of our venerated tests — such as the X^2 tests, t tests, analysis of variance, and so on — are among the more suspect procedures. Analysis of variance, for example, has been used to investigate the influence of dress (Hamid, 1969) and attractiveness (Miller, 1970) on impression, and since analysis of variance is closely akin to W (Winer, 1962, pp. 136-8), it can be suggested that such an approach, by ignoring subjective factors, tends to underestimate the importance of the variables which it set out to investigate. As a first step in minimising these problems, we would suggest the adoption in general of correlational procedures, with these ranging from simple intercorrelations through factor analysis and some of the recent and very promising multidimensional scaling procedures and multivariate statistics. And on the basis of the data which constitute this book (i.e. the data on body build and dress taken together), we would suggest, as a second step, that trait vocabularies should be constructed so as to contain a good deal of redundance, either as antonyms, synonyms, near synonyms, etc., to ensure that potentially important traits do not inadvertently appear in isolation — factor analysis, etc., will not function as palliatives unless they are provided with suitable data. Here, of course, redundance in the trait vocabulary must be tempered by the limits of acceptable statistical practices, an appreciation of the psychological dimensions which need to be tapped, and practical considerations with respect to length and the availability of testing time.

As a final caution, however, it may be anticipated that some concepts, such as Wife, are so unique and complex in their interrelationships with traits and subjects as to be inextricable by 'automatic' procedures. It may be that some concepts will not be fully appreciated or understood unless they are singled out for special treatment, such as visually examining the distributions of individual Σd^2s composing their intercorrelations, and considering how, in turn, these features relate to differences and similarities between particular groups of subjects. It will be recalled that various aspects of this problem were touched upon earlier (e.g. Sections 2.2.1, 2.3.1 and 3.6.5).

3.8. Sex differences in personal stereotyping

In this section we again take up the continuing issue of sex differences in stereotyping, noting that we have already found seven differences in consensus. Fortuitously, two of the concepts for which there were sex differences in concordance — Like Best/Like Least — are also among those specially selected, as antonyms, for the testing of personal stereotyping, thereby providing us with a certain degree of direct evidence concerning the relationship of sex differences to social and personal stereotyping.

3.8.1. Procedures for comparing men and women on personal stereotyping

Consistent with our view that intercorrelations arising between antonyms represent total stereotyping, the problem posed here is to find or devise some satisfactory method of comparing the respective intercorrelations of the male and female groups. Considering that the present data are based on rankings, it follows that the intercorrelations between antonyms can be most easily computed as mean Spearman *rhos*, and that the basic datum for describing individual subjects will be again, as in Section 3.7.1, their own *rho*s (expressed in the form of Σd^2). To ascertain if the mean *rho*s for the antonyms differed according to the sex of the subjects, the 50 individual *rho*s (25 for each sex) were compared in a Mann-Whitney U test in a manner similar to the described in Section 3.6.3.

Table 3.9

Summary of Correlations between Antonyms (*rho*s) and U Tests Used to Test for Sex Differences in Personal Stereotyping

	*Rho*s Between Antonyms[1]		Sex Differences		
Antonym Pairs	Males[2]	Females[2]	U	z	p[3]
1. Like-Least/-Best	.85	.74	266	.90	.36
2. Young/Old	.58	.60	301	—.22	.82
3. Leader/Follower	.41	.56	264	—.94	.34

1. Negative signs omitted from *rhos*.
2. All six *rhos* found to be significantly different from zero by means of Kolmogrov-Smirnov one-sample tests (Stewart et al., 1974).
3. Two-tailed probabilities.

3.8.2 Sex differences in personal stereotyping — A failure to confirm

The testing of differences between intercorrelations was carried out separately for each of the three pairs of antonyms, and the resulting means, *U*s, and *z* equivalents (with probabilities) are presented in Table 3.9. In examining Table 3.9 it is immediately evident that none of the observed differences approach the levels required for rejecting the null hypothesis — namely that men and women, taking both personal and social components into account, do not differ in the extent to which they stereotype — indicating that men and women are more or less equal in total stereotyping. Considering, however, that the present data are based on only three isolated examples, it would seem unwise to make excessive generalisation from them.

Coming back to the problem of consensus, the present results represent something of a paradox. It would seem that women, while more diverse in attributing both Attractiveness and Unattractiveness than are men, are at the same time nearly as reliable or personally consistent when required to perform the same task twice. Turning to the two remaining pairs of antonyms, where the sex differences in concordance were less dramatic (e.g. Table 3.7), we find an essential confirmation of this conclusion.

3.8.3. Implications of the failure to find sex differences

In so far as there is a well documented (e.g. Winer, 1962, pp. 124-32) relationship between consensus and reliability, these data represent something of a paradox, but as Winer is quick to point out (p. 128), the expected relationship assumes that there are no systematic differences between judges. From this vantage, it seems reasonable to suggest that the present sample of female subjects are either more heterogeneous than the males or are possessed of some form of systematic bias which gives rise to subjective stereotyping.

Assuming that this interpretation is correct, it still remains to be seen whether such biases or heterogeneity are characteristic of women in general or whether they represent a once only occurrence, being unique to the present sample as a result of, say, errant sampling. This issue, of anomalous sampling and generality, has been partly resolved by our two later English studies, both of which show that the most important findings of the present investigation have been replicated there, at least in general terms.

Whatever else, it seems clear from these findings that random responding is not a generally adquate explanation for sex differences in social stereotyping or other instances of reduced consensus. Indeed, in looking at these and other comparable data (see Section 2.3) one truly wonders if there is ever a legitimate rationale for making face value interpretations of small or nonsignificant *W*s.

3.9 Correlations between traits — An examination of the way in which traits are construed and structured

Having examined the more important aspects of social stereotyping and trait attribution, we can now turn to a second and somewhat different feature of these data, namely, the correlations between traits. In keeping with other investigators (e.g. Bruner et al., 1958; Cronbach, 1958; Hays, 1958; Koltuv, 1962; Passini & Norman, 1966), we will proceed under the assumption that the observed correlations represent the way in which persons expect traits to co-exist in Others — that the patterns of correlations represent implicit expectations concerning the organisation of personality in Others, including both acquaintances and strangers. And while Norman (1963) and Kuusinen (1969) have shown that these implicit expectations show an unexpected degree of consensus and can be elicited by a wide range of stimuli (including samples of handwriting), it is worth noting that this problem has not been sufficiently scrutinised in the context of stereotyping, where the available correlations have been examined only superficially, if at all.

In view of this deficiency we have undertaken to investigate the nature of the correlations between traits here, and again, in several later locations (see Section 5.9 and Chapter 8). By way of preview, it can be suggested that the intercorrelations in question may serve several important functions: to shed additional light on previously observed sex differences; to undertake an initial consideration of conceptual stereotyping; and to provide for further clarification of the proposed close relationship between stereotyping and person perception.

3.9.1. Trait intercorrelations — Computational procedures and transformations

Because of the nature of these data (i.e. based on rankings) it was decided to compute the intercorrelations as *mean Spearman rho*s, as has been described graphically in Section 2.3.

To do this, we take a pair of traits and compute the correlation (i.e. *rho*) between them for each subject. This set of correlations, one for each subject, is then averaged to give the mean *rho* statistic. This process is repeated for every pair of traits, and when completed yields a set of 105 mean *rho*s for each sex (i.e. $(n^2-2)/2$ correlations for each sex). The mean *rho*s from the US study, which we will simply refer to as correlations, are shown in Table 3.10. The correlations for the female subjects are shown in the upper triangle of this Table.

Because correlation coefficients (e.g. *rho*s) are not, in the proper sense, additive we have introduced two further steps into the computation of mean *rho*s to correct for this difficulty. First, and recalling that most common correlation coefficients, such as *rho*, are in fact cosines, each individual *rho* — as derived from individual subjects — is *transformed into the angle to which it corresponds* in the trigonometric sense. Next, the angles are summed and divided by the number of subjects to obtain the *average angle*, and as a final step, transformed back into a *cosine*, which represents the mean Spearman *rho*s as presented in Table 3.10. This transformation has been discussed in more detail in one of our earlier papers (Stewart et al., 1975, p. 460), but essentially represents a technical improvement over the straight averaging of individual *rho*s (Slater, 1972, p. 46) and results in a slightly larger mean *rho*. Thus, in a few instances, where it was considered desirable to compare obtained samples of *rho*s with their corresponding theoretical distributions (as in Tables 2.4, 3.8 and 3.9 for example), we have not employed this angular transformation, and consequently the values of mean *rho*s presented here will be slightly larger than their earlier counterparts.

3.9.2. Trait intercorrelations obtained for male and female subjects in the American study

Because of the realistic supposition that there might be sex differences in the trait intercorrelations of the US study it seemed best to present them separately for each sex in Table 3.10, with the data from the female subjects being above the diagonal. Following Bendig (1956; Hartley, 1953) the significance of the individual mean *rho*s was ascertained by reference to the usual *z* procedure (Edwards, 1950, p. 136; McNemar, 1969, pp. 157-8).

In examining Table 3.10, it can be seen that 120, or slightly more than one half of the correlations, are significantly different from zero in two-tailed tests.

There are several general features worth noting in Table 3.10. First, and as mentioned earlier (see Section 2.3), each of the 15 concepts comprising the US trait vocabulary give rise to at least one (or more) intercorrelations which are larger than its observed coefficient of

Table 3.10

Intercorrelations[1] between Concepts: U.S. study, 25 Subjects of each Sex, Females in Upper Triangle

	1	2	3	4	5	6	7	8	9	10	11	12	13	14	15
1. Prostitute		—15	26*	—03	07	46‡	43‡	44‡	23*	37‡	—35†	07	35†	—27*	36‡
2. Old	—25*		—21	21	07	—46‡	—40‡	—68‡	—15	—33†	61‡	19	—58‡	13	—43‡
3. Wife	34†	—56‡		—13	—23*	50‡	36‡	35†	42‡	26*	—46‡	—18	43‡	—34†	37‡
4. Prudish	—19	21	—33†		—03	—08	—10	—01	—30†	—23*	23*	—09	—25*	13	—21
5. Alcoholic	08	—16	14	06		—11	—11	—17	—15	—07	—01	06	—06	01	—04
6. Sister	35†	—57‡	56‡	—28*	—02		62‡	71‡	12	17	—64‡	—15	71‡	—21	53‡
7. Successful	28*	—52‡	66‡	—35‡	00	50‡		66‡	22	55‡	—59‡	07	57‡	—52‡	46‡
8. Young	24*	—67‡	59‡	—14	21	51‡	50‡		04	29†	—60‡	—01	60‡	—26*	56‡
9. Mother	21	13	—05	—22	07	07	04	—36‡		35†	—15	—02	18	—23*	20
10. Leader	24*	—40‡	52‡	—11	08	27*	56‡	34†	02		—26*	18	24*	—62‡	47‡
11. Like Least	—46‡	69‡	—81‡	27*	—08	—60‡	—70‡	—71‡	12	—55‡		24*	—82‡	22	—64‡
12. Homosexual	09	11	—04	23*	26*	—17	—02	—03	11	17	15		—22	—17	03
13. Like Best	39‡	—60‡	82‡	—34†	11	66‡	72‡	62‡	—10	55‡	—91‡	—11		—27*	63‡
14. Follower	—05	30†	—39‡	31‡	14	—13	—52‡	—17	15	—48‡	38‡	06	—14		—40‡
15. Self	30†	—31†	56‡	—33†	05	34†	53‡	29†	—07	41‡	—59‡	—03	59‡	—52‡	

* $p < .05$. †$p < .01$ ‡$p < .001$ [1]Decimal points omitted

concordance (W, e.g. Table 3.3). Earlier, it was suggested that this discrepancy probably reflects the operation of subjective factors, but regardless of interpretation the present results clearly indicate that W tends to underestimate the degree of stereotyping present in most sets of data.

Second, W, when it is small but significant, does not seem to be a particularly good predictor of either the strength or number of significant intercorrelations in which a trait will participate. Prostitute, for example, which has a W roughly comparable with those of either Alcoholic or Homosexual, does in fact yield many more significant intercorrelations than either of these, with this difference being specially pronounced in the data of the male subjects. The trait of Prudishness might be thought to illustrate the same principle as Prostitute, but this is somewhat questionable because of its marginally larger W. Taken collectively, these observations serve well to highlight the problematical nature of small Ws and their interpretation.

3.9.3. Interpretations and implications of trait intercorrelations

Here, in accordance with Cronbach (1958) and others (e.g. Asch, 1952; Bruner et al., 1958; Koltuv, 1962; Ryle, 1975), significant correlations between traits are construed to be a reflection of the way in which our judges expect these traits to co-vary in Others. Taking an example from our own data, it can be seen that a relationship is perceived to exist between being a Leader and being Successful (r_m = 0.56, r_f = 0.55), implying that our subjects expect these traits to alter systematically — both higher, both lower, or both unchanged — as they consider various target persons. It is noteworthy that several of the earlier investigators (e.g. Newcomb, 1931; Thorndike, 1920) adopted somewhat different points of view towards such correlations — treating them as 'logical errors' or 'halo effects' — because they were much larger than could be expected on the basis of objective evidence (Koltuv, 1962, pp. 1-2; Mason, 1957), but even these somewhat variant interpretations do not diminish the potential importance of such associations in social interaction and our understanding of social behaviour (Marks, 1965; Ryle, 1975; Slater, 1976; Tagiuri & Petrullo, 1958).

On the other hand, a simple bivariate correlation between traits may obscure other important considerations, such as whether the relationship between traits is conditional (A implies B, but not vice versa) or unconditional (A implies B, B implies A), or whether one trait is more 'central' or salient than the other (Asch, 1946; Wishner, 1960). Moreover, it sometimes happens that male and female subjects yield apparently equivalent associations between traits (i.e. *r*s of comparable magnitude) which are later shown to derive from entirely different considerations. We find, for example, that the correlation between Leader and Successful decreases markedly for male subjects (from 0.56 to 0.28) when Attractiveness is partialled out (see Sections 3.9.8 & 3.9.9 for details), but remains largely unaffected for the females, decreasing from 0.55 to just 0.52. Without debating the generality of this finding, it is clear that our female subjects have employed different criteria than those of the males — possibly focusing more on Potency or Masculinity than Physical Attractiveness — in relating the concepts of Successful and Leader to female target persons (Krech & Crutchfield, 1948, p. 437; Mason, 1957). Clearly there are a number of considerations, such as conditionality, centrality and latent sex differences, which one must bear in mind when examining the intercorrelations presented in Table 3.10, and attempting to extrapolate from them to other circumstances.

In looking at Table 3.10, it is quickly evident that Attractiveness and Unattractiveness enter into a majority of the larger correlations, of say 0.60 and greater, with this trend being considerably more pronounced in the case of the males. Traditionally, such a finding would be dismissed as nothing more than a 'halo effect', but in view of the large amount of more recent research showing physical attractiveness to be one of the key variables in social interaction (see Chapter 4), the present results seem to be worthy of further consideration, and may even be seen as additional confirmation of this somewhat unpopular thesis (Aronson, 1969). In common with the majority of studies (see Demer & Thiel (1975) for exceptions), greater Attractiveness is perceived by our subjects to imply other positive qualities, such as being desirable as a Wife, a Leader, Successful, and Young rather than *Old*. There is also a positive correlation between Physical Attractiveness and Prostitute, but in light of the extreme range of our target persons the rationale behind this association appears to be self-evident.

Before, however, concluding that Attractiveness is the sole feature moderating trait inferences, it is worthwhile to point out that subsequent analyses (see Sections 3.9.8 & 5.10) have revealed a second variable, alluded to above as Potency or Masculinity, which also serves as a basis for inferences. This variable finds expression in correlations involving traits such as Follower, Young, Maternal and Self, although the exact nature of the influence varies with the two sexes. While our data show this constituent to be a secondary feature of social image, it is possible that other trait vocabularies may bring it into greater prominence.

Considering that Table 3.10 contains some 120 significant intercorrelations, it is not feasible to discuss them individually here. Additional examples will be found in the sections which follow, and later, in Chapters 5, 6 & 8. Between these various sources, one should find sufficient information to clarify most questions concerning these intercorrelations and the interpretations which can be applied to them.

3.9.4. Sex differences in the association and inference of traits

Because one of our prime aims was to investigate as many potential instances of sex differences as possible, and encouraged by our earlier findings of sex differences in both trait attribution (Section 3.5.3) and concordance (Section 3.6.4.), it seemed obligatory to compare the intercorrelations presented in Table 3.10 for the presence of sex differences. On the basis of Hartley's (1953) demonstration, that it was acceptable to employ Fisher's *z* transformation with mean *rho*s, we used the procedures outlined by McNemar (1969, pp. 157-8) in making the 105 individual comparisons which were required. The results are presented in

Table 3.11

Summary of the Trait Intercorrelations which were found to yield Significant Sex Differences in the U.S. Study

Traits	Males	Females	z_{sex}	p^{1}_{sex}
1. Wife/Old	—.56	—.21	2.57	.01
2. Wife/Alcoholic	.14	—.23	2.30	.03
3. Wife/Successful	.66	.36	2.55	.01
4. Wife/Young	.59	.35	1.95	.05
5. Wife/Mother	—.05	.42	3.05	.002
6. Wife/Like Least	—.81	—.46	3.86	.001
7. Wife/Like Best	.82	.43	4.27	.001
8. Homosexual/Prudish	.23	—.09	1.99	.05
9. Young/Alcoholic	.21	—.17	2.36	.02
10. Young/Sister	.51	.71	1.99	.05
11. Young/Mother	—.36	.04	2.55	.01
12. Young/Self	.29	.56	2.05	.05
13. Mother/Leader	.02	.35	2.12	.04
14. Mother/Follower	.15	—.23	2.36	.02
15. Leader/Like Least	—.55	—.26	2.16	.03
16. Leader/Like Best	.55	.24	2.29	.03
17. Like Best/Like Least	—.91	—.82	2.27	.03

[1]Two-tailed probabilities.

Table 3.11, and here, as in earlier sections, we have employed two-tailed probabilities in determining the significance of sex differences.

The summary of sex differences displayed in Table 3.11 show one marked exception from the previous findings in one important respect — that unlike concordance (Section 3.6.4.) and trait attribution (Section 3.5.3.), which disclosed sex differences in only a few quite specific traits, the present intercorrelations involve 14 out of the total of 15 traits, with only Prostitute showing no sex differences. On closer examination, however, it can be seen that each of the intercorrelations displayed in Table 3.11, except only one (namely Young/Sister), involve at least one trait which has evidenced sex differences in either or both of the two earlier tests. Upon reflection, however, this finding is perhaps not so surprising, in that one would not expect traits which had not previously evidenced sex differences to suddenly manifest them when paired in an intercorrelation — noting that in the case of the one exception (i.e. Young/Sister), both traits had shown strong trends in the direction of sexual differentiation. Nonetheless, it is interesting that some intercorrelations which involve a strongly sex typed concept such as Wife/Successful, show sex differences, while other pairings, which appear vis à vis to be equally likely candidates (e.g. Wife/Follower), fail to do so. And while we do not have any ready explanation for these findings in general, nor the interesting variations which they display, it does seem probable that intercorrelations will prove to be one of the more efficient and straightforward methods for investigating sex differences in future studies.

It can also be seen in Table 3.11 that the male subjects yielded the larger intercorrelations somewhat more frequently than did the females, i.e. in 11 out of the 17 instances of sex differences. However, this observation should be tempered by noting that the present trait vocabulary is small, and may show some unintentional biases which in some way favour the male subjects.

In line with our earlier comments, we will not, here, attempt to interpret these various sex differences, except for a few by way of example. In light of the importance of the various sex differences which have in combination grown out of the English and American studies, the more central of these data have been collected together for detailed consideration in Chapter 6.

Taking up one of the more important sex differences to serve as an example, we find that the Mother/Wife intercorrelations differ quite substantially between the male (r = -0.05) and female subjects (r = 0.42), with this difference being largely unaffected by the partialling out of

Attractiveness (in Table 3.13). Considering the males first, it is clear that the mean intercorrelation (-0.05) is not significant, and we can safely conclude that there is no *general* tendency for the male subjects to perceive the role of Wife as being particularly similar to that of Mother. Having thus ruled out group trends for the males, the possibility of *personal stereotyping* or *contradictory social stereotying* was next appraised in accordance with the procedure suggested in Section 2.4.1, but the resulting F of 1.43 ($df = 24/\infty$, $.10 < p < .05$) fell slightly short of the value required for the 5 per cent level.

For the sake of illustration, however, we shall treat the observed variance ($s^2 = 351.0$) as if large enough to require interpretation. From Section 2.4 we know that inflated variances arise when samples of *rho*s contain unexpectedly large proportions of sizable positive and negative correlations (e.g. the distribution of the sample is bimodal or platykurtic). Such an occurrence suggests that for some appreciable segment of the male subjects the roles of Wife and Mother were perceived to be *either* markedly consistent with one another, *or* markedly incompatible with one another, and that fewer small, noncommitted correlations were obtained than expected. To be somewhat more precise — and recalling that the males were much more concordant on Wife (W = 0.53) than Mother (W = 0.21) — we can infer that these subjects are concordant in their positive perception of Wife, but heterogeneous in their evaluations of Mother, with some showing strong approval and others denigrating this role.

The data from the female subjects do, however, provide an entirely different picture — with the concordances for both Wife (W = 0.17) and Mother (W = 0.23) being relatively small, but at the same time revealing a quite reasonable intercorrelation (r = 0.42) between the two. As we have considered elsewhere (Sections 2.3 and 3.7.1 for example), the finding of appreciable intercorrelations in conjunction with low concordances is *prima facie* evidence of subjective stereotyping, but begs the question of whether we have encountered two or three stereotypes (i.e. multiple stereotypes) or a set of strongly articulated roles where there are nearly as many 'images' (i.e. personal stereotypes) as there are subjects.

Notwithstanding our present inability to specify the number of stereotypes involved in the relationship between Wife and Mother, there are a few general observations which are in order here. First, the finding of subjective stereotyping (be it either multiple or personal stereotyping) implies that the concepts in question are undergoing, either jointly or independently, some type of transition, either of social implication or cultural definition. And second, the present findings of a modest intercorrelation indicate that irrespective of their more or less differentiated perspectives, the female subjects do see either a general relationship (i.e. a modest correlation across many subjects) between Mother and Wife or, alternatively, that a smaller subset of subjects perceive a relatively strong relationship between the two but with their own influence (i.e. high mean intercorrelation) being diluted by the alternative responding of the equally large or more numerous body of dissenting subjects. In other words, the present correlation ($r = 0.42$) could be obtained even if approximately one half of the subjects had perceived the role of Mother as being totally unrelated to that of Wife, provided of course that the remaining subjects displayed individual correlations between Mother and Wife at a level of approximately 0.85 each.

Having ascertained that the relationship between Wife and Mother is apt to be based on subjective rather than social stereotypes, we can extend this line of enquiry further by attempting to specify the underlying nature of the stereotypes with somewhat more precision — e.g. whether the stereotypes are based on, say, Evaluation, description (i.e. congruence) or inference, etc. — by the use of partial correlations. By referring to Table 3.13, we find that the partialling out of Attractiveness only reduces the correlation between Mother and Wife from 0.42 to 0.39, from whence we can conclude that only about 5 per cent of the observed relationship is due to Attractiveness (Ferguson, 1959, p. 291). In view of this finding it seems reasonable to conclude that the stereotypes which enter into the association between these two traits will ultimately be found to be descriptive or functional in nature, rather than Evaluative. And while it does appear that our female subjects are equating the roles of Mother and Wife through such features as inferred age, apparent fecundity, lack of frailty or quality of inferred character, it is very likely, as shown by Wiggins, Hoffman & Taber (1969), for example, that different subjects seize upon particular facets which they, as individuals, find most relevant to their own conception of Wife and Mother, and weigh them accordingly in arriving at their judgements.

The data from the females manifests a broad relationship between Mother and Wife which is thought to be primarily descriptive or functional in nature, and almost entirely devoid of Evaluation. Although not overwhelming in magnitude, the attitude towards Mother does seem to be generally positive, at least to the extent that it can be inferred from the correlations at hand (cf. Mother / Attractive, Mother/ Leader, etc.). Noting that there is also a moderate correlation ($r = 0.43$) between Wife and Attractive — which, equally importantly, is virtually independent from that between Wife and Mother — it can be tentatively suggested that the Mother/Wife relationship is due primarily to the responding of a particular subset of female subjects. In other words, there may be one group of female subjects who perceive Wife to be strongly allied with Mother, a second, who associate Wife with Attractive, and yet a third subset for whom we have, so far, established no firm basis of association (if any). If one equates the maternal association with traditional attitudes, and the attractiveness based relationship with modern or transitional attitudes, then a marked similarity can be found with the recent dichotomy in the role of Wife posited by Broverman and his colleagues (Broverman et al., 1970, 1972; Vogel et al., 1970, 1975).

3.9.5. An examination of conceptual stereotyping in the US data

Earlier it was proposed that intercorrelations between traits or concepts can serve to indicate whether conceptual stereotyping is occurring — that is, whether an intrinsically complex, abstract or multifaceted concept is being employed as though it represented some much more simple or concrete entity. In the earlier location, we argued that large intercorrelations between terms or concepts with only a marginal commonality of meaning could, because the participating concepts must be divested of their more broad raning implications, stand as evidence of conceptual stereotyping.

Accordingly we have abstracted, from Table 3.10, all the intercorrelations which approach or exceed the value of 0.70 (in absolute terms) so that they could be viewed collectively in Table 3.12. While the 'cutting score' of 0.70 is, of course, arbitrary, it should be recognised that the correlations in question are, because of attenuation due to unreliability, rather conservative estimators of the 'true' relationships which they represent. Moreover, it can be safely assumed that some appreciable proportion of the subjects do, in fact, evidence individual correlations which are well in excess of the observed means — raising at the same time the important question as to whether there are systematic differences in the degree to which various subjects display conceptual stereotyping. From this point of view, it is evident that the notion of conceptual stereotyping is closely akin to that of cognitive complexity (e.g. Vannoy, 1965).

Before turning to the more specific problems, it is probably worth while to note, with one exception, that all the intercorrelations shown in Table 3.12 involve either Attractiveness or Unattractiveness. In the present context, it seems that if conceptual stereotyping does occur, it is due to the usurpation of fine nuances of meaning and inference by Evaluation. Undoubtedly, most readers will have noticed, in addition, that these results are consistent with the phenomenon of 'halo effect', which is so often mentioned in the context of person perception and stereotyping. And while we would not disagree with this conclusion, it should be pointed out that recent research has given rise to the notion that Evaluation is one of the most salient variables in person perception and social interaction, making it imperative that we treat 'halo effects' as cognitive realities of major importance, and not merely brush them aside as 'inconveniences' or test artifacts.

With this background in mind, we can turn to two pairs of intercorrelations — namely Wife and Attractive, and Old and Unattractive — which are suggestive of conceptual stereotyping. Both are derived from the male subjects. In the case of Wife and Attractiveness ($r = 0.82$), it would appear that the male subjects, when contemplating potential mates, hold physical attractiveness in mind as a primary consideration, and relegate such matters as homemaking, child rearing, and perhaps to a lesser extent, even personality to positions of secondary importance. Clearly, it would be rash to make such sweeping claims solely on the basis of our own data (replicated in the English studies, however), but there is a growing body of contemporary data which also points in very much the same direction.

The concept of Old presents a rather different picture from that of Wife. Here, since our subjects were for the most part young, we can dismiss any notion of direct or immediate ego involvement, but none the less a mainly Evaluative relationship is seen to emerge. While we have no direct evidence on this matter, it can be hypothesised that the immediate reaction to encountering an elderly stranger is one of aversion.

Table 3.12

Intercorrelations with Values approaching or greater than 0.70

Concepts	r[1]	Sex	Concepts	r[1]	Sex
Wife/Attractive	82	Males	Young/Unattractive	—70	Males
Wife/Unattractive	—81	Males	Old/Unattractive	69	Males
Successful/Attractive	72	Males	Sister/Young	71	Females
Successful/Unattractive	—70	Males	Sister/Attractive	71	Females

[1]Decimal points omitted.

Not having a definite statistical criterion for conceptual stereotyping makes the whole notion somewhat problematical, but it is hoped that the concept can, with due consideration, be firmly established within a sound methodological framework.

3.9.6. Articulation and consistency in stereotyping — a point of comparison with person perception

Here, in comparison with person perception, stereotyping faces a dilemma akin to that of Scylla and Charybdis — too little consistency would imply chaotic or whimsical responding, while excessive consistency might be indicative of an unrealistic dominance by factors such as Evaluation or 'halo effects'. We shall consider these alternatives below, relying primarily on the US intercorrelations (presented in Table 3.10) for our analysis. Before setting off, however, it should be clearly borne in mind that the considerations raised here apply mainly to the stereotyping of body build and dress and, although we hope that they apply in other circumstances, they may or may not be representative of all possible instances of stereotyping.

It is perhaps most convenient to begin with the problem of low consistency or low association between traits. It is assumed that the lack of a systematic basis for evaluating the various traits would result in a preponderance of small and nonsignificant intercorrelations. However, the finding of 120 significant intercorrelations out of a total of 210 goes a long way towards supporting the notion of a sytematised basis of stereotyping.

With this background in mind it seems, then, only reasonable to conclude that there is a systematic cognitive framework within which stereotyping is carried out. And indeed, this supposition is in good agreement with results found for stereotyping in other, rather different circumstances (e.g. Gardner et al, 1968). Moreover, these findings strengthen our contention that there is a close relationship between person perception and stereotyping. Next, we must examine the nature of the underlying cognitive structure, with the purpose of determining if it represents more than a 'halo effect' or homogeneous instance of Evaluation.

This can be carried out in two rather different ways. First, we can enquire as to whether there is an excess of large correlations, this being a condition which is presumed to originate from 'halo effects' (e.g. Koltuv, 1962). Second, we can investigate the data to ascertain whether any other basis for judgement, i.e. other than Evaluation, has been employed here.

Because the present data are based on a restricted number of subjects, this latter analysis will be carried out withthe aid of partial correlations rather than a factor analysis (see Section 5.9).

Turning first to the problem of whether or not there is an unexpectedly high frequency of exceptionally large correlations, we can go back, momentarily, to Table 3.12, from whence it will be recalled that only eight correlations approached or exceeded the arbitrarily chosen level of 0.70. Furthermore, the absolute value of the median correlation is only approaching the value of 0.27. So, on these two counts, it seems reasonable to conclude that there is no evidence suggestive of exaggeratedly large intercorrelations in these data.

Having established this point, we can now turn our attention to the problem of ascertaining just what are the bases that are involved in arriving at these stereotypic judgements. And since it was decided to approach this problem through the use of partial correlations (cf. Koltuv, 1962), the first issue at hand was that of selecting the variable (i.e. trait) which would provide for the most efficient partialling — e.g. the one which is presumed to make the largest contribution to the greatest number of correlations. In looking at Tables 3.10 and 3.12 it was obvious that either Like Best or Like Least were the prime candidates for this function, and accordingly, Like Best was partialled out of the correlations presented in Table 3.10. In the light of this decision, it is appropriate, here, to recall that the subjects were asked to use an aesthetic standard when rating the targets for Attractiveness in order to establish a broad or external frame of reference for the concept (see Section 3.4.4). Table 3.13 shows the resulting partial correlations, presented separately for the two sexes, with the data from the females in the upper triangle (i.e. above the diagonal).

The most striking feature of Table 3.13 is that we have, by this partialling operation, reduced the number of significant correlations from 120 to just 33 each. This drastic reduction does, at once, vindicate our choice of Like Best as the most salient or most ubiquitous of the fourteen variables (disregarding, of course, its antonym, Like Least). In this context, it is interesting to note that Like Least still continues to yield five significant partial correlations, supporting the notion that semantic opposites, such as Most and Least Attractive, are not necessarily in perfect logical or psychological juxtaposition (Stewart et al., 1974, p. 871). In any event, it seems quite clear that Attractiveness forms the basis for a substantial 'halo effect' by making a notable intrusion into approximately 72 per cent of the significant correlations shown in Table 3.10.

Table 3.13

Intercorrelations between the U.S. Traits with Attractiveness Partialled Out. Correlations due to the Female Subjects are Shown in the Upper Triangle[1]

	1	2	3	4	5	6	7	8	9	10	11	12	14	15
1. Prostitute		07	13	06	10	32*	30*	31*	18	31*	—12	16	—19	19
2. Old	01		05	08	04	—08	—10	—51‡	—06	—24	29*	07	—03	—10
3. Wife	03	04		—03	—23	31*	15	13	39†	19	—21	—10	—26	14
4. Prudish	—07	—02	—10		—05	14	05	18	—27	—18	05	—15	07	—07
5. Alcoholic	04	—12	09	10		—10	—09	—17	—14	—06	—10	05	—01	00
6. Sister	13	—24	04	10	—12		37†	50‡	—01	00	—14	01	—03	15
7. Successful	00	—09	18	—16	—11	05		48‡	15	52‡	—26	24	—46†	16
8. Young	00	—44†	18	16	18	17	10		—09	19	—24	16	—13	29*
9. Mother	27	09	06	—27	08	18	16	—38†		32*	00	02	—19	11
10. Leader	03	—06	14	10	02	—15	28*	00	09		—11	25	—59‡	42†
11. Like Least	—28*	29*	—27	—10	05	00	—16	—45†	07	—14		11	00	—28*
12. Homosexual	15	05	09	21	28*	—13	09	05	10	28*	12		—24	22
14. Follower	01	28*	—49‡	28*	16	—05	—61‡	—11	14	—49‡	62‡	04		—23
15. Self	09	13	16	—17	—02	—08	19	—12	—01	13	—16	04	—55‡	

$^*p < .05$ $^\dagger p < .01$ $^\ddagger p < .001$ [1]Decimal points omitted.

What should we make of this 'halo effect' — does it represent an intractable difference between stereotyping and person perception? For a variety of reasons we do not perceive this to be the case. First, and as mentioned earlier, there is now accumulating evidence (see Section 1.3) that Evaluation and 'halo effects' do play a very important role in both person perception and some types of social interaction. Second, we have already seen that the correlations in question are of only moderate size, and are not, on average, appreciably larger than those which survive partialling. And third, which is most important, the partial correlations do, in themselves, indicate that there are at least one or more independent cognitive factors which can co-exist with Evaluation — which are capable of serving as independent bases for framing judgements in the context of stereotyping. Consequently, we shall explore the nature and implications of those correlations in more detail below.

With the hindsight provided by the English studies, it is somewhat less difficult to undertake a provisional classification of the 33 significant partial correlations. In looking at Table 3.13 it is evident that the concepts of Leader, Follower and Successful do, as a group, occasion the largest number of significant correlations, and thus become our most interesting candidate for being an independent basis of judgement. In considering the implications of these three attributes, as well as the factor structure derived from the English data (see Section 5.9.3), it is reasonable to suppose that these particular items represent a quality or connotation much like that of Potency. Here, then, is the suggestion that observers are not only concerned with locating stereotypic target persons along a 'Good-Bad' dimension (i.e. Evaluation), but are, in some circumstances, equally or more concerned with assessing their competence or potential for authority (i.e. Potency) as well.

It seems that the present data are well articulated in spite of being based on stereotyping, with the subjects not only attending to Evaluation, but responding at least to Potency as well. This finding is in good accord with the expectations concerning person perception. More important, however, these results indicate that the cognitive factors called into play by a test based on stereotyping are very much dependent upon the nature and content of the trait vocabulary employed. Indeed, it could be argued that it is possible to create a stereotyping test in which Evaluation is entirely absent and thereby preclude the evocation of any 'halo effect', at least in the sense that the term is usually employed. It is also worth while to note that these results were obtained from tests based on body build, which we feel are, perhaps, less salient (and more prone to 'halo effects') than those based on differences in dress (see Chapters 7 and 8).

3.9.7 Sex differences in trait association when target persons have been 'equated' for Attractiveness — a finding in favour of women's perceptiveness

In accordance with the rationale presented earlier (see Section 3.9.6), we have compared the partial correlations presented in Table 3.13 — showing the degree of correlation which would be expected if the targets had all been of equal Attractiveness — to see if men and women differ in these expectations. The nineteen instances in which sex differences were found are summarised here, in Table 3.14. As discussed earlier one-tailed probabilities were used in compiling this particular Table.

One of the most evident features of Table 3.14 is that, unlike earlier,

Table 3.14

Correlations which show Sex Differences following the Partialling out of Attractiveness — US Data

Pairs of Traits	Males[1]	Females[1]	z	$p<$	Larger r
1. Successful/Prostitute	.00 (.28)	.30 (.43)	1.88	.05	Females
2. Successful/Sister	.05 (.50)	.37 (.62)	2.06	.025	Females
3. Successful/Young	.10 (.50)	.48 (.66)	2.57	.005	Females
4. Successful/Leader	.28 (.56)	.52 (.55)	1.76	.05	Females
5. Follower/Old	.28 (.30)	—.03 (.13)	1.93	.05	Males
6. Follower/Wife	—.49 (—.39)	—.26 (—.34)	1.64	.05	Males
7. Follower/Self	—.55 (—.52)	.23 (—.40)	2.34	.01	Males
8. Follower/Mother	.14 (.15)	—.19 (—.23)	2.03	.025	Females
9. Leader/Prostitute	.03 (.24)	.31 (.37)	1.77	.05	Females
10. Leader/Prudish	.10 (—.11)	—.18 (—.23)	1.72	.05	Females
11. Leader/Self	.13 (.41)	.42 (.47)	1.93	.05	Females
12. Young/Prostitute	.00 (.24)	.31 (.44)	1.95	.05	Females
13. Young/Alcoholic	.18 (.08)	—.17 (—.07)	2.15	.025	Females
14. Young/Sister	.17 (.51)	.50 (.71)	2.30	.025	Females
15. Young/Mother	—.38 (—.36)	—.09 (.04)	1.88	.05	Males
16. Wife/Alcoholic	.09 (.14)	—.23 (—.23)	1.97	.025	Females
17. Wife/Sister	.04 (.56)	.31 (.50)	1.71	.05	Females
18. Wife/Mother	.06 (—.05)	.39 (.42)	2.14	.025	Females
19. Prudish/Homosexual	.21 (.23)	—.15 (—.09)	2.22	.025	Males

[1]For ease of reference, the unpartialled rs from Table 3.10 are shown within the parentheses.

the female subjects do, here, yield the majority of large (partial) correlations, providing the superior correlation in fourteen out of the nineteen comparisons. This finding is almost the exact opposite of those observed earlier, in Tables 3.10 and 3.11 for example, where the men were found to provide the majority of large correlations.

Recalling that the particular partialling operation employed here attempts, statistically (McNemar, 1969, p. 184), to equate the six target persons for Attractiveness, the implications of the present difference between the sexes seems quite clear — namely that differences in Attractiveness have a much greater net influence on the male subjects than on the females when forming their judgements or making inferences about the female targets. Alternatively, it could be said that the female subjects, in formulating their judgements, are more responsive to those aspects of the targets which are in themselves unrelated in Attractiveness — that they are, vis à vis males, more likely to respond to the non-evaluative aspects of female targets and, in this sense, may be capable of making finer discriminations.

Notwithstanding that the data from adolescent boys and girls have also occasioned a comparable sex difference in the utilisation of Evaluative cues (Powell, Stewart & Tutton, 1974), it would probably be unwise to generalise these findings too far since we have never employed male target persons. It is possible that this relationship depends upon the sex of the targets, and that the present outcome would be reversed, i.e. with males being less influenced by Evaluation, if the gender of the targets had also been reversed.

3.10 The differential stereotyping of similar physiques

In this final section we shall take up the problem of ascertaining by how much targets must differ in order to alter their impressions. And while this is an important problem, it seems to have been almost entirely neglected in research. Here, the finding of fine discrimination between targets would be in line with our supposition that person perception and stereotyping are related processes.

3.10.1 Small differences in body build and their implications for impression — a neglected topic

In this section we raise, and try to answer, a question so far neglected by the literatures: by how much must physiques differ to be stereotyped differently? This problem has important practical implications as well as being of some theoretical interest. If physiques have to be grossly different to arouse divergent social expectations then it would imply that only a few extreme human shapes would be 'caricatured'. Hence the stereotyping of physiques, as a factor in social image and social interaction, would be trivial except for the persons having one of these extreme physiques. On the other hand, if diverse expectations can be aroused by only slightly different physiques than the stereotyping of physique would be a much more pervasive social phenomenon. For example, we might say that the initial interaction between strangers will be partly determined by the perception of each other's physique, amongst other informational cues such as manner of dress. A brief review of the current literature on physique stereotyping shows why the present problem has not been solved.

First, several studies have only used examples of extreme physiques, presumably to maximise the likelihood of demonstrating the stereotying phenomenon (Dibiase & Hjelle, 1968; Lerner, 1969; Lerner & Pool, 1972; Lerner & Schroeder, 1971; Miller et al., 1968; Staffieri, 1967; Strongman & Hart, 1968; Wells & Siegel, 1961). Typically, these authors describe their stimuli (physiques) in terms of Sheldon's (1942) morphological system, hence using an extreme endomorph, mesomorph and ectomorph. Second, the studies that do use more than three physiques present highly summarised results (Brodsky, 1954; Kiker & Miller, 1967; Miller & Stewart, 1968). These abbreviated results consist of coefficients of concordance (W); analysis of variance reporting a single F; or a reporting of just the physique rated highest on a particular concept; all of which lose information. For example, given six physiques, a significant W of 0.33 can imply (1) that one physique was given an extreme rating while the remaining five physiques received random ratings, or (2) that several of the physiques were discriminated between, but at a fairly weak level. Thus in the present situation we cannot tell, for example, whether two ectomorphs are always stereotyped identically or whether an ectomorph and endomorph are always stereotyped differently. However the aim of these studies has been to show that physiques can be stereotyped, a fact which is almost overproved and needs no further confirmation. Now, the gross phenomenon of stereotyping and social image must be broken down, so that both its perceptual basis and its social/personal significance can be understood (Bourke, Stewart & Miller, 1973).

We can at this point consider Sheldon's influence upon the stereotyping research. First, Sheldon (1942) has published an atlas of 'standard' physiques, allowing researchers to communicate about the stimuli used without publishing pictures of them. Second, there is the influence of Sheldon's hypothesised relationship between overt behaviour and physique as described by his morphology (Biller & Liebman, 1971; Child, 1950; Walker, 1962): some authors implicitly or explicitly reasoning that the stereotyping of somatotypes would tend to substantiate Sheldon's claims.

However, despite these two reasons why the physique stimuli used should be selected to be representative of Sheldon's morphological dimensions, it has to be made clear that as yet we have no evidence that these dimensions are the perceived aspects, the cues, having psychological meaning and eliciting stereotypes. There is a danger, though, that this assumption will be made since researchers have forced stereotypes on to Sheldon's dimensions by (1) limiting the number and range of physiques used, and (2) by obscuring possible inconsistencies in stereotypes with their abbreviated results. In other words, a relationship between Sheldonian dimensions and social expectations has not been demonstrated, as it might have been if the dimensions had been systematically varied and plotted against stereotype. It is possible that the informational cues that evoke expectation, or social image, cannot be described by his dimensions. We will return to this point when discussing the results.

As it is, Stewart, Tutton & Steele (1973) have explicitly, and Sleet (1969) implicitly, already questioned the assumption that there are no stereotyping differences between similar physiques. In presenting complete data on six physiques they note, for example, that their two primarily ectomorphic figures received markedly different ratings on several concepts. Here, we will systematically examine this observation. We will analyse the data from an endomorphic, a mesomorphic and an ectomorphic pair of physiques. Each of these pairs looks superficially similar being high on just one of Sheldon's dimensions, but at a closer look they can be quite easily distinguished (see Appendix I). If stereotypes or impressions are based upon subtle cues then we would expect the members of each pair to be stereotyped differently. If, on the other hand, stereotypes are based on a rough, overall use of Sheldon's dimensions, then the members of the pairs should evoke very similar stereotypes.

3.10.2. Fine grained stereotyping: a confirmation via analysis of variance (ANOVA)

As our starting point we used the data presented in Tables 3.4 and 3.5

which were analysed as follows. The data for each pair of physiques was analysed in a mixed model ANOVA. The concepts of Follower, Old and Like Best, being antonyms of Leader, Young and Like Least (Stewart, Steele & Powell, 1973), were reversed so as not to force an interaction effect that one would predict on an *a priori* basis. A summary of the three ANOVAs, one for each pair of physiques, is presented in Table 3.15.

One of the main effects, Physique (P) was significant for all three analyses, showing that subjects differentiated clearly between the two members of the pairs. A nonspecific P effect has already been established by previous research with the use of *W* (Stewart, Tutton & Steele, 1973), but it must be remembered that *W* does not show where differences are. The interactions between Physiques and Concepts (P x C) were also found to be significant, but only for the endomorphic and ectomorphic pairs. These interactions indicate that members of these pairs were seen as more or less different on particular concepts. The main and interaction effects (P and P x C) are, of course, interdependent, being influenced by the choice of concepts and the direction of their scoring. The mesomorphic figures, although generally seen as different as indicated by the singificant P effect, maintained a fairly constant

Table 3.15

Summary Tables of the three analyses of variance associated with the three pairs of similar physiques

Source		Endomorphs		Mesomorphs		Ectomorphs	
	df	*MS*	*F*	*MS*	*F*	*MS*	*F*
Sex (S)	1	.1	—	.6	—	1.1	—
*S*s within groups	48	3.8	3.04	1.5	—	4.8	2.27
Physiques (P)	1	133.2	88.25†	21.4	11.86*	16.4	7.56†
P x S	1	.2	—	.6	—	22.3	10.23†
P x *S*s within groups	48	1.5		1.8		2.2	
Concepts (C)	14	90.7	38.96†	13.6	7.34*	79.0	28.39†
C x S	14	2.6	1.13	1.4	—	4.3	1.55
C x *S*s within groups	672	2.3		1.9		2.8	
P x C	14	18.1	14.48†	2.3	1.34	39.7	18.81†
P x C x S	14	1.0	—	1.7	—	2.8	1.33
Residual	672	1.3		1.7		2.1	
df and *SS*s (Total)	1499	4363.8		2824.0		5425.2	

$^*P < 0.01$. †$P < 0.001$.

difference — probably due to the large number of average ratings these physiques received, as reflected in the total *SS*s.

The Sex (S) main effects were not significant, indicating that the ratings by male and female subjects were, in general, quite similar. The Physique and Sex (P x S) interactions were significant for the ectomorphic pair only, indicating that the sex of the judge influenced the ratings given to each of these physiques across several of the concepts. As Stewart, Tutton & Steele (1973) have pointed out, sex differences are only liable to occur on specific concepts. In addition, however, the present results suggest that sex differences in stereotyping are confined to particular physiques as well as specific concepts.

The Concept (C) main effects were also significant for all three analyses, indicating that subjects differentiated clearly between concepts; that some concepts were seen as related to body build whereas others were not. The significance of these main effects can, of course, be altered considerably by the particular concepts chosen. The present results are consistent with those of Stewart, Steele & Miller (1970), who have shown that, in regard to stereotyping, there are significant differences between both concepts and subjects.

3.10.3 Similar physiques — a comparison of impressions based on t tests

So that we could see more clearly where the pairs of physiques were seen as different, a *t* test was performed for each pair of similar physiques on each concept. Table 3.16 gives the mean rank for each physique on each concept; the smaller the rank the more agreement with the concept. Table 3.16 also gives the *t* for each difference in mean rank and indicates the significance of the *t*s. Since 45 *t* tests were performed we would expect, by chance, less than three to be significant at the 0.05 level and less than one at the 0.01 level. The number of significant *t*s was thus greatly in excess of the number expected by chance.

The general result of the *t* tests is, as with the analyses of variance of the previous section, that the members of each pair are seen as different, particularly in relation to the endomorphic and ectomorphic pairs. Further, it should be noted that every one of the concepts yields at least one significant difference between similar physiques.

3.10.4 Fine grained stereotyping — discussion and implications

The most important finding to emerge is that the superficially similar pairs of physiques have been clearly differentiated in terms of ascribed behaviour. The implication is that physiques have undergone a 'fine grained' analysis; subtle differences have been perceived and

Table 3.16

Mean rank (*MR*) and Standard Deviation (*SD*) of Six Physiques on 15 Concepts. A *t* Statistic of Differences between Similar Physiques is also included

Concepts		Endomorphs			Mesomorphs			Ectomorphs		
		1	2	*t*	3	4	*t*	5	6	*t*
Like Least	MR	2.60	1.42	6.90d	3.82	3.36	2.11a	4.30	5.50	4.80d
	SD	1.05	0.93		1.26	1.06		1.46	0.97	
Like Best	MR	4.44	5.48	7.18d	3.42	3.52	0.39	2.74	1.40	4.25d
	SD	0.91	1.07		1.34	1.09		1.45	0.88	
Wife	MR	3.92	4.94	2.29a	3.44	3.44	0.00	3.38	1.88	5.32d
	SD	1.29	1.58		1.50	1.30		1.74	1.32	
Young	MR	4.50	5.14	2.83c	3.50	3.66	0.74	2.16	2.04	0.27
	SD	0.91	1.26		1.11	1.15		1.99	1.05	
Successful	MR	4.18	5.54	6.29d	2.56	3.38	3.16c	3.54	1.80	6.13d
	SD	1.10	0.97		1.31	1.29		1.72	0.88	
Sister	MR	4.20	5.22	4.32d	3.52	3.80	1.40	2.30	1.96	1.14
	SD	1.01	1.33		1.36	1.14		1.69	1.24	
Leader	MR	4.12	5.26	4.59d	2.26	2.72	1.47	4.02	2.62	5.73d
	SD	1.22	1.17		1.47	1.11		1.74	1.32	
Old	MR	2.52	2.12	1.75	3.82	3.30	2.42b	4.36	4.88	1.80
	SD	1.25	1.52		1.14	1.15		2.07	1.15	
Self	MR	3.80	5.42	9.53d	3.14	3.18	0.42	3.12	2.34	3.43c
	SD	1.31	1.11		1.37	1.26		1.95	1.42	
Follower	MR	3.12	2.12	4.55d	4.48	4.06	1.34	2.82	4.40	5.78d
	SD	1.38	1.47		1.40	1.41		1.78	1.41	
Mother	MR	2.48	3.84	5.61d	3.04	3.30	1.00	4.92	3.42	5.64d
	SD	1.49	1.66		1.67	1.43		1.38	1.63	
Prostitute	MR	3.50	4.80	4.67d	3.00	3.48	2..04a	3.24	2.85	1.27
	SD	1.51	1.67		1.48	1.40		1.80	1.68	
Prudish	MR	3.48	3.26	0.54	3.60	3.86	0.83	2.40	4.40	6.36d
	SD	1.27	1.83		1.59	1.34		1.89	1.65	
Homosexual	MR	3.64	3.88	0.98	2.84	3.12	0.84	3.32	4.20	2.53b
	SD	1.29	1.94		1.50	1.42		2.01	1.67	
Alcoholic	MR	3.40	3.78	1.23	3.52	3.70	0.64	2.64	3.96	4.22d
	SD	1.48	2.11		1.28	1.11		1.97	1.83	

a = $p < 0.05$.   b = $p < 0.02$.   c = $p < 0.01$.   d = $p < 0.001$.

differentially interpreted. Two endomorphs, say, might have exactly the same morphological rating but still be stereotyped differently if the distribution of the fat over the body differs. Fatness of the breasts, buttocks and legs (Bourke, Stewart & Miller, 1973; Wiggins & Wiggins, 1969), for example, may be linked with different attributes. The finding of stimulus differentiation suggests one reason why knowing Sheldon's somatotype of a particular physique will be a poor indication of its associated stereotypes; for Sheldon's system is essentially a summary description.

In this particular study, Sheldon's somatotype alone does not adequately predict stereotyping differences between similar physiques. This is made clear by considering that the mesomorphs differed by four points on Sheldon's system (i.e. 3-6-2 vs. 1-7-1), whereas both the endomorphs and the ectomorphs differed by only two points. Despite their greater difference, the mesomorphic pair were stereotyped much more similarly than the remaining pairs. It suggests there are specific features of body build (such as squareness of the shoulders, perhaps) which evoke stereotypes but which cannot be described by a summary, overall assessment of the body as provided by Sheldon's somatotypes. It is clear that the subjects were not responding to morphological difference *per se*, but to the nature of that difference. Thus, for any concept, certain differences in physique will be potent even if small, whereas other differences may be irrelevant however large.

A second finding pertaining to the relationship between Sheldon's dimensions and stereotype is that the concepts used in this study tended to bear a nonlinear relationship to Sheldon's dimensions. This is made clear by observing that both the endomorphic and ectomorphic pairs have one 'fatter' and one 'thinner' member and seeing in each case which of them more suits a particular concept. The question is: if the fatter endomorph suits a concept more, then does the fatter ectomorph also suit that concept more? And similarly for thinness. The answer is no, for all concepts except Homosexual and Alcoholic. In fact, for the remaining 13 concepts, if the fatter endomorph suits a concept more then the thinner ectomorph suits it more, and vice versa. It suggests we have a U or inverted U shaped curve for every concept in relation to the general dimension of fatness. Further, this U function implies that the extremes of a physique dimension will generally be evaluated negatively, normality being more highly valued.

A third finding reiterating that a small physical difference can cause large stereotypic differences is that on nine of the concepts the mean ratings of each physique were not grouped in somatotype pairs, but showed some overlap. This is especially evident on Prudish and Alcoholic, where the two ectomorphs were rated as highest and lowest, bracketing the other physiques, demonstrating how two very similar figures can receive widely divergent ratings on a particular concept if differing on a crucial feature. Similarly, two extremely different physiques on Sheldon's system may not be rated differently on a particular concept as long as they share such a crucial feature, as can be observed in the concept Leader.

In concluding the comments on Sheldon's system, we can say that it is relevant to expectations because it indicates gross difference. The system does not, however, provide a sufficiently rich psychological or conceptual framework for the perceptual basis of stereotyping. Such a framework will be concerned with the wider problem of how people perceive complex stimuli. It will refer to overall aspects of physique (e.g. 'extremeness') and to more particular aspects (e.g. 'squareness of shoulders'). Further, it must relate, at least potentially, to the characteristics of the perceiver.

The finding of stimulus differentiation and use of multiple cues suggests that the characteristics of the perceiver will influence the stereotype that he holds. As Shranger & Altrocchi (1964; Wiggins et al., 1968, 1969) discuss, an important source of individual variability in the judgement process may well be differences in the cues chosen as bases for judgement. At a simple level one might hypothesise, for example, that the extrovert will utilise more cues, hence differentiating more strongly between people, because for him people play an important role in his life style. A further source of individual variability will be in the interpretation of a particular cue once it has been perceived. The significant Sex x Concept interaction may well be a demonstration of this phenomenon. The problem of cue selection and interpretation has been taken up in another paper (Powell, Tutton & Stewart, 1973; Stewart, Steele & Powell, 1973), where it has been shown that social and subjective factors account for approximately equal portions of the variance observed in stereotyping (see Section 3.7.2). Thus there is considerable social consensus in the selection and interpretation of morphological cues, since on the present data we found mostly significant *W*s (see Table 3.3). The significance and impact of which subjective interpretations are capable has been partially borne out by observing the belief systems of clinical patients (Watts, Powell & Kullick, 1973). Here, two of the patients interpreted their own physiques as being of the kind that would suggest femininity to others. In other words, both patients made assumptions about other people's stereotypes, presumably based upon their experience in interacting with others and upon their own stereotypes. The interesting thing was that one patient thought he looked feminine because his wrists, chest and waist were too thin; the other because his wrists, chest and waist were too fat. In both cases a major factor causing them to negatively evaluate their body was that they perceived it as being of an extreme shape.

As a final point, it is thought that by demonstrating how expectations will exist for many different, normal physiques, and not just the three caricatured types, this analysis makes a social-expectational model of the relationship between overt behaviour and physique more plausible. Such a model has been considered by Lindzey (1965), the view being that behaviour can be modified by, and become congruent with, social expectations. In contrast, Sheldon (1942) posited a genetic relationship between physique and behaviour. Probably an interaction model combining these two views will eventually be found most appropriate.

It is appropriate to close this chapter with the material on fine grained stereotyping as it provides further confirmation of the lack of clear demarcation between person perception and stereotyping. To recapitulate, we have found more differentiation between targets, inferences and concepts than one would expect if the traditional views of stereotyping were wholly correct. We also found that Attractiveness, which in its present guise is thought to represent Evaluation, is probably the most salient and ubiquitous factor in judging body build and inferring traits. Accordingly, we have devoted the whole of the following brief chapter to a review of this topic and some of its more important ramifications.

4 Physical Attractiveness as a Factor in Social Perception and Behaviour

4.1 Introduction

There has never been any doubt that physical appearance is a most important factor in social interactions. Nevertheless it seems that experimenters have been reluctant to investigate external attributes of the individual while eager to theorise about less observable characteristics. Why physical appearance has been so disregarded as an area of research interest is difficult to ascertain. One suggestion is that of Aronson (1969): 'It may be that, at some level, we would hate to find evidence indicating that beautiful women are better liked than homely women — somehow this seems undemocratic.' Whether or not it is our concern with equality and fairness for all, or whether it is a more underlying distaste for the study of morphology as suggested by Lindzey (1965) it is certain that physical appearance, and particularly physical attractiveness, has received relatively little attention in the psychological literature of the past. This book goes some way towards redressing that balance and in the following section we shall discuss physical attractiveness and some of its effects on the individual in areas of development, personality and social issues.

4.2 The physical attractiveness stereotype

Within each culture there are definite beliefs about what constitutes physical beauty. But besides the criterion of a few tape measurements in the Miss World and Mr Universe competitions, there are very few objective standards with which to classify what is considered physical attractiveness. Unfortunately, there have been relatively few attempts to study the components of beauty or the stereotypes of attractiveness. Those that have been made have been beset by the problem of quantifying opinions on physical attractiveness. Too many studies in this area have been made relying on the experimenter's subjective assessment of what is considered beautiful. Another problem of such investigations is the distinction which must be drawn between individual components of beauty versus the overall picture. It is questionable as to how meaningful are the studies which isolate one aspect or characteristic from the whole. Do people react to any of the physical attributes individually or do they only react to the total scenario? By testing subjects for their perceptions of one aspect of the total gestalt, while keeping the others constant, are we in fact creating a false judgement situation? The results of our own work would suggest that it is possible to isolate body shape from other characteristics and effectively study perceptions of that variable in isolation.

There is also now an amount of work on the effects of the height variable on subjects' rating of physical attractiveness. Feldman (1971) for example cites a number of surveys and studies to support his claim that in American society height is an important component of the attractiveness of men. The studies report that short men are penalised economically and in their job opportunities and have special dating problems. There is also evidence that in American politics the attraction people feel for a politician is directly related to his height (e.g. Berkowitz, Nebel & Reitman, 1971; Kassarjian, 1963; Ward, 1967).

An interesting study carried out in Australia was that of Wilson (1968) who found a significant relationship between authority status and perceptual distortion of size. The higher the status the greater was the perceived height of the stimulus person. This finding was in line with that of Dannenmaier & Thumin (1964) and of Koulack & Tuthill (1972) who found that perceived height increased as social distance decreased.

While height may be an asset for men, it can be a liability for women since it is a widespread belief in the Western world that the woman must be smaller than the man in a dating partnership. This means that short men and tall women have problems in date or mate selection, a factor supported by the Stolz & Stolz (1951) study which showed that when adolescent boys are worried about their height, they are worried by their shortness, whereas adolescent girls who worry about height are concerned by their tallness.

Facial attractiveness has also been studied for evidence of stereotyping. In this country Iliffe (1960) obtained rankings for 'prettiness' of twelve photographs of women's faces from over 4,000 readers of a national daily newspaper. He found that the attractiveness of preferences remained relatively constant irrespective of age, socio-economic status or geographical location or respondent. The Kopera, Maier & Johnson (1971) study also looked at female facial attractiveness and found consistent stereotyping by all the college student judges irrespective of sex.

In terms of overall physical attractiveness investigators also report the existence of reliable stereotypes. The studies of Murstein (1972),

Berscheid et al. (1971) and Cavior & Dokechi (1971) have all found evidence of a stereotypic perception of overall beauty across subjects of differing ages and sex.

It is apparent from these studies that despite beliefs of individual differences in views of beauty and the assertion that 'beauty is in the eye of the beholder', there is considerable evidence of a widespread agreement in the level of attractiveness of others. However, the Cross & Cross (1971) study, although finding considerable consensus of opinion about the perception of facial beauty, did also find evidence of individual stereotypes. That is to say although the most popular stimulus face was chosen as best by 207 judges there was no face that was never chosen and the least popular face was chosen by four judges. So there is some evidence for the romantic hope that everyone is found attractive by at least somebody.

4.3 The development of the physical attractiveness stereotype

At what age do stereotypes of physical attractiveness first develop? Our own work suggests that stereotypes exist at a very early age but that changes occur in some stereotyped beliefs as the child develops. The studies of Lerner & Gellert (1969) and of Gellert, Girgus & Cohen (1971) looked at stereotyping abilities of nursery school children towards body size. They found that not only were the children able to distinguish between their peers on the dimension of body build, but they also exhibited a stereotypic aversion to the chubby stimulus figures. So there is some evidence that even is preschool children stereotypic connotations are given to at least one aspect of physical attractiveness.

Physical attractiveness has also been shown to be related to popularity in preschool children (Dion & Berscheid, 1972). This study examined the relationship between physical attractiveness and popularity in two groups of preschool children, the younger aged 4.4 to 5.4 years and the older 5.5 to 6.1 years. Resuls showed that the unattractive boys in the sample were also the least popular regardless of age. For the girls, however, some changes took place with age. In the younger age group the unattractive girls were more popular than their attractive peers, whereas in the older group the attractive girls were significantly more popular than the unattractive girls. One possible explanation for this change with age can be made in terms of the increased emphasis on the importance of attractiveness for females with increasing age.

This study also found that attractive children, regardless of sex, were perceived to be more independent and self-sufficient than unattractive children. So that perception of social behaviour as well as popularity seems related to physical attractiveness.

There are a number of possible explanations for these relationships. First, of course, it is possible that the relationships exhibited are based on actual behaviour, so that the unattractive boys may be unpopular because their behaviour is hostile, aggressive or in some other way unpopular, and the popular boys may be popular because their actual behaviour is popular. An alternative explanation for the relationship is that the children have learned the physical attractiveness stereotype and construe behaviour in an appropriate manner (Sigall & Ostrov, 1975). So that, for example, an aggressive act by an unattractive boy is seen as bullying whereas it is construed as bravery when the same act is performed by an attractive child. Without further research it is impossible to credit either explanation. However, it is important to examine the implications of both.

If the relationship between attractiveness and popularity is based on actual behaviour rather than perceptual distortion, then one must speculate on the origins of such behavioural differences between attractive and unattractive children. Are they the result of the stereotypes held by, and subsequent discriminating behaviour of, socialising adults such as parents and teachers? Are children of differing attractiveness levels treated differentially by adults and their behaviour thus moulded to fit the adult's stereotypic expectations? Just as sex differences exist due in large part to the socialising influences, similarly differences between attractive and unattractive children could occur due to differential social role stereotyping on the part of the adults. Or is the child himself fulfilling the expectations of those around him? If he and his peers have learned the stereotypic notions of behaviours associated with the physical attractiveness continuum, then he may simply be conforming with the behaviour he knows is expected of him.

If the relationship between attractiveness and popularity is attributed to a learned stereotypic conception of behaviours associated with various levels of attractiveness, then the consequences may be far reaching. The physical attractiveness of a child may play a large part in his social acceptance and development. A child's self concept, his methods of social interaction and his relationships with others may all be affected by the child's reception by his peers (Sigall & Landy,1973).

4.3.1 The effects of the physical attractiveness stereotype

Stereotyping of any sort is a way of categorising our conceptions, and of reducing uncertainty by generalising. So, for the observer, the act of stereotyping is a convenient information providing device. For example, if we believe that all red headed people have bad tempers then on first meeting a red head we believe we know something about his personality even before introduction and with that knowledge can predict certain aspects of his behaviour. But what of the observed? What is the effect on him of such stereotypes?

We have already mentioned the effect on a child of the physical attractiveness stereotype and its relationship to popularity. A child's behaviour may change to conform with the stereotypes held by his peers and the adults in his life. Furthermore the socialisation process may discriminate between children of differing attractiveness levels, so that different behaviour is expected of attractive and unattractive children. So, for example, the Dion (1972, 1973) study of adults' attitudes towards transgression in children of differing levels of attractiveness found that unattractive children were perceived to possess an antisocial nature and were thought more likely than attractive children to commit transgressions in the future.

Further evidence of the effect on socialisation of attractiveness comes from the study of Clifford and Walster (1973) which showed that the more attractive a child was the higher the educational potential a teacher attributed to him (where photographs of unknown children were presented to the teachers). So it would seem that the effect of physical attractiveness stereotype reaches even into educational development. This finding of a positive relationship between physical attractiveness and perceptions of intellectual or educational potential is seen for its full significance when it is combined with the evidence that there is a positive relationship between a teacher's attitude towards a student and that student's subsequent achievement (Palardy, 1969; Rist, 1970). This means the attractive student is more likely to be viewed favourably by his teacher and is therefore more likely to achieve educational success than his less attractive peers.

Attractiveness can also be an asset when faced with the judicial system. A study by Efran (1974) of a simulated jury task found that physically attractive defendants were evaluated with less certainty of guilt and were recommended less severe punishment than the unattractive defendants. Furthermore, the belief of 'What is beautiful is good' received support from the work of Dion et al. (1972). The results suggest that not only are physically attractive persons assumed to possess more socially desirable personalities than those of lesser attractiveness, but it is presumed that their lives will be happier and more successful.

There is little evidence that these suggestions of personality differences between attractive and unattractive people are valid. A study by Wilson & Brazendale (1976) showed unattractive girls to be more religious, puritanical and opposed to sexual freedom. But there is very little other evidence of this difference. However, the Kaats & Davis (1970) study which found that attractive women gave more favourable descriptions of themselves suggest perhaps that they do feel more subjective happiness than unattractive women. An interesting finding from the Berscheid et al. (1972) study was that women who were attractive in college were less happy in their forties than the women who were less attractive in their younger days. And it is suggested that this is consistent with the notion that happiness depends upon the result of the comparison of one's current state with previous states: the less attractive woman may have a less demanding comparison level to contend with than the attractive.

A recent study by Crisp & McGuinness (1976) should be mentioned here. This study, although not directly concerned with physical attractiveness, examines certain psychological characteristics that are related to a person's weight and fatness. Looking at a middle aged population these experimenters found a relation between certain psychoneurotic characteristics and the degree of obesity exhibited by the subjects. Given that other studies, including our own, have found the obese physique to be considered unattractive, the findings are relevant to the subject of the personality characteristics of unattractive versus attractive people. Crisp & McGuinness found that the obese people in their sample were much less anxious; and, in the case of men, much less depressed than the rest of the population.

The impact of physical attractiveness is specially felt in 'first impressions'. Increasing familiarity with a person lessens the importance of his physical appearance in the social interaction. Most studies of physical attractiveness and its relation to other variables (e.g. Mathews et al., 1972) have been done in a 'first impression' format. It is possible that it is only at this stage of social interaction that physical attractiveness is particularly relevant and that its impact decreases as other knowledge and impressions about the person become known. But even if this is so it would seem likely that the physical attractiveness stereotype has some enduring effect on the individual.

4.4 Physical attractiveness and heterosexual attraction

Mention must be made of the importance of physical attractiveness in heterosexual behaviour such as dating and spouse selection. A number of studies almost exclusively conducted in America have investigated these areas (e.g. Brislin & Lewis, 1968; Tesser & Brodie, 1971; Walster et al., 1966) and all have found evidence of the considerable importance of physical attractiveness as a determinant of attraction in blind dating or computer dating situations. Physically attractive men and women are strongly preferred in heterosexual dating relationships and physical attractiveness is of major significance for both sexes' dating choices.

However, despite an overall tendency to prefer the physically attractive, it seems that men and women differ in the importance they attach to physical attractiveness in heterosexual relationship (Stroebe et al., 1971). Evidence that women place less emphasis on the attractiveness level of their partner than do men comes from various sources. The Berscheid et al. (1971) study indicated that physical attractiveness is more highly related to a woman's popularity than it is to a man's. The Coombs & Kenkel (1966) study of college students showed that compared to women, men consistently reported that they place greater stress on physical attractiveness in making date selection.

The relative levels of attractiveness of both people appears to be important in the choice of a dating partner. Although the physically attractive are preferred, the perceiver's own physical attractiveness level seems to have a moderating effect on the selection process. This is in accordance with the 'matching hypothesis' (Goffman, 1952) which proposes that men and women of comparable levels of social desirability tend to pair off in marriage or dating behaviour. One aspect of a person's social desirability is his level of attractiveness and studies have investigated whether the matching principle could be applied to couples when physical attractiveness is considered in isolation from these other aspects. The Berscheid et al. (1971) study examined physical attractiveness levels in dating choices and found support for this hypothesis. It ws found that while the physically attractive dates were markedly preferred by all, within this trend the less attractive men and women tended to choose the less attractive dates and the more attractive individuals tended to choose the more highly attractive date.

A possible explanation for this is fear of rejection on the part of the less attractive. That is to say the less attractive individual might choose a less attractive date because he felt his chances of acceptance were higher than with the more attractive. Berscheid et al. (1971) looked at this possibility by varying the salience of the likelihood of rejection by the date choice but found no evidence for it. However, a study by Huston (1973) found that men perceived their chances of social acceptance to be less with attractive women and, furthermore, that their subjective probability of rejection may affect the likelihood of their approaching such women.

There is also some evidence that as well as in dating situations the matching hypothesis seems to hold in the choice of long term or marital partners. Murstein (1972) examined the degree of similarity in attractiveness levels of 99 couples who were either engaged or 'going steady' and compared this with a control group of randomly paired couples. Evidence of matching along the physical attractive dimension was found; the physical attractiveness level of the engaged or going steady couples was significantly less discrepant than those of the artificially paired couples.

5 The English Studies

Broadly speaking, the pair of studies to be reported here are a direct continuation of the US study. Their main purpose is to replicate some of the more important of the earlier findings — especially those to do with sex differences in sex role perception — with a larger and more diverse sample of subjects and thus increase their generality. In addition, the increased sample sizes have made permissible certain types of analyses — such as factor analysis for example — which were precluded in the smaller US study.

5.1 Origin and construction of the English test formats

While analysing the US data, the opportunity arose to examine stereotyping and person perception in a large number of subjects. This necessitated the abandonment of face to face testing, as used previously, in favour of a booklet presentation.

In the course of considering alternative formats, it was also decided to adopt a semantic differential procedure for Study 1. However, certain peculiarities were observed in an appreciable number of individual test protocols. Specifically, some subjects would, for particular concepts, assign the same rating or grade, such as '7' (most unlike) or '4' (equivocal or uncertain), to each of the six target persons, which is the functional equivalent of avoiding or evading the necessity of making a discriminating judgement. This phenomenon appeared to be specially frequent on certain concepts, such as Self and Ideal Self, where male subjects were required to make cross-sex identifications, or on emotive concepts, such as Homosexual or Alcoholic.

Needless to say, this finding of 'evasive responding' — which had not been reported in a number of largely comparable studies (Jenkins, 1971; Miller et al., 1968; Wells & Siegel, 1961) — gave rise to a good deal of concern, and motivated us to undertake Study 2, which is based on ranking rather than rating. By this means it was hoped to ascertain in what way, if any, the format — ranking or grading — influences the general outcome of the studies. Here, the aim is not to compare the numerical values arising from the two studies, but rather to observe if they give rise to the same broad implications concerning matters such as sex differences and social role perception.

Grading, as compared to ranking, gives rise to several important differences such as the option to use parametric statistics and the facilitation of response biases, which may represent either an 'advantage' or a nuisance, depending upon the scope and interests of the research in question.

Looking more closely at the latter issue, it is important to notice that the grading or semantic differential format is open to various response biases — such as extreme responding or acquiescent responding — which are lost (i.e. prevented from occurring) in the comparative method of ranking. In raising the issue of response biases, it is necessary to recognise that we are now dealing with a set of tendencies whose domain is far more extensive than that of person perception — that while the various response biases may introduce complications into person perception, their range of influence may extend even more strongly into other diverse fields such as, for example, styles of social interaction, personality assessment, and so on. To be more specific, it has been shown that response biases arise from personality variables, such as anxiety (Osgood et al., 1957, p. 229) and neuroticism (Chetwynd-Tutton, 1974, p. 202), as well as other classes of differences like intelligence and gender (Kerrick, 1954; Miller, 1974). From this standpoint, the measurement of response biases may be viewed as being more relevant to personality theory and the assessment of subjects, and less directly related to, or indeed incidental to, person perception as such.

5.2 The English subjects

Across the two English studies, data were duly collected from 369 subjects over an 18 month period, with a few tests (i.e. six) being spoilt through noncompletion. These two studies, referred to simply as Study 1 and Study 2, were designed to be as similar as possible — i.e. utilising the same trait vocabulary and target prsons, both presented in booklet form with written instructions, etc. — within the stricture that the former study was based on rating or grading, while the latter was based on ranking. The occupational characteristics of the subjects, which are fairly representative indicators of social class and educational background, are presented in Table 5.1.

With the exception of those subjects with a 'commercial' background (see Note, Table 5.1), the vast majority of subjects are persons who were recruited to serve in one of the many research studies being carried out in the Department of Psychology at the Institute of Psychiatry. Basically our data, with few exceptions, were obtained largely with the co-operation of our colleagues, who includes our tests within the batteries of tests required for their own research purposes.

What one chooses to make of the dissimilarity between the samples of subjects depends largely upon how the relationship between the two tests is visualised — whether as a precise methodological comparison or whether as a conceptual replication. Since it is more or less impossible to make direct comparisons between statistics based on ranking and grading (i.e. mean ranking versus mean rating, or product-moment correlations with Spearman *rho*s, etc.), it seems altogether more reasonable to consider Studies 1 and 2 as being conceptually related rather than as an attempt to evaluate different methodologies. From this standpoint, the two groups of subjects appear to be suitable for carrying out the required comparisons in an unbiased manner.

As for the ages of the subjects, these are presented in Table 5.2 according to sex. Finally, regarding the degree of remuneration for participating, the bulk of subjects are about equal in the proportions

Table 5.1

Distribution of English Subjects of Studies 1 and 2 According to their Sex and Occupations

	Study 1		Study 2		
Occupations	Male	Female	Male	Female	TOTALS
1. Traditional	11	9	14	8	42
Skilled Worker (Male	11	—	14	—	25
Housewife (Female)	—	9	—	8	17
2. Commercial[1]	8	30	18	17	73
Clerical	2	24	4	11	41
Administrative	6	6	14	6	32
3. Social Welfare	14	15	10	6	45
4. Nursing	1	44	1	18	64
5. Medical, Dental and Biological Sciences	35	9	27	10	81
6. Psychological	22	20	8	8	58
Experimental	10	4	3	4	21
Clinical	12	16	5	4	37
Totals	91	127	78	67	363

1. Provided by a small publishing house and a firm of quantity surveyors specifically for these studies.

being paid and unpaid. In the case of paid subjects, the rates vary from about 40 pence ($1.00) per hour to approximately £1 ($2.40) per hour.

It is hoped that this summary of our subjects is sufficiently detailed to make realistic replications possible, while at the same time indicating which important groups were under represented in our samples. Clearly, efforts will need to be made to include more 'working class' subjects in future studies, and at the same time, to increase the mean ages of the subjects who participate.

5.3 Method — target persons, trait vocabulary, instructions, etc.

5.3.1 The targets as modified for the English studies

The six physiques serving as targets here were derived, with slight modifications (see below), directly from those used in the earlier US study — for reference, they are reproduced, exactly as employed in the English studies, in Appendix I. As would be expected, we have continued to designate each of the modified targets by the same number with which they were earlier identified in the US study — e.g. the most obese physique is referred to as 'physique 2' or 'target 2' both here and in the US study.

As was mentioned earlier the six targets were chosen to form three distinct pairs — an Endomorphic pair, a Mesomorphic pair and an Ectomorphic pair — according to Sheldon's somatic morphology. One member within each pair was more moderate for the component in question, while the remaining member was more extreme — this relationship can be seen quite clearly in both Table 5.3 and Appendix 1. Table 5.3 also contains our stimulus numbers, ranging from 1 to 6, the approximate

Table 5.2

Mean and Median Ages of the English Subjects according to Sex

	Mean Age — (SD)	Median Age
1. Male Subjects — Study 1 (n = 91)	24.91 (7.18)	24.17
2. Female Subjects — Study 1 (n = 127)	24.10 (5.76)	23.00
3. Male Subjects — Study 2 (n = 78)	24.75 (6.69)	23.36
4. Female Subjects — Study 2 (n = 67)	25.60 (8.26)	24.25

somatotype as provided by Sheldon and the page and figure number of the physiques as they are presented in Appendix 2 of the original source (Sheldon, 1940, 1963). In viewing Table 5.3, it can be seen that we have moved away from a strict adherence to Sheldon's terminology, interchanging it with the more commonplace terms of Obese, Thin and Muscular — a move prompted by the greater descriptive power of the commonplace terms, as well as the failure of the US study to show any appreciable degree of accord with Sheldon's notions (cf. Powell et al., 1974; Stewart et al., 1973; p. 814).

The physiques, as presented in Appendix I, differ from those used in the US study in several important ways. First, only frontal or full face view were used in the English studies as some of the US subjects commented that the profile and full face poses did not, in their judgement, correspond very well. Since these physiques are the creations of an artist rather than the photographs of actual persons, these comments concerning compatibility seemed to warrant further consideration and, in the absence of evidence to the contrary, we decided to omit the profile views altogether. Moreover, it seems reasonable to speculate that profile and frontal views could be providing different sets of cues, with differing degrees of salience — say, posture or breast development as opposed to shoulder width — which could be, or appear

Table 5.3

Characteristics of the Six Somatotyped Female Physiques serving as Target Persons in the US and Later Studies

As Pairs	Stimulus[1]	Classification	Somatotype	Location[2]
Obese	1	Moderate Endomorph	6-3-2	Fig. 102
	2	Extreme Endomorph	7-3-1	Fig. 104
Muscular	3	Moderate Mesomorph	3-6-2	Fig. 99
	4	Extreme Mesomorph	1-7-1	Fig. 101
Thin	5	Extreme Ectomorph	1-2-7	Fig. 97
	6	Moderate Ectomorph	1-3-6	Fig. 98

1. Throughout our studies these stimulus numbers have been used in a consistent manner, each number applying only to one physique, e.g. the mention of Physique 1 or Target Person 1 is *always* in reference to the moderate endomorph with a 6-3-2 somatotype.
2. Figure numbers refer to the location of the original physiques in Sheldon (1940, 1963).

to be, contradictory even if derived from photographs of the same person in different poses. Until this interesting research problem has been more thoroughly investigated, it may be the wisest course to employ only frontal or profile poses singly, and to avoid the various combinations that are found in Sheldon (e.g. 1942, 1954) and elsewhere.

In the second place we decided to 'improve' upon our targets by eliminating some of the detail — such as fat folds, creases and extraneous features — so that the target persons became better balanced for detail and complexity. This 'retouching' also allowed us to 'paint out' the facial detail and some aspects of the hair, which proved to be more satisfactory than the method of masking used in the original US study.

5.3.2 The English trait vocabulary

Because of time constraints, it was necessary to reduce the length of the trait vocabulary in the English studies from 15 items to 10. In addition the US study indicated that several of the concepts in that trait vocabulary might be more or less superfluous — that a concept such as Sister, while performing well enough in its own right, did not seem to shed any additional light on our primary research problems or long term issues (see, for example, the discussion of Sister in Chapter 6). Others, such as Leader and Follower, were, in the view of the present constraints, simply too redundant (i.e. inefficient) for inclusion in the present studies.

The revised trait vocabulary is shown in Figure 5.1. It should be noted that the left hand trait was used for the ranking format.

5.3.3 Procedure

To facilitate testing under a wide variety of circumstances the two English studies were designed around self contained, self explanatory test booklets.

The front page of each test booklet, whether Method 1 or 2, consisted of instructions which were sufficiently detailed to make the tests essentially self administered in most instances. In some circumstances, when it was not implicitly understood, subjects were specifically informed that they could take as much time as they desired to complete the test.

The instructions employed with Method 1 (e.g. Study 1), which is based on grading as in the semantic differential, were a simplification of those used by Miller et al. (1968), and later by Jenkins (1971). For Method 2 (i.e. Study 2), it was necessary to devise a new set of instructions following as closely as possible those of Method 1 as the differences between rating and ranking will permit.

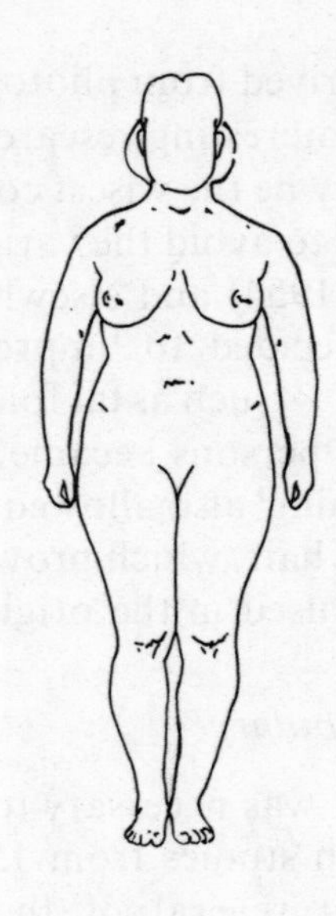

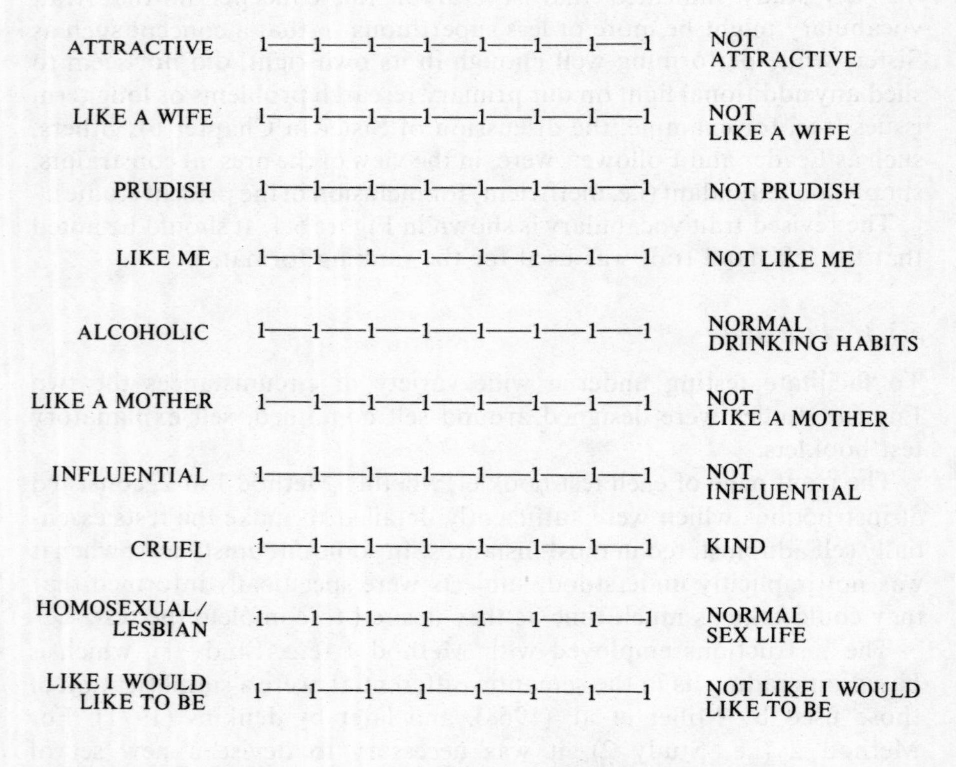

ATTRACTIVE
1—1—1—1—1—1—1—1
NOT ATTRACTIVE
LIKE A WIFE
1—1—1—1—1—1—1—1
NOT LIKE A WIFE
PRUDISH
1—1—1—1—1—1—1—1
NOT PRUDISH
LIKE ME
1—1—1—1—1—1—1—1
NOT LIKE ME
ALCOHOLIC
1—1—1—1—1—1—1—1
NORMAL DRINKING HABITS
LIKE A MOTHER
1—1—1—1—1—1—1—1
NOT LIKE A MOTHER
INFLUENTIAL
1—1—1—1—1—1—1—1
NOT INFLUENTIAL
CRUEL
1—1—1—1—1—1—1—1
KIND
HOMOSEXUAL/ LESBIAN
1—1—1—1—1—1—1—1
NORMAL SEX LIFE
LIKE I WOULD LIKE TO BE
1—1—1—1—1—1—1—1
NOT LIKE I WOULD LIKE TO BE

Figure 5.1 Sample page from Semantic Differential Format showing Target I.

The tests themselves were xeroxed on standard A 4 paper (i.e. 295-mm x 210-mm). For Study 1, each page of the test proper displayed one of the six target persons, centred at the top of the page with ten 7-point scales immediately below (i.e. one page per target person). The scales themselves, reading from top to bottom, were ordered as follows — Attractive, Wife, Prudish, Self, Alcoholic, Mother, Influential, Cruel, Homosexual and Ideal Self (exact terminology given in Figure 5.1). A typical page from the grading method (i.e. Study 1) is shown in Figure 5.1.

In Study 2, each page of the test presented the six target persons simultaneously, ranged across the page longways, with a box beneath each target for writing their respective ranking. The item on which the targets were to be ranked was presented above them, centred just below the top margin of the page (i.e. one page per item from the trait vocabulary). A typical page from the ranking method is shown in Figure 5.2. For this method, the targets were always ranged across the page in a fixed order — this being Targets 4, 3, 2, 6, 1 and 5, reading from left to right.

In preparing the individual test booklets for either study, the six or ten pages were randomised according to a table of random numbers, resulting in a unique random ordering for each individual subject. Here, it is well to note that this procedure results in a random ordering of targets in Study 1 (but with a fixed ordering scales or items), and a random ordering of items in Study 2 (but with a fixed ordering of targets). Moreover, on viewing the first test page, subjects in Study 1 are confronted by the entire trait vocabulary (while continuing in ignorance of the remaining targets), whereas subjects in Study 2 are treated in a converse manner, becoming aware of the entire range of targets upon viewing the first page, but remaining unenlightened concerning the vocabulary items to follow. The precise effect of these procedural variations remains uncertain and should be the subject of future investigation.

Before leaving this topic, it must be stressed that the targets serving in Studies 1 and 2 were, except for their differing arrangements or layout on the test pages, in every respect identical — both sets corresponding exactly with those presented in Appendix 1.

5.4 Trait attribution as reflected in the mean ratings or mean rankings of the English subjects

As we have seen from the detailed analysis of the American data in

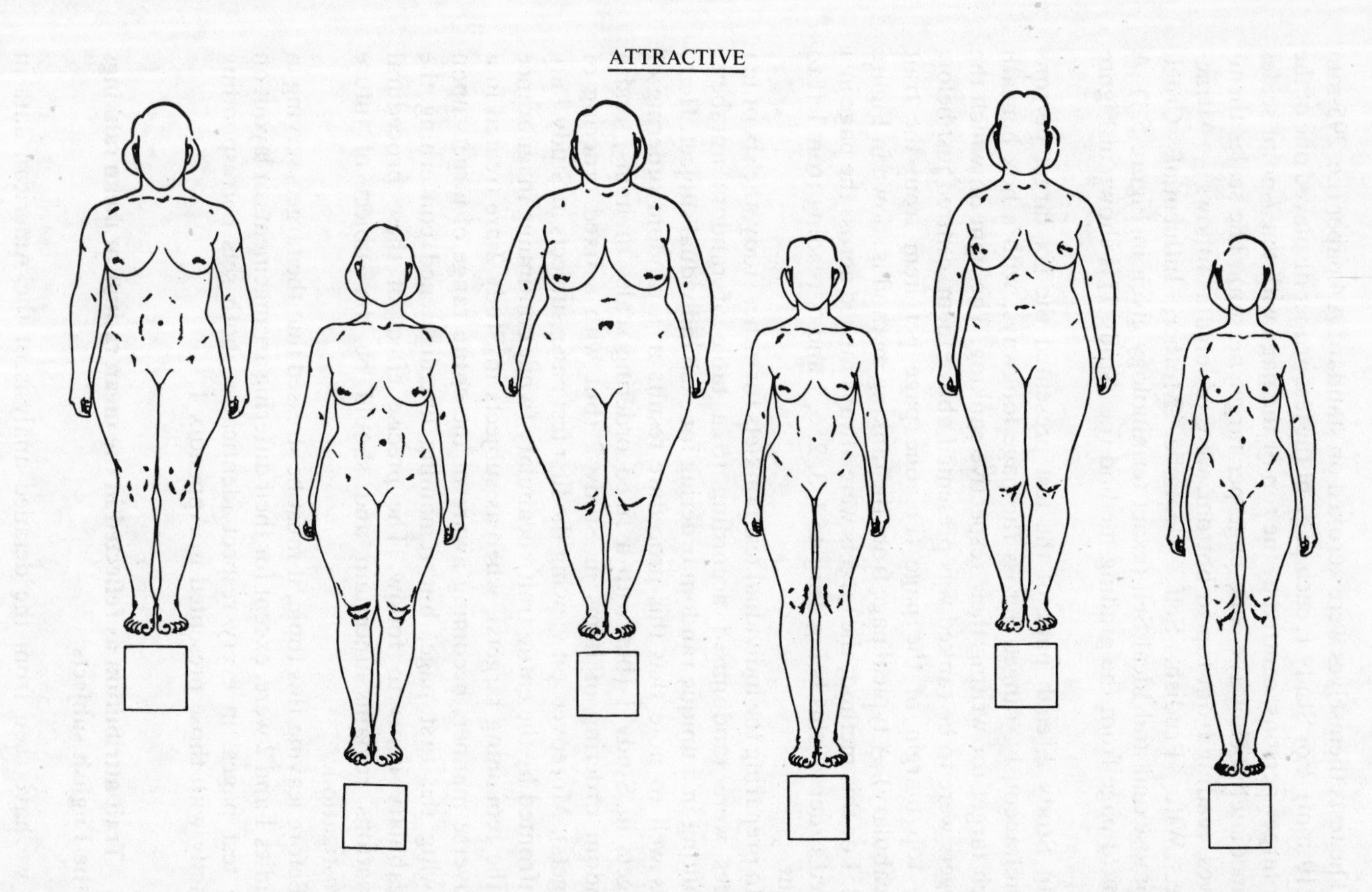

Figure 5.2 Sample page from the Ranking Format showing all six Targets as used in the U.K. studies.

Chapter 3, the attribution of traits to individual targets (i.e. group means) are among the most useful and representative data which can be obtained. Indeed, as we have pointed out earlier, many otherwise useful studies have been almost totally emasculated through their failure to report means with sufficient detail. Accordingly, we shall begin here with a consideration of the means and variances and the trait inferences which they represent.

Because they provide an essential background for the graded data, we will first examine the data derived from the ranking format, or as it is otherwise known, Study 2.

Table 5.4

Mean Ranks and Variance for Six Physiques Ranked by 78 Male Subjects on 10 Concepts*

Concepts		Physiques					
		1	2	3	4	5	6
Attractive	Mean	4.5	5.9	2.7	4.4	2.2	1.4
	Variance	0.5	0.2	0.5	0.6	1.3	0.3
Ideal Self	Mean	4.5	5.9	2.5	4.0	2.6	1.6
	Variance	0.7	0.2	0.5	1.2	1.6	0.8
Self	Mean	4.0	5.8	2.5	3.7	2.9	2.1
	Variance	1.4	0.5	0.8	1.9	2.7	2.1
Wife	Mean	4.1	5.6	2.5	4.4	2.7	1.7
	Variance	0.9	1.0	0.8	1.1	2.6	0.9
Mother	Mean	2.4	4.4	2.7	3.4	4.7	3.5
	Variance	1.7	2.2	1.6	3.1	2.6	2.2
Influential	Mean	3.9	5.0	2.6	3.5	3.7	2.3
	Variance	1.6	2.4	1.6	2.3	3.4	1.7
Alcoholic	Mean	2.9	3.1	3.7	3.0	3.9	4.4
	Variance	2.2	4.2	1.3	1.8	4.3	2.1
Cruel	Mean	3.3	3.8	3.4	2.5	3.9	4.1
	Variance	2.3	3.5	2.1	2.1	3.9	2.3
Homosexual	Mean	3.3	4.3	3.2	2.6	3.5	4.1
	Variance	2.0	3.2	2.1	2.2	3.9	2.5
Prudish	Mean	3.5	3.9	3.6	3.6	2.8	3.7
	Variance	2.2	3.8	1.6	2.4	3.8	3.2

* The smaller the mean ranking, the closer the agreement between the physique and the concept.

5.4.1 Trait inferences based on rankings: Study 2

The mean rankings and variances for each target on all ten trait vocabulary items are presented in Tables 5.4 and 5.5, which represent, respectively, male and female subjects. Following the convention used throughout this book, a small mean score indicates a closer agreement between trait and target than does a large score. Immediately below the means are presented the respective variances, which in one sense serve to show how consensual have been the rankings ascribed to the targets for the various items — with a small variance implying that the subjects 'agree' in their judgements on the particular trait in question.

In view of the large number of entries contained in Tables 5.4 and 5.5,

Table 5.5

Mean Ranks and Variance for Six Physiques Ranked by 67 Female Subjects on 10 Concepts*

Concepts		Physiques					
		1	2	3	4	5	6
Attractive	Mean	4.3	5.9	2.9	4.6	1.9	1.5
	Variance	0.5	0.1	0.4	0.7	1.1	0.3
Ideal Self	Mean	4.2	5.9	3.0	4.6	1.8	1.5
	Variance	0.6	0.1	0.2	0.6	1.2	0.3
Self	Mean	4.0	5.9	2.5	4.2	2.7	1.7
	Variance	1.3	0.1	0.8	0.9	2.2	0.8
Wife	Mean	3.3	5.0	2.7	4.4	3.4	2.3
	Variance	2.2	2.7	1.4	1.6	2.8	2.1
Mother	Mean	2.1	3.9	2.7	3.8	5.0	3.6
	Variance	1.4	3.2	1.9	2.4	1.8	1.8
Influential	Mean	3.5	4.9	2.3	3.4	4.0	3.0
	Variance	1.9	3.0	1.6	2.3	2.9	2.2
Alcoholic	Mean	2.8	3.0	3.5	2.8	4.3	4.6
	Variance	2.1	3.6	1.5	1.8	3.9	1.9
Cruel	Mean	3.4	4.4	3.1	2.3	3.7	4.1
	Variance	2.4	3.2	1.8	2.2	3.7	1.6
Homosexual	Mean	3.6	4.2	2.8	2.4	4.0	4.0
	Variance	2.1	3.5	1.3	2.3	3.5	2.4
Prudish	Mean	3.1	3.8	3.5	3.6	3.3	3.8
	Variance	2.0	3.4	2.0	2.9	4.1	3.0

* The smaller the mean ranking, the greater the agreement between the physique and the concept.

it is not possible to consider the individual means and variances with the thoroughness of which they are deserving. Indeed, this is perhaps a task which is better left to those investigators who have a particular interest in the details of the relationship of body build to behaviour.

The problem of significance — i.e. whether a particular trait is, in fact, perceived to be more characteristic of some target persons than others — is, in essence, the same as that of testing for social stereotyping, i.e. that consensus is always accompanied by differences in mean rankings. In view of the equivalence between the Coefficient of Concordance (W) and Friedman's (X_r^2) test for differences between mean ranks (Haggard, 1958; McNemar, 1969; Winer, 1962, p. 136), it can be inferred from the Ws found in Section 5.6.1 below, that attributions to targets differed significantly on all the concepts except Prudish, where only the data from the males proved to be significant. Notwithstanding 19 confirmations out of 20 tests, it must be remembered that a significant W or X_r^2 only guarantees that one out of the several possible comparisons between means (e.g. 15 in the case of 6 target persons) is significant, and even then, that this one difference may be of negligible practical importance.

Since it is shown in later analyses (i.e. of correlations and the factor analyses based on them) that the data contained in Tables 5.4 and 5.5 are possessed of a structure which can be expressed in a summary form, the need to make individual comparisons is greatly reduced, except perhaps in those circumstances where one is investigating an issue specifically related to some particular aspect of body build. Certainly, there does not seem to be any pressing need to carry out all or even a majority of the tests and comparisons which are implicit in these data — visual inspection should suffice in most instances.

5.4.2 Trait attributions as inferred from mean ratings based on a seven step Semantic Differential format: Study 1

Moving from ranking to data based on ratings, it is worth bearing in mind that most of the points raised in the preceding section — e.g. that means are inversely related to strength of inference or that a large variance implies low levels of consensus, etc. — also apply here with equal force. The earlier considerations are not, however, altogether adequate for a description of ratings, which introduce some new variables — with certain of them, such as the freedom to employ parametric tests, being beneficial, and others, such as a greater openness to response biases, being more of a mixed blessing. The relative importance of these advantages and disadvantages will become more evident as we proceed through these data.

Before taking up the data, however, it is important to note that we have, in respect to the optimum conditions for the analyses of variance which are to follow, randomly discarded a sufficient number of female subjects to equalise the sexes with 91 subjects in each of the two groups. Consequently the mean ratings presented here, in Tables 5.6 and 5.7, are each based on 91 subjects. Moreover, this reduction in numbers also applies to all the Sections (i.e. 6.4 to 6.7) which draw, directly or indirectly, upon the analyses of variance presented below in Table 5.8.

Considering that smaller mean ratings imply a closer relationship, it can be seen that the male subjects do, for example, perceive Target 6,

Tale 5.6

Mean Ratings* and Variances for Six Physiques rated by 91 Male Subjects on 10 Seven-Point Scales (English Study 1: Rating)

Traits		Target Persons					
		1	2	3	4	5	6
1. Attractive	Mean	5.9	6.9	4.2	5.4	3.7	2.5
	Variance	1.6	0.2	3.2	2.2	3.6	2.2
2. Wife	Mean	4.0	5.4	3.4	4.0	4.0	3.2
	Variance	3.2	3.3	2.5	2.8	3.0	2.7
3. Prudish	Mean	4.3	3.9	4.4	4.5	3.7	4.8
	Variance	2.1	2.9	2.1	2.1	2.5	2.3
4. Self	Mean	6.0	6.7	6.0	6.0	5.3	4.4
	Variance	2.0	0.5	2.1	2.0	3.7	4.2
5. Alcoholic	Mean	4.5	3.8	5.3	5.0	5.5	6.0
	Variance	2.6	3.0	1.8	2.6	2.4	1.6
6. Mother	Mean	2.7	3.9	3.4	3.5	4.7	4.0
	Variance	1.9	3.4	2.5	3.2	3.2	3.1
7. Influential	Mean	4.5	5.3	3.8	3.8	4.1	3.4
	Variance	2.6	3.0	1.7	2.3	2.6	2.1
8. Cruel	Mean	5.0	4.9	4.5	4.3	4.3	5.0
	Variance	2.5	2.3	1.6	2.0	2.2	1.4
9. Homosexual	Mean	5.1	4.7	5.1	4.6	5.0	5.6
	Variance	1.7	1.9	2.4	3.0	2.4	1.9
10. Ideal Self	Mean	6.2	6.8	5.6	5.8	5.4	4.5
	Variance	1.3	0.4	2.8	2.3	2.9	4.9

* The smaller the mean rating, the closer the relationship between the target person and the trait in question.

who in addition is judged to be the most Attractive, as best suiting the role of Wife (Mg = 3.2). In contrast, the females regard Targets 1 and 6 (most Maternal versus most Attractive) as both being equally suited to this role (M_gs = 3.0). Subsequently, this sex difference in the perception of the role of Wife — which is reminiscent of the US data — will be shown to be significant.

The variances — which reflect the extent to which subjects have ascribed similar ratings — range from a minimum value of 0.10, for the ratings of Target 2 (the most obese) on Attractiveness in the female data, to a maximum of 4.9, for the ratings of Target 6 (slender, but not excessively so) on Ideal Self in the male data. By way of possible explanation, the exceptionally large variance exhibited by the male subjects in their ratings of Target 6 suggests that they are fairly evenly divided on the suitability of this physique as an ideal for men.

5.4.3 The analysis of variance — a vehicle for assessing discrimination between targets, sex differences in trait attribution and concordance

Because these data are based on grading rather than ranking, it is possible to employ an analysis of variance (ANOVA) to determine if the differences between the observed means are, in fact, significant. The utility of the ANOVA does not, however, stop here, but in addition allows one to test for sex differences in these means and also provides the statistical basis (namely mean squares and error terms) required for measuring concordance. Just how these various ends are achieved will become clear in the discussion of main effects and interactions which is to follow.

As a compromise between clarity and efficiency, we have adopted a Two (Sexes) by Six (Targets) model of ANOVA, with repeated measures, for the present application. Since a three-way model was eschewed, it is necessary to repeat the present analysis for each of the 10 constructs. Every repetition yields two main effects — one for Sex and one for Targets — plus an interaction term for the combined influence of Sex and Targets. The functions and implications of each of these three terms will be discussed below.

Main effects for targets. In their most immediate aspects, these main effects (i.e. their F ratios), show whether or not the subjects (N.B. males and females combined) have discriminated significantly between two or more of the target persons on any particular construct — whether, for example, certain targets differ in degree of Attractiveness or, say, credibility as a Mother.

While we have already acknowledged (in Section 5.4.1) that significant differences between mean ratings or mean rankings are indicative of social stereotyping in circumstances such as these, it is important to recognise that the constituents of these main effects can, as described in Section 5.6.2, be used to compute the $\bar{r}$ statistic — the average intercorrelation between subjects — which is for graded data the exact equivalent of *W*, the coefficient of concordance (Winer, 1962, p. 138). The availability of $\bar{r}$ is noteworthy because it provides a convenient description of the degree of concordance in a form comparable to *W*, i.e. as a correlation rather than a (sic) *F* ratio.

Table 5.7

Mean Ratings* and Variables for Six Physiques rated by 91 Female Subjects on 10 Seven-Point Scales (English Study 1: Rating)

Traits		Target-Persons					
		1	2	3	4	5	6
1. Attractive	Mean	5.9	6.9	4.5	5.8	3.5	2.2
	Variance	1.7	0.1	2.0	1.9	3.5	1.5
2. Wife	Mean	3.0	4.3	3.1	4.1	3.8	3.0
	Variance	3.0	4.1	2.4	3.1	3.4	2.6
3. Prudish	Mean	4.5	4.3	4.4	4.4	4.2	5.0
	Variance	3.2	4.3	3.0	3.0	3.4	2.7
4. Self	Mean	6.1	6.7	5.1	5.8	4.4	3.3
	Variance	1.7	0.8	2.8	2.5	3.3	2.8
5. Alcoholic	Mean	4.9	4.0	4.9	4.7	5.4	5.4
	Variance	2.6	3.9	2.4	2.9	2.7	2.3
6. Mother	Mean	2.6	3.9	3.0	4.0	4.3	3.6
	Variance	2.4	3.4	2.8	3.6	3.3	3.3
7. Influential	Mean	4.4	5.0	3.4	3.5	4.2	3.2
	Variance	3.0	3.6	2.0	2.6	3.3	2.0
8. Cruel	Mean	5.3	5.3	4.4	4.1	4.4	4.9
	Variance	2.1	2.5	2.6	2.9	2.1	2.0
9. Homosexual	Mean	5.5	5.0	4.9	4.3	5.2	5.8
	Variance	2.0	2.1	2.8	3.4	2.5	1.9
10. Ideal Self	Mean	6.1	6.9	5.7	6.2	4.1	3.1
	Variance	1.9	0.2	2.2	1.6	4.2	3.7

* The smaller the mean rating, the closer the relationship between the target person and the trait in question.

Interaction — sex x targets. In the present circumstances, the finding of a significant Sex/Target interaction implies that the male and female subjects apply similar standards when rating certain of the targets but employ different standards when rating others. An interaction would arise if, for example, male and female subjects agreed in their ratings of Attractiveness for certain targets, but then went on to show marked disagreement on others. Basically, a significant interaction implies that sex differences in stereotyping are selective — applying more to some target persons than others (see Section 3.10.2).

Main effects for sex of judge. A significant difference arises here whenever one sex is predisposed to give generally higher (or lower) ratings than the others. An instance of this type can be observed in Tables 5.6 and 5.7, where the females are seen to rate a majority of targets (i.e. five out of six) as better suiting the role of Wife than did their male counterparts. It could be said, here, that the females have a more realistic attitude towards the role of Wife than is true of the males.

Unfortunately, it is not always clear if results of this type arise out of true differences in social perception (as we believe to be the case with Wife) or from sex differences in nonsocial response sets (Miller, 1974). In light of this potential for ambiguity, the sex differences implied by the three significant main effects observed here — on Wife, Self and Ideal Self — must be interpreted with a certain degree of caution.

5.4.4 ANOVAs — results

The 10 ANOVAs — each based on a 2 x 6 design (i.e. Sex x Targets) with repeated measures on Targets — are summarised in Table 5.8. The degrees of freedom (*df*s) reported here reflect the reduction in number of female subjects, from 127 to 91, noted above.

Discrimination between targets. In looking at Table 5.8, it can be seen that all ten main effects for differences between targets, with *F*s ranging from 287.69 to a low of 7.36, are significant beyond the .001 level. On this basis, it is safe to conclude that each construct has given rise to at least one comparison in which two of the six means are significantly different from one another. In the case of the larger *F*s, it is likely that several out of the 15 possible comparisons will yield significant differences, but for reasons stated above, in Section 5.4.1, we will not undertake a pair by pair comparison of targets here.

In terms of social perception, these results imply that some persons will, on the basis of body build alone, be judged to be different from

Table 5.8

Summary of 10 Analyses-of-Variance (1 per Concept) of Ratings assigned by Male and Female Subjects as a function of Sex of Judges and Differences between Target Persons: UK Data

Concepts	Differences in Ratings due to Sex of Judges				Differences in Ratings due to Target Persons				Differences in Ratings due to Interaction (Sex X Targets)			
	MS	*Error*	*F**	*p*<	*MS*	*Error*	*F*†	*p*<	*MS*	*Error*	*F*†	*p*<
1. Attractive	0.03	3.28	0.01	NS	506.65	1.76	287.69	.001	4.08	1.76	2.32	.05
2. Wife	54.97	4.19	13.12	.001	75.72	2.76	27.40	.001	10.83	2.76	3.92	.01
3. Prudish	13.19	3.68	3.59	NS	19.35	2.63	7.36	.001	2.25	2.63	0.85	NS
4. Self	65.28	4.68	13.94	.001	188.66	1.90	99.27	.001	12.29	1.90	6.47	.001
5. Alcoholic	4.11	5.22	0.79	NS	75.26	2.03	37.04	.001	5.83	2.03	2.87	.05
6. Mother	6.16	4.38	1.41	NS	78.26	2.73	28.63	.001	6.23	2.73	2.28	NS
7. Influential	11.90	3.99	2.98	NS	84.51	2.29	36.98	.001	1.17	2.29	0.51	NS
8. Cruel	1.12	3.35	0.34	NS	29.58	1.95	15.21	.001	2.56	1.95	1.52	NS
9. Homosexual	1.47	3.94	0.37	NS	34.02	2.00	16.98	.001	3.65	2.00	1.82	NS
10. Ideal Self	38.86	5.16	7.53	.01	217.15	1.80	120.58	.001	27.16	1.80	15.03	.001

*df = 1/180 †df = 5/900

others, i.e. present different expectations. On the other hand, and irrespective of statistical significance, some of the differences observed in Tables 5.6 and 5.7 suggest that the influence of body build on social perception is, in some instances, of negligible practical importance (e.g. on Prudish, Cruel and Homosexual). Before, however, accepting this conclusion at face value, it is important to remember, as noted in Sections 2.3, 3.7.2 and 5.6.1, that the true impact of stereotyping is, in most instances, better estimated on the basis of intercorrelations than by group means and the measures of concordance (i.e. *W*s and r_S) which are derived from them.

Lastly, the confirmation here of a significant differentiation between targets on all the constructs presages a later finding; that each of these same 10 items also gives rise to a social stereotype which can be related, either directly or indirectly (e.g. via inferred attractiveness), to differences in body build. The issue of social stereotyping and concordance, as measured by the $\bar{r}$ statistic, is discussed at length in Section 5.6.4 below.

Sex by target interactions — selective sex differences in social perception. The finding of five significant interactions — for Attractive, Wife, Self, Alcoholic and Ideal Self — implies that the male and female subjects differ significantly in their evaluations of one or more target persons in each of these instances. In attempting to clarify the nature of these interactions, an examination of Table 5.9 (p.148) — which presents a summary of the *t*s resulting from the pair by pair testing of means for sex differences — shows the present interactions to be the result of the occasional, apparently circumscribed sex differences. On the concept of Wife, for example, the males and females are found to differ significantly only in their ratings of the two obese targets, treating the remaining four targets in an even handed manner. Since no compelling trends are evident in Table 5.9, we are led to conclude that these interactions arise from differences in the way the two sexes conceptualise these particular roles and traits — that interactions are more likely to reflect specific differences in social learning than highly generalised sex differences in cognition or social perception. (N.B. Response biases may play some part in the differences arising from Self and Ideal Self.) On the other hand, and as already noted in Section 3.10.2 above, there seems to be some slight tendency for sex differences to centre more on the slender targets (i.e. 5 and 6) rather than on their more substantial compatriots.

5.4.5 Mean rankings versus mean ratings: the result of admitting or excluding response biases

If one chooses to contrast the data arising from ranking with those from grading (i.e. Tables 5.4 and 5.5 versus 5.6 and 5.7) it is quickly apparent that the degree of discrimination between targets is more clearcut in the former than the latter. Using data from the male subjects to illustrate this point, it can be seen on the concept of Wife, for example, that the mean rankings range from 1.7 to 5.6, a span which is equivalent to 78 per cent of the scale, while the comparable figure for mean ratings is only 38 per cent of the scale, with means ranging from 3.2 to 5.4. This type of discrepancy is of more than merely passing interest for, as we shall see below, it has consequences which reappear throughout the various analyses of graded data.

While recognising that rating scales are open to a wide variety of difficulties (e.g. Cronbach, 1955; Osgood et al., 1957, pp. 229-36; Woodworth & Schlosberg, 1954), we would suggest that the reduced discrimination observed here is a direct result of the less structured quality of ratings. In a rating task, one can, as noted earlier (see Section 5.1) adopt an evasive or noncommittal strategy — e.g. by restricting endorsements to scale midpoints or the ends of scales with the greatest social desirability, etc. — whenever faced with judgements which are perceived to be ambiguous, difficult or threatening. The conditions which encourage this type of responding must, however, lie in the nature of the task at hand, for Woodworth & Schlosberg (1954, pp. 251-65) have suggested that comparable results may be expected from ranking and rating when the required discriminations are simple or involve stimuli familiar to the subjects. Looking at the problem from a somewhat different perspective, there is some evidence to suggest that ranking is a more natural or preferred method of carrying out comparisons (Slater, 1965).

Irrespective of the fact that the broader aspects of this problem are discussed below, in Section 5.6.5, it is worth noting that the present differences raise the question of whether ratings allow subjects to eschew discriminations of which they are capable, or whether ranking forces them to make discriminations between differences which would be otherwise trivial. Whatever the final answer to this controversy, it will be seen below that scaling and ranking lead to the same broad conclusions, albeit with somewhat greater clarity in the case of ranking. In view of the moderate advantages inherent in ranking, it is interesting that many large scale studies (e.g. Jenkins, 1971; Osgood et al., 1957; Warr & Knapper, 1968) have adopted grading procedures without a serious consideration of the available alternatives (Cohen, 1973).

5.5 Sex differences in trait attribution

In the sections which follow, the differences in the way in which men and women have attributed traits to the various target persons will be compared through the medium of *t* tests (i.e. comparing mean ratings or mean rankings). And while the number of *t* tests required (i.e. 60 for each study) do present certain problems, such as the fixing of appropriate significance levels, this approach still seems to be the most efficient means of pinpointing sex differences, so that they can be isolated and easily characterised. (The problem of appropriate significance levels is, however, largely eliminated by the finding, as in the US study, of a numerically small set of significant differences which are, in a statistical sense, quite large.)

5.5.1 Sex differences in trait attribution observed with the semantic differential format: Study 1

The 60 *t* tests for sex differences arising from Study 1 are found in Table 5.9. These tests are based upon the data shown in Tables 5.6 and 5.7.

In examining Table 5.9, it can be seen that the grading format has yielded 10 significant sex differences, with seven of the 10 *t*s being significant at or well beyond the .01 level. It is also worth noting that an additional nine comparisons, such as that concerning Target 4 on Mother, would have been significant if we had been in the position to employ one-tailed probabilities.

Turning to a more or less typical example, we find that the male subjects have rated Target 1 (i.e. the moderately obese target) as being much less suitable or desirable as a Wife than have the females.

5.5.2 Ranking and trait attribution — the sex differences observed in Study 2

As in the preceding section, the data from the male (N = 78) and female subjects (N = 67) have been compared by applying *t* tests. Since we are here dealing with mean rankings, rather than mean ratings as above, it may seem unusual that we are employing a parametric test, such as the *t*. But recalling that we are making comparisons between independent groups and dealing with one target person at a time, it is evident that these data are not particularly different from those routinely submitted to *t* tests (except, of course, for the irrelevant fact that they are integers). The 60 *t* statistics growing out of this comparison are shown in Table 5.10, and again two-tailed probabilities have been employed here to demarcate sex differences. The *t* tests are, themselves, derived from the data presented in Tables 5.4 and 5.5.

In inspecting Table 5.10, it can be observed that 11 of the 60 *t*s are significant, with 6 of these *t*s being significant at or beyond the 1 per cent level. If one-tailed tests had been justified, it is possible that as many as an additional 6 *t*s would also have been significant.

In considering one of the more typical examples, it is evident that the male subjects consider Target 6 (also judged to be the most Attractive) to be more suiting or approximating to the role of Wife than do the females ($t = -2.88$, $p < .01$). Since, as was mentioned in the preceding section, the more detailed aspects of interpretation are treated at length elsewhere (e.g., Section 4.4 and Chapter 6), we can turn to an overview of these results.

5.5.3 *Sex differences in attribution: perspectives provided by a joint consideration of the two English studies*

If the sex differences occurring in Tables 5.9 and 5.10 are considered

Table 5.9

Sex differences (i.e. *t* tests) between the mean ratings ascribed to six target persons by 182 male and female subjects in groups of equal size (English Study 1, based on grading)**

Traits	Target Persons					
	1	2	3	4	5	6
1. Attractive	—0.17	—0.60	—1.09	1.83	0.98	1.91
2. Wife	3.99‡	3.73†	1.05	—0.43	0.87	0.92
3. Prudish	—0.82	—1.46	—0.14	0.32	—2.02*	—1.03
4. Self	—0.65	0.36	3.89†	0.79	3.06†	3.97‡
5. Alcoholic	—1.70	—0.68	1.85	1.16	0.51	2.56†
6. Mother	0.56	0.20	1.64	—1.93	1.65	1.58
7. Influential	0.53	1.14	1.88	1.23	—0.26	0.99
8. Cruel	—1.56	—1.78	0.88	0.66	—0.05	0.23
9. Homosexual	—1.63	—1.48	0.69	1.41	—0.52	—1.07
10. Ideal Self	0.94	—0.53	—0.47	—2.12*	4.61‡	4.54‡

* $p < .05$ † $p < .01$ ‡ $p < .001$

** Two-tailed *t* tests based on 180 degrees of freedom. A negative *t* value indicates that the males perceived the target under consideration to be more closely related to the trait than did the female subjects.

simultaneously, it becomes evident that some of the trends anticipated by the American study gain a certain degree of support. First, it is evident that the significant sex differences are distributed very unevenly among the various concepts — with Wife, Self, and Ideal Self being the recipients of an inordinately large proportion of them. This eventuality was anticipated in the US study (Stewart et al., 1973, p. 811; see Section 3.1) and, indeed, prompted the adoption of an extended trait vocabulary. At that time, it was reasoned that sex differences might only arise from concepts in which one or the other of the sexes had a greater degree of commitment or a different type of involvement, such as in sex roles.

In a later analysis of the US data (namely Powell et al., 1974, p. 412; see Section 3.10), it was also observed that sex differences seemed to accrue unevenly to target persons as well as concepts, with Targets 5 and 6 being especially well founded in this respect. Here, we find at least limited support for this supposition, noting that Targets 5 and 6 do evidence just about twice as many sex differences in attribution as any other Target when the two Tables are considered at the same time. As Targets 5 and 6

Table 5.10

Sex Differences in Trait Attribution due to the *Rankings* of the 78 Males and 67 Females serving in the Second UK Study — as tested by *t* statistics for independent groups[1]

Traits	Target Persons					
	1	2	3	4	5	6
1. Attractive	1.67	—0.71	—1.78	—1.47	1.64	—1.09
2. Wife	3.77‡	2.58*	—1.13	—0.89	—2.54*	—2.88†
3. Prudish	1.65	0.31	0.44	0.11	—1.62	—0.34
4. Self	0.23	—1.12	0.28	—2.55*	0.76	2.02*
5. Alcoholic	0.41	0.30	1.00	0.89	—1.18	—0.84
6. Mother	1.44	1.80	0.13	—1.45	—1.21	—0.42
7. Influential	1.80	0.36	1.41	0.39	—1.01	—2.97†
8. Cruel	—0.39	—1.96	1.28	0.81	0.61	0.00
9. Homosexual	—1.25	0.33	1.85	0.79	—1.55	0.38
10. Ideal Self	2.22*	0.00	—5.12‡	—3.82‡	4.05‡	0.82

* $p<.05$ † $p<.01$ ‡ $p<.001$.

1. Two-tailed *t* tests based on 143 degrees of freedom. A negative *t* indicates that the males perceived the trait as better suiting the target than did the females.

are the most Attractive ones, this excess of sex differences may reflect the difference in degree to which males and females depend upon Evaluation in forming their judgements of female target persons.

Coming back, momentarily, to the appropriateness of multiple *t* tests as a research strategy, we think that the utility of this 'piecemeal' approach is well illustrated by observations such as the above. Of course, such discrete results as are obtained by multiple *t*s do need to be verified when possible by overall procedures, such as the analysis of variance, which provide better estimates of their collective significance.

5.6 Social stereotyping in the English studies

5.6.1 Social stereotypes arising from the ranking format: the results from Study 2

The measurement of concordance is a much more tractable problem with data generated by rankings, so we shall start the survey of results with a consideration of Study 2, which is, of course, based on ranking. Here, Concordance is taken to be representative of the degree of social stereotyping present in the data and can be most easily evaluated by computing Coefficients of Concordance (*W*) for each of the items constituting the trait vocabulary.

It will be recalled that *W* is equivalent to the average correlation between all the possible pairs of subjects when their rankings of targets are compared two at a time (i.e. the average of 2,211 rank order correlations in the case of our 67 female subjects). *W* is, of course, most easily obtained by means of a formula rather than by direct calculation. Disregarding for the moment that a small 'adjustment' is required to make *W* exactly equivalent to the average intercorrelation between subjects, it is, by way of illustration, expected that if pairs of subjects were drawn at random from one of our groups, the observed correlations between their rankings would, on average, approximate to the value of *W* obtained for the group as a whole. In other words, a large *W* indicates that the subjects' rankings were, in general, reasonably similar, while a small *W* implies that the various individual rankings have little in common with one another (see Appendix III for an extended discussion of *W*).

In the present context, the magnitude of *W* can be taken as an indicator of the extent to which subjects have drawn similar inferences from the various aspects of body build which are available to them. The apparent simplicity of this statement should not, however, blind one to the actual complexity of process which underlies the inference *per se* — it is, for example, possible that subjects may draw similar inferences but do so on the basis of entirely different aspects of body build.

Turning to the stereotypic aspects of these data, it is usually assumed that social stereotyping has occurred when arbitrary cues or differences are seen to result in the consensual or concordant attribution of traits and qualities. Here, because some of the factors which appear to mediate stereotyping, such as attractiveness, have been shown to be salient in many circumstances (see Chapter 1), we would argue for the substitution of the term 'minimal' for that of 'arbitrary'. In other words, attractiveness, because it exerts a very real influence over behaviour, cannot in a practical sense be considered to be entirely arbitrary. In any event, the finding of concordance does imply that cultural factors and social experience have operated in such a manner as to enable subjects to make consensual inferences concerning body build and behaviour.

In the actual treatment of the data, the coefficients of concordance have been calculated with the inclusion of a small correction to adjust for the nonadditive nature of the underlying or constituent correlations (Stewart et al., 1975) and in consequence are referred to as *CW*s rather than *W*s in Table 5.11. Except to increase the observed values by about 12 per cent, this adjustment does not alter any of the properties of *W* discussed above. Here, the significance testing was carried out by the remarkably flexible *F* procedure suggested by Edwards (1950; Maxwell, 1964). Bearing these considerations in mind, we can turn to the data proper, which are presented in Table 5.11.

One of the most striking features of Table 5.11 is that 29 out of the 30 *CW*s are significant, and of these, 28 are significant at or beyond the .001 level. Or viewed from a slightly different perspective, it might be said that all the concepts except four (namely Alcoholic, Cruel, Homosexual and Prudish) display levels of concordance which are meaningful in their own right and are of more than heuristic interest. So, in the broadest sense, it can be concluded that there are social stereotypes for both the target persons and the traits, which in some cases may be strong enough to be of practical importance (cf. Tutton et al., 1974). And as we shall see later (in Section 5.7), there are relatively marked sex differences in these data.

The present results can be contrasted and compared with the US data in several different ways. In the first place, the overall pattern of results is quite similar, with concepts such as Attractive (for men), Self (for women) and Wife (for men) displaying quite high levels of concordance.

But, turning to a contrast, we find that the largest of the US concordances are smaller than their English counterparts. Considering that the US subjects were, with respect to social class and education, considerably more homogeneous than the English sample, these results are somewhat surprising. Indeed, they suggest that matters of social class and education may be of specific significance to person perception, and that our great reliance upon university students as subjects may be, in a subtle sense, more detrimental to our studies than we had previously realised.

Before turning to the consensus and stereotyping observed in graded data (i.e. Study 1), it is worth recalling that measures of social stereotyping (such as *W* or *CW*) tend, because they exclude subjective factors, to provide an underestimate of the degree of total stereotyping present in the data (see Chapter 2). While the design of the present study does not make provision for a direct appraisal of the degree of

Table 5.11

Coefficients of Concordance obtained for Male and Female Subjects by the Method of Ranking

	Men		Women		Total	
Concepts	*CW*	F^1	*CW*	F^2	*CW*	F^3
1. Attractive	.85	324.1†	.86	306.5†	.86	621.3†
2. Ideal Self	.77	179.8†	.88	327.6†	.81	412.3†
3. Self	.58	76.4†	.72	126.8†	.64	186.5†
4. Wife	.66	109.8†	.34	27.7†	.50	107.6†
5. Mother	.28	25.3†	.34	27.9†	.30	51.1†
6. Influential	.30	27.8†	.26	19.2†	.27	44.3†
7. Alcoholic	.12	9.1†	.20	13.6†	.16	21.8†
8. Cruel	.10	7.5†	.19	13.4†	.14	19.4†
9. Homosexual	.12	9.2†	.17	11.7†	.14	19.6†
10. Prudish	.05	3.7*	.02	1.5	.03	4.2†

[1] *F*s evaluated against 5 and 383 degrees of freedom.
[2] *F*s evaluated against 5 and 328 degrees of freedom.
[3] *F*s evaluated against 5 and 718 degrees of freedom.
*Significant at the .05 level.
†Significant at the .001 level.

underestimation, it is possible to derive some notion of the magnitude by looking ahead to the intercorrelations (see Table 5.16) and comparing them with their corresponding *W*s. Using this approach, the degree of underestimation appears to be fairly severe, ranging from perhaps as much as 10 to 60 per cent in the case of several of the moderately large *CW*s. If we had applied r^2 or z transformations rather than using raw correlation coefficients, these comparisons would have been even more invidious, but the observed attenuation seems to be reasonably in line with that observed in the American study.

5.6.2 *The measurement of concordance in data based on ratings: background*

As we have just seen, one can immediately fall back upon Kendall's coefficient of concordance (*W*) when needing to measure stereotyping in ranked data. Indeed, *W*, as a statistic, was specifically designed to cope with this type of problem. And while it may appear that no such convenient 'standard' approach is available for graded data as is required here, Winer (1962, pp. 124-32 and 136-8) has shown that conventional analysis of variance can, in fact, be used to obtain the same information (i.e. the average intercorrelation between all possible pairs of subjects) as that available from the coefficient of concordance. Indeed, this approach — based on analysis of variance — yields a good deal more information than does *W*, including such things as an evaluation of sex differences in mean ratings, as estimate of reliability, etc.

Here one may wonder how the analysis of variance, which is basically a parametric technique, can yield the same information as *W*, which is nonparametric in nature and based on ranking, but it is only necessary to recall that the coefficient of concordance is, in fact, a specialised form of analysis of variance (cf. Haggard, 1958; McNemar, 1969, pp. 435-7; Winer, 1962, pp. 136-8); illustrating that in spite of seemingly radical differences in the approach to the measurement of social stereotyping, Studies 1 and 2 are, in fact, virtually identical (with respect to analysis) and could, data permitting, yield results which show an exact numerical correspondence. This point, concerning the potential equivalence of *W* and the analysis of variance, cannot be too strongly emphasised, for, as we shall see below, Study 1 does, in fact, give rise to very different estimates of concordance (i.e. generally smaller) than those derived from Study 2 — diferences which must, therefore, grow out of the unlike demands of ranking and grading, rather than the methods of analysis *per se*. Next, we shall consider the statistical procedures required for estimating concordance from analyses of variance.

5.6.3 *The statistical procedures required for deriving estimates of concordance ($\bar{r}$) from the analysis of variance*

It has long been recognised that the mean squares (MS) which compose an analysis of variance can serve not only as a test of significance, as is embodied in the *F* ratio, but in addition they can be employed to provide an estimate of reliability. And while it is probably less well known (and correspondingly less often required), the same mean squares (MS) can be used to provide an estimate of the mean intercorrelation between all possible pairs of subjects ($\bar{r}$), giving rise to a statistic which is the exact equivalent of *W*. The relationship between mean squares (MS) used to derive $\bar{r}$ is shown in the following equation:

$$\text{Mean Intercorrelation } (\bar{r}) = \frac{MS_{stimuli} - MS_{res}}{MS_{stimuli} + (N-1)\, MS_{res}}$$

where $MS_{stimuli}$ refers to the Mean square between stimuli (i.e. targets), N for the number of subjects, and MS_{res} to the mean square for the residual or error term (see Table 5.8). Accordingly, we used this relationship to ascertain the extent of concordance in the graded data arising from Study 1.

5.6.4 *Social stereotyping and consensus in Study 1: results*

The indices of concordance ($\bar{r}$) for the rating data from Study 1 are shown in Table 5.12, with individual $\bar{r}$s for each sex, and again for the combined group. Significance was evaluated by means of *F*s, and it can be seen from the *df*s that these data have been obtained from the equilibrated sex groups, consisting of 91 subjects each (as required for the analyses of variance).

Again, as with Study 2, one of the foremost features of Table 5.12 is that all the traits show some degree of social stereotyping (i.e. concordance) — with 29 of the 30 $\bar{r}$s being significant well beyond .001 level. On the other hand, it is noteworthy that a number of the obtained $\bar{r}$s are, irrespective of their extreme statistical significance, too small to be of practical importance (e.g. Cruel, Prudish, etc.). Indeed, these data do not, as a whole, yield an impression of strong social stereotyping.

Before drawing any hard and fast conclusions, however, it is probably worth turning to the intercorrelations between traits, presented below in Table 5.16, to estimate as best we can just what are the limits for total stereotyping. It will be recalled that intercorrelations tend to represent both social and personal stereotypes simultaneously, and thereby provide a comprehensive estimate of the influence of stereotyping on the judgements in question. In looking at the intercorrelations between traits, we find that all the traits, except Attractiveness as judged by the males, yield intercorrelations which are in the region of one and a half to seven times greater in magnitude than their corresponding $\bar{r}$s. With the advantage of this new information, it can be argued that the graded data from Study 1 do, in fact, exhibit reasonable levels of total stereotyping (i.e. trait intercorrelations), while, on the other hand, the expression of social stereotyping seems to be restricted in some manner.

Again, as in the US study and Study 2 here, the 'deviant' traits (namely Alcoholic, Cruel and Homosexual) are observed to be among the least consensual items in the trait vocabulary. Here, however, because of the generally lower levels of concordance, the contrast between these and the more desirable traits is not so pronounced as in the earlier data. This tendency for disapproved traits to be low in concordance has also

Table 5.12

Social Stereotyping in Graded Data — Tested by means of $\bar{r}$, a Parametric Equivalent of the Coefficient of Concordance

Concept	Men		Women		Total	
	$\bar{r}$	F^1	$\bar{r}$	F^1	$\bar{r}$	F^2
1. Attractive	.58	127.7†	.64	162.1†	.61	287.7†
2. Ideal Self	.33	45.8†	.49	87.0†	.40	120.6†
3. Self	.31	41.8†	.36	52.1†	.35	99.3†
4. Wife	.16	18.3†	.10	11.0†	.13	27.4†
5. Mother	.16	18.0†	.12	13.3†	.13	28.6†
6. Influential	.16	18.1†	.17	19.9†	.17	37.0†
7. Alcoholic	.27	35.0†	.09	9.9†	.17	37.0†
8. Cruel	.07	7.9†	.09	10.1†	.07	15.2†
9. Homosexual	.06	7.0†	.11	12.2†	.08	17.0†
10. Prudish	.06	6.7†	.03	3.7*	.03	7.4†

[1]df = 5/90
[2]df = 5/180
*Significant at or beyond the .01 level.
†Significant at or beyond the .001 level.

emerged from our later studies, where adolescents evaluated the implications of differences in attire (see, for example, Tables 7.2 and 7.3).

5.6.5 *Differences in the estimates of concordance: a comparison of the results obtained from grading and ranking*

Here we will compare measures of concordance (i.e. CW with $\bar{r}$s) in an attempt to clarify further the differences arising from the grading (i.e. semantic differential) and ranking formats. Unfortunately, as the exact relationship between CW and $\bar{r}$ is not known, this comparison will have to be carried out by inspection. On the other hand, we do know that CW and $\bar{r}$ should yield comparable results when the data upon which they are based are of equivalent quality. In other words, if the graded data should show the clearcut discriminations between the targets that are 'forced' by the ranking procedure (e.g. few tied scores in the individual gradings), then there should be little difference between CW and $\bar{r}$. To facilitate the required comparisons, the observed CWs and $\bar{r}$s have been reproduced in an abbreviated form in Table 5.13.

In looking at Table 5.13, it is found that $\bar{r}$ exceeds the value obtained by CW in only one important instance, that being the concordance of male subjects on Alcoholic. Or from the opposite point of view, CW exceeds $\bar{r}$ in 26 out of 30 instances but, except for the difference mentioned above, the remaining three instances of superior $\bar{r}$ are trivial (cf. Prudish). More important, however, than the sheer frequency with which CW is greater than $\bar{r}$, is the actual magnitude of the observed differences — with 16 of the 30 comparisons showing CW to be anywhere from approximately 100 to 300 per cent larger than the corresponding $\bar{r}$.

Now we can ask just what are the practical implications of these differences. Before embarking on this problem, a few remarks are in order. First, it should be noted that there are no intrinsic differences between mean ratings and mean rankings in the present context (i.e. with no absolute zero point) — as is pointed out by Woodworth & Schlosberg (1954, pp. 257-61). Both represent equivalent measures of 'distance' between stimuli and are open to the same interpretations. Second, and turning to an aspect of CW and $\bar{r}$ which we have not touched on before, both, being intraclass correlations, can be said to indicate the proportion of variance attributable to the variable or trait under consideration (e.g. Hays, 1963, pp. 423-6; McNemar, 1969, pp. 435-7). According to this point of view, the listing for Attractiveness for the male subjects in Table 5.13 implies that this trait accounts for as much as 85 per cent of the variance in the rankings, but only 58 per cent of the variance in the case of the ratings. This seems to be quite a large difference, considering that mean ratings and mean rankings constitute equivalent entities.

Depending, then, upon which type of data was available, one could draw very different conclusions concerning the relative contribution of social stereotyping to impression formation or social image. These marked differences are, of course, related directly to the differences in range of means discussed earlier. It also seems likely that this 'shrinkage' will militate against the finding of sex differences in the concordance of graded data, at least in so far as they are represented in a summary statistic, such as $\bar{r}$ or W, which does not take into account the finer structure of the data.

Turning to what is probably the single most important issue in this section, we are now in a position to focus on the primary point of difference between the grading and ranking procedures with a reasonable degree of precision. To recapitulate, we know that the methods of analysis are counterparts to one another, that the mean ratings and mean rankings are equivalent, and that CW and $\bar{r}$ are subject to the same interpretation with respect to variance explained. By design, the trait vocabulary and target persons are identical in the two studies. And last, the sampling of subjects is seen to be virtually identical — so that we do not, in fact, have any reason to suppose that one group was any more predisposed towards social stereotyping than the others.

Table 5.13

A summary of the Indices of Concordance Derived from the Rating ($\bar{r}$) and Ranking (CW) Formats

Concepts	Males		Females		Total	
	CW	$\bar{r}$	CW	$\bar{r}$	CW	$\bar{r}$
1. Attractive	.85	.58	.86	.64	.86	.61
2. Ideal Self	.77	.33	.88	.49	.81	.40
3. Self	.58	.31	.72	.36	.64	.35
4. Wife	.66	.16	.34	.10	.50	.13
5. Mother	.28	.16	.34	.12	.30	.13
6. Influential	.30	.16	.26	.17	.27	.17
7. Alcoholic	.12	.27	.20	.09	.16	.17
8. Cruel	.10	.07	.19	.09	.14	.07
9. Homosexual	.12	.06	.17	.11	.14	.08
10. Prudish	.05	.06	.02	.03	.03	.03

Given this background, it is only reasonable to assume that the differences between the two methods arise at the time that the subjects are formulating and/or recording their judgements. And knowing that ranking is a highly formalised procedure, which thereby excludes many of the more common response biases, it is necessary to conclude that grading, by its very flexibility, is liable to contamination through a variety of biases — such as extreme responding, displaced responding, or noncommittal responding — and therefore elicits confounded (i.e. low) estimates of social stereotyping.

In taking a closer look at the effects of these biases, it will be recalled that ranking and rating have shown Attractiveness to account for, respectively, 85 and 58 per cent of the variance explained, indicating that ranking leaves just 15 per cent of the variance unaccounted for, while rating leaves nearly one half unaccounted for, with 42 per cent remaining to be explained by factors other than Attractiveness. Consequently, we would suggest that the biases adumbrated here, and possibly others, account for a good proportion of the discrepancy between the 15 and 42 per cent of unexplained variance mentioned above, and likewise for the other major discrepancies occurring in Table 5.13.

Since it is known that ranking procedures can provide results which are broadly comparable with those based on other scaling techniques (cf. Woodworth & Schlosberg, 1954), it is reasonable here to ask why our experimental manipulations have resulted in such marked discrepancies. And while we have no definite answer, it can be suggested that ranking is a more 'natural' (i.e. commonplace or habitual) operation than is grading (Slater, 1965). Viewed thus, it is possible that the rating task, because of its greater novelty or ambiguity vis à vis ranking, may have resulted in higher levels of anxiety or uncertainty, which in turn caused the subjects to evidence various of the well known response biases or other anomalies of scale checking behaviour (e.g. Osgood et al., 1957, pp. 229-36).

Irrespective of the final explanation, it seems reasonable to suggest that ranking, because of its freedom from contamination by extraneous (i.e. noncognitive) response biases, is, in many instances, the more appropriate format for studies of person perception and stereotyping. In amplifying upon this caution, it is worth while to point out that some trait intercorrelations (such as those presented in Table 5.16) could be spuriously inflated by 'shared' response biases, which arise more or less independently of the qualitative implications of the traits in question. In other words, two traits which are in themselves uncorrelated could evidence a correlation simply because they evoke comparable response biases (i.e. alike for given raters, but more or less different from rater to rater) when each is encountered. Indeed, in comparing the intercorrelations for graded and ranked data (below, in Tables 5.16 and 5.17), we find a number of instances where grading yields larger intercorrelations than does ranking, but only for those traits which show lower levels of concordance — namely Prudish, Cruel and Homosexual — causing one to speculate whether this somewhat unexpected 'turn about' is a result of an irrelevant association between response biases being superimposed upon a true, but modest, association between shared meanings or inferences.

5.7 Sex differences observed in the concordances of the English subjects

In view of the findings of the US study and their broader implications, it can be said that sex differences in consensus are among the most important topics to be touched upon here. It will be recalled from Chapters 2 and 3 that variations in consensus have the potential to be prime indicators of a wide variety of circumstances and conditions — including, but not limited to sex differences in social learning and role expectations, role conflicts, social change, and at the extreme, social or personal disorganisation — depending upon the level of analysis which one chooses to employ.

5.7.1 The evaluation of sex differences in concordance in graded data — Study 1

Considering that the *r*s derived from the semantic differential format (via analyses of variance — see Section 5.4.3) do, in fact, represent true instances of averaged product-moment correlations, it seems entirely reasonable that they should be tested for sex differences in the manner outlined by McNemar (1969, pp. 157-8). In this approach, significance is expressed in terms of *z* statistics, and these, along with the constituent $\bar{r}$s, are presented in Table 5.14 below.

Because of the prior experience derived from the US data, we were able to frame some of the predictions as one-tailed tests, with it being predicted in advance that the male subjects would show greater concordance on Attractive, Wife, Homosexual and Alcoholic. For the female subjects it was expected that they would evidence greater concordance on the concepts of Self and Ideal Self, while Mother, Influential, Cruel and Prudish, either because they were being employed for the first time or because they had failed to yield clearcut sex differences in the US study, were requiring of two-tailed tests. Of course, the same considerations apply equally to the choice of one- or two-tailed probabilities in the testing of sex differences between the coefficients of concordance arising out of Study 2. Whether one- or two-tailed tests have been employed will be clearly indicated in Table 5.14 below.

5.7.2 The assessment of sex differences in ranked data — a major departure from the procedures available for the analysis of the earlier US data

In the time intervening between the completion of the US study and the present undertaking, various statistical properties and relationships have come to light (as detailed in Appendix III) which show that *W*s derived from independent groups can be tested for differences in a manner much like that employed with more commonplace correlations. In other words, these developments allow us to make direct comparisons between *W*s — to determine if sex differences are present — without resorting to the somewhat cumbersome procedures employed in the US study.

Because the theoretical background and numerical procedures required for the direct comparison of *W*s have been described in detail in Section III-4 of Appendix III, a brief outline will suffice here. As a first step, it is necessary to transform the observed *W*s by taking their square roots, by which they are changed into a closely related statistic (i.e. $\bar{r}_{iM}$) which approximates to the distribution of Fisher's *z*s. After obtaining the square roots, it is only necessary to find the equivalent *z*s by means of Fisher's formula (or with slightly less accuracy, by means of Tables), and conclude the comparison by computing a standard score (i.e. *z*) for differences between average correlations in the usual manner (Edwards, 1950, p. 136; McNemar, 1969, p. 158). All the required formulae are shown in Appendix III. The one- and two-tailed probabilities of the standard scores can be obtained by consulting one of the common tables of Cumulative Normal Probabilities.

5.7.3 Sex differences in concordance: results from Studies 1 and 2

The tests for sex differences in concordance are summarised in Table 5.14, which portrays the data obtained from both of the UK formats; grading and ranking. As indicated in Section 5.7.1 above, four of the items considered here — namely Mother, Influential, Cruel and Prudish — were requiring of two-tailed tests, while the remaining six items were, on the basis of the US data, considered to be suitable for the more powerful one-tailed tests.

In looking at Table 5.14, it can be seen that only five of the twenty comparisons have yielded differences which are significant; two in which the males were the most concordant, and three in which the females predominated. Considering that the formats exhibit sex differences with approximately equal frequencies — i.e. two for rating versus three for ranking — format does not appear, at first glance, to be a crucial variable. It is noteworthy, however, that the differences arising from ranking are seen to yield levels of significance which are well in excess of those provided by the rating format.

Recalling that we were able to make predictions in the case of twelve comparisons (i.e. six one-tailed comparisons for each of the two formats), we can enquire as to how well these have fared. The results of these particular tests are summarised in Table 5.15.

Table 5.14

Sex Differences in Social Stereotyping: a Summary of the two UK Studies

	Semantic Differential				Ranking[2]			
Concept	$\bar{r}_m$	$\bar{r}_f$	z_{sex}	p_{sex}	$\sqrt{W}_m$	$\sqrt{W}_f$	z_{sex}	p_{sex}
1. Attractive[1]	.58	.64	—1.12	ns	.92	.93	—0.39	ns
2. Ideal Self[1]	.33	.49	2.28	.025	.87	.94	3.69	.0005
3. Self[1]	.31	.36	0.66	ns	.76	.85	2.59	.005
4. Wife[1]	.16	.10	0.71	ns	.81	.58	4.83	.0005
5. Mother	.16	.12	0.48	ns	.53	.58	0.81	ns
6. Influential	.16	.17	0.12	ns	.55	.51	0.54	ns
7. Alcoholic[1]	.27	.09	2.18	.025	.35	.45	—1.24	ns
8. Cruel	.07	.09	0.24	ns	.32	.44	1.44	ns
9. Homosexual[1]	.06	.11	—0.59	ns	.35	.41	—0.80	ns
10. Prudish	.06	.03	0.35	ns	.22	.14	0.88	ns

1. As described in the text, *ps* are based on one-tailed probabilities for both the semantic differential and ranking data. A negative *z* indicates that the observed difference was opposite to that predicted.
2. As required for the present *z* test, the observed *W*s are transformed to square roots — this new statistic ($\sqrt{W}$) being interpretable as the average of the *N* correlations arising from the comparison of each individual ranking with the single set of target means (see Appendix III for a full discussion).

From an examination of Table 5.15, it is evident that our predictions were confirmed without qualification in five out of the twelve instances considered. Two more tests show differences in concordance which accord with predictions, but fail to achieve acceptable levels of significance. Turning to the contradictory results, there are five occasions in which the observed results are the reverse of those anticipated, but none of these reversals approaches significance, with the largest of the 'contrary' *z*s being of a magnitude expected to occur about one time in four on the basis of chance alone ($z = 1.24$, $p < .22$). In view of the fact that the predictions employed here were derived from a study which differed in many important respects from the pair at present under consideration, the observed degree of replication seems, in a general way, satisfactory.

On the other hand, the rather inconsistent patterns of sex differences revealed by ranking and grading suggest that some important questions remain to be answered before the measurement of concordance and social stereotyping can be treated as a cut and dried issue. In the face of these discrepancies it is necessary to ask whether grading, which introduces a whole host of sundry biases, is less efficient at disclosing sex differences than is ranking. Whether grading is a less satisfactory means of assessing concordance and sex differences in social stereotyping

Table 5.15

Instances of Agreement and Disagreement between the Twelve One-Way Tests and Their Antecedent Expectations Concerning Sex Differences in Concordance

Items[1]	Direction of Difference[2]	Results of Test	Number of Tests per Outcome
2b, 3r, 4r, 7g	As Predicted	Significant	5
3r, 4g	As Predicted	Non-Significant	2
1b, 7r, 9b	Reversed	Non-Significant	5
None	Reversed	Significant	0

[1]b = both formats, g = grading only, r = ranking only.
[2]Predictions of direction made in accordance with the US data.

seems, then, to remain an open question, but our opinion tends to favour ranking in this application.

Turning to the last of the general considerations, it is apparent that sex differences are not excessively frequent. In view of our supposition, i.e. that rather special circumstances are required to bring about alterations in concordance (see in particular Sections 2.2 and 2.3.1), this outcome is not entirely unexpected, and indeed has been discussed on several earlier occasions (e.g. Stewart et al., 1973, p. 811; see also Sections 3.1 and 3.6.5).

5.7.4 *Implications of the replicated and nonreplicated sex differences observed here*

Having looked at the more general implications of sex differences in concordance, we can now turn our attention to the individual items and the consequences which they suggest. Because of their more pervasive spheres of influence and generality, the concepts of Wife, Self, Ideal Self and Attractiveness will be examined in greater detail here.

Self and Ideal Self. The female subjects were observed to be more concordant than the males in three out of the four comparisons involving these constructs, the single exception being the concept of Self as evaluated on the semantic differential format. Recalling that the female subjects in the US study were also found to be more concordant on Self, the present replications begin to suggest that this is an expected rather than exceptional sex difference. Since it is not immediately clear as to why the women should be more concordant than the men, we will consider some of the possible causes and contributory factors below.

If the masculine attributes of body build were not so well represented in the targets as the feminine features, then it would be understandable that the males should experience more confusion and display lower concordances on Self and Ideal Self. In view, however, of Sheldon's (1940, 1963) claim that these six target persons encompass the full range of human types, both male and female, this argument does not seem to provide the whole answer. A similar reduction of concordance might be noted if the samples of male subjects were nonrepresentative with respect of body build but this argument seems unlikely in the face of three replications.

Looking then to explanations which are more purely psychological in nature, it is possible that a certain, perhaps sizable proportion of the male subjects respond inappropriately — selecting slender rather than muscular somatotypes — because the muscular targets, when presented in the guise of women, create such unfavourable impressions. Should such a bias be operative in the male subjects it is inevitable, as discussed in Section 2.2.1, that concordance will be reduced. The underlying problem seems, then, to be one of cross-sex discrimination on the part of the male subjects.

Recalling that muscularity is a valued trait in male targets, a partial answer might be obtained if subjects were to be tested for Self and Ideal Self on sets of both male and female targets. In any event, the notion of a psychological explanation is consistent with the observation that male subjects find the task of evaluating Self and Ideal Self particularly disturbing when required to use female targets as the standards of comparisons (see Sections 5.1 and 5.9.4 for background and a further discussion of this problem).

Wife — a partial replication of an important sex difference in social role perception. Both formats show the males to be more concordant on this concept than are the females, but unfortunately the difference is not significant in the case of grading. Considering that other data derived from the grading format — such as the intercorrelations between Wife and Mother, Wife and Attractiveness, etc. — indicate clear sex differences in the evaluation of this construct, it seems reasonable to suggest that it is the presence of idiosyncratic (i.e. nonconsensual) response biases which are responsible for the low levels of concordance and the consequent failure to observe sex differences in the social stereotyping of this construct. Should this supposition prove to be correct, it serves to illustrate how easily the grading format can be confounded by extraneous response biases, and thus render equivocal results.

Moving on to the ranking format, we encounter a difference between the males ($W_{\text{Wife}} = 0.66$) and females ($W_{\text{Wife}} = 0.34$) which is, in both magnitude and direction, quite similar to that found in the US study — a replication which is all the more interesting because of the altered circumstances of the US/UK studies. Recalling that we have argued at length against the plausibility of explaining instances of low concordance on socially salient constructs by invoking notions of random or disinterested responding (see Sections 2.3 and 3.7.2, or Stewart et al., 1974, p. 868), the considerations put forward in the case of the US data seem equally appropriate to the present circumstances.

Briefly, we suggested in the case of the US study that the female subjects were less concordant than the males, not because of random responding or limited insight but rather because of a greater diversity of attitude and expectations concerning what is constituted by the role of Wife. And while the data from the US/UK studies cannot be considered to be final on this point, there is a strong suggestion from the correlational data that the females perceive the role of Wife to be either home and family orientated in a traditional manner, or focus more strongly on the social aspects of the husband/wife interaction and their involvement in peer group activities. This latter conception is less traditional and probably comes closer to that point of view espoused by the males than does the former. We are not, however, alone in this point of view, as the Brovermans and their colleagues (e.g. Broverman et al., 1972; Vogel et al., 1970, 1975) have arrived at a similar conclusion in spite of using an entirely different procedure and experimental approach. Some of the causes and implications of such a bifurcation in social roles has been discussed in a general way in Section 2.2.2, while the more specialised topic of sex differences in the perception of family roles has been summarised in Chapter 6 below.

Sex differences in the social stereotyping of physical attractiveness: a failure to confirm. In looking at Table 5.14, it can be seen, contrary to predictions from the US data, that the female subjects were, in both instances, slightly more concordant in their judgements of Attractiveness of body build than their male counterparts. In so far as neither difference is significant, nor that significance was obtained when the two studies were combined as independent replications in the manner suggested by Maxwell (1961, p. 73), it seems reasonable to conclude that the two sexes do not, as tested here, differ in their appreciation of Physical Attractiveness. Irrespective of the fact that this outcome is at variance with the US data on consensus, it is important to recognise that it does not in any way infirm the idea that men and women draw dissimilar inferences from physical attractiveness or weigh its importance in an unequal manner (Berscheid et al., 1971; Coombs & Kenkel, 1966).

Here we can only speculate as to why the US/UK results are at odds with one another, but one of the more suspect areas may well be that of the way in which the targets were reproduced and presented. In the case of Attractiveness — which is one of the more palpable or immediate qualities — it is reasonable to expect that the graphical quality with which the target is reproduced and its ability to convey detail will exert a marked influence over the degree of Attractiveness perceived to be present. While the differences between the US and UK stimuli have been discussed in detail (see Section 5.3.1), it is worth noting that the UK targets differed from their US equivalents by being larger, having better black/white contrast, and a generally more professional appearance. What is probably more important, however, is the fact that the UK study utilised only a single full face pose for each of the targets, while the US study employed two poses: the above mentioned full face pose along with a second pose representing the target in profile.

Against this background — and noting that the profile representations are generally less attractive than their full face counterparts — it does not seem unrealistic to posit that it is the absence of the profile pose which is responsible for the more consensual attribution of Attractiveness encountered in the UK data (i.e. $W_{UK} = 0.79$, $W_{US} = 0.57$). Considering that concordance has been related to reliability (e.g. Frijda & Philipszoon, 1963; Winer, 1962, pp,. 124-32), and reliability to ambiguity (Frith & Lillie, 1972) it does not seem too fanciful to suggest that the observed differences in concordance arise because the US targets were more ambiguous than the later reproductions, with the most likely sources of ambiguity being (1) the somewhat poorer quality of the US graphics, and (2) the uncertainty arising out of the disparities between the full-face and profile poses.

In connection with this problem, and the failure to replicate the US results, it would be interesting to know if ambiguity is a condition which brings about a greater reduction in concordance for women than men in the judgement of Attractiveness of female targets — a not entirely implausible suggestion in the light of somewhat greater responsiveness on the part of males to differences in attractiveness (see Chapter 4). Likewise, it would be useful to know which, if any, personality variables enter into the resolution of discrepant information relating to attractiveness.

5.8 Trait associations and the implicit structure of social perception

In this section we shall be concerned with the correlations between traits and the inferences which can be drawn from them. Trait inter-correlations can be expected to illuminate several different types of problems, such as sex differences in the conception of social roles, conceptual stereotyping, and indeed the relationship of stereotyping to person perception. In contrast to the earlier treatment of trait associations, which was based on only 25 subjects of each sex, it is possible to carry out factor analyses in an attempt to isolate the more salient features of social perception present here.

Table 5.16

Trait Intercorrelations Obtained by means of the *Semantic Differential Format* (UK Study 1). The Correlations shown here are based on 91 Males (in lower triangle) and 127 Females (in upper triangle)

	1	2	3	4	5	6	7	8	9	10
1. Attractive		.35‡	—.18‡	.74‡	—.35‡	.07	.38‡	—.02	—.29‡	.85‡
2. Like A Wife	.53‡		—.04	.33‡	—.19‡	.57‡	.18‡	—.17‡	—.34‡	.29‡
3. Prudish	—.24‡	—.20‡		—.19‡	.03	—.06	—.12*	.13*	.22‡	—.17‡
4. Like I Am	.50‡	.27‡	—.19†		—.34‡	.15†	.32‡	—.06	—.31‡	.74‡
5. Alcoholic	—.49‡	—.34‡	.14*	—.29‡		—.23‡	—.13*	.17‡	.33‡	—.29‡
6. Like A Mother	—.05	.43‡	—.12*	—.03	.00		.09	—.34‡	—.38‡	.08
7. Influential	.43‡	.24‡	—.17†	.26‡	—.23‡	.10		.14†	.02	.33‡
8. Cruel	—.05	—.16†	.15*	—.04	.13*	—.27‡	.14*		.47‡	—.08
9. Homosexual	—.32‡	—.37‡	.20‡	—.21‡	.26‡	—.25‡	—.10	.33‡		—.31‡
10. Like I Would Like To Be	.59‡	.24‡	—.25‡	.51‡	—.32‡	—.05	.34‡	—.08	—.23‡	

$^*p < .05$ †$p. < .01$ ‡$p. < .001$

5.8.1 Computation of the intercorrelations

The present trait intercorrelations were obtained by the same method as described in Sections 2.3 and 3.9.1. As mentioned earlier, each of the 45 intercorrelations is computed by averaging a number of Spearman *rho*s (i.e. one r_S per subject), while at the same time applying Slater's (1972) correction to compensate for the non-additive nature of correlation. Since, as is seen in Appendix III the same general conditions are valid for parametric data as well as those based on rankings, the intercorrelations were computed in the same way for the graded data from Study 1.

The correlations thus obtained are presented in Table 5.16, which represents the graded data from Study 1, and 5.17, which shows the correlations obtained by ranking (i.e. Study 2).

To ascertain if the observed correlations differed significantly from zero, *z*s (i.e. relative deviates) were computed by means of the single-group variant of formula III-6 in Appendix III (see McNemar, 1969, pp. 157-8, for further details). Because of the generality of this procedure, it was applied to both the parametric and ranked data alike. Irrespective of the similar treatment, the test for the graded data was considerably more discriminating because of the larger sample size.

Considering the data from both studies and sexes as a whole, it can be seen that the vast majority of correlations differed significantly from zero. To quantify this matter, Tables 5.16 and 5.17, taken together, provide 118 correlations which are significant at or beyond the .05 level (two-tailed tests) — representing some 66 per cent out of the total of 180.

While many of the more specific implications of the finding of a large number of significant trait intercorrelations in data from stereotyping were treated earlier (in Sections 3.9.2 and 3.9.3) and are generally applicable here, it is probably worth while to reiterate the single most salient implication — namely that stereotyping is shown by this finding to be systematic and not determined by the 'minutia' or idiosyncrasies of particular concepts. Assuming that this conclusion is true, it should be even more evident in the factor analyses which are to follow, and further strengthens the contention that stereotyping and person perception are essentially similar processes.

Since the more specific implications have been discussed in detail in Section 3.9 we will not repeat them here, but rather take up a new issue — that of whether grading and ranking provide comparable intercorrelations.

Table 5.17

Trait Intercorrelations Obtained by means of the *Ranking Format* (UK Study 2). The Correlations shown here are based on 76 Males (in lower triangle) and 67 Females (in upper triangle)

	1	2	3	4	5	6	7	8	9	10
1. Attractive		.58‡	.01	.85‡	—.49‡	—.09	.33‡	—.13	—.07	.97‡
2. Wife	.86‡		.02	.59‡	—.22†	.40‡	.34‡	—.21†	—.11	.57‡
3. Prudish	.04	.01		.06	.11	.10	.16*	.10	.07	.03
4. Like I Am	.74‡	.66‡	.10		—.44‡	.05	.39‡	—.11	—.09	.85‡
5. Alcoholic	—.37‡	—.29‡	.00	—.29‡		.12	—.14*	.21†	.21†	—.48‡
6. Like A Mother	.10	.22‡	—.07	.17†	—.08		—.20†	—.08	.04	—.11
7. Influential	.52‡	.54‡	.04	.42‡	—.19†	.17†		.10	.12	.29‡
8. Cruel	—.24‡	—.20†	.16*	—.05	.24‡	—.09	.06		.43‡	—.10
9. Homosexual	—.06	—.10	.03	.07	.28‡	.05	.13	.50‡		—.09
10. Like I would Like To Be	.90‡	.75‡	.03	.79‡	—.41‡	.10	.50‡	—.15*	.01	

*p. < .05 †p. < .01 ‡p. < .001

5.8.2 Rating v. ranking — quantitative differences in trait attribution

Even a cursory glance at Tables 5.16 and 5.17 is enough to give the impression that they differ from one another in several important ways. In comparing the two Tables it is obvious that large correlations — say, those in the top 20 per cent of the samples — are almost always much larger when expressed in ranking than in grading. Here, some of the prime examples are Attractive/Self, Self/Ideal Self, and Attractive-/Wife — where the relative diferences persist even in the fact of appreciable sex differences. In a somewhat contradictory manner, the second difference arises out of the fact that grading evidences many more significant intercorrelations than does ranking — 71 versus 47 to be precise. On examining the Tables in question, it was found that ranking gives rise to more small nonsignificant correlations — as exemplified by those arising from Prudish, Cruel and Homosexual — than does the grading format. In regard to these small correlations, it can be suggested (see Section 5.6.5) that the grading procedure yields correlations which reflect common (.e. joint) response biases as well as shared meanings or reciprocal inferences. Reasoning in the same vein, it is also possible that response biases, such as a reticence towards using the highest or lowest ratings, may play some role in limiting the highest values achieved relative to ranking.

To assess whether these differences were relevant or not, we computed correlations between the correlation coefficients due to the two different formats. On the basis of this procedure, the following correlations were obtained — $r_{male} = 0.87$, $r_{female} = 0.90$, and $r_{total} = 0.89$ — suggesting that grading and ranking provide results which are generally similar. As would be expected, the means and variances of these arrays were also found to be comparable. These results should not, however, blind one to the fact that pairwise comparisons (e.g. male subjects on Wife and Ideal Self, $r_R = 0.75$, $r_G = 0.24$) do show some discrepancies between methods which are unexpectedly large — differences which might prove to be crucial to specific research hypotheses. While it is evident that a further investigation of this issue is required, it seems most reasonable to conclude that the choice of format should be determined primarily by the specificity or generality of would-be research hypotheses and related considerations.

5.8.3 Sex differences in trait associations: a confirmation of sex differences in the conception of certain sex roles.

One of our prime concerns here is to ascertain if it is possible to replicate the rather provocative sex differences found in the US study (see Section 3.9.4). These, it will be recalled, involved the relationships between the constructs of Wife, Mother and Physical Attractiveness — with the male subjects perceiving the contingency between Attractiveness and the role of Wife more strongly than did the female subjects and the females, for their part, perceiving a greater similarity between the roles of Wife and Mother than did the males. Clearly, if these stereotypic role perceptions do impinge on social interactions or mould the social institutions which they represent, their consequences could be widespread and of considerable importance. Accordingly, we consider an attempt to replicate them to be one of the most noteworthy aims of the present study.

Assessment of differences. Notwithstanding that our interest was centred primarily on the three traits mentioned above, we felt nonetheless that the implications of the other potential sex differences are of sufficient importance to warrant the testing of all 90 intercorrelations (45 from each format) for possible differences. In light of the discrepancy in size of correlations introduced by the use of two formats (see Section 5.8.2 immediately above), it followed that comparisons could only be carried out between those data emanating from the same format, lest differences due to methods and sex become totally confounded. Because of the large

Table 5.18

A Summary of the Trait Intercorrelations obtained from the *Semantic Differential Format* (Study 1) which were found to yield Significant Sex Differences — data based on 91 Males and 127 Females

Constructs	Males	Females	z_1-z_2	p_{sex}
1. Attractive/Like A Wife	.53	.35	.22	.01
2. Attractive/Like I Am	.50	.74	—.40	.001
3. Attractive/Alcoholic	—.49	—.35	.17	.05
4. Attractive/Ideal Self	.59	.85	—.58	.001
5. Like A Wife/Prudish	—.20	.04	.16	.05
6. Like A Wife/Alcoholic	—.34	—.19	.16	.05
7. Like A Wife/Like A Mother	.43	.57	—.19	.02
8. Like I Am/Like A Mother	—.03	.15	—.18	.05
9. Like I Am/Ideal Self	.51	.74	—.39	.001
10. Alcoholic/Like A Mother	.00	—.23	.23	.01
11. Cruel/Homosexual	.33	.47	—.17	.05

number of tests required here, it was decided to employ two-tailed probabilities for all comparisons.

Turning to particulars, differences between the intercorrelations originating from male and female subjects were, as a first step, transformed to Fisher's *z*s, and then submitted to Formula III-6 as shown in Appendix III. Because of the generality of this procedure, it was employed with both sets of data in exactly the same way, irrespective of format. All the comparisons yielding differences with a (two-tailed) probability of 5 per cent or less are shown in Tables 5.18 and 5.19, which represent, respectively, grading and ranking.

Results and implications. In examining these Tables, it can be seen that a total of 24 significant differences were found — 13 due to ranking and 11 due to grading — out of the combined 90 comparisons. Considering that six of these were significant beyond the .001 level, five beyond the .01 level, three beyond the .02 level and 10 beyond the .05 level, it is obvious that the present results greatly exceed the five or so differences which would be expected on the basis of chance alone. It is also interesting to note that the rating procedure, irrespective of the greater power afforded by its larger data base, was somewhat less successful at detecting sex

Table 5.19

A Summary of the Intercorrelations which were found to differ significantly for Male and Female Subjects tested by means of the *Ranking* format: Study 2, 78 Males and 67 Females

Constructs	Males	Females	z_1-z_2	p_{sex}
1. Attractive/ Like A Wife	.86	.58	.63	.001
2. Attractive/ Like I Am	.74	.85	—.31	.005
3. Attractive/ Like A Mother	.10	—.09	.19	.05
4. Attractive/ Influential	.52	.33	.23	.02
5. Attractive/ Ideal Self	.90	.97	—.62	.001
6. Like A Wife/ Like A Mother	.22	.40	—.20	.05
7. Like A Wife/ Influential	.54	.34	.25	.01
8. Like A Wife/ Ideal Self	.75	.57	.33	.001
9. Like I Am/ Alcoholic	—.29	—.44	.24	.01
10. Like I Am/ Ideal Self	.79	.85	—.19	.05
11. Alcoholic/ Like A Mother	—.08	.12	—.20	.05
12. Like A Mother/ Ideal Self	.10	—.11	.21	.05
13. Influential/ Ideal Self	.50	.29	.25	.01

differences than was the ranking procedure, even with its considerably smaller data base. Implicit in this comparison is the status of the subjects, which we have already shown to be comparable in all more important respects (see Section 5.2).

Comparing these results with those of the US study (p.100) in a general way, it is again found that each and every one of the traits are involved in at least one intercorrelation which shows sex differences. In the US study, the comparable figure was 14 out of 15, or 93 per cent. Here once more is this interesting contrast between concordance, with its rather circumscribed sex differences, and the more generalised intrusion of sex differences into trait associations and inferences. Indeed, on this basis one might be tempted to conclude that a few rather specific differences in role conceptions have, in turn, a rather widespread influence on patterns of association and, in a broader sense, the resultant cognitive structure. In a less speculative vein, these findings reinforce the notion that trait intercorrelations may prove to be one of the more efficient means of investigating the rather will o' the wisp phenomenon of sex differences (e.g. Taft, 1966, p. 7; Warr & Knapper, 1968).

The constructs of Wife, Mother and Attractiveness. Here the pivotal concepts is that of Wife, and gives rise to two intercorrelations of particular interest, namely Wife/Attractive, which is predicted to be higher for men than women, and Wife/Mother, for which women are expected to show the larger correlation. Looking at Tables 5.18 and 5.19, it can be seen that these expectations were borne out in both sets of data, with all four comparisons yielding significant differences in the predicted directions, irrespective of test format. Considering that these relationships have been verified three times — in two different countries and by differing methods in each study — it seems evident that we should begin to look more closely at these findings and what they purport.

Turning briefly to the implications, we have suggested, both here (e.g. Chapter 4 and Section 3.9.7) and elsewhere (e.g. Tutton et al., 1974), that the exaggerated emphasis which male subjects place on Attractiveness is one of the more unfortunate legacies of our cultural background, a position which is strongly supported by the material presented in Chapter 4. These attitudes may become a serious source of dissatisfaction when the demands of reality, such as ageing or the bearing and raising of children, force changes which are at variance with the unrealistic expectations.

On the part of the females, we have proposed that the observed pattern of results is most readily explained by positing the existence of two different role conceptions for the construct of Wife — one emphasising attractiveness and allied social functions, and the other, in a more traditional mould, laying stress upon child rearing and housewifery (e.g. Stewart et al., 1973 — see also Sections 3.9.6 and 5.7.4) — which may, in the extreme, prove to be incompatible. The contrast between the rather low levels of concordance and the more moderate intercorrelations provide reason to believe that the female subjects endorce these two different conceptions of Wife with approximately equal frequencies, or as an alternative explanation, that they are amalgamating the two orientations in such a manner as to produce highly individualistic (i.e., nonconcordant) constructs to suit their individual needs and circumstances. Whatever the actual state of affairs, an extreme adherence to either position — social or traditional — may prove to be just as problematical as is the excessive emphasis on attractiveness evidenced by some of the men.

While the remaining sex differences in association are not directly involved with the testing of our main thesis, it is obvious that certain of them, such as the males' more definite attribution of Influence to Attractiveness (in Study 2), do serve a corroborative function. In view of the fact that the US data also reveal a comparable sex difference — viz., in the correlations between Attractive and Leader — it is evident that the two sexes also differ in their appreciation of the influence of physical attractiveness on instances of social behaviour outside the sphere of the immediate family (e.g. Shaw & Wagner, 1975). This finding also suggests that men and women may react differently in encounters with attractive females (e.g., Krebs & Adinolfi, 1975).

Finally, it is apparent from Tables 5.18 and 5.19 that correlations involving either Self or Ideal Self account for 11 of the 24 sex differences observed here. And while some of these differences are seen to be quite interesting, it is well to remember that judgements involving cross-sex discriminations of Self are open to distortions on at least two counts: evaluative biases in the case of ranking formats (see p. 105), combined with 'non-committal' responding in the case of grading (see Section 6.1). Consequently, the correlations involving the males' judgements of Self and Ideal Self should be approached with some caution, at least until the influence of these potentially aberrant factors are better understood. Irrespective of these difficulties, other studies (Bourke, et al., 1973; Miller, et al., 1971) have shown that targets derived from Sheldon (1954; 1963) can provide meaningful results for Self when the targets and judges are of the same sex, implying that we can approach the data provided by the females, here, with fewer reservations. These issues are considered further in the following section.

5.8.4 *Conceptual stereotyping in the UK data*

Earlier, in Sections 1.2.2 and 3.9.7, it was suggested that conceptual stereotyping occurred whenever two traits or concepts, each with their own distinct set of implications and connotations, came to be treated, in practice, as if they were synonyms. In an operational sense, conceptual stereotyping should result in exceptionally large intercorrelations between the affected traits or concepts.

Using the same arbitrary criterion as in Section 3.9.7 above, eleven correlations — three based on graded data, and eight on ranking — were found which exceeded the required magnitude of 0.70. These correlations are presented in Table 5.20, and are seen to involve four concepts — Attractiveness, Wife, Self and Ideal Self — out of the ten employed. In respect to this Table, it should be noted that the male subjects tested with the semantic differential format (i.e. grading) failed to provide any correlations large enough to qualify for inclusion here, their largest being 0.59 for Attractive/Ideal Self. Bearing this somewhat surprising feature of Table 5.20 in mind, one gains the impression, in keeping with the discussion in Section 5.9.2 above, that ranking is a somewhat more efficient means of detecting conceptual stereotypes than is grading.

Sex differences in conceptual stereotyping. Depending upon whether one chooses to focus on the size or numerousness of the correlations,

Table 5.20

Correlations of a sufficient magnitude (i.e. > 0.70) to be suggestive of conceptual stereotyping

Trait Pairs	Males Ranking	Females Ranking	Females Grading
Attractive/Self	0.74	0.85	0.74
Attractive/Ideal Self	0.90	0.97	0.85
Self/Ideal Self	0.79	0.85	0.74
Wife/Attractive	0.86	—	—
Wife/Ideal Self	0.75	—	—

Table 5.20 also suggests that the females are, in a proportional sense, slightly more prone to conceptual stereotyping than are the males. Recalling, however, that this is opposite to the trend found in the US data (see Section 3.9.7), it is probably nearest the truth to say that there is no evidence, at yet, for any generalised sex differences in this respect.

Conceptual stereotypes involving the construct of Wife. In keeping with the position set out in Chapters 3 and 4, we are assuming here that physical attractiveness has, for many of the male subjects, come to be the most salient feature in construing the role of Wife, and hence in evaluating potential partners. While many of the practical implications of this bias are discussed in Chapter 6 and elsewhere, it is worth mentioning, in brief, one of the more specifically cognitive, and hence covert, aspects of this conceptual stereotype, namely that the males' one-sided emphasis on attractiveness may result in a corresponding lack of awareness of those activities, responsibilities, skills, expectations, attitudes and so on, which constitute an adequate representation of the role of Wife.

Conceptual stereotypes involving the images of Self and Ideal Self. In looking at Table 5.20, it can be seen that there is only one correlation, namely Wife/Attractive, which does not involve either Self or Ideal Self as one of the variables. This fact, combined with the knowledge that the targets tend towards the extremes of body build, raises the possibility that these correlations are in some degree artifactual. Irrespective of this possibility, it will be seen below that the concepts of Self and Ideal Self still provide several interesting inferences which cannot be dismissed on the basis of artifact alone. Moreover, the finding of comparable relationships in our adolescent data also argues against the likelihood of a serious qualitative artifact (see Table 8.5).

Starting with one of the more clearcut results, the correlations between Attractive and Ideal Self indicate in a remarkably unambiguous fashion that for both males and females alike the physique which is most desirable is that which is most Attractive — that both sexes perceive the slender targets as being closest to their ideals in the present circumstances. And while the data from the female subjects are consistent with the findings presented in Chapter 4 and elsewhere (e.g., Berscheid & Walster, 1974; Black, 1974; Byrne, Ervin & Lamberth, 1970), those of the males present something of a paradox, running contrary to a not inconsiderable number of earlier studies which have consistently shown that the ideal male body-form is muscular or mesomorphic rather than slender as indicated here (cf., Dibiase & Hjelle, 1968; Jenkins, 1971;

Miller, et al., 1968; Wells & Siegel, 1961). In view of these earlier studies, the present rejection of the mesomorphic body-type by the male subjects appears to represent a disorientation brought about by the necessity of making a cross-sex discrimination, implying that males may encounter some difficulty in extrapolating male characteristics from female physiques.

Turning to a more detailed consideration of this proposition, it may be that the male subjects are deterred from making the more appropriate, role-consistent judgements because of the marked positive evaluation which accrues to the slender female physiques — that the greater appropriateness of the muscular targets is nullified by the 'halo effect' created by the attractiveness of the slender targets. In a somewhat corresponding manner, Bourke, et al. (1973) found that female subjects with high Lie-Scores (on the EPI) tended to overestimate the physical attractiveness of their own physiques relative to objective criteria, such as physical measurements, suggesting that the 'pull' of attractiveness can be significant even in same-sex discriminations.

The physical 'Self' as a stereotypic construct. In view of the problems posed by the concepts of Self and Ideal Self in our own data (see Sections 6.1, 6.9.3 and 6.94), it is not unnatural to ask how they are performed in studies comparable to ours — where subjects have been required to evaluate their own physiques through comparisons with a limited set of supplied targets which serve as 'standards.' In taking up these data it is necessary, as indicated above, to distinguish between those which have required cross-sex discriminations, and those in which the gender of the targets and subjects have been congruent.

Beginning with those studies requiring only same-sex discriminations, it is possible to cite Bourke, et al. (discussed at the close of the preceding section) and Miller, et al. (1971) as constructive instances of this procedure, which are all the more important to the present issue because of their use of targets comparable to ours, i.e., derived from Sheldon. Noting that Bourke, et al. has been discussed above, we can turn directly to Miller, et al., who found that male subjects with elevated schizophrenia (*SC*) scores on the *MMPI* tended to perceive themselves (veridically or otherwise) as being more slender or fragile than other groups of otherwise comparable subjects. This finding is complimented by Arnhoff and Damianopoulos (1964), who found that schozophrenics exhibited a marked inability to recognise photographs of their own bodies when presented along with those of a set of heterogeneous strangers. In marked contrast, normals were almost always correct in their choices, notwithstanding that they reported a degree of certainty or uncertainty roughly comparable with those of the schizophrenics. Lastly, and in quite a different context, Schonbuch & Schell (1967) found that both over- and under-weight subjects show systematic distortions in Self perception, believing in both instances that they were heavier than was objectively correct. This bias was not observed in subjects of normal weight.

Turning to cross-sex discrimination, Fillenbaum (1961) found that one's own standing on weight and height influenced same-sex judgements (in the manner of assimilative projection), but not cross-sex judgements; implying that inferences drawn about Self from cross-sex data may be less valid or informative than those derived from same-sex discriminations. On the other hand, Jenkins (1971) has found that cross-sex discrimination did not in any way deter her *female subjects* from attributing traits to *male targets* on the basis of assumed similarity. Here each of the 140 male and female subjects completed four 68-item semantic differentials; one for themselves, and one for each of three male target persons — a mesomorph, an endomorph, and an ectomorph. On comparing the semantic differentials it was found that the patterns of attribution were significantly more alike for Self and the target chosen as Most Like Self than for either of the two physically less similar targets. Indeed, in spite of the cross-sex discriminations, the females evidenced a stronger assumed similarity bias than did certain of the male subjects (i.e. the ectomorphic group). A study by Mintz (1956) dealing with the estimation of age also confirms that cross-sex conditions need not invalidate Self attributions, but it is worth noting that Fillenbaum was concerned with features of the person which are more circumscribed than those treated by either Jenkins or Mintz.

In looking at these studies, and in particular those which are most similar to ours (viz. Bourke et al., 1973; Jenkins, 1971), it is clear that conceptions of Self do find expression in the judgement of simple stimuli, where even a gross similarity in body build is sufficient to evoke a significant degree of assimilative projection (Jenkins, 1971). Moreover, these same data also show, as suggested in Section 1.3.5 above, that the conceptions or stereotypes of Self obtained in these circumstances differ significantly from conceptions of Others. Looking ahead, however, our own data (in Section 8.9.2) show that it is not only possible to elicit Self attributions by means of stereotyping, but in addition that the Self stereotype is intimately related to social behaviour and attitudes. On the basis of these observations, we must conclude that the Self stereotype is one of the more interesting and ubiquitous of psychological constructs, irrespective of the difficulties sometimes encountered in its elicitation.

5.9 Factor analyses: an examination of the cognitive structure and implicit expectations underlying the inferences drawn from body build

By employing a factor analyss, it is possible to ascertain if the relationships evident in a correlation matrix can be explained by recourse to a smaller set of variables. In other words, one can determine if a number of significant correlations are, in fact, dependent upon the operation of a single variable or factor.

In view of the large number of significant correlations observed in our UK data, it was decided to submit each of the four obtained correlation matrices (as shown in Tables 5.16 and 5.17) to a factor analysis — i.e. a principal components analysis, followed by rotations — as a final stage of data reduction. We chose to use four independent analyses so that differences due to sex would not be confounded with differences arising out of the two different test formats employed in the UK studies. As an added advantage, the original correlation matrices are reduced to a numerically smaller and more manageable set of factor loadings.

The objective of such a set of analyses is to isolate, if possible, the two or three higher order features of cognition — perhaps best thought of as 'qualities' in the case of body build — which mediate the more restricted inferences and expectations which constitute the manifest aspects of social perception. If the results of the partialling of the US intercorrelations (see Section 3.9.6) serve as a reasonable guide, then it might be anticipated that the present analyses will yield at least two factors, the larger representing Social Desirability or Evaluation, while the smaller factor may well correspond with Masculinity or Potency. Whatever the nature of the results, it is important to realise that the obtained factors are probably general in nature — i.e. could be derived from targets which differed in respects other than body build — and therefore represent ubiquitous aspects of social perception. On the other hand, it was noted earlier (see Section 1.4.2) that the apparent salience (i.e. the variance accounted for) may depend upon the type of targets employed — that, for example, Activity is of primary importance in the judgement of hands, while Evaluation predominates in judgements of facial expression (Gitin, 1970, p. 275). Bearing these observations and qualifications in mind, we can turn to the data at hand.

5.9.1 Analysis and results

The correlations portrayed in the above mentioned Tables were submitted to four individual factor analyses, according to whether the subjects were male (M) or female (F), or whether tested by means of grading (G) or ranking (R). The four analyses, that is MR, FR, MG and FG, were carried out on the University of London's CDC 6600 computer by means of the SPSS package of Northwestern University, with these analyses being followed by Varimax rotations from the same source. Principal factors yielding eigenvalues of less than 1 were excluded from further analysis.

For reasons which were outlined earlier (see Section 5.2), it was not possible to arrange circumstances so that the same number of subjects would be included in each of the four analyses. The actual numbers employed are as follows: MG = 91, FG = 127, MR = 78 and FR = 68. Since at first glance the numbers of subjects appear to be on the small side, it is important to remember that the data were collected under conditions of repeated measures, increasing the stability of the correlations by a factor of approximately 1.8 here. In other words, the sampling errors associated with the correlations in question are more representative of larger groups — estimated as MG = 163, FG = 230, MR = 140 and FR = 122 — than those listed above. Viewed from either perspective, however, the sample sizes clearly exceed the ratio of 3 subjects per variable which is sometimes suggested as the lower limit of sample size for factor analyses.

The results of the analyses are presented in Tables 5.21, which show the four principal components solutions, and 5.22, which portray the Varimax rotations. As an aid to interpretation, the rotated factor loadings are also depicted graphically in Figures 5.3 to 5.6.

It was, as a first step, necessary to determine which set of results — the principal factors or the rotated factors — would provide the most satisfactory basis for the following discussion. In looking at Tables 5.21 and 5.22, it can be seen that there is little difference in the variance accounted for by the two different approaches, with the principal components having just a slight edge in this respect. When, on the other hand, *W*s are used to ascertain the degree of similarity of the factors elicited from the groups (i.e. the similarity of the four patterns of loadings on, say, the first factor), it is evident, from Table 5.23, that the rotated factors have a clear advantage in this respect. In other words, the patterns of loadings exhibited by the four groups are, except for a minor reversal on the first factor, more alike one another following rotation than before it.

Since the greater similarity between groups enables one to deal more succinctly with the results, it was decided to adopt the solution based on rotations for the present discussion. In examining the relevant Tables, it

Table 5.21

Unrotated Principal Components Obtained from the Four Groups Constituting the UK Studies — Males/Ranking (MR), Females/Ranking (FR), Males/Grading (MG) and Females/Grading (FG)

	LOADINGS[1]											
	1st Component				2nd Component				3rd Component			
Traits	MR	FR	MG	FG	MR	FR	MG	FG	MR	FR	MG	FR
Attractive	94	94	83	84	00	00	26	39	—07	—21	00	—05
Wife	89	73	67	59	01	16	—34	—33	08	43	34	51
Prudish	04	03	—43	—29	27	44	12	02	—70	11	09	58
Self	83	91	64	81	19	09	29	30	—06	—08	—17	—06
Alcoholic	—49	—59	—61	—53	40	36	—08	12	16	19	15	01
Mother	23	07	22	43	02	38	—73	—64	70	80	47	43
Influential	63	45	52	41	31	52	29	42	12	11	53	33
Cruel	—24	—23	—24	—29	79	62	64	68	—10	—50	50	34
Homosexual	—08	—17	—54	—59	83	68	44	52	20	—34	20	28
Ideal Self	92	93	70	82	07	—01	32	36	—08	—23	—19	—12
% — Variance	40%	37%	33%	35%	17%	16%	16%	18%	11%	14%	10%	11%

1. Decimal points omitted.

Table 5.22

Factor Loadings Obtained from the four groups constituting the UK Studies — Males/Ranking (MR), Females/Ranking (FR), Males/Grading (MG), and Females/Grading (FG)

	LOADINGS[1]											
	Factor — I				Factor — II				Factor — III			
Traits	MR	FR	MG	FG	MR	FR	MG	FG	MR	FR	MG	FG
Attractive	93	96	85	91	—20	—02	05	—11	—01	03	20	08
Wife	87	59	39	30	—16	—19	—09	—01	12	60	72	79
Prudish	12	00	—35	—24	14	31	22	55	—73	34	—20	25
Self	85	90	73	84	01	—01	—02	—16	—03	18	—02	12
Alcoholic	—40	—61	—61	—37	50	28	—14	26	06	22	—11	—29
Mother	20	—14	—20	00	08	—11	—19	—19	70	87	85	86
Influential	68	40	46	57	20	32	51	34	12	47	40	14
Cruel	—07	—09	—05	12	80	82	83	74	—22	—11	—15	—31
Homosexual	09	—08	—35	—22	85	78	53	70	08	05	—36	—38
Ideal Self	92	96	79	89	—12	—01	—02	—17	—02	01	—03	05
% Variance	39%	36%	29%	30%	18%	16%	13%	16%	11%	15%	16%	18%

1. Decimal points omitted.

is also evident that the factors become more distinctive following rotation, an outcome which is consistent with the objective of rotation to yield a 'simple structure'. The principal component solutions are retained (in Table 5.21) because they represent, in a statistical sense, the most efficient and elegant factorisation of the correlations at hand and, in addition, illustrate the configuration of component loadings before they are altered by the somewhat arbitrary process of rotation. Moreover, there are a few investigators, such as Slater (1967), who feel that rotations are superfluous.

5.9.2 Overall considerations — differences due to formats, gender of subjects, etc.

In the light of the relatively large correlations between the various sets of correlation coefficients which were factored in the present analyses (r_{males} = 0.87, $r_{females}$ = 0.90, and r_{total} = 0.89 — see Section 5.8.2 for details), it seems reasonable to anticipate that the resulting patterns of factor loadings should be quite similar in the four analyses. This expectation is confirmed in Table 5.23, which shows that a sizable coefficient of concordance was obtained for each of the three factors being considered here — indicating that the ordering of traits by magnitude of loading was reasonably predictable from group to group. Indeed, the suggestion of group by group consistency is not contradicted

Table 5.23

Agreement between patterns of loadings Before (Principal Components, *PC*) and After Rotation (Rotated Factors, *RF*). Agreement expressed as Concordance Coefficients (*W*) and Mean Spearman *Rhos* (r_s) between groups (MR, FR, MG, and FG)

	Factors/Components					
	I		II		III	
Solutions	*W*	r_s	*W*	r_s	*W*	r_s
Before Rotation (*PC*)	0.97	0.96	0.69	0.58	0.52	0.36
After Rotation (*RF*)	0.93	0.91	0.81	0.75	0.73	0.64

by an inspection of the loadings themselves, in Table 5.22. Recalling that each of the four groups is entirely independent of one another, and that two markedly different methods of testing were employed, the present results are, by their consistency, remarkably encouraging.

Irrespective of this overall correspondence between the analyses, a visual inspection of the loadings presented in Table 5.22 reveals some disparities which are large enough to be suggestive of sex differences, differences due to format, or in some instances differences originating in an interaction between gender and format. One of the more notable sex differences is illustrated by the pattern of loadings obtained for Prudish on Factor III (F III). Format differences are apparent on Wife (F I), Homosexual (F III) and Prudish (F I). Lastly, indications of interactions (Sex x Format) are to be found on Wife (F III), Mother (F I) and Influential (F III).

In view of the notorious difficulties encountered when attempting to evaluate differences between factor loadings, the present examples are put forward as tentative or illustrative, rather than as proven cases. Should these or similar instances be confirmed in subsequent studies, it seems reasonable to suppose that those concerning sex differences in perception, and those arising from format, may be open to relatively straightforward and useful interpretations. On the other hand, the differences involving interactions between gender and format seem to be quite obscure, and even if confirmed may prove difficult to explain in a useful or satisfactory manner.

Having looked at some of the broader or more quantitative aspects of these factor analyses, we are now in a better position to take up the problem of attempting to identify or name the observed dimensions. This endeavour should also serve, at the same time, to indicate in what manner the present results relate to the more ubiquitous features of social perception considered in the final third of Chapter 1.

5.9.3 Qualitative features: some possible interpretations for the observed factors

Before embarking on the discussion proper, it needs to be recognised that there are three somewhat interdependent qualifications which bear directly on the present concern. First, the interpretation or 'naming' of factors is, as pointed out by Rosenberg & Olshan (1970, pp. 625-6; Gifford, 1975, p. 728), a fairly arbitrary matter — depending very much upon which of the larger loadings one chooses to focus (e.g. Gibbins, 1969). Second, and as is well known, the outcome of any factor analysis depends very largely upon its 'input parameters', with the trait vocabulary being especially important in this respect. Third, and more germane to the present circumstances, we purposely limited the number of items in our trait vocabulary to suit the conditions of testing (see Section 5.3).

In the light of these qualifications, and the limitations which they impose upon the present task, it is understandable that our comments and interpretations should be viewed here as having a 'provisional status', with the uncertainty being greatest for Factors II and III. Bearing these reservations in mind, we can turn to the factors themselves, noting that the Figures presented on pages 186 and 187 are probably more useful for depicting qualitative features than are Tables 5.21 and 5.22.

Factor I: an expression of Social Desirability and/or Evaluation. In looking at Factor I, we find a cluster of traits relating to Self and Attractiveness at one extreme, balanced by an array of the remaining seven traits which, in each analysis, is terminated by Alcoholic at the opposite extreme. Since Cruel and Homosexual are also found in proximity with Alcoholic, we feel justified in considering Factor I to be an expression of Social Desirability, Evaluation or Personal Desirability. The contiguity of the Mother concept to the deviant concepts would, on the face of it, seem to contradict this interpretation but, as we have pointed out in earlier sections, there does seem to be an actual denigration of this concept by our subjects, both here and in the US study (N.B. The ages of the subjects may play some part in the lack of acceptance of this concept).

In a related manner, one could ask why the traits of Homosexuality and Cruelty were perceived to be less objectionable than those of Alcoholism or, indeed, being a Mother. One of the more reasonable explanations seems to be that the physical attractiveness of body build is simply not salient for these two particular traits, but rather that their attribution depends upon other features of physique, as is discussed in connection with Factor II below.

One of the more interesting questions to be posed by Factor I is whether differences in all types of attractiveness — including, say, facial attractiveness as well as the more abstract construct of 'psychological attractiveness' — would yield a dispersion of traits comparable to that observed here. The studies by Kuusinen (1968; 1969) and Norman (1963; Passini & Norman, 1966) suggest that we might expect a good deal of generality, but ultimately this is an issue which will be answered only by additional research.

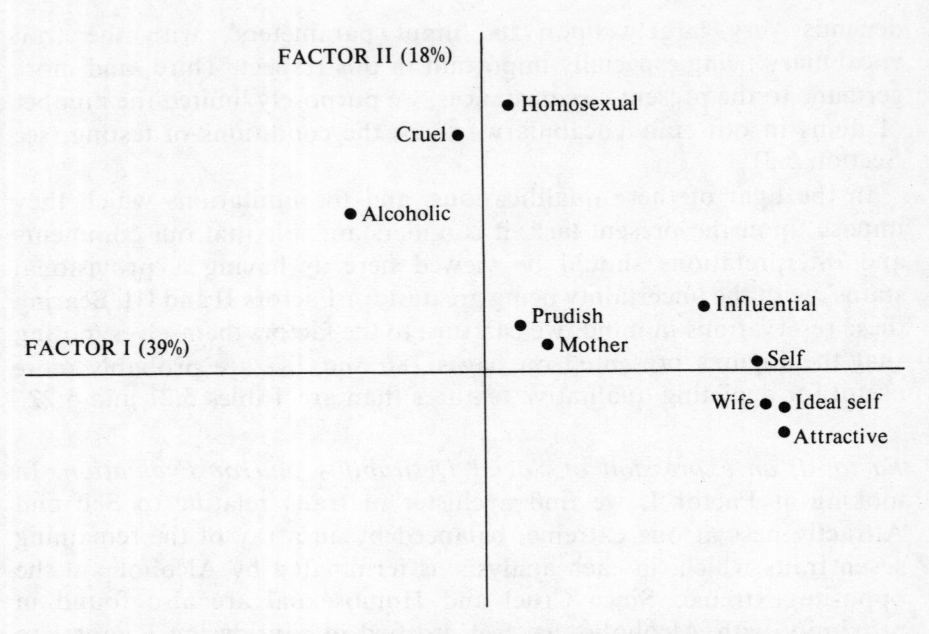

Figure 5.3 Trait space obtained for 78 males tested by means of ranking.

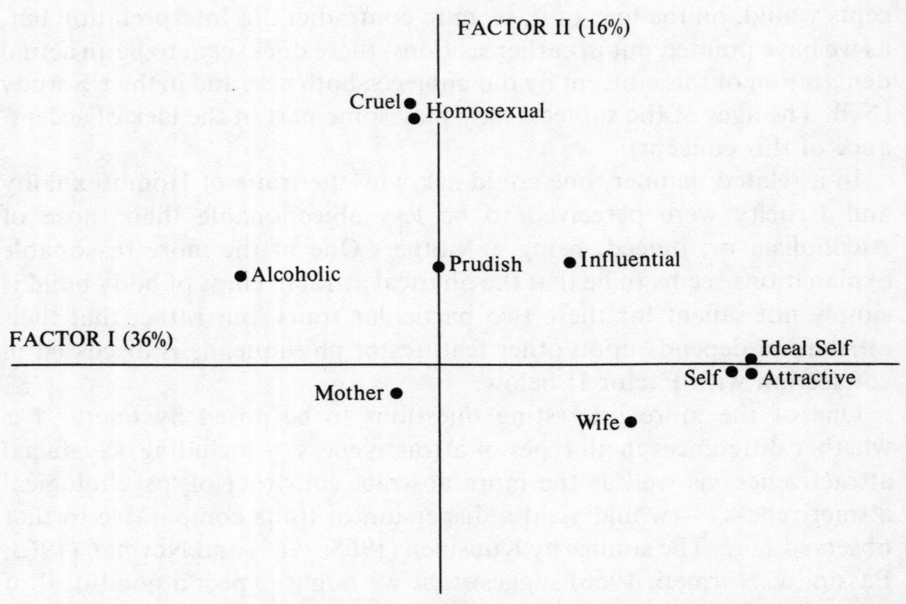

Figure 5.4 Trait space obtained for 67 females tested by means of ranking.

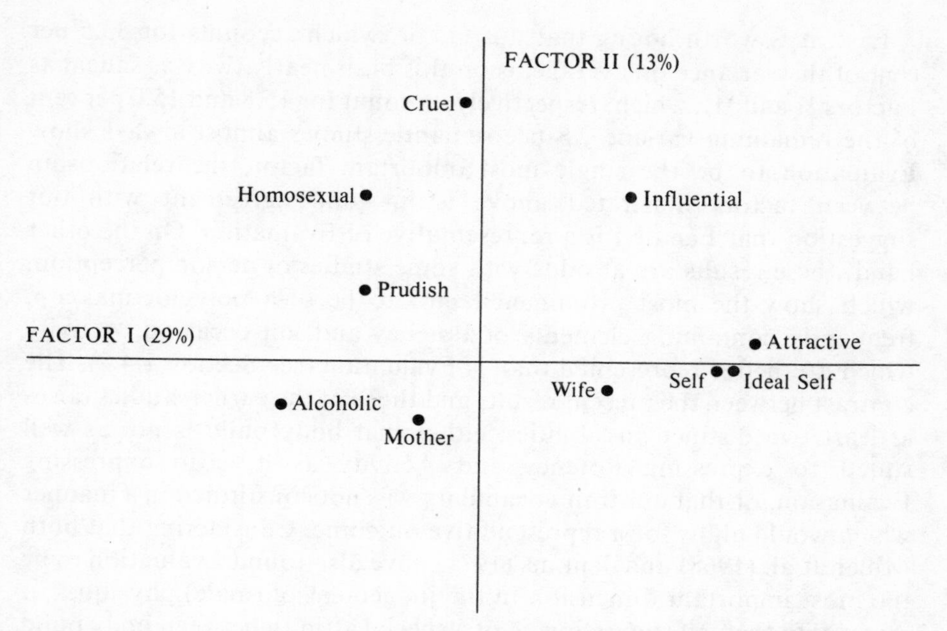

Figure 5.5 Trait space obtained for 91 males tested by means of semantic differential.

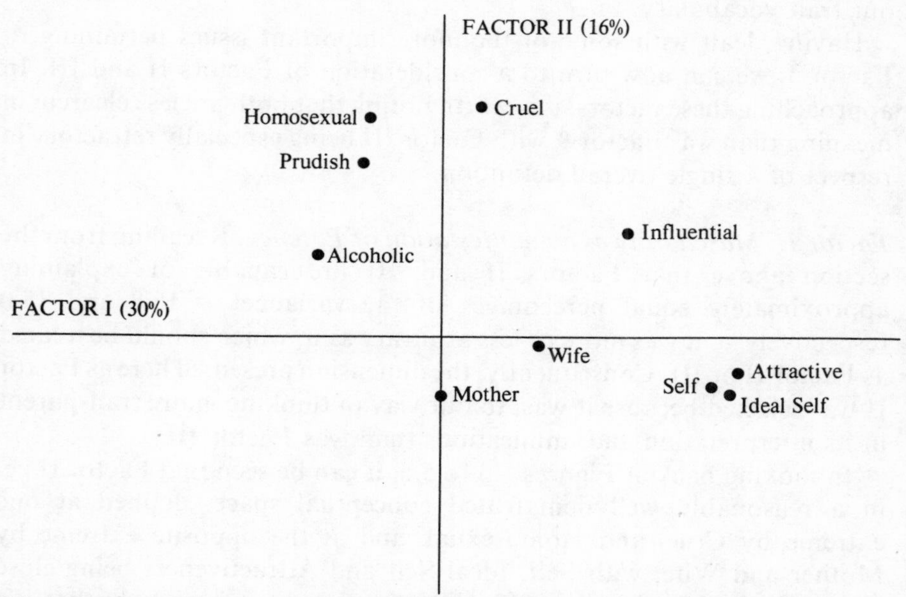

Figure 5.6 Trait space obtained for 127 females tested by means of the semantic differential.

Last, it is worth noting that this factor, which accounts for 33.5 per cent of the variance on average, is on this basis nearly twice as salient as Factors II and III, which, respectively, account for 15.8 and 15.0 per cent of the remaining variance. Since semantic studies almost always show Evaluation to be the single most important factor, the relationship between factors illustrated above is in good agreement with our suggestion that Factor I is a representative of Evaluation. On the other hand, these results are at odds with some studies of person perception, which show the most prominent factor to be of a polyglot makeup, frequently containing elements of Potency and, on occasion, Activity which are better represented than is Evaluation (see Section 1.4.2). The contrast between the present results and those of the earlier studies raises at least two distinct possibilities: either that body build is not as well suited to expressing Potency and Activity as it is to expressing Evaluation, or that our trait vocabulary was not constituted in a manner which would allow for a representative outcome. Considering that both Miller at al. (1968) and Jenkins (1971) have also found Evaluation to be the most important dimension in the judgement of (male) physiques, it seems that the first suggestion — of a special affinity between body build and Evaluation — is likely to be the more powerful explanation. It is clear, however, that both Potency and Activity are underrepresented in our trait vocabulary.

Having dealt with some of the more important issues pertaining to Factor I, we can now turn to a consideration of Factors II and III. In approaching these factors, it is worth noting that both are less clearcut in meaning than was Factor I, with Factor III being especially refractory in respect of a single overall definition.

Factor II: Masculinity as a manifestation of Potency. Recalling from the section above that Factors II and III are capable of explaining approximately equal percentages of the variance — 15.8 and 15.0 respectively — it was more or less arbitrary as to which should be treated as Factor II or III. Consequently, the dimension presented here as Factor II was selected because it was, to our way of thinking, more transparent in its interpretation and implications than was Factor III.

In looking back at Figures 5.3 to 5.6, it can be seen that Factor II lies in a reasonably well demarcated conceptual space, defined at one extreme by Cruel and Homosexual, and at the opposite extreme by Mother and Wife, with Self, Ideal Self and Attractiveness being close companions of the sex roles. While the first impression might be that of a dimension representing 'deviancy', we think that there are certain features of these data which militate strongly against this interpretation. First, Influential, which is a nondeviant trait, loads in all four instances towards the Cruel/Homosexual pole of this dimension. Second, Alcoholic, which is a deviant trait, displays a rather inconclusive pattern of loadings on this factor. And third, had we scored the graded data for Kind rather than Cruel — thereby reversing the signs of the correlations — it is most likely that we would now be observing a dimension characterised by Kind versus Cruel at the extremes (see Figure 5.1 for details of the rating format).

Based on these considerations, we would suggest that Factor II is most correctly envisaged as a reflection of concepts such as Cruel/Kind, Tough/Tender, Masculine/Feminine or Hard/Soft, or in a broader sense, a dimension based on Potency rather than deviancy. As a descriptive scale in social perception (see Section 1.4.2), we prefer the notion which embraces Masculinity/Femininity, because this interpretation is the one most consistent with the attribution of Success, Leadership, Influence, Cruelty and Homosexuality to the more masculine (i.e. mesomorphic) target person in both the US and UK studies. As in the case of Factor I, the correctness of this suggestion and the scope of its implications (i.e. the range of traits moderated by this factor) will only be fully appreciated as additional data become available.

Assuming that the above interpretation is the correct one, it is somewhat surprising to find that male and female subjects evidence loadings for Self and Ideal Self which are approximately equal on this factor. If Factor II does reflect Masculinity/Femininity, it is only natural to expect the loadings relating to the physical status of the males to be closer to the Masculine pole than are the equivalent loadings of the female subjects. We have encountered this anomaly before — in connection with Conceptual Stereotyping (p. 163) — where it was observed that the correlations of Self and Ideal Self with Attractiveness (a feminine 'ideal') were larger than expected for the male subjects.

On this earlier occasion, it was argued that the influence of Evaluation was sufficiently great as to cause the male subjects to nominate the slender, more Attractive female targets for Self and Ideal Self, rather than the more suitable (i.e. role congruent), but less well-received mesomorphic targets. Bearing in mind that Factors I and II are, as constituted here, orthogonal to one another, the net effect of this bias is, of course, to shift the male loadings for Self and Ideal Self from Masculinity towards Evaluation, just as has been observed. Indeed, if one looks at the correlations in Tables 5.16 or 5.17, it can be seen that this shift is inevitable.

As indicated in the earlier discussion, we do not have a ready explanation for the cause of this bias, but it would seem to offer some interesting research possibilities. It is worth noting, in this context, that the male subjects evidenced more reticence and embarrassment than the female subjects when requested to identify their actual physical selves by means of comparisons with drawings of nude females. Why this task should prove to be more 'threatening' for males than females is somewhat difficult to understand.

On the basis of these considerations, we continue to feel justified in treating Factor II as an expression of Masculinity/Femininity, with a secondary implication of Potency. Returning to the initial impression — that Factor II might represent 'deviancy' — it is entirely possible, in view of the known sex differences in the frequency of anti-social behaviour (e.g. Cowie et al., 1968), that certain types of deviant acts may, ultimately, come to be arrayed along this dimension in an ancillary fashion. As with Factor I, however, the veracity of these considerations and speculations awaits confirmation or refutation on the basis of later research and, more especially, on the employment of larger trait vocabularies.

Factor III: the Maternal Construct. To put Factor III in a proper perspective, it is necessary to turn back to Table 5.22, in which the rotated factor loadings are displayed. It can be seen that the most notable positive loadings are those arising for the construct of Mother, with all four groups, irrespective of format or gender, showing large, comparable loadings. Indeed, in looking across this Table, it can be seen that neither of the preceding factors — Evaluation or Potency — has extracted an appreciable proportion of variance from this construct. As we shall see below, there are several other sets of loadings — those of Wife and Cruel being most notable among them — which are also consistent with the interpretation of this being a Maternal factor.

The concept of Wife yields the second most salient set of loadings here, and thus tends to confirm the Maternal nature of this factor. Considering that significant correlations between Mother and Wife were found for three out of the four groups tested (i.e. except for males tested by means of ranking), it does not come as a surprise to find that Wife is one of the more important constituents of this factor. Indeed, as far as the female subjects are concerned, this relationship had been anticipted in some of the earliest discussions of the US data (e.g. Stewart, Steele & Miller, 1970; Stewart et al., 1973).

The one unexpected aspect of these results is, however, the magnitude of the loadings, especially that observed for the males tested by means of grading. Considering that in every instance except one (i.e. females tested by grading), the correlations between Attractive and Wife are of considerably greater magnitude than those between Mother and Wife, it was expected that the construct of Wife would manifest its largest loadings on the Evaluative factor. In sharp contrast to these expectations, the present results imply that the construct of Wife is characterised by a greater proportion of non-Evaluative than Evaluative variance.

Because this conclusion contrasts so strongly with the data which have preceded it, we thought it necessary to have a further look at the procedures employed here. As a first step, we consulted the original unrotated principal components (Table 5.21) and found the expected relationship, with the concept of Wife loading most strongly on the Evaluative dimension irrespective of gender or format. Moreover, the female subjects show larger residual loadings on the remaining two components, in agreement with the supposition previously made that they exhibit a greater range of alternative conceptions for this construct. (N.B. The Maternal component appears to be represented by the second component for the grading format (MG, FG), and the third component for the ranking format (MR, FR) in Table 5.21).

Bearing these differences in mind, it is evident that it is the process of rotation which is responsible for the rather unprecedented pattern of loadings for Wife on Factor III — that rotation has, in approximating to a 'simple structure', created a configuration which appears to be less plausible or satisfactory in a psychological sense. Since it is well known that the problem of rotations can be approached in a variety of ways (e.g. by Promax, Varimax, Quartimax, etc.) and that all solutions are to a certain extent arbitrary, we shall assume that the principal components analyses are, in this particular instance, more representative. And while changes of this magnitude are not without precedent (e.g. Frijda & Philipszoon, 1963, Table 1), it is somewhat worrying that two 'standard' and closely related treatments of the same data should have such different implications.

Assuming that we have selected the correct alternative, the present results are consistent with our previous discussions, where it was suggested that women perceive a closer, less Evaluative relationship between the roles of Wife and Mother than do the male subjects. In view, however, of the large number of only partially understood influences converging upon this factor — i.e. differences due to format, gender of judges and rotations — it does not seem useful to attempt to proceed much beyond this one general observation. In a more qualified sense, the rotated data do suggest that the concept of Mother is, irrespective of its social importance, a somewhat isolated construct, sharing little variance with Evaluation and Potency. While the isolation observed here might arise from methodological considerations, such as the limited size of our trait vocabulary, it is important to notice that this quality is also mirrored (in a reduced degree) by our adolescent female subjects (in Table 8.6, Factor III), in what appears to be a factor characterised by Mother, Wife and Self. The adolescent males do not give rise to a comparable factor, providing additional support for the notion that there are likely to be sex differences in the perception of sex roles.

Factors derived from physiques: summary and conclusions. Whether looking at rotated or unrotated loadings, it is evident that Factor I represents Evaluation, and accounts for approximately twice as much of the variance as either of the remaining two factors. As compared with other studies of social perception, Evaluation may be especially prominent here because of the unavoidable relationship between body build and aesthetic quality. It was also suggested that this aesthetic factor also contributed to some of the observed sex differences.

Factor II is not quite so clearcut in its implications as was its predecessor but one of the more plausible interpretations is as a dimension representing Masculinity/Femininity. While the loadings would not, by themselves, be entirely adequate to support this conclusion, the argument is considerably strengthened by the finding that the most salient traits (namely Cruel, Influential and Homosexual) are also those having the strongest associations with the masculine or mesomorphic target persons. As pointed out by others (see Section 1.4.2), Masculinity/Femininity may, in fact, represent the more general quality of Potency.

The third factor — with its composition changing in response to formats, gender and rotation — is clearly the most problematical of the three factors to be considered here. While the rotated solution suggested a conceptual synthesis of Wife and Mother, we have opted for a more purely Maternal construct as that being most consistent with all the available evidence (e.g. unrotated loadings, underlying correlations, sex differences, etc.). In this case, the concept of Wife is, again, seen to be predominantly Evaluative in quality, but more so for male judges.

Notwithstanding that Factors II and III have proved to be somewhat difficult to specify or particularise within the constraints of the present trait vocabulary, it may still be true that they represent relatively general or ubiquitous cognitive dimensions. To put this issue in proper perspective, it is necessary to recall, from Table 5.23 that the four groups, which in essence comprise four independent replications, show a substantial degree of consensus on each of the two factors (W_{II} = 0.81, W_{III} = 0.73, $ps < .001$). In view of the relatively indefinite and unstructured quality of the stereotyping task, the elicitation of comparable factor from four independent groups implies that these are reasonably commonplace dimensions. Given that these patterns of loadings have been replicated four times, and also appear to have close relatives in the US study and certain of the Adolescent data, it does not seem premature to suggest that they can be replicated again and, assuming that a larger trait vocabulary is employed, that they can be identified with more certainty than is possible here.

In Chapter 8, the reader will encounter a new set of factor analyses — based on children's and adolescents' judgements of target persons who differ in manner of dress — which bear a rough correspondence with those presented here, and which automatically invite comparison. While there are sufficient differences in subjects, targets and trait vocabulary to preclude a direct or quantitative comparison, it is nonetheless possible to contrast them on a more qualitative basis, such as ease of interpretation, etc. In carrying out such a comparison, it is quickly evident that the latter factor analyses are in almost every respect more incisive and straightforward than are these. Before entirely dispensing with body build, however, it is worth noting that the data from body build and dress appear to encompass two somewhat different sets of cognitive dimensions, implying that tests based on body build may be more appropriate than dress to certain types of problems. It would be instructive, in this context, to obtain data simultaneously for both types of target from a single sample of subjects who evaluate both on the same set of constructs. As it stands, however, we feel that tests involving differences in dress and attire are, in most circumstances, the more promising of the two approaches — being credible across a wider range of constructs and appearing, as stimuli, to be less contrived and out of place than nudes.

6 Sex Roles And Sex Role Stereotyping

6.1. The concept of sex role stereotyping

This chapter is devoted to a detailed investigation of sex role stereotyping as it occurs in our data. With the stereotyping of sex roles we are following a division posited by Brodsky (1954) and Krasner et al. (1964), being concerned with the stereotyping of an abstract notion rather than a concrete characteristic. However, the end result of the stereotyping process is the same; that is to say persons are categorised and attributed certain characteristics because they have some single factor in common. In this respect sex role stereotyping is similar to racial, religious and occupational stereotyping (Braun, 1962; Cauthen et al., 1971; Gahagan, 1933), being the stereotyping of a person because they belong to a particular social group. So if you occupy the role of, say, Wife, Mother or Father, there are attitudes, characteristics and opinions, etc. which are expected to go with that role. To carry the process a step further, it should also be possible, by a close examination of stereotypes, to determine which characteristics go together to form the 'ideal' role — whether Mothers should be Kind or Strict; Wives be Retiring or Sensuous.

We singled out sex role stereotyping from other types of group stereotyping to discuss in detail here for several reasons. First, we feel that it has particular relevance and importance to problems of today, such as changing attitudes towards women in society and more longstanding problems such as those concerned with marital harmony (Luckey, 1960a, b). Second, a consideration of the published literature shows that this area has been relatively under researched; racial and religious stereotypes, important and all pervading as they are, have had an enormous amount of print devoted to them (e.g. Cauthen et al., 1971), yet sex role stereotypes, although subject to a considerable amount of controversial discussion and active dialogues, seem to have escaped much real scientific enquiry and evaluation. Third, it is only in the stereotyping of sex roles that there is any clear indication that the sex of our subjects influences the way in which they perceive target persons and others. In other words, the differences between men and women on judging traits are larger and more frequent on the sex role concepts such as Wife and Mother then they are on traits such as Successful or Influential, which are more 'unisex'.

Against this background we will begin here with a review of the research that has been done by others, not by giving a detailed description of all investigations, but rather by indicating the areas that have been researched, the findings concerning the stereotyping of sex roles, and the methods employed. In more detail, we will then describe our own research findings and emphasise how the understanding and awareness of sex role stereotypes can be especially relevant to certain areas of social adjustment such as marital discord and role transition.

6.2. Research on sex role stereotyping

At the most general level, sex role stereotyping studies have confined themselves to looking simply at those characteristics which are associated with a person because of his sex, listing which traits are commonly associated with women and which with men. Some of the most thorough research in this area has been carried out by a group of workers in Worcester, Massachusetts. (See Broverman et al., 1970, 1972; Clarkson et al., 1970; Rosenkrants et al., 1968; Vogel et al., 1970). This team has developed a questionnaire to assess individual's perceptions of 'typical' masculine and feminine behaviour, consisting of 122 items which are evaluated on a 60-point scale according to their representativeness of masculinity and of femininity. They reported results from testing nearly 1,000 subjects and found that a strong consensus of opinion about the attributes associated with men and women existed, which cut across all subjects irrespective of their sex, age, religion, marital status or educational background.

Characteristics ascribed to men were more often positively valued or more socially desirable than those ascribed to women (see also Bieliauskas,1965; Salzman, 1967). The positively valued masculine traits formed a cluster of related behaviours such as competence, rationality and assertion; a relative absence of these traits characterised the stereotypic perception of women who were seen as dependent, passive, illogical, etc. The positively valued female traits also formed a cluster, which in this case was suggestive of warmth and expressiveness. Such things as gentle, tactful and quiet were included here (see also Douvan & Adelson, 1966; Pinter & Fortano, 1944; Vroegh, Jenkin, Black & Hendrick, 1967).

The Worcester data are representative of the many studies to have found results of this nature, and overall it is the characteristics attributed to the male personality which are more highly valued by both sexes than those attributed to the female. In the Sherriffs and McKee (1957) study, women were regarded as 'guilty of snobbery and irrational and unpleasant emotionality'. Similar results are those of Kitay (1940), Fernberger (1948), McKee & Sherriffs (1957, 1959), and Lunneborg (1970, 1972). Interestingly, the female sex role is devalued by women just as strongly as by men. Goldberg (1968) showed very clearly that women downgraded the work of professionals of their own sex and considered them inferior to males of equivalent intellectual standards.

In an interesting study, Wiley (1973) attempted to refute some of the traditionally held beliefs of the passivity of women and of the aggressiveness of men. The study was of cooperative behaviour in a game setting involving subjects of both sexes where differing levels of verbal and nonverbal communications were allowed. There was no difference between males and females in cooperative behaviour when no verbal communications were allowed. When verbal communication was allowed, however, the traditional male-female pattern appeared with the male taking the dominant role and the female the passive role.

So, overall, we must conclude that in the UK, North America and, most probably Australia and New Zealand, females have certain stereotypes associated with them which are generally negatively valued attributes and that men are seen as the stronger and more esteemed sex. The question as to why such stereotypes have become associated with the sexes is the subject of much debate and controversy (e.g. Mosher, 1968; Sistrunk & McDavid, 1971). Whether women are socialised into becoming passive, dependent persons or whether they are inherently so, is still a point of issue with some people (e.g. Selcer & Hilton, 1972). But no one can deny the socialising influences of the enormous amount of stereotyping of the sexes which is present in children's books, stories and games. Nor can one deny the potential importance of parents' expectations (i.e. stereotypes) concerning how boys and girls ought to differ, even at quite young ages (e.g. Faggot, 1973a). Therefore it must come as no surprise to find that awareness of sex roles (Hartup & Zook, 1960; Schell & Silber, 1968) and preferences between them (Hartup et al., 1963; Pollis & Doyle, 1972) are present even in preschool children.

Yet, pervasive as they are, the entire blame cannot be laid on children's books, parents' stereotypes or the advertising media, since child rearing practices represent another domain of influences which are more or less independent of the former influences; while children's books and parents can communicate an aberrant social image of idealised sex roles to children, other factors, such as differential discipline and punishment, can have equally marked effects. In this vein, Wallach & Caron (1959), after finding that girls, independent of IQ, use narrower cognitive categories than do boys, suggested

> that for girls there has been a generalization of fear of independence from the sphere of action to that of cognition. Concepts are subject to social regulation as much as behavior, and because girls have been made reluctant to overstep the behavioral boundaries prescribed by authority, so they are loath to be expansive in the realm of concepts.

In a later study, dealing with number of categories rather than width of categories, Reich (1968) also found women to differ from men; women using, under some conditions, fewer categories. In this instance, Reich attributed the difference to developmental factors as women reported having significantly less 'cognitive experience' in childhood than did men. Glixman (1965) also reports finding sex differences in the use of categories, but in the opposite direction, a not unusual occurrence in an area where differences have been tenuous and difficult to replicate (Warr & Knapper, 1968, pp. 185-90).

Whether or not one accepts these explanations of sex differences being due to differences in discipline or experience, there is an accumulating body of evidence suggesting the existence of sex differences in cognition (Gerace & Caldwell, 1971; Wolfgang, 1968); perception (Sandstrom, 1953; Willemsen & Reynolds, 1973); and problem solving (Sweeney, 1953).

Turning to our own research, the methodology adopted in our American and English studies has enabled us to examine the stereotyping of various sex roles by a relatively indirect method, i.e. in a person perception context. It need only be said here that, by including various sex roles as traits or concepts in the tests, we were able to look, not only at the relationship between body build and sex roles, but also between sex roles and the other descriptive and evaluative traits (e.g. Attractive, Alcoholic, etc.), and so obtain a fairly detailed overview of the stereotyping of sex roles themselves.

By examining groups of male and female respondents separately we were able to explore any sex differences in the stereotyping of sex roles which might appear. Sex differences, it will be recalled, were anticipated, in part, on the basis of the studies carried out by Miller et al. (1968) and Hamid (1968), although the specific nature of the sex differences could not, themselves, be anticipated.

Initially, the three sex roles to be investigated (in the American study) included the concepts of Wife, Mother and Sister but, in the later studies,

Sister was omitted because it produced no real findings of interest — it being heavily saturated with evaluation and correlating 0.69 with Attractive in the American study. On the other hand, the data to be presented show the concept of Sister to be useful as a broadly neutral or nonspecific indicator of evaluation which might serve as an alternative to Attractive when the latter term is inappropriate or too obvious.

6.3. Sex role stereotyping — results from the American study

In our first study, based on 50 US subjects and reported in detail in Chapter 3, substantial evidence was provided for the stereotyping of the sex roles of Wife, Mother and Sister. As the ranking methods had been used, the existence of social stereotypes of the highly divergent female physiques was tested by computing coefficients of concordance (W). The three sex roles were, as is shown in Table 6.1, all significantly stereotyped at or beyond the .01 level.

The interesting finding to emerge from this analysis was that the male subjects were consistently more concordant in stereotyping the Wife concept than were the women. This finding led us to examine in more detail how the sex roles had been attributed to each target person by the male and female subjects as separate groups. Table 6.2 shows the mean ranking given the physiques for the sex role concepts. As can be seen the greatest discrepancy between the sexes concerned the Wife role — the women saw the obese physiques as more likely to be Wives than did the men, whereas by way of contrast the males perceived the slender target persons as more likely to be Wives than did the female objects.

We then went on to look at the intercorrelations between the sex role concepts and the other concepts and traits included in the study — the method of computing the mean intercorrelations has been described earlier, but it may be recalled that comparisons between correlations were made on the basis of differences between z equivalents (see Bendig (1956, p. 77), Edwards (1950, p. 136), and Hartley (1953) for the details of this procedure).

Turning to the correlational data, which are presented in Table 6.3, we find that the men showed a greater correlation between Like Best and the Wife concept than do the women. It can also be seen that this relationship is, in a corresponding manner, reversed for Wife and Like Least — i.e. the observed correlation being negative in this case — while preserving the sex difference observed above. The men also perceived the Wife role as being less related to Old but more to Alcoholic, suggesting

Table 6.1

Coefficients of Concordance by sex for sex role constructs and *U* resulting from sex difference (American Study)

	Men			*Women*			*Mann Whitney U*		
Construct	*W*	*F*	$p^1 <$	*W*	*F*	$p^1 <$	*U*	*z*	$p^2 <$
Wife	0.53	27.1	.001	0.17	4.9	.001	135	3.44	.0005
Mother	0.21	6.4	.001	0.23	7.2	.001	276	0.71	.30
Sister	0.40	16.0	.001	0.45	19.6	.001	272	0.79	.30

1. Indicates social stereotyping when *p* is less than .05.
2. Indicates a sex difference in social stereotyping, if significant.

Table 6.2

Comparison (via t tests) of the differences in the Mean Rankings originating from Male and Female Subjects for three Sex Role Concepts — Wife, Mother and Sister

	Sex Roles								
	Wife			Mother			Sister		
Target Persons	Men	Women	t^1	Men	Women	t^1	Men	Women	t^1
1. Moderately obese	4.24	3.60	1.79	2.48	2.48	0.00	4.20	4.20	0.00
2. Extremely obese	5.56	4.32	2.98†	3.64	4.04	—0.85	5.24	5.20	0.11
3. Moderately Muscular	3.36	3.52	—0.37	2.84	3.24	—0.85	3.28	3.76	—1.26
4. Extremely Muscular	3.68	3.20	1.32	3.20	3.40	—0.49	3.84	3.76	0.25
5. Extremely Slender	2.56	4.20	—3.76‡	4.84	5.00	—0.41	2.32	2.28	0.08
6. Moderately Slender	1.60	2.16	—1.52	4.00	2.84	2.67†	2.12	1.80	0.91

* $p < .02$ † $p < .01$ ‡ $p < .001$

1. t tests based on 48 degrees of freedom and evaluated on the basis of two-tailed probabilities.

Note: The lower the numerical value of the mean, the greater the appropriateness of the sex role to the traget person.

Table 6.3

Sex Differences in the Intercorrelations arising from the Sex Role Concepts of Wife, Mother and Sister

	Correlations with *Wife*				Correlations with *Mother*				Correlations with *Sister*			
Constructs	Men	Women	z	p^1_{sex}	Men	Women	z	p^1_{sex}	Men	Women	z	p^1_{sex}
Like Least	—.81	—.46	3.86	.001	.12	—.15	1.66	NS	—.60	—.64	0.40	NS
Like Best	.82	.43	4.27	.001	—.10	.18	1.73	NS	.66	.71	0.58	NS
Wife	—	—	—	—	—.05	.42	3.05	.002	.56	.50	0.51	NS
Young	.59	.35	1.95	.05	—.36	.04	2.55	.01	.51	.71	1.99	.05
Successful	.66	.36	2.55	.01	.04	.22	1.12	NS	.50	.62	1.08	NS
Sister	.56	.50	0.56	NS	.07	.12	0.31	NS	—	—	—	—
Leader	.52	.26	1.90	NS	.02	.35	2.12	.04	.27	.17	0.64	NS
Old	—.56	—.21	2.57	.01	.13	—.15	1.73	NS	—.57	—.46	0.92	NS
Self	.56	.37	1.50	NS	—.07	.20	1.67	NS	.34	.53	1.45	NS
Follower	—.39	—.34	0.35	NS	.15	—.23	2.36	.02	—.13	—.21	0.50	NS
Mother	—.05	.42	3.05	.002	—	—	—	—	.07	.12	0.31	NS
Prudish	—.33	—.13	1.30	NS	—.22	—.30	0.53	NS	—.28	—.08	1.27	NS
Homosexual	—.04	—.18	0.87	NS	.11	—.02	0.55	NS	—.17	—.15	0.13	NS
Alcoholic	.14	—.23	2.30	.03	.07	—.15	1.35	NS	—.02	—.11	0.55	NS
Prostitute	.34	.26	0.54	NS	.21	.23	0.13	NS	.35	.46	0.81	NS

that as compared to female subjects they would prefer Wives not to be too 'hidebound', or alternatively, that drinking is in general more acceptable to men than women. Concerning the Mother role, the women saw it as more related to 'youth' and 'success', and more likely to be a Leader and less likely to be a Follower than did men. However, the most substantial difference between the sexes was in the relationship between the Wife and Mother roles — the women seeing them as two highly related roles, whereas the men assigned to them a slightly negative relationship, suggesting that men perceive these two roles as more or less unrelated.

There were no significant sex differences in the corresponding correlations for the Sister role, indicating that the differences observed for Wife and Mother are not due specifically to the way in which male and female subjects handle evaluative traits.

6.4. Sex role stereotyping in the enlarged English sample — a continuation and replication

The findings from the preliminary American study indicated that important differences might exist between men and women in the perception of the two primary roles of Wife and Mother. Consequently, it was decided to include these two sex roles in the final list of 10 concepts which was devised for use on the English sample.

Following a pattern of analysis similar to that employed on the US study, the data were examined from the point of view of establishing the existence of the social stereotyping of Wife and Mother, and then of studying related sex differences in detail.

The first stage in the analysis was to look for evidence that the two sex roles were, in fact, being stereotyped — that the subjects were attributing the traits to the target persons in a consensual or concordant manner. Since these data were based on a seven-point rating scale (i.e. semantic differal format) rather than ranking as in the earlier US study, it was possible to employ two-way analyses of variance on these data, and thereby examine the influence of the sex of the judges upon the ratings more directly than in the case of rankings. The Summary Tables for Mother and Wife are presented in Table 6.4, where each concept is represented by its own separate analysis of variance (see Section 5.4.3 for details). It should be noted that these data are based upon 91 men and 91 women, subjects being randomly discarded from the latter group to equate the sample sizes.

Table 6.4

Summary of Analyses of Variance for the Concepts of Wife and Mother

Concepts	Difference in Ratings due to Sex of the Judges				Differences in Ratings due to Target Persons				Differences in Ratings due to Interaction (Sex X Targets)			
	MS	*Error*	*F**	*p*	*MS*	*Error*	*F*†	*p*	*MS*	*Error*	*F*†	*p*
2. Wife	54.97	4.19	13.12	.001	75.72	2.76	27.40	.001	10.83	2.76	3.92	.01
6. Mother	6.16	4.38	1.41	NS	78.26	2.73	28.63	.001	6.23	2.73	2.28	NS

* df = 1/180 † df = 5/900

In looking at this Table, it can be seen in the middle section (Differences in ratings due to target persons) that both of these sex roles show highly significant social stereotypes — that the subjects, both male and female, are within their own groups consensual in attributing different degrees of Maternalness and Wifeliness to the various target persons. These data indicate that there are physical criteria for these two social roles which have a basis in social expectations.

Turning next to sex differences in the general style of rating (i.e. irrespective of differences between target persons), which is presented in the first section of Table 6.4 (Differences in ratings due to sex of the judges), it can be seen that there is a significant sex difference for Wife but not for Mother — a finding which is broadly commensurate with the American study. In this case the significant F implies that the female subjects tended, in contrast to the males, to rate all the target persons as somewhat more 'like a Wife' irrespective of the differences in body build. In other words, the women in the present study were less critical (i.e. discriminating) of the wife role with respect to body build than are the male judges — a difference which may reflect the male's (supposed) more active role in mate selection.

The results from the Mother concept, on the other hand, indicate by their lack of significance that men and women are, in general, about equal in the readiness with which they attribute Maternalness to various female target persons — that women do not, in fact, perceive traits of maternalness as more common or widespread than do the male subjects in the present study. This result is a little bit surprising in view of the fact that motherhood represents something of an ideal, at least to a certain proportion of women. It is possible that different results would be obtained from an older or more family orientated sample of female subjects.

Continuing on to the last portion of Table 6.4 (Differences in ratings due to the interaction of sex by targets), we find again that there is a significant difference for Wife, but not for Mother. In this context a significant difference implies that judges have applied a different criterion to the judgement of the various targets as a function of their own sex — that the men in the present sample perceive some of the target persons as more suiting or less suiting the Wife role than do the female judges. While the exact nature of these discrepancies will be considered in detail in the next paragraph, it is interesting to note that men and women do not show an interaction in their judgement of the Mother role: considering that men tend to devalue the mother concept, one might expect that they would attribute maternalness and nonmaternalness in a different pattern from that of the female judges who are, or should be, somewhat more sympathetic to the role of Mother. On the other hand, this lack of interaction is consistent with the absence of positive evaluation of the Mother concept which was apparent in the factor analyses of the data from the female subjects (see Figures 5.4 and 5.6).

Accordingly, we then went on to examine the observed stereotypes in more detail, by establishing which roles were commonly attributed to which of the various body builds. Table 6.5 shows the mean ratings given to the six target persons by men and women for the two sex roles.

As is partially anticipated by the interaction between Sex and Targets discussed above, significant differences between the males and females were present on Targets 1 and 2 for the concept of Wife. Here, as in the US study, the male subjects perceived the more obese physiques as less likely to be Wives than did the females.

Table 6.5

Comparison (via t tests) of the Differences in the Mean Ratings originating from Male and Female Subjects for two Sex Role Concepts — Wife and Mother

	Sex Roles					
	Wife			Mother		
Target Persons	Men	Women	t[1]	Men	Women	t[1]
1. Moderately obese	4.04	3.00	3.99**	2.69	2.57	0.56
2. Extremely obese	5.36	4.32	3.73**	3.95	3.89	0.20
3. Moderately muscular	3.37	3.13	1.05	3.36	2.97	1.64
4. Extremely muscular	4.03	4.14	—0.43	3.45	3.98	—1.93*
5. Extremely slender	4.01	3.78	0.87	4.75	4.31	1.65
6. Moderately slender	3.20	2.98	0.92	4.04	3.63	1.58

* $p \approx .05$ ** $p < .001$.

1. t tests based on 180 degrees of freedom and evaluated on the basis of two-tailed probabilities.

Note: The lower the numerical value of the mean, the greater the appropriateness of the sex role to the target person.

Somewhat surprisingly the concept of Mother also gives rise to a nearly significant sex difference on Target 4. The t, of 1.93 — which indicates that the males are more likely to perceive Target 4 as maternal — falls just short of the 5 per cent level of significance for a two-tailed test (the F ratio for Interaction shown in Table 6.5, being 2.28, reflects this marginal state of affairs as it is almost significant with $df = 5/900$). This difference was not observed in the US data, while in addition, we failed to replicate the sex difference concerning Target 6's rating on Mother, although the relevant test ($t = 1.58$, $df = 180$) did reach the 6 per cent level in a one-tailed test (i.e. the observed difference was in the direction predicted from the US study). In view of our failure to replicate this difference in the second UK study, it is difficult to decide whether women really consider the most Attractive target (e.g. 6) to be more suiting the maternal role than do the men, but the balance of evidence does seem to favour this conclusion.

In considering the sex differences arising in the US and UK studies, it must be remembered that the target persons and the way in which they

Table 6.6

Summary of the Intercorrelations between the Sex Roles of Wife and Mother and the remaining eight Constructs, shown with the *z*s used to test for Sex Differences

	Correlations with 'Wife'				Correlations with 'Mother'			
Traits	Men	Women	z_{sex}	p^{1}_{sex}	Men	Women	z_{sex}	p^{1}_{sex}
Attractive	.53	.35	2.83	.005	—.05	.07	—1.52	NS
Prudish	—.20	—.04	—2.05	.04	—.12	—.06	0.76	NS
Like I Am	.27	.33	—0.83	NS	—.03	.15	—2.28	.03
Alcoholic	—.34	—.19	—2.04	.04	.00	—.23	2.95	.004
Influential	.24	.18	0.79	NS	.10	.09	0.13	NS
Cruel	—.16	—.17	0.13	NS	—.27	—.34	0.97	NS
Homosexuel	—.37	—.34	—0.43	NS	—.25	—.38	1.82	NS
Ideal Self	.24	.29	—0.68	NS	—.05	.08	1.64	NS
MOTHER	.43	.57	—2.37	.02	—	—	—	—

[1]Two-tailed probabilities.

are portrayed have both been considerably altered between the US and the UK study. Consequently it is not surprising that there is not a one to one correspondence between the sex differences observed in the two studies. On the other hand, the most important sex difference — that concerning the appropriateness of the obese targets to the role of Wife — was replicated with a high degree of confidence.

Continuing with the English study, the analysis then went on to examine the relationships (i.e. correlations) between the sex role concepts and the remaining eight descriptive and character traits. The 34 relevant correlations are presented separately for the sexes in Table 6.6 where the significance testing has been carried out by means of z tests.

Starting our discussion with the concept of Wife, sex differences were found to alter significantly the extent of association between this sex role and three of the eight remaining traits, these being Attractive, Alcoholic and Prudish. Roughly speaking, the men perceived the role of Wife as being more closely associated with that of Attractiveness, and more distant to those of Alcoholic and Prudish, than did the women in the sample. Taken at face value, this difference in attribution seems to indicate a generally more positive or more idealised (or possibly critical) evaluation of the role of Wife by men than by women.

On taking up the Mother concept we find, however, something of a reversal — with the female subjects giving a more affirmative valuation to the Mother role than did the males. Specifically, the female judges perceived the role of Mother as being more congruent with physical Attractiveness, their own Selves and Ideal Selves, and less socially deviant in terms of Alcoholism and Lesbianism than did their male counterparts, who were less critical in this instance. Before moving on, however, it is worth noting that the sex differences involving Attractiveness and the Ideal Self are based on correlations which are sufficiently small in absolute terms to require cautious interpretation.

Turning to the relationship between the Mother and Wife concepts, it can be seen in Table 6.6 that, as compared with the male subjects, the females have indicated their expectation of a closer correspondence between the roles of Wife and Mother. That a comparable difference was found in the earlier US study seems to confirm that this is one of the more important sex differences in sex role perception, having potential relevance to both practical (e.g. marital adjustment) and theoretical issues (e.g. sex differences in social development). In respect of this important topic, we can note in advance that this particular sex difference was replicated for a third time in the study to be discussed immediately below.

6.5. The second English study — additional confirmation of sex differences in sex role typing

Because of certain unexpected aberrations arising out of the semantic differential format, it was decided to undertake the testing of a further sample of English subjects ($N = 145$) — retaining the same target persons and concepts, but employing instead a slightly modified version of the ranking procedure which had served efficiently in the US study. For convenience this study has been referred to as 'Study 2' and those particular aspects which bear on sex role stereotypes and sex differences in role perception will be related below.

In the light of the success of the previous two studies, it is not surprising that this study also yielded some interesting data on sex role stereotyping and gender differences in the evaluation of sex roles. We will begin the discussion by considering the essential, but sometime equivocal, problem of consensus or social stereotyping.

In accordance with the return to the ranking format, social stereotyping was evaluated with the aid of the coefficient of concordance (*CW*) — with the *CW* for the sex roles of Wife and Mother being presented in Table 6.7

In examining these data, it can be seen that the male and female

Table 6.7

Comparing the Sex Differences in Social Stereotyping of *Wife* and *Mother* by means of *z* tests between Coefficients of Concordance (*CW*s)

Sex Role Concepts	Coefficients of Concordance (*CW*s) Males[1]	Females[2]	Combined[3] Sexes	Sex Differences z_{sex}	p_{sex}
Wife	0.66*	0.34*	0.50*	4.86	.001
Mother	0.28*	0.34*	0.30*	—0.76	NS

*$p < .001$ (significance is indicative of social stereotyping).
[1] $n = 78$.
[2] $n = 67$.
[3] $N = 145$.

subjects have both stereotyped these two sex roles to a significant degree, but with the males showing a much higher level of social stereotyping for the concept of Wife than that of Mother. In comparing the two sexes the males are, as in the previous two studies, substantially more concordant in their judgements of the role of Wife than were the females, with this difference being significant at the .001 level. Here, then, we have further evidence that the males and females construe the notion of Wife in differing ways, with the heterogeneity evidenced in the performance of the female subjects being suggestive of a greater sensitivity to the alternative roles available to, or expected of, the married woman. This finding also suggests that some aspects of socialisation may have been less uniform for women than men.

Moving next to the attribution of sex roles to the individual target persons, the data for the male and female subjects are shown in Table 6.8, which displays the mean rankings of the individual physiques for the concepts of Wife and Mother. Again the results were similar to those of our previous studies, with the female subjects displaying a much broader range of acceptance in their attribution of the Wife role to the various target persons. In contrast, the male subjects perceived the thinner, more Attractive targets to be more congruent with their notions of Wife, and showed a correspondingly strong rejection of the obese targets. As we have noted immediately above and on several earlier occasions, the apparent 'blunting' of the social perception of Wife by the females may not stem so much from their uncritical attribution of this concept, but rather that we are, in reality, dealing with a mixed social stereotype, in which one aspect leans towards the notion of motherhood, and the other, alternative conception towards the ideal of a younger, more social (e.g. outgoing) Wife, in whom physical attractiveness is a particularly important trait or quality.

With respect to sex differences in attribution, the concept of Mother was unremarkable; a finding which is consistent with the relative absence of sex differences observed in the previous two studies. Here, the only clear trend across all three studies seems to be the female subjects' greater reluctance to attribute maternal qualities to Target 4, which is the most muscular or masculine of the six. It would be tempting to conclude that the culturally defined role of Mother (e.g. Secord & Jourard, 1956) is simply too important to be admitting of marked sex differences, but the generally low levels of concordance accruing to the concept of Mother in our own studies is at variance with this notion. If the concept can differ markedly between persons, it seems reasonable that it could equally differ systematically between the sexes.

Table 6.8

Sex Differences in the Attribution of 'Mother' and 'Wife' to the various Target Persons by 78 Males and 67 Females tested on the Ranking Format

Target Persons	Mean Rankings and *t*s for Wife				Mean Rankings and *t*s for Mother			
	Men M^* S^2	*Women* M^* S^2	$t^1_{sex} <$	$p^2_{sex} <$	*Men* M^* S^2	*Women* M^* S^2	$t^1_{sex} <$	$p^2_{sex} <$
1. Moderate Endomorph	4.1 (0.9)	3.3 (2.2)	3.77	.001	2.4 (1.7)	2.1 (1.4)	1.44	NS
2. Extreme Endomorph	5.6 (1.0)	5.0 (2.7)	2.58	.01	4.4 (2.2)	3.9 (3.2)	1.80	NS
3. Moderate Mesomorph	2.5 (0.8)	2.7 (1.4)	—1.13	NS	2.7 (1.6)	2.7 (1.9)	0.13	NS
4. Extreme Mesomorph	4.4 (1.1)	4.4 (1.6)	—0.89	NS	3.4 (3.1)	3.8 (2.4)	—1.45	NS
5. Extreme Ectomorph	2.7 (2.6)	3.4 (2.8)	—2.54	.02	4.7 (2.6)	5.0 (1.8)	—1.21	NS
6. Moderate Ectomorph	1.7 (0.9)	2.3 (2.1)	—2.88	.004	3.5 (2.2)	3.6 (1.8)	—0.42	NS

1. *DF*s = 143. A negative *t* indicates that the males found the target to be more appropriate to the role than did the women.
2. Two-tailed probabilities.
* The lower the value of the mean, the greater the agreement between the trait and the target.

The correlations from Study 2 involving the sex roles of Wife and Mother are shown in Table 6.9. From this Table it can be seen that the male and female subjects differ significantly in their attributions of Physical Attractiveness, Ideal Self and Ability to Influence to the concept of Wife, with the degree of association being greater for men than women in all three instances. These findings are, again, reminiscent of the more positive or more demanding evaluation of the hypothetical Wife by males which was observed in the earlier studies.

The concept of Mother also provided three sex differences, but here, as in the previous two studies, the participating correlations (excepting those between Mother and Wife) were generally of such small magnitude as to raise serious doubts concerning the appropriate interpretation. In attempting to understand this failing, it may be cogent to point out that our studies based on differences in dress and attire (see Chapters 7 and 8) yield considerably more robust Mother stereotypes and correlations than are observed here — suggesting that the implications of dress and fashion may be considerably more salient for this concept than are differences in body build. In view of the importance of the Mother

Table 6.9

Intercorrelations between the Sex Roles of Wife and Mother and the other Traits, shown with the *z*s used for test for Sex Differences

Traits	Correlations with Wife				Correlations with Mother			
	Men	*Women*	z_{sex}	p^1_{sex}	*Men*	*Women*	z_{sex}	p^1_{sex}
Attractive	.86	.58	6.52	.001	.10	—.09	1.97	.05
Prudish	.01	.02	—0.10	NS	—.07	.10	—1.76	NS
Like I Am	.66	.59	1.19	NS	.17	.05	1.26	NS
Alcoholic	—.29	—.22	—0.77	NS	—.08	.12	—2.07	.04
Influential	.54	.34	2.58	.01	.17	.20	—0.32	NS
Cruel	—.20	—.21	0.11	NS	—.09	—.08	—0.10	NS
Homosexual	—.10	—.11	0.10	NS	.05	.04	0.10	NS
Ideal Self	.75	.57	3.36	.001	.10	—.11	2.18	.03
MOTHER	.22	.40	—2.07	.04	—	—	—	—

1. Two-tailed probabilities.

concept, this particular problem is clearly deserving of further investigation.

6.6 Discussion of sex role findings

At this point we can sum up the findings from all three studies. Throughout all aspects of the analysis there was repeated evidence of the discrepancy between men's and women's evaluations of the Wife and Mother roles. Primarily, the men consistently gave a more positive valuation to the concept of 'Wife' since they saw the fatter and less attractive physiques as less likely to be wives and they gave a higher valuation to the 'Wife' role in terms of its relationships with the other positively valued traits. In contrast the women tended to give a more positive valuation to the 'Mother' role than did the men, though this finding was not as pervasive. The women tended to see the less extreme and more attractive physiques as more likely to be mothers and to exhibit higher relationships between the 'Mother' construct and the positively valued constructs.

The second major finding concerned the relationship between the two roles, for the women saw relatively little conflict between 'Wife' and 'Mother' but the men saw the two roles very differently.

There are two aspects of these findings which may have importance in terms of marital harmony. One is the discrepancy *per se* found between men and women in their perceptions of the 'Wife' and 'Mother' roles for it can be realistically hypothesised that shared perceptions between husband and wife of these two basic roles are important for marital harmony. Hicks & Platt (1970) have described the family as a matrix of defined, interlocking and interdependent roles, such that within this frame of reference congruence of role perception as well as compatibility between role expectation and actual fulfilment would generally be associated with high levels of marital happiness. Experimental evidence concerning the importance of shared stereotypes is provided by the Dewrey & Rae (1969) study, where it was shown that a shared conception of masculinity between husband and wife was an important factor in marital success. Studies by Luckey (1960a, b, c) and that of Stuckert (1963) have found that it is important for marital satisfaction that the wife accurately perceives her husband's perception of himself, but not important in itself that the husband accurately perceives the wife's self perception. In a similar study Kotlar (1965) found that congruence of perception was significantly related to husbands' and couples' marital adjustment, but not to wives' adjustment.

The second factor of importance to marital harmony in our findings was the nature of the discrepancy exhibited by the men in their evaluations of the 'Wife' and 'Mother' roles. Here the problem of role transition and ability to cope with changed perceptions becomes the important influence on the marital relationship (Pineo, 1961, 1969). The birth of the first child is a traumatic event in the life of any couple but for many fathers it is a time of particular adjustment strain. Not only must a man adjust to a certain degree of displacement in his wife's affections and attendances but he must also adjust his perception of his wife's role so that it now incorporates the maternal role as well. It can be hypothesised that if a man's stereotypes of the 'Wife' and 'Mother' roles are not too discrepant then the transition should be relatively easy. If, on the other hand, he holds differing evaluations of these two basic roles, then the adjustment necessary may be quite difficult for him to make.

The man faced with such changed circumstances finds his wife is now fulfilling two roles for which he has conflicting stereotypes. To overcome this conflict he either adapts his stereotype of one or both of the roles until they are seen as compatible, or, more likely, he changes his perception of his wife until she fits in more with his stereotype of a mother, and this is equivalent to devaluing his wife. When a man takes this latter alternative and the woman is unaware of her husband's change of perception, then marital discord may result and seriously affect the continuity of the relationship. Further research is needed to discover how effective counselling would be in modifying these perceptions and avoiding or relieving marital distress.

It is interesting to speculate on the development of such differences in men's and women's perceptions. In a previous study (Powell et al., 1973) it was shown that young boys of nine or ten valued the 'Mother' role more positvely than did girls of the same age. For adolescents the value of the 'Mother' role was about the same for boys and girls. And now in this study the findings show that in adulthood the 'Mother' role is devalued more for males than females. So it appears that there is a general downward trend in attitudes towards the 'Mother' role from childhood to adulthood for both males and females. However, whereas the trend tends to flatten out for females about adolescence, it continues to descend for males, dropping below that of the females and resulting in the discrepancy in evaluations in adulthood.

Concerning the relationship between the two social roles; for both boys and girls 'Wife' and 'Mother' were seen as less similar in early childhood than they were in adolescence. But again after adolescence there was a sharp drop in the relationship for men whereas for women the degree of relationship stayed fairly constant. So again it appears that the crucial time for the development of this difference between men and women is in the years between adolescence and early adulthood.

7 The Social Consensus of Judgement in Childhood

7.1 The Interpretation of Physique by Children

There is ample evidence from our own and others' work that physique can be a potent elicitor of impressions and stereotypes in adulthood. The consensual evaluation of body type is not, however, a purely adult characteristic, since there are a number of studies showing that physique creates socialised impressions from early in childhood. For example, Lerner & Gellert (1969) found that 5 year old female children were distinctly averse to the endomorphic build, although unequivocal stereotyping was not generally evidenced. Subsequently, during the elementary school ages, body build stereotypes become well pronounced, as a brief review of some of the major studies will demonstrate.

7.1.1. Consensual judgement of physique

In one of the few children's studies concerned with female physique Caskey & Felker (1964) demonstrate this early stereotyping. In their study 75 school girls, 15 in each grade from 1 to 5 (6 to 10 year old), were individually shown silhouettes of a female endomorph, mesomorph and ectomorph. As each of 40 adjectives was read out, the children indicated which of the three target persons it best suited. Of the 40 adjectives, 30 were assigned nonrandomly to the stimuli. The results of this study can be compared with that of Staffieri (1967). Here, 90 male children, 18 at each age level from 6 to 10 years, assigned 39 adjectives to silhouettes of a male endomorph, mesomorph and ectomorph. Half the children viewed adult silhouettes, and half child silhouettes; but since patterns of responding did not differ for the two groups, they were combined for the purposes of analysis. All except two of the adjectives were assigned nonrandomly.

7.1.2. Evaluative judgements of physique

From the above two studies, a generally coherent picture of the evaluation likely to be placed by an observer upon a particular same sex body type can be formulated.

Endomorphic girls seem unlikely to be ideally chosen as best friends by their fellow girls. First, their appearance is hardly perceived as conducive to approach responses; that is, untidy and sloppy, ugly and dirty.

Second, anticipated personality is also negative, given lazy, stupid, mean, unkind and chattering traits. The resultant perception is that of a timid, lonely, unhappy individual who, perhaps not unreasonably, has something to worry about.

Mesomorphic girls do not provoke strong reactions amongst their peers. The dominant perception is simply that of a strong and healthy girl, with an unworried, forceful personality to match.

Ectomorphic girls are rated the most positively of the three body build types. A clean, tidy and pretty exterior, together with a quiet, kind and clever personality, provide the Best Friend image. A happy person with many friends, she might only have second thoughts about her sick and weak looking frame.

Turning to the male peer analysis of endomorphic boys, they are probably best described as the architype 'dumb slob'. A dirty, untidy, sloppy and ugly first impression is expected to conform with the unintelligent, lazy, forgetful, cowardly and mean personality it clothes. He is perhaps seen as trying to get his own back on people, rather than just sit back and take abuse; through the lying, cheating, impolite, dishonest and argumentative behaviours attributed to him. As with the endomorphic girl, he is seen as a sad and lonely figure.

Mesomorphic boys are seen as the direct opposite of the endomorphs. They are perceived as having their pick of friends. This is not simply because they have a physically dominating appearance, good looking, strong, fit and healthy, and not withdrawing from fights, for personality attribution is also favourable; unworried, helpful, polite, honest and truthful.

Ectomorphic boys sound more human. Nervous, weak and sick constitutionally, they would understandably rather not fight, nor risk that possibility by talking too much or arguing. Thus interpersonally their perceived mode of operating is sneakily. But outwardly, they are clean and tidy, and do not have the mean streak of the endomorph. Another sad, rejected figure, however.

One obvious question is whether these descriptions fit with the physique-behaviour relationships that Sheldon has tried to delineate by objective means. There is no straightforward answer to this since the traits employed in the stereotyping studies are not exactly those that Sheldon investigated. Further, the physiques used in the stereotyping studies were all extreme representations of somatotypes, and as such the results cannot always be extrapolated to cover more average builds (Powell et al., 1974) since extreme physiques seem to have characteristics that are a function of extremity rather than of a particular somatotype.

Notwithstanding these limitations, however, there are two points in the comparison of stereotyping with objective studies where differences emerge.

First, mesomorphic boys are perceived as almost paragons of virtue, whereas Sheldon (Glueck & Glueck, 1956) has shown mesomorphy to be clearly associated with delinquency. The discrepancy may not be as great as it seems, however, if one posits that it is the physically more mature boys who are expected to represent group standards of behaviour. In certain subcultures standards clearly fringe on the delinquent, especially those involving toughness, daring and a lack of respect for authority. In such situations the mesomorph, the leader, may be at greater risk in terms of being apprehended.

Second, in the stereotyping results there is a clear trend for all good qualities to be attributed to a single figure, whereas socially favourable traits are apparently spread throughout Sheldon's somatotypes when objective measures are taken. In fact this finding of clustering positive traits may well be a function of restricting attributional choice to only three figures but it does raise the possibility, to be taken up in the next chapter, that stereotyped perceptions are simplified by reducing within stimulus inconsistency, denying that both good and bad qualities can coexist within the same individual.

Returning to the evaluations placed on particular physiques, it is obvious that the above stereotypic sketches should not be applied rigidly with reference to any particular individual but treated as extreme caricatures. This is partly due to the experimental method itself: only extremes of body build were used as target persons; only one example per body type was employed, thus ruling out an analysis of within somatotype variation; cues such as clothing and facial appearance were not present, which would modify body build influences; and the one choice forced choice method does not allow the individual subject to quantify the relative differences between targets on a given trait. Within these limitations, however, there is a clear cut preference for the ectomorphic female and the mesomorphic male.

This result has further been found replicable. Staffieri (1972) reports a study of 120 boys from 8 to 12 years old who assigned one of four figures (extreme endomorph, mesomorph, ectomorph and a dysplatic physique) to each of 36 behavioural descriptions similar to those of Staffieri (1967). The mesomorph was again 'all things good', the endomorph was seen as a socially unfavourable character, and finally the ectomorph appeared socially submissive.

In fact, the stereotypes remain reasonably constant through older age levels of children and adolescents. Lerner (1969b) traced this pattern. In his study 50 male volunteers formed three groups — pre-puberty (mean age 10.7 years, n = 15); post-puberty (mean age 14.9 years, n = 15) and end of pubertal growth spurt (mean age 19.5, n = 20). The subjects were shown pictures representing an adult male endomorph, mesomorph and ectomorph, one of which had to be assigned to each of 30 behavioural descriptions selected from Brodsky (1954). The three groups did not differ significantly in their stereotypes of the three physiques and again, the mesomorph is fit and courageous, most wanted as a friend; the ectomorph is socially submissive, timid and in a precarious mental state; and, of course, the endomorph continues friendless, spending time abusing his body with nicotine and alcohol. There is one further point of interest in this data. Although Lerner's subjects agreed that the mesomorph has enough positive assets to be most wanted as a friend, it also seems he has enough negative qualities such that who would be least preferred as a friend is in doubt. His superior qualities would be too much for some people, perhaps. The lack of consensus upon the trait 'least preferred as a personal friend', is also influenced by a fairly even division between subjects as to whether they could endure best an obese or a frail person as a friend. The lack of consensus on this trait cannot reasonably be put down to unreliable responding, since in all other respects the traits form coherent patterns. Rather, it could be a function of the fact that it reflects a personal statement as to the qualities one dislikes in others (unlike, say 'have the fewest friends' which is a statement relating the target to a group of others, not to the subject himself). It suggests that although there may be a shared conception of generally desirable qualities, we are idiosyncratic about the qualities in an individual that would lead us to reject them.

7.1.3. Comparison of children's and adults' evaluations of physique

The studies cited so far thus indicate that children of all ages from 6 to 19 years hold largely similar attitudes towards distinctive body types. In contrast to this lack of age differences in the stereotypes held, there is a clearcut sex difference; males prefer the mesomorphic build in boys and girls the ectomorphic type for their own sex, the endomorph, however, remaining for both sexes at the bottom of the pile.

There is the question of whether the children's stereotypes match those of adults. The girls' perception of the ectomorphic figure as most attractive is clearly maintained into adulthood, as can be seen by comparing the traits Ugly and Pretty in Caskey & Felker's study, with the traits Like Least and Like Best in a study by Stewart et al. (1973). In the Stewart study, 25 adult female college students ranked six female physiques (two endomorphs, two mesomorphs and two ectomorphs) from most to least suiting Like Least and Like Best, with instructions to judge upon an aesthetic rather than imputed personality basis. The two endomorphs were least liked, followed by the two mesomorphs and finally by the two ectomorphs. This order of preference was exactly reversed, as would be expected, on Like Best. The order of preference in Caskey & Felker's study for the traits Ugly and Pretty was respectively identical. Similarly, boys' physique preferences are present in adulthood. Table 7.1 compares on matchable traits Staffieri's study with that of Sleet (1969), in which 45 adult males ranked 12 male figures (three each of somatotype extremes and three combined dominance figures). The Table gives for each pair of traits the rank order of somatotype suitability as ascertained by each study. As can be seen, a high degree of concordance between the studies is evidenced.

It is difficult to say exactly when these socially stereotyped perceptions of physique become apparent. Certainly, the five year old girls in Lerner & Gellert's (1969) study, as has been mentioned, did not demonstrate clearcut stereotyping. Similarly Staffieri (1967) found that the male preference for mesomorphy was not evidenced in 4 to 6 year olds. But at these ages a possible confounding effect is the ability of the child to perform the experimental task (understand fully the instructions, etc.), the extent of this problem being difficult to assess.

Table 7.1

Results of adult males viewing male physiques (Sleet, 1969) compared with boys viewing male physiques (Staffieri, 1967) on Traits common to both studies

		Rank Order					
		Sleet			Staffieri		
Sleet	Staffieri	1	2	3	1	2	3
Not lazy	Lazy	Mes	Ect	End	End	Ect	Mes
Best liked	Best friend	Mes	Ect	End	Mes	Ect	End
Well adjusted	Worries	Mes	Ect	End	Ect	End	Mes
Attractive physique	Good looking	Mes	Ect	End	Mes	Ect	End
Physically fit	Healthy	Mes	Ect	End	Mes	Ect	End

However, the important practical point is that as soon as the child formally becomes a social animal, that is within the school setting, the stereotypes are strong; liable to be an influence upon social interaction, friendship formation and so on. Hence the obese child, the physically mature child and the frail child are immediately cast into socioexpectational moulds. The effects of such expectation cannot be overestimated (Kelvin, 1969), such that if there is a genetic link between somatotype and behaviour/personality, within a few years any 'real' associations are liable to be severely disguised by cultural modelling.

There are many studies relating social pressure to behaviour. For example, Biller & Liebman (1971) found that boys' body build was more related to sex role adoption (i.e. public) than to sex role preference (i.e. that can be kept private). Also Hartup et al. (1963) found that young boys took longer orientating towards attractive, but sex inappropriate, toys when one of the experimenters was present, than when left alone to choose toys. Incidentally, but interestingly, young girls did not show such reticence when in adult company, reflecting, perhaps, the social acceptance of 'tomboy' behaviour.

Thus it will come as no surprise to find that the physically mature boy is actually found to have more friends, to be more respected, and to achieve more leadership, than the immature boy (Jones & Bayley, 1950), or that boys with inadequate physique are likely to have neurotic worries centring on their build, feelings of social inadequacy and loss of self esteem, to the extent that hormone treatment and plastic surgery are considered viable therapies (Schonfeld, 1950).

Unfortunately, there is scant information regarding the age at which the personal physical attributes of an individual begin to have an effect upon his behaviour. In fact the process probably commences when children begin to utilise physical information in part to determine their sociometric choice. For example, suppose attractiveness is used as one criterion of approach and friendship formation, then obviously unattractive children would acquire fewer friends. Now the experients and studies within the area of personality judgement show quite convincingly that friends are attributed more favourable traits than are non-friends. Thus children who have been 'gated out' due to their physical attractiveness will therefore be adversely labelled and judged. The types of behaviour that rejected children show would only confirm the biased labelling, thus reinforcing their negative evaluation. In other words, the association between attractiveness and undesirable traits could equally be a result of peer rejection as it could be a cause of it, while both processes serve to confirm each other. The example of attractiveness was not chosen fortuitously, for there is some evidence that even in very young children it predicts friendship choice (Dion & Berscheid, 1974).

In this study, Dion examined the relationship between physical attractiveness and peer perception at a very early age, 4 to 6 years. Seventy seven children in all were subjects, attending the same nursery school, subdivided into two age ranges, the younger 4 years 4 months to 5 years 4 months, and the older 5 years 5 months to 6 years 10 months (*N*s of 37 and 40 respectively). The 38 girls and 39 boys were distributed evenly through the two age ranges. Each child was interviewed individually, utilising a board on which was mounted separate photographs of each of his classmates.

First, each child was asked to indicate three peers whom he liked, and three whom he disliked. In this manner a Total Popularity Index (Moore, 1967) was constituted for each child, being the number of positive choices received from peers minus the number of negative choices.

Next, each child nominated a member of his group as exhibiting certain social-behavioural traits read out by the experimenter (e.g. Find the one who: is not afraid of things, cries a lot, always wants to be the best, scares you).

In a separate part of the study, the attractiveness of each child was evaluated. Fourteen adult judges (7 male) rated each child on the basis of his photograph from Very Attractive to Very Unattractive on a 5-point scale. The judges were unacquainted with the children and with the other aspects of the study.

Essentially the results show that attractive males were more popular than the unattractive males. This pattern was also evident in the girls although not until the older age range. In terms of more specific behaviours, attractive children were nominated more independent and self sufficient that unattractive children; while unattractive children were more often nominated the aggressive, antisocial, nonconforming descriptions.

Here then, a pattern emerges of 'attractive is good'. Now, in relation to body build, clearly this is one aspect of physical attractiveness, along with the other cues, as in the Dion study, of dress, face, expression, hair, etc. Turning to physique behaviour stereotypes, one is obliged to ask the question 'Are mesomorphic males (or ectomorphic girls) rated positively on most traits because of the fact of their mesomorphy or because of their judged attractiveness?' Clearly, it is highly possible that attractiveness mediates the stereotyping of the physique-behaviour relationships. An attractiveness mediated model of body build stereotyping has at least two points in its favour:

1. In order to stereotype physique at a young age, children need not learn the multiplicity of supposed relationships between body and behaviour, just simply what is attractive and order all other value judgements about that knowledge.
2. Attractiveness is a highly socialised concept at a very early age, as witnessed by the extremely high consensus on this concept in the stereotyping studies previously quoted, thus consensus on all other value judgements will be apparent. Each child does not have to acquire for himself the same physique behaviour beliefs as most of his peers — just the same opinion as to what is attractive.

Thus much of the stereotyping data can be explained by having the child learn two 'facts': first, attractive is good, and second, mesomorphy is attractive (or for girls, ectomorphy is attractive). This does not place too great a load on the cognitive abilities of even the youngest child. The one further judgement a child has to make is whether a given trait is 'good', which may depend upon such factors as the sex of the child, the opinion of his or her reference group and the sex of the target. For example, both male and female ectomorphs are stereotyped as Quiet. Since the female ectomorph is given generally positive evaluations, Quiet may be interpreted as a 'good' trait for girls. On the other hand, male ectomorphs have a somewhat negative evaluation overall, suggesting that Quiet is seen as a not so good trait in boys. One can see, therefore, how traits attributed to physiques might not always be a direct function of the physique itself.

A prediction consequent upon the above reasoning would be that traits that have no clearly defined degree of social desirability in either a positive or negative direction will tend not to be stereotyped strongly. To test this, stereotyping stuides would preferably take independent measures of the desirability of each trait, rather than relying on a *post hoc* analysis of the relationships between traits.

In conclusion, it can be suggested that the learning of physique stereotypes will be a multifaceted process involving the acquisition of adult and peer labels concerning classes of physique. A 'class' of physique may be defined not only in terms of somatotype, but also in terms of another factor such as 'attractiveness' which might in some situations cut across somatotypes. Attribution of traits might further be influenced by extraphysique factors such as semantic, implicit relationships between labels and the social desirability of the traits in question. The part that learning by direct observation plays is unclear. Observational, 'objective' evidence is liable to be biased by initial expectations such that one only searches for or notices confirmatory instances — strongly emotive stereotypes being notoriously difficult to negate. Selective observation may, therefore, maintain rather than initiate a stereotype.

7.2 The use of socionormative criteria of judgement

In the previous section it was shown that stereotyped perceptions of body build develop in early childhood and persist throughout adulthood. The studies cited do not however, demonstrate any developmental pattern of social responding. Does consensus increase with age concomitant with social experience? Do traits show differential patterns of consensual development? Is there a sex difference in degree of stereotyping? These questions have not yet been answered, first because of the relative insensitivity of the one-choice forced-choice method and second because cross-sectional studies giving exactly the same test to different ages and specifically analysing for consensus are lacking in the literature, as noted by Cauthen et al. (1971).

Therefore, as a pilot study in the area, Powell et al. (1973) carried out what will be referred to as Study I. Briefly, there were four groups of children:

Young Boys (YB)	$n = 52$,	Mean age = 10.4 years
Young Girls (YG)	$n = 52$,	Mean age = 10.3 years
Adolescent Boys (AB)	$n = 52$,	Mean age = 15.5 years
Adolescent Girls (AG)	$n = 52$,	Mean age = 15.4 years

The children were required to rank six distinctively dressed female figures (Appendix II) from most to best suiting each of eleven personality and behavioural traits (Table 7.2).

7.2.1. Hypotheses regarding age and sex differences in Study I

In Study I, there were two major hypotheses with respect to consensual responding that were under investigation:

H(1) The older children will show more consensus on this social judgement task than will the younger children.

There is no direct evidence bearing on this question, but it seems reasonable that if clothes have an arbitrary social meaning, then this meaning has to be learned, a time consuming process culminating in the adult pattern of being able to manipulate dress deliberately to convey certain impressions.

H(2) Male children will show more consensus in their judgements than will female children.

Bearing on this hypothesis is the finding of Stewart et al. (1973), that adult women hold more individual opinions about female physique than do men. There is a similar sex difference indicated in Hamid's (1968) study of dress perception in adults. Finally, in Staffieri's (1967) study on males evaluating physique, there were more highly stereotyped traits than in the female counterpart study of Caskey & Felker (1964).

7.2.2. Results — consensus within age and sex groups

In order to assess consensus, a Coefficient of Concordance (*CW*, see Section 5.6.1) was computed for each of the four groups on each of the eleven traits. As a general assessment of the results, it can be noted that the mean *CW* for each group was as follows:

Table 7.2

*CW*s for Young Boys (YB), Young Girls (YG), Adolescent Boys (AB) and Adolescent Girls (AG) on each Trait, and the significance of Age and Sex Comparisons of *CW*

	*CW*s				*Sex*[1]		*Age*[1]	
Traits	YB	YG	AB	AG	YB *vs* YG	AB *vs* AG	YB *vs* AB	YG *vs* AG
Likes Parties	.415	.476	.570	.520	NS	NS	.03	NS
Like A Wife	.227	.385	.256	.298	.03	NS	NS	NS
Steals From Shops	.140	.177	.243	.319	NS	NS	NS	.04
Liked by Men	.219	.251	.481	.459	NS	NS	.001	.01
Clever	.167	.281	.355	.356	NS	NS	.01	NS
Like A Mother	.369	.307	.313	.352	NS	NS	NS	NS
Strict	.148	.088	.426	.378	NS	NS	.001	.001
Good looking	.289	.170	.353	.332	NS	NS	NS	.03
Argues A Lot	.087	.032*	.094	.091	NS	NS	NS	NS
Liked By Women	.210	.078†	.197	.206	.03	NS	NS	.04
Like I Will Be	.171	.160	.214	.158	NS	NS	NS	NS

* *W* not significant.
† *W* significant at the .01 level. All remaining *W*s significant at the .001 level.
[1]Probability levels for these comparisons being given one-tailed since direction is predicted in text.

Young Boys (YB) = 0.222
Young Girls (YG) = 0.219
Adolescent Boys (AB) = 0.318
Adolescent Girls (AG) = 0.315

Sex and age differences were evaluated for significance using the *z* test described in Section 4 of Appendix III and presented in Table 7.4 with one tailed probability levels since direction of differences has been predicted. Clearly, the marked age differences and negligible sex differences support H(1) and reject H(2), and indeed of the 22 age comparisons of individual *CW*s, nine reached statistical significance in the predicted direction, while only two were significant for sex comparisons (one favouring boys and one girls).

Turning to the original hypotheses, it is clear that H(1) is supported: there is a gradual trend with age towards greater consensus in social judgement. The implications of this finding are at least threefold. First, children are becoming less egocentric in their perception, a trend noted in other contexts by Inhelder & Piaget (1958). Second, although Kelly has stressed the use of grids in the determination of idiosyncratic patterns of perception, they can be equally meaningfully used to ascertain the extent to which perceptions are social in nature. Third, a test and methodology has been described that is sensitive to group and individual differences in social learning.

With respect of H(2), it is equally clear that this was not supported; boys did not show more consensus than the girls. There are several possible reasons for this, the most likely of which has been suggested by Stewart et al. (1973); sex differences are liable to be both trait and stimulus specific. Comparing the Stewart study with Study I; Stewart found higher male consensus on Attractive and Wife but no such difference was found in Study I on Good Looking and Like a Wife. The differences between the studies, almost identical methodologically, could be attributed to either the differences in stimuli (physique as opposed to clothes) or to age (adults as against children). However, in another methodologically similar study, Hamid (1968) examined clothes perception in adults and still found the Stewart result of higher male consensus on physically attractive. Thus the age of the subjects in Study I seems the prime influence upon the lack of sex difference. It seems that females learn to hold invididual views of female attractiveness at some stage through adolescence and early adulthood.

7.2.3. Replication and extension — Study II

In order to increase our understanding of the type of stereotyped perceptions liable to be applied to clothes and in order to elucidate sex differences, if any, a second study of stereotyping in childhood was undertaken (Study II). In this instance 108 boys (mean age 14.7) and 76 girls (mean age 14.6) ranked the six figures of Study I on 20 traits. The traits consisted of the 11 used in Study I interspersed with 9 new ones that centred around social activity, an aspect of interpersonal judgement liable to be closely related to clothing. The 20 traits are listed in Table 7.3 presented with their associated *W*s for boys, girls and, since the boys and girls differed in both mean age and numbers, a group of boys matched for age and number with the girls. Difference in consensus between the matched boys and girls was ascertained using the z test procedure, and the significance of the resultant P is indicated, this time using two tailed probabilities since Study I shows we should not expect sex differences.

There are several points in these data to bring out. First, considering only those traits that were used in both Studies I and II, the children of Study II showed higher consensus than the younger children of Study I. Thus the hypothesis of increased social responding with age is again supported. The only contraindications are that Study II boys stereotyped the figures rather less on the traits Good Looking, Likes Parties, and Like I Will Be. However one must expect some random fluctuations, and, more important, local social group differences are superimposed upon the age trend.

Second, comparing the consensus shown in Study II with that of the adolescents of Study I, children similar in age but differing in physical location, the boys in both studies show similar group conformity. The girls, however, tend to show higher consensus in Study II, suggesting that here we have a socially more cohesive group of girls. Perhaps their environment is rather more uniform, perhaps their group has rather more mutual or reciprocal friendship structures, perhaps the individual characteristics of the groups members are different. It is difficult to select groups matched according to such criteria but certainly the relationship between social structure and social learning in an aspect of stereotyping that deserves to be high on the list of future research priorities. The parameter of individual differences or characteristics is taken up in a later chapter.

The third point concerns sex differences in degree of concordance. The girls in Study II showed trends towards greater consensus on 14 of the 20 traits. These trends do reach significance on 5 occasions whereas the boys have significantly higher *W*s on only 2 traits. One is left with the indication of greater agreement amongst the females. Therefore, there has been no support in our work for the original hypothesis of higher male consensus; rather, in fact, some evidence to reverse that prediction has been found. It may be that during early adolescence children reach a peak of socially determined perceptions prior to the transition into an adult world. At this time, length of acquaintanceship with the childhood reference group will be maximal, and thus maximal learning would be anticipated. Thereafter, the child leaves his childhood world; he moves towards leaving school and is old enough to start being accepted by early adult groups. This is especially relevant to the present results, because of earlier social and sexual maturity in females. It is possible, therefore, that

Table 7.3

CWs for boys, matched boys, and girls in Study II, and the significance of the differences in *CWs* between matched boys and girls.

Trait	Boys (*N*=108)	Matched Groups Girls (*N*=76)	Matched Groups Boys (*N*=76)	P_{diff}
Likes Parties	.369	.507	.356	.02
Fights With Other Girls	.521	.655	.526	.03
Like A Wife	.323	.397	.381	ns
Stays Out Late	.299	.309	.368	ns
Steals From Shops	.323	.513	.306	.005
Liked By Men	.282	.346	.288	ns
Doesn't Do What Her Mother Says	.471	.446	.427	ns
Clever	.502	.542	.477	ns
Agrees With Sex Before Marriage	.569	.366	.600	.001
Like A Mother	.358	.404	.398	ns
Has Lots Of Boyfriends	.373	.317	.432	ns
Strict	.358	.433	.405	ns
Likes Discos	.440	.328	.496	.02
Good Looking	.225	.315	.267	ns
Likes Tough Boys	.460	.409	.469	ns
Argues A Lot	.160	.386	.149	.001
Like I Am	.060	.075	.060*	ns
Liked By Women	.226	.399	.223	.02
Likes Kissing	.376	.281	.412	ns
Like I Will Be	.084	.213	.110	ns

* $p. \lesseqgtr .01$. All remaining *ws* significant at the .001 level.

girls reach this peak earlier than do the boys, and that our results reflect this. If all the children were tested again in a year's time, say, one could predict lower female consensus because of their social movement away from childhood referents, and still higher male consensus because of another year of intragroup experience. Obviously, a year by year analysis will be needed in the future to plot precise trends in conformity to peer perceptions.

Our fourth point is that there seems to be a pattern to the kind of traits on which boys show higher consensus. They are Likes Kissing, Has Many Boyfriends, Likes Discos, Stays Out Late, Agrees With Sex Before Marriage, and Likes Tough Boys. These are all vaguely 'immoral' traits. In fact if the reader jumps ahead slightly to Figure 8.1 in the next chapter, it will be seen that these traits all fall into one quadrant of a two-dimensional factor space. This quadrant concerns a type of sociable behaviour that is rather 'loose' in nature. It does seem as if our males in Study II were particularly concordant as to the kind of woman who will be sexually responsive. Given the importance of predicting accurately, but with only very limited firsthand information on which to base such predictions, this could account for the adolescents falling back on indirect evidence such as group opinion. Hence the present high levels of consensus on these particular traits are a clear indication of the communicative function of dress (e.g. McKeachie, 1952).

As a final point in this section, it is encouraging to find amongst this abundance of stereotypes that the children in both Studies I and II preserved distinctive identities for themselves. Levels of concordance on Like I Am and Like I Will Be were generally quite low. Essentially this suggests that we had as many 'types' of children as we had stimuli, therefore considerably enhancing the generality of our findings.

7.3. The Social Image of Female Dress

7.3.1 The influence of clothes

There is obviously more to clothes than their purely functional purpose would suggest; they communicate information about a person, leading to value judgement and differential behavioural and expectational responses on the part of the observer.

One of the more studied aspects of this information transmission is the way in which social groups conform to an idiosyncratic mode of dress, such that an individual can be quite accurately labelled or categorised according to his or her reference group. This pattern of social or reference group conformity is not only apparent at the extremes (e.g.

school uniform against brolly and bowler) but also when the possible range of dress is restricted, such that if labelling is to take place it has to be based upon rather subtle cues, such as colour of shirt or the difference between long and short sleeved sweaters. To illustrate the pattern of reference group conformity in matters of dress, Clum & Eicher (1972) analysed the dress and friendships of 241 high school students. They found both boys and girls dressed more like their appropriate reciprocal friendship structure (their group of mutual friends) than like the rest of their school class. Incidentally, the students in this study, which took place in the rural Midwest of the United States, were conforming or conservative overall, it would seem from the given description of, for example, the 'typical' girl; 'dressed in solid brown A-line dress which was 1-2 in. above the knees. She also wore plain nylon hosiery with loafers and had slightly curled medium length hair'. Hence this result was not with a highly fashion conscious group, using 'fashion' in a commercial sense. It points up the fact that 'fashion' has at least two meanings: (i) up to the minute, (ii) a subgroup arbitrary definition.

An interesting follow up was made of the Clum & Eicher (1972) study, by Littrell & Eicher (1973). The longitudinal aspect of Littrell's analysis made possible the investigation of transfer between the mutual friendship groups. Essentially, they found that 'opinions about clothing and appearance seem to be important in the process of movement from social isolation to social acceptance'. However, despite the fact that the girls in another study agreed that clothing played an important role in their school in terms of accepting someone, there was no agreement on why clothing was important (Hendricks et al., 1968), other than the frequent comment 'first impressions count'.

In fact, the first impression aspect of clothes seems to be of considerable importance, as Eicher and Kelly (1972) highlight. Studying high school girls by questionnaire and interview, they found that 'according to the girls . . . it is dress first, then personality, then common interests that lead to the pursual of friendships'. Thus clothing seems a prime consideration in the determination of initial approach responses and could lead to the situation found by Ostermeier & Eicher (1966) that the best dressed girls in high school are most popular with other girls; they simply have more opportunities to find friends. Eicher & Kelly (1972) also touch on the fact that first impression does not mean general impression, since a highly articulated visual analysis is made. As they put it 'while money is usually cited as the reason for "poor" dressing, our findings suggest that a misunderstanding of how to put together the fashion package is equally responsible'. In this respect Kelly & Eicher

(1970) give examples of minute observation such as 'she over teases her hair'.

In Eicher & Kelly (1972), it seems that lower social class girls could wear virtually the same clothes as higher social class girls, but still be judged as 'not dressed right', 'they tried to wear the latest fashions but did not quite know how'. The lower class girls tended to overdo things; which can be fatal as a typical statement from the girls in Hendricks et al.'s (1968) study suggests 'if it's . . . extreme, then this would have a negative effect on popularity'. Finally, to indicate how trivial attention to dress can be, even the wrong coloured bobby socks can lead to rejecting responses (Allen & Eicher, 1973). In the light of this, a mismatched outfit would seem a hanging offence.

Turning from Midwest high schools to the 'real' world, several studies have demonstrated how behavioural interaction is influenced by clothes (Raw, 1976). Here, it would seem that people respond most positively towards others who are similarly dressed. Suedfeld et al. (1971) made use of a Washington peace demonstration mainly attended by young people. A female experimenter dressed as a 'hippie' was able to solicit more signatures for an antiwar petition than a 'straightly' dressed female experimenter. Also, more subjects signed without looking at the petition, and more unsolicited signatures were attracted. In a similar study, somewhat better controlled, Lambert (1972), in London, found that a female experimenter, when dressed tidily rather than untidily, found people more likely to answer market research questions. People can also be better persuaded to part with money as a consequence of dress. Emsuiller et al. (1971) showed that people are more willing to lend a dime for a telephone call to a person if they are similarly dressed.

Clothes will even influence whether an individual will violate the law or risk his life, demonstrated by Lefkowitz et al. (1954). Here pedestrians were more liable to cross at traffic lights when the pedestrian signal said 'Wait' if a high status smartly dressed man modelled, than if a scruffy model was used.

However, even though clothing affects how we attend to our own wellbeing, it does not seem to affect the concern shown over the wellbeing of another. At the same peace demonstration mentioned earlier, Suedfield et al. (1972) found that subjects were just as willing to help a 'hip' person feeling ill as a conventional person, to the extent of providing bus fare or help home. But it is worth mentioning that another manipulation did have an effect upon helping behaviours. 'Ill' people who wore 'Support Nixon' badges rather than 'Dump Nixon' badges received less helping behaviour, and this was even before Watergate. The inverse relationship between Nixon and altruism deserve further research.

Looking at a slightly different aspect of attire, namely tattoos, Taylor (1968) in an investigation of Borstal girls, found that tattoos were used to communicate a variety of messages. The 'messages' included (1) rejection of the nondelinquent social world, (2) masculine and homosexual tendencies, (3) prior incarceration at a Borstal (e.g. the tattoo 'B.O.G.' meant Borstal Old Girls), and (4) sexual willingness (e.g. the tattoo 'LIMP' was an abbreviation for 'Love is my profession').

7.3.2 Social image of figures in Studies I and II

In terms of our own studies, it has been shown so far that the children in Studies I and II rank ordered the six stimulus figures on a variety of traits with generally high consensus. Hence children use fairly similar criteria when judging whether a particular style of dress should be labelled in a particular way. The precise location of each figure on each trait, the social image of each style, is given in Tables 7.4 and 7.5. Also included is the variance of each judgement, which obviously is a rough guide to the certainty of a figures position, the extent to which the group tend to attribute the same rank.

In fact it will be seen that each figure has a distinctly different 'character'. A brief profile of the figures summarising the information from all the children in Studies I and II, regardless of age and sex, illustrates this. Figure A, dressed in trousers and shirt, provoked rather mixed reactions, few of them particularly extreme, and in this respect resembled the mesomorphic female in the physique perception tests. She is not really a man's woman, not very good looking, and not likely to have many boyfriends; but she is likely to be quite popular with other women, with her somewhat wifely and motherly qualities. Of her negative qualities, these tend to be behavioural, not being above fighting or stealing. She is an average person, someone with whom many of our subjects could identify with, especially the children in Study I.

Figure B, the miniskirted female in tightly clinging sweater, represents the number of significant differences is above the number one would expect by chance, but there is clearly no indication of a general sex difference in the attribution of traits to figures. This finding was confirmed in a more qualitative manner by computing *CW*s at the a commonly seen fashion, at its height in England about eight years ago. The miniskirt is still a potent article of clothing, the keynote being its sexual connotations. The figure is particularly liked by men, good looking, and likely to have many boyfriends; the probability of explicit

Table 7.4

Mean Rank and Variance of each figure on each trait, for the four groups of Study I (*ns* = 52)

		A		B		C		D		E		F	
		Mn	Var	Mn	Var	Mn	Var	Mn	Var	Mn	Var	Mn	Var
Likes Parties	YB	3.1	2.0	3.3	1.4	1.6	1.4	3.5	2.5	5.3	1.1	4.2	2.1
	YG	4.0	1.7	3.2	1.3	1.3	0.8	3.6	2.1	5.2	1.5	3.8	2.0
	AB	3.5	1.4	2.1	0.9	2.2	1.9	2.8	1.7	5.5	0.9	4.9	0.9
	AG	4.0	1.2	2.8	1.1	1.7	1.8	2.6	1.4	5.2	1.4	4.8	1.7
Like A Wife	YB	2.5	2.0	3.8	2.5	3.2	3.3	4.9	1.4	3.9	2.5	2.7	2.2
	YG	2.1	1.6	3.3	1.6	4.2	2.6	5.2	0.9	3.8	2.4	2.4	1.9
	AB	2.8	2.5	4.1	1.8	2.9	2.7	5.0	1.1	3.8	2.8	2.5	2.4
	AG	2.6	2.3	3.9	2.3	3.8	2.2	4.7	1.5	4.0	2.7	1.9	1.6
Steals From Shops	YB	3.3	2.1	3.2	2.1	4.7	2.5	2.8	3.0	3.2	3.4	3.9	2.2
	YG	3.1	2.8	2.9	2.2	4.8	2.2	2.6	2.0	3.7	3.6	3.8	1.8
	AB	2.6	2.1	2.9	2.2	4.8	2.0	2.6	1.8	4.2	3.6	3.4	2.9
	AG	2.6	2.0	2.2	1.7	4.9	1.5	3.1	2.3	4.5	2.2	3.8	2.5
Liked By Men	YB	3.0	1.8	2.8	2.8	2.7	2.7	3.3	3.0	4.8	2.1	4.3	1.6
	YG	3.9	1.8	2.6	2.1	2.4	2.3	3.2	2.7	4.7	2.5	4.3	2.0
	AB	3.6	2.2	1.8	1.4	3.3	1.9	2.2	1.6	5.1	1.5	4.7	1.6
	AG	4.1	1.6	2.5	1.5	2.3	1.8	2.3	1.4	4.8	2.1	5.0	1.4
Clever	YB	3.2	2.3	4.1	1.9	3.7	2.3	4.4	2.7	2.3	3.2	3.3	2.5
	YG	3.1	1.6	3.7	2.1	4.2	2.4	4.7	2.3	1.8	2.2	3.5	2.2
	AB	3.7	2.1	4.6	1.5	3.1	2.2	4.8	1.5	1.8	2.5	3.0	1.7
	AG	3.7	1.9	4.7	1.9	3.2	2.1	4.6	1.5	1.6	1.7	3.2	2.3
Like A Mother	YB	2.8	1.8	4.1	1.9	2.6	2.7	5.3	0.8	3.8	2.5	2.4	1.6
	YG	2.6	2.3	3.8	2.0	3.7	2.7	5.0	1.4	3.8	2.2	2.1	1.8
	AB	2.9	1.8	4.4	1.4	3.0	2.1	5.0	1.4	3.6	2.6	2.1	2.9
	AG	2.7	1.7	4.1	2.0	3.6	2.4	4.9	1.4	3.8	2.3	1.8	1.9
Strict	YB	3.5	2.0	4.2	1.7	3.7	3.2	4.2	3.0	2.3	2.8	3.0	2.5
	YG	3.5	2.0	4.0	2.6	3.7	3.2	4.0	2.7	2.5	3.2	3.4	2.6
	AB	3.6	2.1	4.8	1.4	3.3	2.1	4.9	1.4	1.8	1.7	2.6	1.5
	AG	3.8	1.6	4.4	1.8	3.5	1.9	5.0	1.4	2.1	2.4	2.3	2.0
Good Looking	YB	2.7	2.0	2.8	2.4	2.5	2.4	3.7	2.4	4.9	1.9	4.4	1.6
	YG	3.6	2.4	2.9	2.1	2.3	2.1	3.7	2.8	4.3	3.3	4.2	2.0
	AB	3.4	2.6	2.1	1.5	2.7	2.1	3.1	1.8	4.8	2.0	4.8	1.6
	AG	3.7	1.8	3.4	2.2	2.0	1.8	2.6	1.5	4.2	2.7	5.0	2.0
Argues A Lot	YB	3.6	3.3	3.8	2.4	4.3	2.6	2.9	2.5	2.9	3.1	3.5	2.3
	YG	3.6	2.4	3.5	2.6	4.1	3.3	3.1	3.0	3.3	3.4	3.5	2.6
	AB	3.6	2.6	3.1	2.9	4.2	2.6	2.6	1.9	3.5	2.8	4.0	3.3
	AG	2.9	2.4	3.0	2.8	4.0	2.1	3.0	3.0	3.9	3.0	4.1	3.0
Liked By Women	YB	2.6	1.9	3.6	2.3	2.4	2.8	4.6	2.0	4.2	2.5	3.6	2.5
	YG	3.0	2.6	3.7	3.0	2.8	2.4	4.2	2.6	3.8	3.0	3.4	2.9
	AB	3.1	2.3	4.0	2.1	2.3	2.4	4.8	1.4	3.5	2.8	3.3	3.4
	AG	2.8	2.4	4.2	2.4	3.3	2.7	4.8	1.8	2.9	3.0	2.8	2.9
Like I Will Be	YB	2.2	2.4	3.5	2.4	3.1	2.7	4.2	1.9	4.3	2.9	3.8	2.5
	YG	2.6	2.1	2.8	2.8	3.2	2.9	4.0	2.4	4.6	2.5	3.8	2.3
	AB	2.6	2.5	2.8	2.8	2.8	1.6	3.9	1.9	4.4	2.8	4.4	2.4
	AG	2.2	2.8	3.4	2.9	3.0	2.8	3.5	2.2	4.0	3.2	4.2	3.2

sexual contact is high. No wonder she is not rated highly in terms of being popular with other women, nor seen as fulfilling the traditional female role of wife and mother.

If Figure B is popular for the 'wrong' reasons, then Figure C is popular for the right reasons. Our formal ballgown figure is again perceived as being attractive and popular with men; staying out late and having a good social life, and a kiss would not be out of the question. But she is a nice girl, does not argue, fight or steal, and likes the right males (not the toughs associated with Figure B). Thus she can maintain her popularity with other women, since she is rather too correct to pose a real threat. To summarise the difference between Figures B and C using the terminology developed in an earlier section, B is an example of Uncontrolled Sociability whilst C is more typical of Controlled Sociability.

Figure D seems someone who would like to imitate Figure B, but does not quite make it. She is not as attractive or as popular with men overall, although she too has many boyfriends. There is nothing much that is appealing about her personality, nor her behaviour, which is seen as argumentative, disobedient and most unintelligent.

Turning to Figure E, the besuited female, she appears the perfect example of Controlled Unsociability. She is characterised by her cleverness and strictness. Men do not like her, but then she does not like men. Sex before marriage and kissing? Never! Her personal restraint extends to her conformity of behaviours, which is very proper, obedient and honest. If a social life exists, it is not at the level of parties and discos.

Finally, Figure F is definitely the wife and mother image, which implies for the children a lack of interest in, and approval of, boyfriends and sex, perhaps consequent upon the perceived loss of attractiveness.

7.3.3 Sex differences in impression formation

One of the first questions addressed was whether boys and girls would differ in the interpretation they place upon clothes. Therefore, taking the data of Study I, sex differences were determined by *t* test comparison of each figure on each trait. Of the 66 comparisons (11 traits by 6 figures) at the younger age levels, only 6 were significant (1 at the .05 level, 4 at the .01 level and 1 at .001). Of the 66 comparisons at the adolescent age, still only 10 were significant (3 at .05, 5 at .01 and 2 at .001). It is apparent that the number of significant differences is above the number one would expect by chance, but there is clearly no indication of a general sex difference in the attribution of traits to figures. This finding was confirmed in a more qualitative manner by computing *CW*s at the younger and older age of the sexes combined, as presented in Table 7.6.

Table 7.5

Mean Rank and Variance of each figure on each trait for the Boys (n = 108) and Girls (n = 76) of Study II

		A		B		C		D		E		F	
		Mn	Var	Mn	Var	Mn	Var	Mn	Var	Mn	Var	Mn	Var
Likes Parties	B	4.0	2.0	3.2	1.4	1.5	1.2	3.6	2.7	4.5	2.3	4.2	2.0
	G	4.7	1.7	3.4	1.3	1.1	0.2	3.5	2.1	4.4	1.9	3.9	2.2
Fights with Other Girls	B	2.3	1.7	2.7	1.7	5.3	1.0	2.2	1.7	4.5	2.3	3.9	1.1
	G	1.7	1.1	2.3	0.9	5.5	0.6	2.9	1.5	4.7	1.2	3.9	1.5
Like A Wife	B	3.7	2.1	4.2	1.7	2.4	2.0	5.0	1.6	3.0	2.8	2.7	2.4
	G	3.7	2.2	3.9	1.7	3.4	2.1	5.2	1.2	2.8	2.5	1.9	1.5
Stays Out Late	B	3.3	2.2	2.5	2.5	3.1	2.9	2.7	2.0	4.9	1.7	4.6	1.6
	G	3.4	2.6	2.8	1.8	2.4	1.9	3.0	2.5	4.8	2.1	4.6	1.9
Steals From Shops	B	2.6	2.1	2.8	1.8	5.0	1.4	2.5	2.5	4.2	2.6	3.7	2.3
	G	2.1	1.8	2.3	1.4	5.4	0.7	3.0	1.8	4.6	2.1	3.7	1.8
Liked By Men	B	4.0	2.3	2.5	2.1	2.4	1.9	3.3	2.5	4.2	2.8	4.6	1.7
	G	5.1	1.6	3.1	2.0	1.9	1.5	3.4	2.3	3.5	2.6	4.1	2.2
Doesn't Do What Her Mother Says	B	2.9	2.1	2.3	1.1	4.5	1.9	2.0	1.6	4.8	1.6	4.4	1.8
	G	2.7	2.0	2.2	1.2	4.4	1.8	2.4	2.1	5.1	1.5	4.2	1.9
Clever	B	4.1	2.0	4.4	1.6	2.9	1.6	5.0	1.3	1.6	1.4	3.0	1.8
	G	4.2	2.8	4.6	1.0	3.2	1.4	4.7	1.5	1.3	0.6	2.9	1.7
Agrees With Sex Before Marriage	B	3.3	1.6	1.8	0.8	4.0	2.0	2.2	1.5	5.1	1.4	4.7	1.3
	G	3.5	2.4	2.2	1.2	3.8	1.8	2.4	2.4	4.9	1.8	4.2	2.3
Like A Mother	B	3.6	2.5	4.4	1.8	2.6	2.1	5.1	1.4	2.8	2.1	2.6	2.1
	G	3.7	2.9	4.3	1.3	3.4	2.0	5.0	1.5	2.7	2.2	1.8	1.4
Has Lots Of Boyfriends	B	3.7	2.0	2.2	1.5	3.2	2.4	2.5	2.0	4.6	2.3	4.8	1.5
	G	4.7	1.6	2.8	1.9	2.2	1.5	2.9	2.4	4.0	2.8	4.4	2.5
Strict	B	3.7	2.2	4.5	1.6	3.5	2.3	4.6	2.1	2.0	2.3	2.6	1.7
	G	3.9	2.3	4.5	1.4	3.6	1.9	4.6	2.0	1.5	0.9	2.8	2.3
Likes Discos	B	3.7	1.4	2.2	1.3	3.5	2.8	2.0	1.7	4.8	1.8	4.7	1.6
	G	4.4	1.6	2.5	1.3	2.9	3.1	2.3	2.2	4.5	2.4	4.4	1.9
Good Looking	B	3.9	2.2	2.6	2.1	2.4	2.2	3.5	2.6	4.0	3.1	4.6	1.8
	G	4.9	1.7	3.9	1.7	2.0	1.2	3.5	2.4	2.9	2.8	3.9	3.0
Likes Tough Boys	B	2.9	2.0	2.4	1.5	4.4	2.0	2.0	1.4	4.7	2.0	4.6	1.5
	G	2.3	2.4	2.5	1.3	4.6	1.7	2.6	2.0	4.6	2.2	4.4	1.6
Argues A Lot	B	3.0	2.8	2.9	1.9	4.5	1.7	2.7	3.2	4.1	3.0	3.8	2.6
	G	2.2	2.0	2.6	1.5	4.9	1.1	2.8	2.1	4.6	2.6	3.9	2.5
Like I Am	B	3.1	3.1	3.2	2.4	3.1	2.4	3.8	2.7	3.7	3.4	4.1	2.6
	G	3.5	3.3	3.7	2.8	3.0	2.0	4.3	2.2	3.0	3.2	3.5	2.9
Liked By Women	B	3.8	2.3	4.0	2.8	2.5	2.0	4.7	1.8	2.7	2.7	3.4	2.5
	G	4.4	2.2	4.5	1.1	2.6	1.9	4.6	2.0	2.3	2.2	2.5	2.0
Likes Kissing	B	3.9	2.2	2.0	1.5	3.0	2.2	2.7	2.3	4.7	2.0	4.7	1.4
	G	4.3	2.1	2.7	1.6	2.5	2.1	2.7	2.5	4.5	2.3	4.3	2.6
Like I Will Be	B	3.2	3.3	3.1	2.3	2.9	2.5	3.8	2.8	3.9	3.1	4.3	2.4
	G	4.1	2.7	4.0	1.9	2.4	1.7	4.4	2.3	2.8	3.2	3.3	2.7

younger and older age of the sexes combined, as presented in Table 7.6.

As can be seen, the *CW*s for the combined sex groups are virtually as high as the sexes considered separately (Table 7.6). Therefore, when boys and girls stereotype clothes they are using the same criteria of judgement, otherwise the combined *CW*s would have fallen sharply. A very similar conclusion can be drawn by comparing the boys and girls of Study II.

Table 7.6

*CW*s obtained by pooling the sexes in Study I: a smaller than expected *CW* for pooled sexes implies that the Boys and Girls have employed different criteria when forming their impressions

	CW boys	*CW* girls	*CW* for Combined Sexes[1] Expected[2]	Obtained[3]	Implications for Criteria
Children					
Likes Parties	0.415	0.476	0.446	0.470	Same
Like A Wife	0.227	0.385	0.310	0.314	Same
Steals From Shops	0.140	0.177	0.159	0.171	Same
Liked By Men	0.219	0.251	0.236	0.247	Same
Clever	0.167	0.281	0.224	0.243	Same
Like A Mother	0.369	0.307	0.337	0.346	Same
Strict	0.148	0.088	0.119	0.127	Same
Good Looking	0.289	0.170	0.229	0.239	Same
Argues A Lot	0.087	0.032	0.060	0.069	Same
Liked By Women	0.210	0.078	0.143	0.151	Same
Like I Will Be	0.171	0.160	0.164	0.172	Same
Adolescents					
Likes Parties	0.570	0.520	0.546	0.582	Same
Like A Wife	0.256	0.298	0.278	0.288	Same
Steals From Shops	0.243	0.319	0.282	0.271	Same
Liked By Men	0.481	0.459	0.470	0.454	Different
Clever	0.355	0.356	0.355	0.396	Same
Like A Mother	0.313	0.352	0.333	0.359	Same
Strict	0.426	0.378	0.401	0.447	Same
Good Looking	0.353	0.332	0.342	0.332	Same (?)
Argues A Lot	0.094	0.091	0.093	0.091	Same
Liked By Women	0.197	0.206	0.201	0.167	Different
Like I Will Be	0.214	0.158	0.187	0.135	Different

1. Unlike *W*s, *CW*s obtained by pooling can, because of their insensitivity to anomalous data (see Stewart et al., 1975), exceed the *CW*s obtained for either of the constituent groups.
2. Obtained by averaging the boys' and girls' *CW*s as *z*s.
3. *CW*s obtained by combining the *raw data* of the two sexes and treating it as a single sample.

7.3.4 *Age differences in impression formation*

A different pattern emerges with regard to age differences. Again *t* tests were used to compare adolescent boys with young boys, and the older with the younger girls. For the boys, of the 66 tests, 16 were significant (11 at .05, 2 at .01 and 3 at .001). For the girls, 21 were significant (11 at .05, 5 at .01 and 5 at .001). Thus there are more significant differences than one would expect by chance, indicating that age is an important factor in the impressions created by different clothes. Briefly, the differences were created for the boys by the older ones seeing Figure B (miniskirt) and Figure D (shorts) as more sociable than did the younger boys, correspondingly seeing Figure C (ballgown) as less sociable. The essential differences for the girls was the way in which the adolescents saw Figure D (shorts) as more sociable than the younger ones (the same trend as for the boys), and saw Figure F (the mother type) as less sociable than did the younger girls (again this trend was found in the boys but only significant for Like Parties).

However, one must be cautious in interpreting the differences in social impressions of the adolescents and young children of Study I as purely due to the age factor. All the papers reviewed earlier regarding conformity to dress style indicated that marked local group differences can be obtained with respect to the evaluation of specific clothes. In fact if the children in Study II are compared by eye with the younger children in Study I, many of the 'age' trends of Study I are not apparent. For example, for boys of Study II see the ballgown figure as slightly more sociable than do the younger boys of Study I. Therefore it is probably more accurate in this particular instance to conceive of the young children and adolescents of Study I and the children of Study II simply as three different social groups whose detailed normative attitudes are dictated by local school convention above and beyond an overall generalised cultural model.

If a conclusion is to be drawn from the three-way comparison of specific dress interpretation, it is that group differences in evaluating people tend to lay primarily along a sociability dimension. This might be restated within the framework of earlier studies. Sociability can in part be defined or assessed as the acceptability of an individual into an observers' reference or social group. Since social groups differ in their dress conventions, and since dress has been shown as an important aspect of acceptability, it follows that the perceived sociability of a particular individual will also differ from group to group.

8 Perceived Trait Relationships

8.1 Introduction

A major difficulty in studying trait associations has been how to represent people's inferences in at least a quasiformal manner, an especially difficult problem when such inferences have been collected as free response data (e.g. Beach & Wertheimer, 1961). This is a problem addressed by Implicit Personality Theory (Rosenberg & Sedlak, 1972), in which the aim is to structurally represent 'implicit' theories of personality as opposed to the 'explicit', formally stated, theories of personality. The former is more likely to predict interpersonal judgement than the latter. This has therefore led to the use of trait vocabularies provided by the investigator, so that cluster, factor and principal component analysis become appropriate. The loss of individual information (such as the type of trait preferentially employed if given choice) is made up for by the gain in terms of interpersonal communalities of trait association. Thus the underlying dimensions of trait association can be defined; a step towards making 'implicit' theories 'explicit'.

8.2 Trait relationships in Study I

The children's Study I can be brought under this general rubric, although obviously limited in scope because of the relatively small number of traits used. Several hypotheses were formulated, born more of intuition than direct experimental information of which there is only a very limited amount concerning children and adolescents.

H(1) Children will distinguish between the primarily social traits, Likes Parties and Good Looking, and the familial traits, Like a Mother and Like a Wife.

H(2) Boys will identify themselves more with the social traits than the familial traits. Girls showing the opposing trend.

H(3) Children will distinguish between two traits with social connotations, but differing in sexual implications: Liked by Men and Liked by Women.

As a preliminary investigation of these hypotheses, four correlation matrices are computed (i.e. one for each of YB, YG, AB and AG) using

Table 8.1 Mean Correlations[1] between traits for Young Boys (YB), Young Girls (YG), Adolescent Boys (AB), and Adolescent Girls (AG), with corresponding significance levels shown in the upper triangle

		1	2	3	4	5	6	7	8	9	10	11
1. Likes Parties	YB	—	001	001	NS	NS	001	001	001	NS	001	001
	YG	—	001	001	05	NS	001	NS	001	001	005	001
	AB	—	001	001	01	001	NS	NS	NS	001	001	001
	AG	—	001	001	001	001	001	NS	NS	001	001	005
2. Liked By Men	YB	48	—	001	NS	NS	001	NS	001	NS	001	001
	YG	54	—	001	NS	NS	001	NS	001	001	001	001
	AB	71	—	001	01	001	NS	05	NS	001	001	001
	AG	75	—	001	005	001	001	NS	NS	001	001	001
3. Good Looking	YB	53	74	—	NS	05	001	001	001	NS	001	001
	YG	52	71	—	NS	NS	001	005	001	NS	001	001
	AB	68	76	—	NS	005	NS	NS	NS	001	001	001
	AG	56	71	—	NS	NS	NS	NS	NS	NS	001	001
4. Like A Wife	YB	06	05	07	—	001	001	001	NS	01	NS	005
	YG	—14	—05	—02	—	001	005	01	NS	001	05	01
	AB	—19	—20	—04	—	001	001	005	001	001	01	02
	AG	—26	—21	—07	—	001	001	05	NS	01	001	01
5. Like A Mother	YB	10	02	16	52	—	001	001	01	005	01	001
	YG	—11	—09	07	66	—	001	001	NS	001	NS	001
	AB	—30	—38	—22	73	—	001	001	001	001	001	NS
	AG	—34	—33	—13	70	—	001	05	005	001	001	NS
6. Liked By Women	YB	35	37	51	35	51	—	001	001	001	05	001
	YG	30	35	58	22	36	—	001	001	02	01	001
	AB	05	—09	12	49	43	—	001	001	001	NS	001
	AG	—29	—25	01	45	49	—	001	05	001	001	001
7. Steals From Shops	YB	—27	—13	—24	—25	—31	—38	—	001	01	05	05
	YG	—12	—09	—23	—19	—28	—28	—	001	005	NS	NS
	AB	02	15	—05	—21	—25	—37	—	001	001	005	NS
	AG	12	08	—15	—14	—16	—32	—	001	001	001	NS
8. Argues A Lot	YB	—25	—31	—43	—12	—20	—47	33	—	05	001	001
	YG	—24	—26	—43	—08	—13	—47	43	—	NS	001	001
	AB	01	02	—01	—37	—35	—36	36	—	001	NS	01
	AG	11	03	—12	—10	—21	—16	36	—	005	NS	NS
9. Clever	YB	—09	00	01	19	22	24	—19	—14	—	05	NS
	YG	—39	—26	—11	29	34	18	—21	—12	—	001	NS
	AB	—39	—48	—29	36	41	44	—46	—27	—	001	NS
	AG	—37	—26	00	19	28	41	—48	—23	—	001	NS
10. Strict	YB	—29	—40	—41	04	20	—16	16	27	14	—	05
	YG	—23	—30	—31	15	12	—19	04	39	25	—	001
	AB	—58	—65	—54	20	33	11	—23	—08	44	—	001
	AG	—45	—47	—38	26	37	33	—24	—07	46	—	NS
11. Like I Will Be	YB	30	42	55	23	29	60	—14	—41	12	—16	—
	YG	35	50	63	19	25	59	—07	—37	03	—30	—
	AB	50	46	64	17	07	27	—08	—20	—03	—31	—
	AG	21	35	48	19	09	27	06	—10	02	—10	—

1. Decimal points omitted from both *r*s and *p*s.

the procedure outlined above in Section 3.9.1. Table 8.1 presents these intercorrelations.

With respect to H(1) it can be seen that Likes Parties is closely allied with Good Looking, and Like a Mother with Like a Wife, and, as predicted, that these social and familial traits show low correlations between themselves with concomitant distinct patterns of implications. In fact the social and familial traits move from relative independence in the young groups to real opposition in the adolescents, who appear to perceive social and family commitments as quite mutually exclusive.

In regard to (H2), the intercorrelations provide support for the notion that boys will identify more with the social than the familial traits (as seen through their respective correlations with Like I Will Be). However, contrary to expectation, so do the girls! Hence it would seem that during adolescence, girls must resolve something of a conflict, inasmuch as they identify with a set of traits that exclude the Wife and Mother roles which they are in reality most liable to assume. Obviously they must revise more favourably their conceptions of Wife and Mother roles: either that or alternatively avoid the roles or, another alternative, assume the roles in a grudging fashion. But there is yet another option, which may, in fact, have been present implicit in these data, that of divorcing the ideas of 'Wives in general' and 'The sort of Wife I will be'. Further research should elucidate patterns of attitude change and rationalisation.

Finally, in support of (H3), the correlations suggest the traits Liked by Men and Liked by Women become more distinct with age. Although both similarly linked to Like I Will Be, Liked by Men is seen primarily as a social trait, and Liked by Women as a familial trait. Liked by Men is thus aligned with sexuality, as had been hypothesised, and this is a trend which increases with age.

8.3 Factor analyses of trait relationships — Study I

Turning to a more formal analysis of the relationships between groups of traits, a principal component analysis approach was employed so as to ascertain the underlying dimensionality of the groups' judgemental structure. Two methods were used to tackle this problem, related but the first based upon the fictional data from a 'typical' subject (i.e. the mean rank of each stimulus figure on each trait — the so called 'consensus grid'), and the second upon the average group intercorrelation matrix.

Considering the first method, a consensus grid was computed for each of the four groups, which formed the input data for Slater's INGRID programme, essentially an unrotated principal component analysis (see

Tutton, 1973, for details). Table 8.2 gives the loadings of each trait upon the first and second components of INGRID, polarised arbitrarily such that Like I Will Be always loads positively. The loadings for each of the four groups is given.

The results generally bear out the inspection of the intercorrelation matrices in regard to H(1), (2) and (3). The first component for all four groups centres about the social/sexual traits of Likes Parties, Liked by Men and Good Looking. For three of the four groups (i.e. except YB) the familial traits of Like a Wife, Like a Mother and Liked by Women load in opposition, together with the other 'unsociable' traits of Clever and Strict, emphasising the perception of family roles as serious and sensible. The finding of a primary dimension that might be labelled 'sociability' supports other findings showing that children describe their peers in terms largely reflecting social attitudes and behaviours (Yarrow & Campbell, 1963). A further term which could describe our primary component is 'extraversion', suggesting a link between our results and at least one explicit theory of personality, that of Eysenck (1947). Indeed,

Table 8.2

Loadings of Each Trait on the First and Second Components of the Principal Component Analyses for Young Boys, Young Girls, Adolescent Boys and Adolescent Girls

	First Component				Second Component			
	YB	YG	AB	AG	YB	YG	AB	AG
% variance	56	51	69	65	34	31	21	18
1. Likes Parties	2.5	2.6	2.8	2.7	−0.8	1.0	1.4	−0.4
2. Liked By Men	1.6	2.0	2.9	2.8	−1.1	0.1	0.2	−0.4
3. Good Looking	2.0	1.5	2.2	2.1	−0.9	0.6	1.0	−0.9
4. Like A Wife	1.1	−1.3	−1.2	−1.6	1.6	2.1	1.4	1.1
5. Like A Mother	1.3	−1.1	−1.8	−1.9	2.1	2.0	1.2	0.8
6. Liked By Women	1.7	0.3	−0.9	−1.6	0.8	1.0	1.6	−0.1
7. Steals From Shops	−1.0	−0.4	1.1	0.8	−0.7	−0.8	−0.9	2.1
8. Argues A Lot	−1.2	−0.3	0.9	0.7	−0.2	−0.6	−0.9	0.9
9. Clever	−0.6	−1.9	−2.3	−1.9	1.4	0.2	0.3	−1.5
10. Strict	−0.8	−0.9	−2.7	−2.5	1.3	0.0	0.2	−0.7
11. Like I Will Be	1.4	0.7	1.1	0.6	0.4	1.2	1.4	0.6

since explicit theories supposedly have an objective reality, they should be evidence in implicit judgement through a process of observational learning.

The second component extracted is more difficult to label, but is more dominated by the familial traits than the social ones. The charactero-logical aspects of the traits, rather than the sociological aspects, seem to have been emphasised, perhaps, with meaning changing slightly for each group.

It was in part due to the confused nature of this second component that the rotated principal component analysis was undertaken. The uncertainty of the nature of the second component, which, in fact, looks to many eyes like an attenuation of the first, is probably due to two factors. First, the number of factors extractable on INGRID is limited to the number of stimuli minus one. Thus in this case all variance has to be forced on to five components. Second, INGRID is an unrotated analysis. Therefore the rotated analysis was additionally employed from which, potentially, a great many factors could be extracted. There is another pertinent difference between the two analyses. The INGRID programme maximises the clustering of stimuli as well as traits, whereas the latter deals with trait relationships only, although of course these relationships were obtained in the first instance through the consideration of the stimuli.

The rotated principal component analysis is presented in Table 8.3. Each group exhibits two dimensions, well defined in terms of factor loadings and very similar between groups. The first factor is sociability, as indicated by Likes Parties, Liked by Men, Good Looking, and, to some extent, Liked By Women; thus stressing being popular and having a good time, in contrast to Strict and Clever roles. The second factor concerns adult family roles, in terms of Like A Wife and Like A Mother, together with Liked By Women, Clever and Strict, to a lesser degree. The two components reflct something of a childhood/adulthood dichotomy as well.

Therefore, H(1) and H(3) again receive substantial support, as with the consensus grid analysis. Also, H(2) was again rejected; for both Boys and Girls, Like I Will Be loaded more heavily on the social component. As has been discussed, this does not necessarily mean that Girls are rejecting the most typical female roles, since the loadings of Like I Will Be on the family role component are not actually negative. Rather, it could be that they are rejecting the stereotype of female roles. However, whether the compromise conception of a socially orientated women's family role can be adhered to in the face of reality, is a different matter. For a start, compatibility probably has to be achieved with the future husband's expectations. Finally, the obvious omission in the present data is a consideration of male adult family roles. Whether boys prefer to adopt a strict, serious paternal role, or to continue enjoying themselves, is a question for future studies.

8.4 Sex and age differences in Study I

Throughout this discussion of implicity personality judgement, it will have been noticed that there are very few marked sex differences or age differences in the configuration of the underlying dimensions. However, if differences do exist in terms of the ranking of the objects on which these factors are based, do these differences fall into a meaningful pattern or are they distributed randomly? Briefly, if the mean rank of each figure on each trait as given by one group is subtracted from the respective means of another group, then one can undertake a principal component analysis of this grid of difference scores, all this being the analysis of the DELTA programme (Slater, 1976). Hence the components along which

Table 8.3

Loadings of each Trait on the first two Rotated Principal Components

	First Component				Second Component			
	YB	YG	AB	AG	YB	YG	AB	AG
1. Likes Parties	.71	.74	.84	.75	—.06	—.22	—.14	—.19
2. Liked By Men	.85	.86	.86	.87	—.15	—.09	—.11	—.12
3. Good Looking	.88	.82	.90	.92	—.01	.03	—.00	.06
4. Like A Wife	—.12	.08	.01	—.01	.73	.86	.97	.90
5. Like A Mother	—.11	.09	—.18	—.14	.85	.86	.90	.83
6. Liked By Women	.45	.55	.20	.02	.59	.37	.47	.66
7. Steals From Shops	—.21	—.15	—.02	—.06	—.45	—.06	.24	.14
8. Argues A Lot	—.51	—.15	—.15	—.15	—.26	.11	—.33	.03
9. Clever	—.19	—.41	—.35	—.15	.56	.50	.11	.07
10. Strict	—.70	—.29	—.70	—.51	.38	.43	.04	.22
11. Like I Will Be	.55	.79	.76	.67	.33	.33	.31	.57

groups differ are obtained. The loadings on the first component for each of the two age and two sex comparisons are given in Table 8.4.

By inspection of this Table, it can be seen that group differences in attribution fall along the same dimensions as the groups' judgemental dimensions. The younger boys and girls differ primarily in their attribution of family role characteristics, the older children in the attribution of the social traits. With respect to age differences in attribution, these fell for both sexes along a social dimension. Therefore, although the four groups in question exhibited approximately the same dimensions of judgement, there were group differences in the application of these dimensions to the evaluation of target persons. Stimuli were placed differently within the same frame of reference, indicating that the same object can have a different meaning for different groups, a question of impression formation which will be taken up in a later section.

Table 8.4

Loadings of Each Trait on the First Component of the Principal Component Analyses of the Differences in Mean Rank of each Figure on each Trait between YB and YG, AB and AG, YB and AB, and YG and AG

	Sex Comparisons		Age Comparisons	
	YB-YG	AB-AG	YB-AB	YG-AG
1. Likes Parties	0.8	0.9	1.7	1.4
2. Liked by Men	0.7	1.4	1.7	1.0
3. Good Looking	0.8	1.7	1.2	1.1
4. Like A Wife	—1.1	—0.7	—0.3	—0.2
5. Like A Mother	—1.0	—0.7	0.0	—0.2
6. Liked By Women	0.0	—0.5	—0.6	—1.1
7. Steals From Shops	—0.3	—0.5	0.3	0.1
8. Argues A Lot	0.1	—0.4	0.9	0.7
9. Clever	—0.4	0.1	—0.9	—0.4
10. Strict	0.0	—0.7	1.2	—1.6
11. Like I Will Be	0.0	0.3	0.9	0.4

8.5 Trait relationships in Study II

We can now turn to Study II, which fills out our knowledge of the factor structure found in Study I because of its enlarged vocabulary of 20 rather than 11 traits. The intercorrelation matrices for the boys and girls in Study II are presented in Table 8.5.

By inspection, these results are a reasonable replication of Study I intercorrelations: the social groupings of Good Looking, Likes Parties, and Liked By Men is again apparent; the so called familial cluster of Like A Mother, Like A Wife, and Liked By Women is evidenced; Clever and Strict are paired; and finally Argues and Steals are related.

As for the new traits, they generally aligned themselves with the dimensional structure of Study I traits. Thus to the social cluster were added Has Lots Of Boyfriends, Likes Kissing, Likes Discos and Stays Out Late; the traits Fights With Other Girls, Likes Tough Boys and Doesn't Do What Her Mother Says, join Steals From Shops and Argues A Lot to provide the tone of a 'deviant' grouping; and Like I Am was strongly associated with Like I Will Be. The position of Agrees With Sex Before Marriage is somewhat unclear, seeming to fall between the social and deviant groups.

A more precise examination of the underlying structure of these intercorrelations was undertaken by performing rotated principal component analyses on Boys and Girls treated separately. Three orthogonal factors were extracted for each group, and the loadings of each trait on each factor, for both Boys and Girls, is given in Table 8.6. Also, for ease of comprehension, Figures 8.1 and 8.2 plot the location of all the traits in a space defined by the first two factors, for Boys and Girls respectively.

Considering the Boys' location of traits first of all, that is, Figure 8.1, it can be seen that their two factors represent two aspects of social behaviour. Factor I will be termed Social Control, refining the previously labelled 'familial' dimension. One pole of this factor is characterised by deviant behaviours (stealing and fighting), by a lack of respect for others' opinions (argues and disobeys mother), and by a preference for similar sounding males (liking tough boys). This 'hard' picture thus indicates a resistance to social controls. At the other pole of this factor there lay the conventional roles of Mother and Wife, the 'soft' trait of Liked By Women, and the mature, orderly traits of Clever and Strict. These latter traits thus reflect both the acceptance by the individual of social norms and the individual's behaviour designed to enforce it in others, i.e. both controlled and controlling.

Table 8.5

Table of Intercorrelations[1] for the Adolescent Boys ($N = 108$) and Girls ($N = 74$) participating in Study II. (Correlations due to the Girls are presented in the Upper Triangle)

Traits	1	2	3	4	5	6	7	8	9	10	11	12	13	14	15	16	17	18	19	20
1. Likes Parties	—	—39*	02	50*	—35*	67*	—04	02	18′	—03	60*	—15	54*	59*	—07	—23*	32*	17′	52*	43*
2. Fights	—26*	—	—32*	20′	77*	—39*	68*	—60*	48*	—36*	—15	—44*	08	—48*	69*	72*	—24*	—60*	03	—50*
3. Like A Wife	19*	—55*	—	—38*	—35*	02	—45*	58*	—43*	80*	—15	50*	—27*	12	—48*	—38*	30*	60*	—27*	42*
4. Stays Out Late	25*	32*	—20*	—	15	45*	47*	—44*	56*	—41*	60*	—53*	61*	30*	43*	25*	17′	—29*	65*	11
5. Steals From Shops	—25*	67*	—45*	29*	—	—34*	70*	—59*	55*	—35*	—13	—45*	17′	—46*	67*	71*	—21′	—52*	06	—45*
6. Liked By Men	53*	—12	11	44*	—20*	—	—08	08	24*	—07	83*	—10	56*	74*	—11	—29*	39*	19′	58*	57*
7. Disobedient	—02	61*	—54*	46*	61*	13	—	—72*	67*	—54*	18′	—62*	36*	—28*	71*	69*	—16	64*	34*	—36*
8. Clever	—05	—60*	52*	—45*	—54*	—11	—65*	—	—62*	63*	—14	74*	—36*	32*	—60*	—60*	37*	68*	—31*	50*
9. Premarital Sex	13	53*	—43*	60*	42*	38*	68*	—65*	—	—51*	47*	—63*	57*	08	63*	54*	—04	—52*	60*	—15
10. Like A Mother	08	—51*	68*	—32*	—47*	01	—59*	62*	—56*	—	—25*	58*	—38*	11	—50*	—36*	27*	68*	—32*	37*
11. Popular With Boys	39*	22*	—22*	56*	17′	60*	45*	—42*	66*	—34*	—	—32*	71*	67*	16	—12	39*	—04	70*	43*
12. Strict	—24*	—37*	40*	—46*	—27*	—31*	—53*	56*	—64*	54*	—55*	—	—39*	08	—48*	—45*	18′	52*	—46*	24*
13. Likes Discos	35*	29*	—28*	55*	29*	51*	56*	—44*	70*	—37*	65*	—58*	—	41*	37*	14	24*	—24*	70*	20′
14. Good Looking	50*	—14′	18*	39*	—15′	75*	06	02	33*	05	58*	—27*	48*	—	—21′	—41*	55*	36*	49*	68*
15. Likes Tough Boys	07	63*	—50*	48*	55*	18*	68*	—66*	71*	—56*	50*	—49*	60*	08	—	71*	—06	—62*	29*	—29*
16. Argues A Lot	—09	47*	—37*	21*	45*	—08	50*	—38*	36*	—35*	16′	—19*	27*	—16′	49*	—	—23*	—64*	13	—47*
17. Like I Am	26*	—04	18*	22*	—12	40*	05	08	14′	04	31*	—16′	25*	51*	07	—02	—	31*	25*	77*
18. Liked By Women	21*	—56*	55*	—24*	—47*	14′	—45*	53*	—45*	51*	—20*	33*	—21*	24*	—48*	—38*	18*	—	—17′	51*
19. Likes Kissing	44*	15′	—13	54*	09	67*	43*	—35*	65*	—26*	71*	—53*	72*	64*	44*	09	34*	—06	—	23*
20. Like I Will Be	35*	—10	18*	25*	—18*	48*	02	10	14′	06	35*	—15′	28*	54*	12	—13	65*	29*	36*	—

′ $p < .01$ two-tailed. * $p < .001$ two-tailed.

1. Decimal points omitted. Some trait-names abbreviated (c.f. Table 8.6).

Turning to Factor II, this will be termed Gregariousness, paralleling the similarly named dimension of Study I. Here, sociability is defined by specific behaviours involving a direct intent to be with people, such as Liking Parties, Having Many Boyfriends, and Going To Discotheques; by having the attributes liable to result in having social encounters, i.e. being Attractive and being Liked by Men; and by being approving of low level sexual activity such as Kissing. The traits used did not include

Table 8.6

Factor Loadings for the adolescent Boys and Girls of Study II

	Factor I		Factor II		Factor III	
	Mal.	Fem.	Mal.	Fem.	Mal.	Fem.
% variance accounted for	33%	29%	25%	28%	9%	18%
Likes Parties	—38	—34	—77	—79	00	—08
Fights With Other Girls	94	95	25	27	11	11
Like A Wife	—64	05	08	17	24	84
Stays Out Late	37	25	—51	—69	11	—17
Steals From Shops	92	98	35	24	17	15
Liked By Men	—27	—30	—88	—88	09	01
Doesn't Do What Her Mother Says	79	81	—13	—11	09	—09
Clever	—67	—43	24	11	19	53
Agrees With Sex Before Marriage	59	64	—49	—44	—03	—08
Like A Mother	—66	—01	17	25	15	82
Has Lots of Boyfriends	22	—01	—76	—91	03	01
Strict	—32	—32	59	34	21	43
Likes Discos	36	22	—63	—77	06	—07
Good Looking	—32	—31	—80	—77	26	24
Likes Tough Boys	84	88	—11	—10	12	05
Argues A Lot	79	90	28	17	22	05
Like I Am	09	32	—10	—45	87	87
Liked By Women	—67	—43	—08	—02	21	49
Likes Kissing	07	19	—84	—79	04	—07
Like I Will Be	05	—06	—26	—54	77	71

sufficient nonsociable ones to define clearly the opposite pole of this factor, but the trait Strict best gives the flavour of unsociability, suggesting an unwillingness to be expansive towards people and a tendency to keep morals under too tight a rein.

It is interesting to view the traits in the light of these Social Control and Gregariousness factors. With Boys, for example, Agreeing With Sex Before Marriage is uncontrolled sociability, while Stealing, Fighting and Arguing reflect uncontrolled unsociability. Considering the other quadrants, Strict implies controlled unsociability, and Liking Parties comes nearest to representing controlled sociability. Here, the difference between the uncontrolled sociability of Going To Discos and the controlled sociability of Liking Parties can be noted. Discos seem to suggest youthful, spontaneous activity, whereas parties are institutions to be found at any age level with varying degrees of formality. Similarly, being Attractive and being Liked by Men suggest an element of control, perhaps because they are attributes which can be utilised at the individuals' discretion, whereas Having Many Boyfriends reflects some lack of control, perhaps because the individual has decided to utilise the mentioned attributes somewhat loosely.

Turning to the trait structure presented by the Girls, this is remarkably similar to the Boys', with three important differences. First, the concepts of Mother and Wife have shifted towards the middle of the Social Control dimension (i.e. becomes less controlled and controlling). Does this represent the beginning of a revaluation of these roles to become congruent with personal preferencs and aspirations? Second, the Self and Future Self concepts are more sociable in nature, possibly due to the greater social/sexual maturity of girls at this age. Third, and this concerns Factor III as in Table 8.6, Girls, more than Boys, align themselves with the female roles of Wife and Mother. This is not, it may be remembered, a result that was found in Study I although predicted. But its appearance here is possibly due to the inreased variety of traits, a condition that may have an effect upon factor structure, by sensitising subjects towards particular aspects of judgement, and giving a greater opportunity for sex diferences in the evaluation of the roles to emerge. This last point is important since it is quite clear that the concepts of Wife and Mother with which the girls associate themselves are in part different from the concepts that the Boys hold. Boys too might have been more prepared to relate themselves to these adult roles if they had evaluated them in a 'better' (i.e. less controlled) manner. In Study I, then, Boys and Girls on a limited sample of traits evaluated Mother and Wife in the same way, and aligned their future self with them in the same way. Thus the

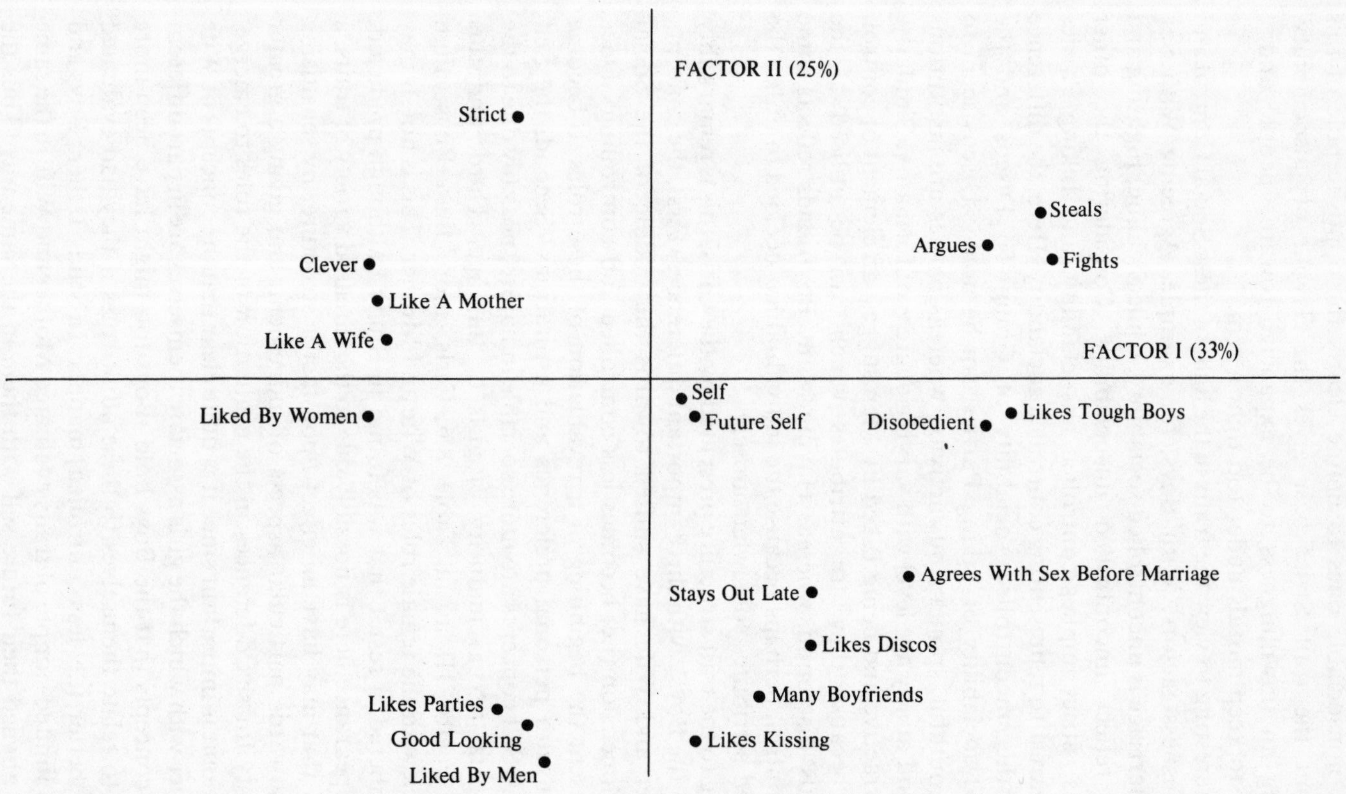

Figure 8.1 Two dimensional trait space (Sociability x Control) for the 108 adolescent boys participating in Study II.

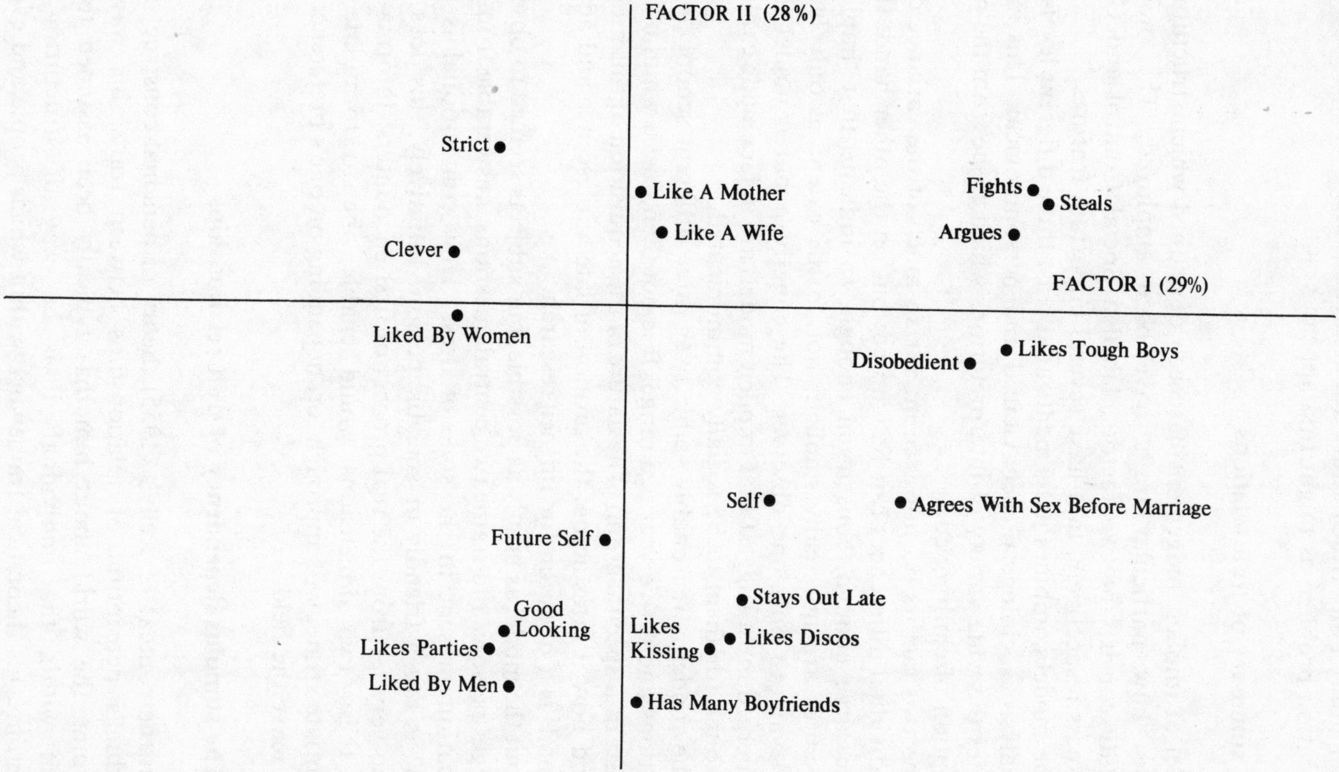

Figure 8.2 Two dimensional trait space (Sociability x Control) for the 74 adolescent girls participating in Study II.

results of Study I and Study II are not as incompatible in respect to this identification problem as might first appear.

8.6 A summary of trait relations

A model of implicit judgement has been developed which structurally describes how particular traits have been employed. The model essentially consists of two factors, labelled Social Control and Gregariousness respectively, that have several important features.

1. The model combines judgements at at least three different levels of analysis: sociological, behavioural and personological. This indicates the wide variety of interpretations which ensue from the perception of clothing cues.
2. The two factors do not account for so much of the variance that individual differences can be ignored; but on the other hand, they are large enough, consensual enough, to indicate that 'implicit' theories are not really implicit, not to the extent of only being relevant to only one observer. The cohesive, shared model that emerged must suggest that implicit models are in fact made explicit enough for them to be socially communicated.
3. The model is reasonably stable over three different school populations and a five year age range. It is not then, just a whim on the part of a specific group. The nature of the acquisition of this model, and how it fares across the turmoil of late adolescence and adulthood, is a question for further research.

To put the model as briefly as possible, our subjects seemed to observe the target persons and frame two central questions, answerable from the information present in the style of dress. How conventional is this person? Is this a friendly or sociable person? Intuitively, this does not seem so very far from the real process of first encounters. Information along these two dimensions would enable one to formulate an appropriate strategy of approach, or, depending on one's preferences, a cue to leave the field.

8.7 The stimulus dependency of trait relationships

Within the context of Kelly's (1955) theory of personal constructs, an individual's perception of relationships between traits, his way of construing the world about him, has typically been assumed to be implicit within that individual. It is his way of structuring his perceptions, his theoretical framework within which people and events can be evaluated. However, the idea that external stimuli are always evaluated within the same, single framework at a given point in time, that seems to follow from a 'one person one model' notion, is worth examining closely. Kelly describes how people's model changes over time as a result of confirmations and rejections of hypotheses, indicating temporal flexibility in the system. But could there also be a certain flexibility regarding different stimuli? This has been found to be the case in regard to another aspect of trait relations, that of cognitive complexity. Flexibility of framework is obviously the case when extremely different stimuli are observed, since different adjectives are used, and it does not make much sense, say, to evaluate objects as if they were people. Flowers, for example, are seldom viewed as more or less intelligent, or more or less sociable. The range of convenience of such constructs does not include inanimate objects, unless by association. But if two objects are appropriately described by the same set of constructs, does it follow that they are evaluated within the the 'same' framework? It is possible that there might be contextual factors regarding two such similar stimuli which could bias the evaluative structure. Could the location of an object within a framework change the nature of that framework?

In terms of our studies, the question posed was whether correlations between traits were the same for each of the six target persons. Normally, a group correlation matrix is computed by averaging across subjects the correlation between each pair of traits. Considering one subject, information from all the stimuli are used to compute the correlations. However, one can equally as well take the figures one by one, in a group situation, correlating for each, rank on one trait with rank on all the others. In this manner, six intercorrelation matrices are computed, one for each target person. This method of obtaining a matrix per stimulus was employed on the data of 91 English males who graded six physiques (two endomorphs, two mesomorphs and two ectomorphs, one of each pair a more extreme example of the somatotype than the other) on ten supplied traits.

It seemed likely that the more different the stimuli, the greater the probability of their being evaluated within a slightly different structure. In terms of the physiques the greatest difference visually seems to be between the ectomorphs and the endomorphs, with an impressive difference in sheer bulk. Since the greatest differences evaluatively also lay between these somatotypes (with the mesomorphs generally falling between them), it was hypothesised that:

H(1)The greatest difference between physiques in terms of perceived trait intercorrelations will be between the endomorphs and the ectomorphs.

H(2)The mesomorphs' correlations will be approximately equidistant from the remaining two somatotypes.

Procedurally, intercorrelations were computed for each physique, then, taking the figures two at a time through all the 15 possible combinations, each respective correlation was compared using z equivalents. The number of significantly different rs for each comparison of physique is tabulated in Table 8.7.

Since each cell in this Table represents 45 comparisons, 675 tests were made overall. Of these the total significant number is 79. Hence this is twice the number one would expect by chance, and the original notion of trait structure changing from stimulus to stimulus receives considerable support.

The distribution of these significant differences is in the direction predicted by H(1) and H(2). The number of significant differences between ectomorphs and endomorphs is 35 (i.e. 6 + 6 + 12 + 11), whereas the number of differences between the mesomorphs and ectomorphs is only half that at 17 (i.e. 3 + 9 + 1 + 4), as is the number of differences between mesomorphs and endomorphs (1 + 4 + 4 + 8). Further, there are only half as many differences between the moderate physiques as the extreme physiques (i.e. 1 + 6 + 3 vs. 8 + 11 + 4), indicating again that the more different or unusual is a stimulus the more likely it is to be viewed within a different trait structure. The evaluation of normal physiques tends to converge upon a single model.

In order to evaluate more exactly what impact different physique has upon trait structure, a rotated principal component analysis was performed for each of the two figures that showed most differences, i.e. the moderate endomorph and the extreme ectomorph. The first two factors extracted for both physiques proved quite similar. There was no radical restructuring. For each physique, the location of each trait within this factor space is presented in figure 8.3.

It can be seen that the first factor roughly corresponds with Attractiveness, a factor which, if given more traits, might have been identified as the Sociability factor described in children's Study I. The second factor is defined by deviant traits, a more precise parallel to the children's second factor of Social Control, which also placed family roles in opposition to socially disapproved behaviour.

Comparing the endomorph with the ectomorph, there are two major instances of shift in trait location, concerning Influential and Prudish. Although these are clearly seen as deviant traits when the endomorph is

Table 8.7

The number of significantly different *r*s when comparing respective trait intercorrelations obtained under six conditions of viewing (six physiques). Each cell represents 45 comparisons[1]

Target Persons[2]	1. Moderate Endomorph	2. Extreme Endomorph	3. Moderate Mesomorph	4. Extreme Mesomorph	5. Extreme Ectomorph
1. Moderate Endomorph	—	—	—	—	—
2. Extreme Endomorph	4	—	—	—	—
3. Moderate Mesomorph	1	4	—	—	—
4. Extreme Mesomorph	4	8	3	—	—
5. Extreme Ectomorph	12	11	1	4	—
6. Moderate Ectomorph	6	6	3	9	3

1. The data were obtained from the 91 males serving in the first UK study (see Chapter 5 for details).
2. Numbers conform to those used in Chapters 3 and 5 and Appendix I.

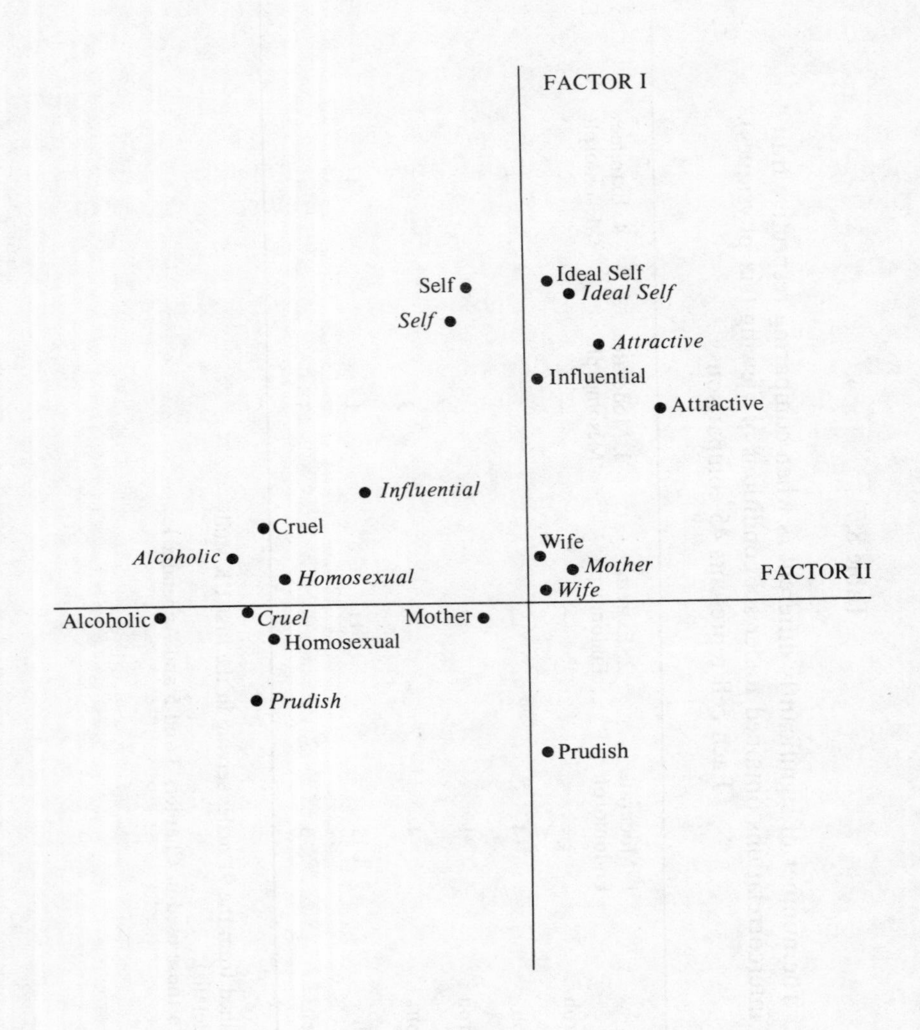

Figure 8.3. The factor structure of traits obtained from 91 male subjects when viewing a moderate endomorph (italics) and an extreme ectomorph (see Chapter 5 for details).

viewed, they are seen as no more deviant than Wife or Mother when considering the ectomorph. Also, in the case of the ectomorph, Influential and Prudish become more polarised about the Self and Attractive dimension. Therefore it would seem that when an unattractive, nonself figure is viewed and evaluated, the undesirable aspects of influence and prudishness are accentuated. When an attractive, selflike physique is evaluated, powers of influence are regarded in a more desirable light (the correlation between Attractive and Influential rises from .19 to .49). At the same time Prudish is treated more as an antonym for Attractiveness, perhaps because of the unsociable implications being accentuated (the correlation between Attractive and Prudish falls from -.17 to -.41). This process described is like someone saying 'my friends and myself are both powerful and attractive people but normally, in other people, power corrupts'.

The extent to which one's implicit personality model is dependent upon the characteristics of the stimulus person is a problem well worth future investigation. At present, we can say that although differences may not be radical, they may be very pertinent. Large changes are only likely when the extremes of stimulus type are evaluated. It is also likely that there will be individual differences in stimulus dependency, concerning, for example, those interpersonal aspects to which an observer is sensitised.

One important question not yet touched upon is whether stimulus dependency of trait correlations can be viewed as a developmental process. If so, then it is difficult to predict as to in which direction the process would move. On the one hand, theories of development often stress increasing articulation or differentiation with age (Werner, 1957), that suggests a likelihood of increasing dependency. In contrast, Kelly's position stresses that based on increasing experience a conceptual model of the world is gradually built up, established and internalised, which suggests a reduction of stimulus dependency with age. Thus the data of children's Study I was approached with an open mind. Since the preceding analysis concerned adult males, only the boys of Study I were considered.

A matrix per stimulus was therefore computed for both the adolescent and the young boys. Considering the adolescents, it was calculated whether any of the six respective correlations for each of the 55 trait pairs differed significantly (roughly equivalent to asking whether the range of the six alternatives was significantly large). It was found that 35 out of the 55 trait pairs showed at least one significant difference between the six alternatives. Thus it can be said that 64 per cent of intercorrelations were to some extent stimulus dependent. Calculating the comparative statistic for the adults, there 58 per cent of intercorrelations showed some dependency. Obviously a comparison between these two percentages must bear in mind the different traits and stimuli used, but at the very least the closeness of the two figures shows that under certain conditions the dependency shown by adults and adolescents can be equal.

The figure by figure analysis was repeated for the younger boys. Only 31 per cent of the intercorrelations showed a degree of stimulus dependency, half that of the adolescents. Therefore the evidence suggests that age leads to increasing stimulus dependency. It seems the younger boys are more rigid in their application of 'rules' of personality and behaviour organisation; their implicit personality theory shows a wider range of convenience. The adolescents and the adults are more prepared to apply different rules to different people.

Finally, to give a concrete example of how the location of a stimulus within a framework can change that framework, it was noticed that when more attractive stimuli were observed there was a trend for the correlation between Self traits and Attractiveness to drop. When the UK adults viewed the grossly obese figure, they rated it as very unlike themselves and very unattractive, and so a high positive correlation of .52 was obtained between Self and Attractive. That is to say that very few subjects would profess to looking like that, and indeed that physiques of that proportion are singularly few in the environment. But when the most aesthetically pleasing target, the moderate ectomorph, was viewed then some subjects saw themselves having a similar body build and some as having a dissimilar body build, while still rating this target as first or second most Attractive. Hence for this most appealing figure, the correlation between Self and Attractive fell to .33. Similarly, the correlation between Ideal Self and Attractive fell from .58 to .42. A comparison of the second least attractive figure with the second most attractive shows precisely the same trend; the correlations fell from .43 to .32, and from .53 to .45 respectively. For the adolescents, the correlation between Like I Will Be and Good Looking fell from .74 for the least good looking figure to .39 for the most good looking. This trend was much slighter for the younger boys, who, as noted, showed less dependency. Their respective correlations were .38 and .34 for the least and most good looking figures.

The pattern is as if when viewing an unattractive person one's own feeling of attractiveness is enhanced. The opposite applies when an attractive figure is evaluated; we have a heightened sense of our own lack of attractiveness. It appears to be a contrast effect. It may well be possible in the future to view implicit personality theory in relation to, for example, adaptation level theories of psychophysical judgement. Parameters such as anchor points and relevancy of cue would assume importance. Careful selection of traits and stimuli will be needed to elucidate the principles of stimulus dependency, and procedures must be developed to assess it in the individual rather than, as here, in the group.

8.8 A note on cognitive complexity

An aspect of cognition which has received some attention over recent years is that of cognitive complexity, a structural concept introduced by Bieri (1955), within the framework propounded by Kelly '1955). Essentially, cognitive complexity is a concept relating to differentiation within, and differentiating powers of, an individual's dimensional system for construing behaviour. As Bieri (1966) puts it, cognitive complexity is the construing of behaviour 'in a multidimensional way', such that a complex person will perceive many facets of others' behaviour, will measure it against several standards, whereas a cognitively simple person, at his simplest, would utilise only one dimension and orientate all other adjectives or descriptions or evaluations about this single criterion. Within the setting of this book, for example, the subject who is able to attribute both good and bad qualities to a target person will be more complex than the observer who assumes and perceives that people are either all good or all bad. The former individual will observe the nuances in people, and hence be able to discriminate well between those in his social universe. The latter's powers of discrimination are not nearly so refined.

Although an appealing idea, complexity has proved an awkward construct, both in terms of its measurement and its implications; even its status as a unitary construct has been brought into question. But the construct's apparent volatility may reflect more our lack of knowledge about important parameters, rather than an inherent instability that would make it a meaningless variable to attach importance to.

In practical terms, complexity has typically been measured by assessing the extent to which an individual's constructs overlap, to which end, to give just one example, the statistic Average Match between Rows (AMR) was developed (Adams-Webber, 1969). As the name of the statistic suggests, a score is derived for each subject by comparing each of his constructs (dichotomously scored) with every other construct and computing the average match. This is obviously an average of crude correlation coefficients. Similar approaches have been used by Bieri

(1955) and Tripodi & Bieri (1963, 1964).

A second method is to compute the amount of variation explained by the first dimension (in factor analytic terms) of a person's cognitive structure. This approach has been used often enough for it now to be referred to as the 'standard' measure (Adams-Webber, 1969). Examples in the literature are rare, but this technique is as noted by Chetwynd-Tutton (1974) prevalent in unpublished doctoral dissertations.

The two approaches described (others have been summarised by Bonarius, 1965) give fairly similar assessments of complexity. In Adams-Webber's (1969) study the AMR score correlated 0.88 with the amount of variance explained by the first component of Kelly's (1963) nonparametric factor analysis; but it will be appreciated that these two measures of complexity were drawn from the same data, that would tend to give a spuriously high correlation between measures. In fact, correlations between measures purporting to assess cognitive complexity are not always high (sometimes, not even always positive!). As an example of this, Vannoy's (1965) factor analysed twenty variables supposed to reflect complexity and did not obtain a single factor. This may reflect the inadequacy of measures, the lack of a unitary complexity dimension, or a mixture of both these reasons.

The literature seems to be drawing the conclusion that first, cognitive complexity is not a unitary concept. Zimring (1971) presents evidence that cognitive simplicity and cognitive complexity represent qualitatively different processes, and are not simply aspects of one dimension, and second, that complexity depends in part upon the nature of the stimulus (Crockett, 1965; Signell, 1966). Thus it is possible for a person to be complex in one aspect of cognition relating to one class of stimuli, but not complex in relation to another which perhaps may have no particular relevance for him. This seems sensible, and not unrelated to Whorf's Hypothesis (Whorf, 1956), which concerns the way in which people from different environments linguistically differentiate aspects of their environment that are of particular importance, Eskimos having many different words for 'snow' for example.

Bearing all these considerations in mind, the cognitive complexity of the children in Study I was investigated being particularly concerned with age and sex differences.

In regard to age differences in complexity, it has been claimed that differentiation is a developmental process (Werner, 1957; Bieri, 1966), but this general principle need not apply to a particular class of stimuli. Children at a very young age might be very concerned about what sort of mud tastes nicest, but not many adults. The particular problem with our stimuli is that they are stereotyped; there is considerable social consensus upon their evaluation, with markedly more consensus at the older age level. This is an important parameter, because it is often tacitly assumed that the social transmission of information leads to its simplification, i.e. that stereotypes are in the traditional viewpoint black and white, that stereotypic perceptions are cognitively simple. This belief yields the following hypothesis, diametrically opposed to that of Bieri (1966):

H(1) Cognitive complexity in dress perception will reduce with age.

Turning to the question of sex differences in complexity, there were no sex differences in stereotyping and so this is not an important consideration. In terms of personal relevance, both boys and girls would seem to have a stake in perceiving the subtleties of dress. Girls have to dress to create an appropriate impression of themselves and boys have to read the cues correctly. Finally, since the literature does not reveal any consistent sex difference in complexity, all the pointers are to the following hypothesis:

H(2) There will be no sex differences in cognitive complexity.

A third hypothesis can be formulated pertaining to the relationship between different measures of complexity, since in our study two can be computed. The first is a refined version of AMR, which is the extent to which subjects perceive correlation between traits, given by the formula Σr^2. The second measure is the amount of variance accounted for by the first component extracted in a principal component analysis, Slater's INGRID. If Adams-Webber's (1969) result is to be replicated, then:

H(3) The perceived degree of correlation between traits will correlate very highly with the size of the first component.

The results of this study, however, were not entirely in line with the hypothesis, as can be seen from Table 8.8 which presents for all four groups of Study I the mean Σr^2 score, the mean percentage of variation explained by the first component, both with the relevant comparisons in terms of t tests, and finally the correlations between these two measures.

The most obvious result is that our two measures of complexity were highly correlated as predicted by H(3), replicating the result of Adams-Webber (1969), to the extent that in the present study they can be treated synonymously. The very high degree of correlation can be attributable to several factors: their computation from the same data; a statistical, computational relationship; a psychological relationship in that they are probably measuring the same entity. But H(3) is the only hypothesis that is supported by the findings.

H(1), that complexity would reduce with age on our test, must be rejected since the Girls clearly increased in cognitive complexity, their degree of perceived overlap between traits becoming smaller and the size of the first component reducing. However, this is not to say that the alternative hypothesis of Bieri (1966) is wholly supported, since the Boys showed reduced complexity in the older age group. Thus neither a stereotyping parameter nor a developmental parameter fully predict the results. The finding of a sex difference in the pattern of development is most probably due to the nature of the stimulus class. Whether the results were dictated by the fact of this being a dress perception test or a female dress perception, or a person perception test or a female person perception test can only be elucidated by further research that systematically manipulates stimulus class. There is already some

Table 8.8

Presenting for the Four Groups of Study I, mean Σr^2, mean per cent variation accounted for by the first Component, Comparisons between Groups by *t* test (Probability two-tailed unless otherwise stated), and the Correlations between the two Measures of Cognitive Complexity

	Young	Adolescent	
	Mean Σr^2		
Boys	18.26	20.42	$p < .05$ (1-tailed)
Girls	19.34	17.00	$P < .05$
	ns	$p < .01$	
	Mean per cent of first component		
Boys	53.76	58.03	$p < .05$ (1-tailed)
Girls	56.22	51.97	$p < .05$
	ns	$p < .01$	
	Correlations of Σr^2 and per cent		
Boys	.9594	.9743	
Girls	.9558	.9577	

evidence of differential patterns of development of complexity dependent upon the nature of the stimulus, Signell (1966) finding, for example, that complexity in nation perception increases with age but remains constant for person perception. It follows from our and Signell's findings that Sex x Stimulus Class interactions will be evident in future research. The present findings allow one important conclusion to be drawn, however. The fact that perceptions of people become more stereotyped does not necessarily imply that those perceptions will show reduced cognitive complexity. Stereotypes do not as a matter of course lead to a simplified view of the world.

Turning to H(2), that there would be no sex differences in complexity, this too must be rejected since the Girls were clearly more complex at the older age level than the Boys. In order to replicate this finding a Σr^2 comparison was made between the Boys and Girls of Study II. Indeed, even with the new traits introduced making it a rather different test, Girls were still significantly more complex ($p. < .01$).

As discussed above, the reasons for this sex difference can only be determined by varying stimulus class. But for the moment, it might be observed that women's clothes have more interpretative meaning for other women than for men, the learning for this taking place through late childhood and adolescence. The women's complaint that her mate has only a blunt appreciation of her dress sense seems to have a basis in reality.

8.9 A note on personality, self and attractiveness

In the preceding sections it has been the consensual aspects of social perception that have been emphasised. However, it must be recognised that individual differences are liable to moderate the perceived relationships between different traits, as in the way the Wife role has been differentially evaluated by the two sexes. Most obviously, one would expect the Self construct to relate to the other traits dependent upon personality, i.e. children should describe themselves on the stereotyping task in a manner consistent with self reported personality.

With a view to substantiating this proposition, the matched groups of 76 children in Study II were administered the Eysenck Personality Questionnaire that yields three personality scores: Psychoticism or Tough mindedness (P), Extraversion (E) and Neuroticism (N) (Eysenck & Eysenck, 1976). The children were also given the Children's Scale of Social Attitudes (Wilson, Nias & Insel, 1972) that assessed Conservatism (C) or orthodoxy of beliefs. Lastly, each child completed a self report scale of antisocial behaviour (ASB) in which various misbehaviours were affirmed or denied (Powell, 1977).

8.9.1 Method

The dimensions of P, E, N, C and ASB were related to trait association in the following manner. First, for each child a rank order correlation coefficient was computed between Like I Am and every other trait (making 19 separate correlations). Then each of the 19 correlations, which might be conveniently labelled 'trait distances', was treated as a variable in its own right and correlated with each of P, E, N, C and ASB. One could tell, therefore, whether the trait distance between, say, Agrees With Sex Before Marriage and Like I Am, varied systematically with, say, Extraversion. If the resulting correlations were positive in this particular instance, it would mean that Extraverts saw themselves as more agreeing with sex before marriage. If the correlation was negative, it would imply the opposite — that Extraverts saw themselves as less agreeing with sex before marriage.

8.9.2 Results for self image

In Table 8.9 we have the details of this analysis of self image, giving all the significant ($p < .05$) correlations between personality factors and trait distances. There is one proviso that should be borne in mind when viewing the results, namely that the boys were being expected to identify their self images through identification with female stimuli. We find, for example, that the girls yield approximately 25 per cent more Self/trait interactions (i.e. 41 versus 31) than the boys, suggesting that the boys may have found this 'cross-sex' identification to be more difficult. And while caution is clearly called for in interpreting these results, it is encouraging to see that the Self/Future Self correlations were nearly as large for boys ($r = 0.65$) as girls ($r = 0.77$) in Table 8.5.

Taking the personality dimensions in turn, we see that the high P girls were distinctly tough and independent — Staying Out Late, Liking Tough Boys and being Disobedient, and also being sexually more liberal, as well as tending to reject adult social roles such as Wife and Strict. High E adolescents, as would be expected, saw themselves as more sociable, but without the 'deviant' vein that runs through the high P picture, e.g. the high E adolescents did not agree more with Sex Before Marriage and Staying Out Late. The N scale had little impact upon the self image of the girls, but seems rather more influential in the case of the boys. Barring the problems posed by cross-sex discrimination as mentioned above, the

Table 8.9

Traits which Judges attribute to themselves as a function of their own personality (P, E, N) or social orientation (C, ASB)
(Only significant correlations are shown[1])

Self as compared with:	Tough Mindedness (P)		Extra-version (E)		Neuroticism (N)		Conserva-tism (C)		Antisocial Behaviour (ASB)	
	Boys	Girls	Boys	Girls	Boys	Girls	Boys	Girls	Boys	Girls
Likes Parties	—	19	19	—	—	—	—28	—19	—	—
Fights	—	—	—	—	—21	—	—	—21	—	—
Like A Wife	—	—19	—23	—	34	—	—	27	—	—
Stays Out Late	—	26	—	—	—	—	—24	—24	25	29
Steals From Shops	—	—	—	—	—	—	—	—20	—	—
Liked By Men	—	27	—	21	—	28	—23	—	—	28
Disobedient	—	19	—	21	—32	—	—	—21	28	—
Clever	—	—	—	—	27	—	20	41	—25	—
Sex Before Marriage	—	30	—	—	—23	—	—22	—28	34	35
Like A Mother	—	—	—	—26	—	—	—	28	—	—
Popular With Boys	—	28	20	33	—21	21	—20	—	21	38
Strict	—	—29	—	—21	—	—	—	41	—22	—27
Likes Discos	—	—	—	28	—	—	—31	—	27	38
Attractive	—	—	—	19	—	—	—	—	—	—
Likes Tough Boys	—	26	—	—	—20	—	—	—32	—	—
Argues	—	—	24	—	—	—	—	—	27	—
Liked By Women	—	—	—	—	26	—	—	24	—	—
Likes Kissing	—	30	—	34	—	—	—22	—33	22	38
Future Self	—28	—	—	—	—	20	—	—	—33	—

1. Decimal points omitted. Because the present correlations involve three variables rather than two, it was decided to table all correlations which exceed the value required for the .05 level in a one-tailed test.

similarity in self/trait interaction between the high N boys and the Conservative girls (to be discused next) is suggestive of a problematical sexual identification in the boys — that high N may be antithetical to a satisfactory gender role adjustment in boys. The C scale gave clearcut results, for adolescents with orthodox, traditional attitudes saw themselves on the stereotyping task as particularly moral. For instance, they saw themselves as Fighting and Stealing less, agreeing less with Sex Before Marriage and Kissing and identified more with the adult roles of Wife and Mother. The ASB questionnaire, like P, provides an impression of toughness and independence, tinged as would be expected with a flavour of deviancy and rebellion. Here, it is interesting to observe that the ASB score has a much greater impact on the self images of boys than does P — suggesting, as one possibility, that some additional variable is involved in the transition from being 'tough minded' to being overtly delinquent.

8.9.3 *Results for Attractiveness*

One of the themes in this book is the importance of Attractiveness in mediating social behaviour. In an attempt to see if personality moderated the subjective definition of Attractiveness in any major way, the personality scales of P, E, N, C and ASB were correlated with the trait distance between Good Looking and each of the remaining traits (exactly as described above). The significant results are presented in Table 8.10.

The ASB, P and C scales proved to have the most impact upon the perception of Attractiveness. Essentially, the tough high-P/high-ASB adolescents found toughness and deviancy more likely to be attractive while the moral high C children were more likely to find conventionality attractive in others.

8.9.4 *Conclusion*

The major finding of this section is essentially one of a crossvalidation between traditional personality tests and the present stereotyping technique as ways of eliciting self descriptions. Indeed, given the oblique nature of the 'questioning' in the stereotyping format, this method of enquiring might be preferred in situations where demand characteristics ought to be kept at a minimum, e.g. it is less easy to see what the 'right' answer should be on a stereotyping test.

Further support for the view that a stereotyping test can elicit accurate self descriptions came from the analysis which showed that individuals

Table 8.10

The Influence of Personality (P, E, N, C and ASB) on the Distribution of Traits which are inferred to Covary with Attractiveness (Only significant correlations are shown[1])

Attractive as compared with:	Tough Mindedness (P)		Extra-version (E)		Neuroticism (N)		Conserva-tism (C)		Antisocial Behaviour (ASB)	
	Boys	Girls	Boys	Girls	Boys	Girls	Boys	Girls	Boys	Girls
Likes Parties	—	—	—	—	—	—	—	—	—	—
Fights	—	19	—	—	—	22	—	—	—	19
Like A Wife	—	—	—	—	—	—	—	—	—	—
Stays Out Late	—	23	—	—	—	—	—23	—	—	—
Steals From Shops	—	25	—	—19	—	—	—	—	—	—
Liked By Men	—	30	—	—	24	23	—21	—	—	32
Disobedient	—	26	—	—	—	—	—	—	—	—
Clever	—23	—	—	—	—	—	—	—	—27	—
Sex Before Marriage	19	29	29	—	—	—	—20	—	19	—
Like A Mother	—	—	—	—	—	—	—	20	—	—
Popular With Boys	—	22	—	—	—	29	—	—	—	20
Strict	—	—23	—	—	—	—	—	—	—	—
Likes Discos	—	—	—	—	—	—	—31	—	—	24
Likes Tough Boys	27	29	—	—	—	—	—33	—	26	—
Argues	—	25	23	—	—	—	—25	—	—	—
Present Self	—	—	—	19	—	—	—	—	—	—
Liked By Women	—	—	—	—	—	—	—	—	—	—
Likes Kissing	—	19	—	—	—	—	—	—	—	—
Future Self	20	—	—	—	—	—	—	—	—	—

1. Decimal points omitted. In view of the fact that the present correlations involve three variables, significance has been assessed by means of one-tailed tests based on a 5 per cent probability.

were more likely to find targets attractive if they attributed to those targets traits that they themselves possessed. This is a well known finding previously described many times using standard personality assessment measures, and so it is highly encouraging for the 'validity' of stereotyping that it should also be replicated here. In a like manner, these results also further the notion that the demarcation between stereotyping and person perception is largely arbitrary in nature, related more to method than results.

Bibliography

Abelson, R.P., & Sermat, V. (1962). Multidimensional scaling of facial expressions. *Journal of Experimental Psychology*, 63, 546-554.

Aboud, F.E., & Taylor, D.M. (1971). Ethnic and role stereotypes: Their relative importance in person perception. *Journal of Social Psychology*, 85, 17-27.

Adams, H.F. (1927). The good judge of personality. *Journal of Abnormal and Social Psychology*, 22, 172-181.

Adams-Webber, J.R. (1969). Cognitive complexity and sociality. *British Journal of Social and Clinical Psychology*, 8, 211-216.

Alfert, E. (1958). Two components of assumed similarity. *Journal of Abnormal and Social Psychology*, 56, 135-138.

Allen, C.D., & Eicher, J.B. (1973). Adolescent girls' acceptance and rejection based on appearance. *Adolescence,* 8, 125-138.

Allport, G.W., & Odbert, H.S. (1936). Trait-names: a psycho-lexical study. *Psychological Monographs,* 47, Whole No. 211.

Allport, G.W., & Postman, L.F. (1958). The basic psychology of rumor. In Maccoby, E.E., Newcomb, T.M. & Hartley, E.L. (Eds.), *Readings in social psychology*. (3rd ed.) New York: Holt, Rinehart & Winston. Pp. 54-65.

Anderson, N.H., & Jacobson, A. (1965). Effect of stimulus inconsistency and discounting instructions in personality impression formation. *Journal of Personality and Social Psychology*, 2, 531-539.

Arnhoff, F.N., & Damianopoulos, E.N. (1964). Self-body recognition and schizophrenia. *Journal of General Psychology*, 70, 353-361.

Aronson, E. (1969). Some antecedents of interpersonal attraction. In Arnold, W.J., & Levine, D. (Eds.), *Nebraska symposium on motivation*. Lincoln: University of Nebraska Press. Pp. 143-177.

Asch, S.E. (1946). Forming impressions of personality. *Journal of Abnormal and Social Psychology*, 41, 258-290.

Asch, S.E. (1952). *Social psychology*. New York: Prentice-Hall.

Bagby, J.W. (1957). A cross-cultural study of perceptual predominance in binocular rivalry. *Journal of Abnormal and Social Psychology*. 54, 331-334.

Baker, B.O., & Block, J. (1957). Accuracy of interpersonal prediction as a function of judge and object characteristics. *Journal of Abnormal*

and Social Psychology, 54, 37-43.
Ball, T.S., & Vogler, R.E. (1971). Uncertain pain and the pain of uncertainty. *Perceptual and Motor Skills,* 33, 1195-1203.
Bannister, D. (1972). Critiques of the concept of 'loose construing': A reply. *British Journal of Social and Clinical Psychology*, 11, 412-414.
Bartlett, F.C. (1932). *Remembering: an experimental and social study.* London: Cambridge University Press.
Bassili, J.N. (1976). Temporal and spatial contingencies in the perception of social events. *Journal of Personality and Social Psychology*, 33, 680-685.
Bayton, J.A., McAlister, L.B. & Hamer, J. (1956). Race-class stereotypes. *Journal of Negro Education*, 25, 75-78.
Beach, L., & Wertheimer, M. (1961). A free response approach to the study of person cognition. *Journal of Abnormal and Social Psychology*, 62, 367-374.
Belanger, R.M., & Sattler, J.M. (1967). Motive to achieve success and motive to avoid failure as a capacity to tolerate uncertainty in a pain producing situation. *Journal of Experimental Research in Personality*, 2, 154-159.
Bender, I.E., & Hastorf, A.H. (1950). The perception of persons: Forecasting another person's responses on three personality scales. *Journal of Abnormal and Social Psychology*, 45, 556-561.
Bender, I.E., & Hastorf, A.H. (1953). On measuring generalized empathic ability (social sensitivity). *Journal of Abnormal and Social Psychology*, 48, 503-506.
Bendig, A.W. (1956) Ranking methodology: the development of a judgmental criterion with clinical case histories. *Journal of Consulting Psychology*, 20, 75-78.
Berkowitz, W.R., Nebel, J.C. & Reitman, J.C. (1971). Height and interpersonal attraction: the 1969 Mayoral election in New York City. Proceedings of the 79th annual convention of the American Psychological Association, 6, 281-282.
Berlyne, D.E. (1960). *Conflict, arousal and curiosity.* New York: McGraw-Hill.
Berscheid, E., Dion, K.K., Walster, E. & Walster, G.W. (1971). Physical attractiveness and dating choice: a test of the matching hypothesis. *Journal of Experimental Social Psychology*, 7, 173-189.
Berscheid, E., & Walster, E. (1974). Physical attractiveness. In Berkowits, L. (Ed.), *Advances in experimental social psychology*. Vol. 7. New York: Academic Press. Pp. 157-215.
Berscheid, E., Walster, E. & Campbell, R. (1972). Grow old along with

me. Mimeographed copies available from the authors.
Bieliauskas, V. (1965). Recent advances in the psychology of masculinity and femininity. *Journal of Psychology*, 60, 255-263.
Bieri, J. (1955). Cognitive complexity-simplicity and predictive behavior. *Journal of Abnormal and Social Psychology*, 51, 263-268.
Bieri, J. (1966). Cognitive complexity and personality development. In Harvey, O.J. (Ed.), *Experience, structure and adaptability*. New York: Springer.
Biller, H.B., & Liebman, D.A. (1971). Body build, sex-role preference, and sex-role adoption in junior high school boys. *Journal of Genetic Psychology*, 118, 81-86.
Black, H.K. (1974). Physical attractiveness and similarity of attitude in interpersonal attraction. *Psychological Reports*, 35, 403-406.
Black, J.D. (1956a). Adjectives associated with various MMPI codes. In Welsh, G.S., & Dahlstrom, W.G. (Eds.), *Basic readings on the MMPI in psychology and medicine*. Minneapolis: University of Minnesota Press. Pp. 151-172.
Black, J.D. (1956b). MMPI results for fifteen groups of female college students. In Welsh, G.S., & Dahlstrom, W.G. (Eds.), *Basic readings on the MMPI in psychology and medicine*. Minneapolis: University of Minnesota Press. Pp. 562-573.
Blood, R.O. (1956). Uniformities and diversities in campus dating preferences. *Journal of Marriage and Family Living*, 18, 37-45.
Blumberg, H.H., DeSoto, C.B. & Kuethe, J.L. (1966). Evaluation of rating scale formats. *Personnel Psychology*, 19, 243-259.
Bonarius, J.C.J. (1965). Research in the Personal Construct Theory of George A. Kelly: Role Construct Repertory Test and basic theory. In Maher, B. (Ed.), *Progress in experimental personality research*. Vol. 2. New York: Academic Press.
Borke, H., & Fisk, D.W. (1957). Factors influencing the prediction of behavior from a diagnostic interview. *Journal of Consulting Psychology*, 21, 78-80.
Bourke, F.J.P., Stewart, R.A. & Miller, A.R. (1973). Personality factors in sexual preference. Paper read at Western Psychological Association, Anaheim, California, April, 1973.
Braun, J.R. (1962). Stereotypes of the scientist as seen with Gordon Personal Profile and Gordon Personality Inventory. *Journal of Psychology*, 53, 453-455.
Brigham, J.C. (1971). Ethnic stereotypes. *Psychological Bulletin*, 76, 15-38.
Brislin, R.W., & Lewis, S.A. (1968). Dating and physical attractiveness:

Replication. *Psychological Reports*, 22, 976.
Brodsky, C.M. (1954). A study of norms for body form-behavior relationships. *Anthropological Quarterly*, 27, 91-101.
Broverman, I.K., Broverman, D.M., Clarkson, F.E., Rosenkrantz, P. & Vogel, S.R. (1970). Sex role stereotypes and clinical judgements of mental health. *Journal of Consulting Psychology*, 34, 1-7.
Broverman, I.K., Vogel, S.R., Broverman, D.M., Clarkson, F.E. & Rosenkrantz, P.S. (1972). Sex-role stereotypes: A current appraisal. *Journal of Social Issues,* 28, 59-78.
Bruner, J.S., Shapiro, D. & Tagiuri, R. (1958). The meaning of traits in isolation and in combination. In Tagiuri, R., & Petrullo, L. (Eds.), *Person perception and interpersonal behavior*. Stanford: Stanford University Press. Pp. 277-288.
Bruner, J.S., & Tagiuri, R. (1954). The perception of people. In Lindzey, G. (Ed.), *Handbook of social psychology*. Cambridge, Mass.: Addison-Wesley. Pp. 634-654
Bush, L.E. (1973). Individual differences in multidimensional scaling of adjectives denoting feelings. *Journal of Personality and Social Psychology*, 25, 50-57.
Byrne, D., Ervin, C.R. & Lamberth, J. (1970). Continuity between the experimental study of attraction and real-life computer dating. *Journal of Personality and Social Psychology*, 16, 157-165.
Carrigan, P.M. (1960) Extraversion-introversion as a dimension of personality: A reappraisal. *Psychological Bulletin*, 57, 329-360.

Cauthen, N.R., Robinson, I.E. & Krauss, H.H. (1971). Stereotypes: A review of the literature 1926-1968. *Journal of Social Psychology*, 84, 103-125.
Cavior, N., & Dokecki, P.R. (1971). Physical attractiveness self-concept: a test of Mead's hypothesis. Proceedings of the 79th annual convention of the American Psychological Association, 6, 319-320.
Cavior, N., & Dokecki, P.R. (1973). Physical attractiveness, perceived attitude similarity, and academic achievement as contributors to interpersonal attraction among adolescents. *Developmental Psychology*, 9, 44-54.
Chaikin, A.L., Derlega, V.J., Yoder, J. & Phillips, D. (1974). The effects of appearance on compliance. *Journal of Social Psychology*, 92, 199-200.
Chetwynd-Tutton, S.J. (1974). Generalised grid technique and some associated methodological problems. Unpublished doctoral thesis,

University of London.
Child, I.L. (1950). The relation of somatotype to self ratings on Sheldon's temperamental traits. *Journal of Personality*, 18, 440-455.
Clark, F.W. (1965). Cue-extremeness and cue-utilization in clinical judgement. Unpublished Master's thesis, University of Oregon.
Clarkson, F.E., Vogel, S.R., Broverman, I.K., Broverman, D.M. & Rosenkrantz, P.S. (1970). Family size and sex-role stereotypes. *Science*, 167, 390-392.
Clifford, M.M., & Walster, E. (1973). The effect of physical attractiveness on teacher expectation. *Sociology of Education* 46, 248-258.
Cline, V.B. (1955). Ability to judge personality assessed with a stress interview and sound-film technique. *Journal of Abnormal and Social Psychology*, 50, 183-187.
Clum, T.L., & Eicher, J.B. (1972). Teenagers' conformity in dress and peer friendship groups. Research Report (No. 156, Home & Family living), Agricultural Experiment Station, March, 1972. East Lansing: Michigan State University. Pp. 1-8.
Cohen, A.R., Stotland, E. & Wolfe, D.M. (1955). An experimental investigation of need for cognition. *Journal of Abnormal and Social Psychology*, 51, 291-294.
Cohen, R. (1973). *Patterns of personality judgement*. New York: Academic Press.
Cook, M. (1971). *Interpersonal perception*. Harmondsworth: Penguin Books.
Cook, M., & Smith, J.M.C. (1974). Group ranking techniques in the study of the accuracy of interpersonal perception. *British Journal of Psychology*, 65, 427-435.
Coombs, C.H. (1960). *A theory of data*. New York: Wiley.
Coombs, R.H., & Kenkel, W.F. (1966). Sex differences in dating aspirations and satisfaction with computer-selected partners. *Journal of Marriage and the Family*, 28, 62-66.
Cowie, J., Cowie, C. & Slater, E. (1968). *Delinquency in girls*. London: Heineman.
Crandall, V.J., & Bellugi, U. (1954). Some relationships of interpersonal and intrapersonal conceptualizations to personal-social adjustment. *Journal of Personality*, 23, 224-232.
Crisp, A.H., & McGuiness, B. (1976). Jolly fat: relation between obesity and psychoneurosis. *British Medical Journal*, in press.
Crockett, W.H. (1965). Cognitive complexity and impression formation. In Maher, B.A. (Ed.), *Progress in experimental personality research*. Vol. 2. New York: Academic Press.

Cronbach, L.J. (1955). Processes affecting scores on 'understanding others' and 'assumed similarity'. *Psychological Bulletin*, 52, 177-193.
Cronbach, L.J. (1958). Proposals leading to analytic treatment of social perception scores. In Tagiuri, R., & Petrullo, L. (Eds.), *Person perception and interpersonal behavior*. Stanford: Stanford University Press. Pp. 352-379.
Cross, J.F., & Cross, J. (1971). Age, sex, race and the perception of facial beauty. *Developmental Psychology*, 5, 433-439.
Crow, W.J. (1957). The effect of training upon accuracy and variability in interpersonal perception. *Journal of Abnormal and Social Psychology*, 55, 355-359.
Crow, W.J., & Hammond, K.R. (1957). The generality of accuracy and response sets in interpersonal perception. *Journal of Abnormal and Social Psychology*, 54, 384-390.
Cureton, E.E. (1958). The average Spearman rank criterion correlation when ties are present. *Psychometrika*, 23, 271-272.
Cureton, E.E. (1965). The average Spearman rank correlation when ties are present: A correction.*Psychometrika*, 30, 377.

D'Andrade, R.G. (1965). Trait psychology and componential analysis. *American Anthropologist*, 67, 215-228.
Dannenmaier, W.D., & Thumin, F.J. (1964). Authority status as a factor in perceptual distortion of size. *Journal of Social Psychology*, 63, 361-365.
Dermer, M., & Thiel, D.L. (1975). When beauty may fail. *Journal of Personality and Social Psychology*, 31, 1168-1176.
DeWolfe, A.S. (1971). Cognitive structure and pathology in associations of process and reactive schizophrenics. *Journal of Abnormal Psychology*, 78, 148-153.
Diamond, S., Balvin, R.S. & Diamond, F.R. (1963). *Inhibition and choice*. New York: Harper & Row.
Dibiase, W.J., & Hjelle, L.A. (1968). Body-image stereotypes and body-type preferences among male college students. *Perceptual and Motor Skills,* 27, 1143-1146.
Dion, K.K. (1972). Physical attractiveness and evaluations of children's transgressions. *Journal of Personality and Social Psychology*, 24, 207-213.
Dion, K.K. (1973). Young children's stereotyping of facial attractiveness. *Developmental Psychology*, 9, 183-188.
Dion, K.K. & Berscheid, E. (1972). Physical attractiveness and social

perception of peers in preschool children. Mimeographed research report available from the authors.
Dion, K.K., Berscheid, E. & Walster, E. (1972). What is beautiful is good. *Journal of Personality and Social Psychology*, 24, 285-290.
Dion, K.K., & Berscheid, E. (1974). Physical attractiveness and peer perception among children. *Sociometry*, 37, 1-12.
Doppelt, J.E., & Wallace, W.L. (1955). Standardization of the Wechsler Adult Intelligence Scale for older persons. *Journal of Abnormal and Social Psychology*, 51, 312-330.
Douvan, E., & Adelson, J. (1966). *The adolescent experience*. New York: Wiley.
Drewery, J., & Rae, J. (1969). A group comparison of psychiatric and non-psychiatric marriages using the interpersonal perception technique. *British Journal of Psychiatry*, 115, 287-300.
Dustin, D.S., & Baldwin, P.M. (1966). Redundancy in impression formation. *Journal of Personality and Social Psychology*, 3, 500-506.
Dymond, R. (1948). A preliminary investigation of the relationship of insight and empathy. *Journal of Consulting Psychology*, 12, 228-233.
Dymond, R. (1949). A scale for the measurement of empathic ability. *Journal of Consulting Psychology*, 13, 127-133.
Dymond, R. (1950). Personality and empathy. *Journal of Consulting Psychology*, 14, 343-350.

Eaves, L., & Eysenck, H.J. (1975). The nature of extraversion: A genetical analysis. *Journal of Personality and Social Psychology*, 32, 102-112.
Edwards, A.L. (1950). *Experimental design in psychological research*. New York: Rinehart.
Edwards, A.L. (1954). *Statistical methods for the behavioral sciences*. New York: Rinehart.
Efran, M.G. (1974). The effect of physical appearance on the judgement of guilt, interpersonal attraction, and severity of recommended punishment in a simulated jury task. *Journal of Research into Personality*, 8, 45-54.
Eicher, J.B., & Dillon, M.L. (1969). Boys' clothing conformity and acceptance. Research Bulletin, Agricultural Experiment Station, April 1969, No. 22. East Lansing: Michigan State University. Pp. 1-15.
Eicher, J.B. & Kelley, E.A. (1972). High School as a meeting place. *Michigan Journal of Secondary Education,* 13, 12-16.

Emswiller, T., Deaux, K. & Willits, J.E. (1971). Similarity, sex, and requests for small favors. *Journal of Applied Social Psychology*, 1, 284-291.

Engel, E. (1956). The role of content in binocular resolution. *American Journal of Psychology*, 69, 87-91.

Estes, S.G. (1938). Judging personality from expressive behavior. *Journal of Abnormal and Social Psychology*, 33, 217-236.

Everitt, B. (1974). *Cluster analysis*. London: Heinemann.

Eysenck, H.J. (1947). *Dimensions of personality*. London: Kegan Paul.

Eysenck, H.J. (1953). *The structure of human personality*. London: Methuen.

Eysenck, H.J. (1967). *The biological basis of personality*. Springfield, Ill.: Thomas.

Eysenck, H.J., & Crown, S. (1948). National stereotypes: An experimental and methodological study. *International Journal of Opinion and Attitude Research,* 2, 26-39.

Eysenck, H.J., & Eysenck, S.B.G. (1976). *Psychoticism as a dimension of personality*. In press.

Eysenck, H.J., Granger, G.W. & Brengelmann, J.C. (1957). *Perceptual processes and mental illness. Institute of Psychiatry-Maudsley Monographs, No. 2. London: Oxford University Press.*

Eysenck, S.B.G., & Eysenck, H.J. (1963). The personality of judges as a factor in the validity of their judgments of Extraversion-Introversion. British Journal of Social and Clinical Psychology, 3, 141-144.

Faggot, B.I. (1973a). Sex-related stereotyping of toddlers' behaviors. *Developmental Psychology*, 9, 429.

Faggot, B.I. (1973b). Influence of teacher behavior in the preschool. *Developmental Psychology*, 9, 198-206.

Faust, M.S. (1960). Developmental maturity as a determinant in prestige of adolescent girls. *Child Development*, 31, 173-184.

Feather, N.T. (1967). Level of aspiration and performance variability. *Journal of Personality and Social Psychology*, 6, 37-46.

Feldman, J.M. (1972). Stimulus characteristics and subject prejudice as determinants of stereotype attribution. *Journal of Personality and Social Psychology,* 21, 333-340.

Feldman, J.M., & Hilterman, R.J. (1975). Stereotype attribution revisited: the role of stimulus characteristics, racial attitude, and cognitive differentiation. *Journal of Personality and Social Psychology*, 31, 1177-1188.

Feldman, S.D. (1971). The presentation of shortness in veryday life — height and heightism in American society: towards a sociology of stature. Paper presented at the meetings of the American Sociological Association, 1971.
Ferguson, G.A.(1959). *Statistical analysis in psychology and education*. New York: McGraw-Hill.
Fillenbaum, S. (1961). How fat is fat? Some consequences of similarity between judge and judged object. *Journal of Psychology*, 52, 133-136.
Fernberger, S.W. (1948). Persistence of stereotypes concerning sex differences. *Journal of Abnornal and Social Psychology*, 43, 97-101.
Friendly, M.L., & Glucksberg, S. (1970). On the description of subcultural lexicons: A multidimensional approach. *Journal of Personality and Social Psychology*, 14, 55-65.
Frijda, N.H., & Philipszoon, E. (1963). Dimensions of recognition of expression. *Journal of Abnormal and Social Psychology*, 66, 45-51.
Frith, C.D., & Lillie, F.J. (1972). Why does the Repertory Grid Test indicate thought disorder? *British Journal of Social and Clinical Psychology*, 11, 73-78.
Frith, U. (1971). Why do children reverse letters? *British Journal of Psychology*, 62, 459-468.
Frith, U. (1974a). A curious effect with reversed letters explained by a theory of schema. *Perception and Psychophysics*, 16, 113-116.
Frith, U. (1974b). Internal schemata for letters in good and bad readers. *British Journal of Psychology*, 65, 233-241.

Gage, N.L. (1952). Judging interests from expressive behavior. *Psychological Monographs*, 66, 18 (whole No. 350).
Gage, N.L. (1953). Accuracy of social perception and effectiveness in interpersonal relationships. *Journal of Personality*, 22, 128-141.
Gage, N.L., & Cronbach, L.J. (1955). Conceptual and methodological problems in interpersonal perception. *Psychological Review*, 62, 411-422.
Gage, N.L., Leavitt, G.S. & Stone, G.C. (1956). The intermediary key in the analysis of interpersonal perception. *Psychological Bulletin*, 53, 258-266.
Gahagan, L. (1933). Judgments of occupation from printed photographs. *Journal of Social Psychology*, 4, 128-134.
Gardner, R.C., Kirby, D.M. & Finlay, J.C. (1973). Ethnic stereotypes: the significance of consensus. *Canadian Journal of Behavioural Science*, 5, 4-12.

Gardner, R.C., Taylor, D.M. & Feenstra, H.J. (1970). Ethnic stereotypes: Attitudes or beliefs? *Canadian Journal of Psychology*, 24, 321-334.

Gardner, R.C., Wonnacott, E.J. & Taylor, D.M. (1968). Ethnic stereotypes: A factor analytic investigation. *Canadian Journal of Psychology*, 22, 35-44.

Gellert, E., Girgus, J.S. & Cohen, J. (1971). Children's awareness of their bodily appearance: A developmental study of factors associated with the body percept. *Genetic Psychology Monographs*, 84, 109-174.

Gerace, T.A., & Caldwell, W.E. (1971). Perceptual distortion as a function of stimulus objects, sex, naivete, and trials using a portable model of the Ames distorted room. *Genetic Psychology Monographs,* 84, 3-33.

Gibbins, K. (1969). Communication aspects of women's clothes and their relation to fashionability. *British Journal of Social and Clinical Psychology*, 8, 301-312.

Gibrat, R. (1966). The culture of science and letters, and the engineer. Proceedings of the 164th Ordinary General Meeting of the Societe Des Ingenieurs Civils De France, British Section, London, May, 1966.

Giedt, F.H. (1955). Comparison of visual, content, and auditory cues in interviewing. *Journal of Consulting Psychology*, 19, 407-416.

Gifford, R.K. (1975). Information properties of descriptive words. *Journal of Personality and Social Psychology*, 31, 727-734.

Gitin, S.R. (1970). A dimensional analysis of manual expression. *Journal of Personality and Social Psychology*, 15, 271-277.

Glixman, A.F. (1965). Categorizing behavior as a function of meaning domain. *Journal of Personality and Social Psychology*, 2, 370-377.

Glueck, S., & Glueck, E. (1956). *Physique and delinquency*. New York: Harper.

Goffman, E. (1952). On cooling the mark out: some aspects of adaptation to failure. *Psychiatry*, 15, 451-463.

Goldberg, P. (1968). Are women prejudiced against women? *Transactions*, 5, 28-30.

Gray, J.E. (1973). Dimensions of personality and meaning in self-ratings of personality. *British Journal of Social and Clinical Psychology*, 12, 319-322.

Grunes, W.F. (1957). Looking at occupations. *Journal of Abnormal and Social Psychology*, 54, 86-92.

Guardo, C.J., & Meisels, M. (1971). Child-parent spatial patterns under praise and reproof. *Developmental Psychology*, 5, 365.

Guilford, J.P. (1959). *Personality*. New York: McGraw-Hill.

Haggard, E.A. (1958). *Intraclass correlation and the analysis of variance*. New York: Dryden Press.
Haire, M., & Grunes, W. (1950). Perceptual defenses: processes
Hamilton, D.L., & Huffman, L.J. (1971). Generality of impression-formation processes for evaluative and nonvaluative judgments. *Journal of Personality and Social Psychology*, 20, 200-207.
Hanno, M.S., & Jones, L.E. (1973). Effects of a change in reference person on the multidimensional structure and evaluations of trait adjectives. *Journal of Personality and Social Psychology*, 28, 368-375.
Hartley, H.O. (1953). Approximate tests for comparisons of rank correlations. Paper read at American Statistical Association, Washington, December, 1953.
Hartup, W.W., Moore, S.G. & Sager, G. (1963). Avoidance of inappropriate sex-typing by young children. *Journal of Consulting Psychology*, 27, 467-473.
Hartup, W.W., & Zook, E.A. (1960). Sex-role preferences in three- and four-year-old children. *Journal of Consulting Psychology*, 24, 420-426.
Hastorf, A.H., & Bender, I.E. (1952). A caution respecting the masurement of empathic ability. *Journal of Abnormal and Social Psychology*, 47, 574-576.
Hastorf, A.H., Bender, I.E. & Weintraub, D.J. (1955). The influence of response patterns on the 'refined empathy score.' *Journal of Abnormal and Social Psychology*, 51, 341-343.
Hastorf, A.H., & Myro, G. (1959). The effect of meaning on binocular rivalry. *American Journal of Psychology*, 72, 393-400.
Hatch, R.S. (1962). *An evaluation of a forced choice differential accuracy approach to the measurement of supervisory empathy*. Englewood Cliffs, N.J.: Prentice-Hall.
Hathaway, S.R. (1956). Clinical intuition and inferential accuracy. *Journal of Personality*, 24, 223-250.
Hays, D.P., & Sievers, S. (1972). A sociolinguistic investigation of the 'dimensions' of interpersonal behavior. *Journal of Personality and Social Psychology*, 24, 254-261.
protecting an organized perception of another personality. *Human Relations*, 3, 403-412.
Hallworth, H.J. (1965). Dimensions of personality and meaning. *British Journal of Social and Clinical Psychology*, 4, 161-168.
Halpern, H.M. (1955). Empathy, similarity, and self-satisfaction. *Journal of Consulting Psychology*, 19, 449-452.
Hamid, P.N. (1968). Style of dress as a perceptual cue in impression

formation. *Perceptual and Motor Skills,* 26, 904-906.
Hamid, P.N. (1969). Changes in person perception as a function of dress. *Perceptual and Motor Skills*, 29, 191-194.
Hays, W.L. (1958). An approach to the study of trait implication and trait similarity. In Tagiuri, R., & Petrullo, L. (Eds.), *Person perception and interpersonal behavior*. Stanford: Stanford University Press.
Hays, W.L. (1963). *Statistics for psychologists*. New York: Holt, Rinehart & Winston.
Hebron, M.E. (1968). A note on the predictive validity of the MPI as tested by a semantic differential technique. *British Journal of Psychology*, 59, 473-474.
Heider, F., & Simmel, M. (1944). An experimental study of apparent behavior. *American Journal of Psychology*, 57, 243-259.
Hendrick, C. (1968). Averaging vs summation in impression formation. *Perceptual and Motor Skills,* 27, 1295-1302.
Hendrick, C., & Costantini, A.F. (1970). Effects of varying trait inconsistency and response requirements on the primacy effect in impression formation. *Journal of Personality and Social Psychology*, 15, 158-164.
Hendricks, S.H., Kelley, E.A. & Eicher, J.B. (1968). Senior girls' appearance and social acceptance. *Journal of Home Economics*, 60, 162-172.
Hess, V.L., & Pick, A.D. (1974). Discrimination of schematic faces by nursery school children. *Child Development*, 45, 1151-1154.
Hewitt, L.E. (1958). Student perceptions of traits desired in themselves as dating and marriage partners. *Marriage and Family Living*, 20, 344-349.
Hicks, M., & Platt, M. (1970). Mental happiness and stability. A review of research in the sixties. *Journal of Marriage and the Family*, 28, 109-123.
Himmelfarb, S., & Senn, D.J. (1969). Forming impressions of social class: two tests of an averaging model. *Journal of Personality and Social Psychology*, 12, 38-51.
Hovey, H.B. (1956). MMPI profiles and personality characteristics. In Welsh, G.S., & Dahlstrom, W.G. (Eds.), *Basic readings on the MMPI in psychology and medicine*. Minneapolis: University of Minnesota Press. Pp. 315-320.
Hudson, J.W., & Henze, L.F. (1969). Campus values in mate selection: A replication. *Journal of Marriage and the Family*, 31, 772-775.
Huston, T.L. (1973). Ambiguity of acceptance, social desirability, and dating choice. *Journal of Experimental Social Psychology*, 9, 32-42.

Iliffe, A.H. (1960). A study of preferences in feminine beauty. *British Journal of Psychology*, 51, 267-273.

Inhelder, B., & Piaget, J. (1958). *The growth of logical thinking from childhood to adolescence*. New York: Basic Books.

Jenkins, M.A. (1971). Stereotyping and other response patterns on racial and somatotype stimuli. Unpublished Master's thesis, University of Southern California, 1971.

Jerdee, T.H. (1961). Supervisor perception of subordinate attitudes. *Dissertation Abstracts*, 22, 334.

Johansson, G. (1973). Visual perception of biological motion and a model for its analysis. *Perception and Psychophysics*, 44, 201-211.

Jones, M.C., & Bayley, N. (1950). Physical maturing among boys as related to behavior. *Journal of Educational Psychology*, 41, 129-148.

Kaats, G.R., & Davis, K.E. (1970). The dynamics of sexual behavior of college students. *Journal of Marriage and the Family*, 32, 390-399.

Kagan, J. (1965). Individual differences in the resolution of response uncertainty. *Journal of Personality and Social Psychology*, 2, 154-160.

Kagan, J., Henker, B.A., Hen-Tov, A., Levine, J. & Lewis, M. (1966). Infants' differential reaction to familiar and distorted faces. *Child Development*, 37, 519-532.

Kaplan, M.F. (1971). Dispositional effects and weight of information in impression formation. *Journal of Personality and Social Psychology*, 18, 279-284.

Kaplan, M.F. (1973). Stimulus inconsistency and response dispositions in forming judgments of other persons. *Journal of Personality and Social Psychology*, 25, 58-64.

Kassarjian, H.H. (1963). Voting intentions and political perception. *Journal of Psychology*, 56, 85-88.

Kates, W.W., & Kates, S.L. (1964). Conceptual behavior in psychotic and normal adolescents. *Journal of Abnormal and Social Psychology*, 69, 659-663.

Katz, D., & Braly, K.W. (1933). Racial stereotypes of 100 college students. *Journal of Abnormal and Social Psychology*, 28, 280-290.

Kelvin, P. (1969). *The bases of social behaviour*. London: Holt, Rinehart & Winston.

Kelley, E.A., & Eicher, J.B. (1970). Communication via clothing:

Implications for home economics teaching. *Forum* (J.C. Penney Co.), 1970, Spring/Summer, p. 23.

Kelly, G.A. (1955). *The psychology of personal constructs*. New York: Norton.

Kelly, G.A. (1963). Non-parametric factor analysis of personality theories. *Journal of Individual Psychology*, 19, 115-147.

Kendall, M.E. (1948). *Rank correlation methods*. London: Griffin.

Kennard, D. (1974). The newly admitted psychiatric patient as seen by self and others. *British Journal of Medical Psychology*, 47, 27-41.

Kerric, J.S. (1956). The effects of manifest anxiety and IQ on discrimination. *Journal of Abnormal and Social Psychology*, 52, 136-138.

Kiker, V.L., & Miller, A.R. (1967). Perceptual judgment of physique as a factor in social image. *Perceptual and Motor Skills,* 24, 1013-1014.

Kirby, D.M., & Gardner, R.C. (1972). Ethnic stereotypes: Norms on 208 words typically used in their assessment. *Canadian Journal of Psychology*, 26, 140-154.

Kitay, P.M. (1940). A comparison of the sexes in their attitudes and beliefs about women. *Sociometry*, 34, 399-407.

Klett, C.J. (1957). The social desirability stereotype in a hospital population. *Journal of Consulting Psychology*, 21, 419-421.

Klett, C.J., & Tamkin, A.S. (1957). The social desirability stereotype and some measures of psychopathology. *Journal of Consulting Psychology*, 21, 450.

Kolers, P.A. (1968). The recognition of geometrically transformed text. *Perception and Psychophysics*, 3, 57-64.

Koltuv, B.B. (1962). Some characteristics of intrajudge trait inter-correlations. *Psychological Monographs*, 76, 33 (whole No. 552).

Kopera, A.A., Maier, R.A. & Johnson, J.E. (1971). Perception and physical attractiveness: the influence of group interaction and group coaction on ratings of the attractiveness of photographs of women. Proceedings of the 79th annual convention of the American Psychological Association, 6, 317-318.

Kotlar, S.L. (1965). Middle-class marital role perceptions and marital adjustment. *Sociology and Social Research*, 49, 283-293.

Koulack, D., & Tuthill, J.A. (1972). Height perception: A function of social distance. *Canadian Journal of Behavioural Science*, 4, 50-53.

Krasner, L., Ullmann, L.P. & Weiss, R.L. (1964). Studies in role perception. *Journal of General Psychology*, 71, 367-371.

Krebs, D., & Adinolfi, A.A. (1975). Physical attractiveness, social relations, and personality style. *Journal of Personality and Social*

Psychology, 31, 245-253.

Krech, D., & Crutchfield, R.S. (1948). *Theory and problems of social psychology*. New York: McGraw-Hill.

Kubiniec, C.M., & Farr, S.D. (1971). Concept-scale and concept-component interaction in the semantic differential. *Psychological Reports,* 28, 531-541.

Kuethe, J.L. (1962a). Social schemas. *Journal of Abnormal and Social Psychology,* 64, 31-38.

Kuethe, J.L. (1962b). Social schemas and the reconstruction of social object displays from memory. *Journal of Abnormal and Social Psychology*, 65, 71-74.

Kurtzberg, R.L., Safar, H. & Cavior, N. (1968). Surgical and social rehabilitation of adult offenders. Proceedings of the 76th annual convention of the American Psychological Association, 3, 649-650.

Kuusinen, J. (1968). Factorial invariance of personality ratings. Unpublished manuscript, Center for Comparative Psycholinguistics, University of Illinois, February 1968. (Mimeographed).

Kuusinen, J. (1969). Affective and denotative structures of personality ratings. *Journal of Personality and Social Psychology*, 12, 181-188.

La Gaipa, J.J. (1971). Stereotypes and perceived ethnic-role specialization. *Journal of Social Psychology*, 85, 285-292.

Lambert, S. (1972). Reactions to a stranger as a function of dress. *Perceptual and Motor Skills,* 35, 711-712.

Landy, D., & Sigall, H. (1974). Beauty is talent: Task evaluation as a function of the performer's physical attractiveness. *Journal of Personality and Social Psychology*, 29, 299-304.

Lee, J.C., & Tucker, R.B. (1962). An investigation of clinical judgement: A study in method. *Journal of Abnormal and Social Psychology*, 64, 272-280.

Lefkowitz, M., Blake, R.R. & Mouton, J.S. (1955). Status factors in pedestrian violation of traffic signals. *Journal of Abnormal and Social Psychology*, 51, 704-706.

Lerner, M.J. (1965). Evaluation of performance as a function of performer's reward and attractiveness. *Journal of Personality and Social Psychology*, 1, 355-360.

Lerner, R.M. (1969a). Some female stereotypes of male body build behavior relations. *Perceptual and Motor Skills,* 28, 363-366.

Lerner, R.M. (1969b). The development of stereotyped expectancies of body build-behaviour relations. *Child Development*, 40, 137-141.

Lerner, R.M., & Gellert, E. (1969). Body build identification, preference and aversion in children. *Developmental Psychology*, 1, 456-462.
Lerner, R.M., & Pool, K. (1972). Body build stereotypes: A cross-cultural comparison. *Psychological Reports*, 31, 527-532.
Lerner, R.M., & Schroeder, C. (1971). Kindergarten children's active vocabulary about body build. *Developmental Psychology*, 5, 179.
Levin, J. (1965). Three-mode factor analysis. *Psychological Bulletin*, 64, 442-452.
Levy, L.H., & Dugan, R.D. (1960). A constant error approach to the study of dimensions of social perception. *Journal of Abnormal and Social Psychology*, 61, 21-24.
Lewis, M. (1969). Infants' responses to facial stimuli during the first year of life. *Developmental Psychology*, 1, 75-86.
Lindgren, H.C., & Robinson, J. (1953). An evaluation of Dymond's test of insight and empathy. *Journal of Consulting Psychology*, 17, 172-176.
Lindzey, G. (1965). Morphology and behavior. In Lindzey, G., & Hall, C.S. (Eds.), *Theories of personality: Primary sources and research*. New York: Wiley. Pp. 344-353.
Lippman, W. (1922). *Public opinion*. New York: Harcourt, Brace & Co.
Little, K.B. (1968). Cultural variations in social schemata. *Journal of Personality and Social Psychology*, 10, 1-7.
Little, K.B., & Schneidman, E.S. (1959). Congruencies among interpretations of psychological tests and anamnestic data. *Psychological Monographs*, 73, 6 (Whole No. 476).
Littrell, M.B., & Eicher, J.B. (1973). Clothing opinions and the social acceptance process among adolescents. *Adolescence*, 8, 197-212.
Loftus, E.F., & Palmer, J.C. (1974). Reconstruction of automobile destruction: An example of the interaction between language and memory. *Journal of Verbal Learning and Verbal Behavior*, 13, 585-589.
LoSciuto, L., & Hartley, E.L. (1963). Religious affiliation and open-mindness in binocular resolution. *Perceptual and Motor Skills*, 17, 427-430.
Luce, D.R. (1956). A survey of the theory of selective information and some of its behavioral applications. Revision of technical report no. 8, Bureau of Applied Social Research, New York.
Luckey, E.B. (1960a). Marital satisfaction and congruent self-spouce concepts. *Social Forces*, 39, 153-157.
Luckey, E.B. (1960b). Marital satisfaction and parent concepts. *Journal of Consulting Psychology*, 24, 195-204.

Luckey, E.B. (1960c). Marital satisfaction and its association with congruence of perception. *Marriage and Family Living*, 22, 49-54.
Luft, J. (1950). Implicit hypotheses and clinical predictions. *Journal of Abnormal and Social Psychology*, 45, 756-759.
Lunneborg, P.W. (1970). Stereotypic aspects in masculinity-femininity measurement. *Journal of Consulting and Clinical Psychology*, 34, 113-118.
Lunneborg, P.W. (1972). Dimensionality of MF. *Journal of Clinical Psychology*, 28, 313-317.
Luria, A.R. (1932). *The nature of human conflicts.* New York: Liveright.
Lyerly, S.B. (1952). The average Spearman rank correlation coefficient. *Psychometrika*, 17, 421-428.

Maher, B.A. (1957). Personality, problem solving, and the *Einstellung* effect. *Journal of Abnormal and Social Psychology*, 54, 70-74.
Manis, M. (1959). Assessing communication with the semantic differential. *American Journal of Psychology*, 72, 111-113.
Marks, I.M. (1965). *Patterns of meaning in psychiatric patients.* Institute of Psychiatry-Maudsley Monographs, No. 13. London: Oxford University Press.
Mash, E.J., & McElwee, J.D. (1974). Situational effects on observer accuracy: Behavioral predictability, prior experience, and complexity of coding categories. *Child Development*, 45, 367-377.
Mason, D.J. (1957). Judgments of leadership based upon physiognomic cues. *Journal of Abnormal and Social Psychology*, 54, 273-274.
Mathews, A.M., Bancroft, J.H.J. & Slater, P. (1972). The principal components of sexual preference. *British Journal of Social and Clinical Psychology*, 11, 35-43.
Maxwell, A.E. (1961). *Analysing qualitative data.* New York: Wiley.
McKeachie, W.J. (1952). Lipstick as a determinant of first impressions of personality: An experiment for the general psychology course. *Journal of Social Psychology*, 36, 241-244.
McKee, J.P., & Sherriffs, A.C. (1957). The differential evaluation of males and females. *Journal of Personality*, 25, 356-371.
McKee, J.P., & Sherriffs, A.C. (1959). Men's and women's beliefs, ideals and self-concepts. *American Journal of Sociology*, 64, 356-363.
McNemar, Q. (1969). *Psychological statistics.* New York: Wiley.
Measey, L.G. (1972). The psychiatric and social relevance of tattoos in royal navy detainees. *British Journal of Criminology*, 12, 182-186.
Meenes, M. (1942). A comparison of racial stereotypes of Negro college

students in 1935 and 1942. *Psychological Bulletin*, 39, 467-468.
Meisels, M., & Guardo, C.J. (1969). Development of personal space schematas. *Child Development*, 40, 1167-1178.
Michotte, A.E. (1950). The emotions regarded as functional connections. In Reymert, M. (Ed.), *Feelings and emotions*. New York: McGraw-Hill, Pp. 114-126.
Miller, A.G. (1970). Role of physical attractiveness in impression formation. *Psychonomic Science*, 19, 241-243.
Miller, A.R. (1967). Ascription of stereotypes based on physique. Unpublished Master's thesis, California State University, Los Angeles.
Miller, A.R. (1969). Analysis of the Oedipal complex. *Psychological Reports*, 24, 781-782.
Miller, A.R., Kiker, V.L., Watson, R.A.R., Frauchiger, R.A. & Moreland, D. (1968). Experimental analysis of phsyiques as social stimuli: Part II. *Perceptual and Motor Skills,* 27, 355-359.
Miller, A.R., & Stewart, R.A. (1968). Perception of female physiques. *Perceptual and Motor Skills,* 27, 721-722.
Miller, A.R., Stewart, R.A., Steele, R.E., Watson, R.A.R., Newhauser, D. & Kiker, V.L. (1969). Perception of physiques as a diagnostic index. Paper read at Western Psychological Association, Vancouver, June, 1969.
Miller, A.R., Stewart, R.A., Steele, R.E., Watson, R.A.R., Newhauser, D. & Kiker, V.L. (1971). Psychopathology and perception of physiques. *Perceptual and Motor Skills*, 32, 475-478.
Miller, G.A. (1956). The magical number seven, plus or minus two: Some limits on our capacity for processing information. *Psychological Review*, 63, 81-97.
Miller, H.L., & Rivenbark, W.H. (1970). Sexual differences in physical attractiveness as a determinant of heterosexual liking. *Psychological Reports*, 27, 701-702.
Miller, P. McC. (1974). A note on sex differences on the semantic differential. *British Journal of Social and Clinical Psychology*, 13, 33-36.
Mills, J., & Aronson, E. (1965). Opinion change as a function of the communicator's attractiveness and desire to influence. *Journal of Personality and Social Psychology*, 1, 173-177.
Mintz, E. (1956). An example of assimilative projection. *Journal of Abnormal and Social Psychology*, 52, 279-280.
Mobbs, N.A. (1968). Eye-contact in relation to social introversion/extraversion. *British Journal of Social and Clinical Psychology*, 7, 305-306.

Moore, M. (1966). Aggression themes in a binocular rivalry situation. *Journal of Personality and Social Psychology*, 3, 685-688.

Moore, S.G. (1967). Correlates of peer acceptance in nursery school children. *Young Children*, 22, 281-297.

Mosher, D.L. (1968). Measurement of guilt in females by self-report inventories. *Journal of Consulting and Clinical Psychology*, 32, 690-695.

Mueller, W.S. (1974). Cognitive complexity and salience of dimensions in person perception. *Australian Journal of Psychology*, 26, 173-182.

Mulaik, S.A. (1964). Are personality factors raters' conceptual factors? *Journal of Consulting Psychology*, 28, 506-511.

Murstein, B.I. (1972). Physical attractiveness and marital choice. *Journal of Personality and Social Psychology*, 22, 8-12.

Mussen, P.H., & Jones, M.C. (1958). The behavior inferred motivations of late and early maturing boys. *Child Development*, 29, 61-67.

Neisser, U. (1967). *Cognitive psychology*. New York: Appleton-Century-Crofts.

Newcomb, T. (1931). An experiment designed to test the validity of a rating technique. *Journal of Educational Psychology*, 22, 279-289.

Niebuhr, H., & Cohen, D. (1956). The effect of psychopathology on visual discrimination. *Journal of Abnormal and Social Psychology*, 53, 173-177.

NORC (1947). Occupational ratings for 90 occupations. National Opinion Research Center.

Norman, W.T. (1963). Toward an adequate taxonomy of personality attributes: Replicated factor structure in peer nomination personality ratings. *Journal of Abnormal and Social Psychology*, 66, 574-583.

Oldfield, R.C., & Zangwill, O.L. (1943). Head's concept of the schema and its application in contemporary British psychology. Part IV. Wolters' theory of thinking. *British Journal of Psychology*, 33, 143-149.

Olds; E.G. (1938). Distribution of sums of squares of rank differences for small numbers of individuals. *Annals of Mathematical Statistics*, 9, 133-148.

Osgood, C.E. (1955). Fidelity and reliability. In Quaster, H. (Ed.), *Information theory in psychology*. Glencoe, Ill: Free Press.

Osgood, C.E. (1966). Dimensionality of the semantic space for communication via facial expressions. *Scandinavian Journal of Psychology*, 7, 1-30.

Osgood, C.E., Suci, G.J. & Tannenbaum, P.H. (1957). *The measurement of meaning*. Urbana: University of Illinois Press.

Osgood, C.E., Ware, E. & Morris, C. (1961). Analysis of the connotative meanings of a variety of human values as expressed by American college students. *Journal of Abnormal and Social Psychology*, 62, 62-73.

Ostermeier, A.B., & Eicher, J.B. (1966). Clothing and appearance as related to social class and social acceptance of adolescent girls. *Quarterly Bulletin of the Michigan Agricultural Experiment Station*, 48, 431-436.

Palardy, J.M. (1969). What teachers believe — What children achieve. *Elementary School Journal*, 168/169, 370-374.

Passini, F.T., & Norman, W.T. (1966). A universal conception of personality structure. *Journal of Personality and Social Psychology*, 4, 44-49.

Peabody, D. (1970). Evaluative and descriptive aspects in personality perception: A reappraisal. *Journal of Personality and Social Psychology*, 16, 639-646.

Pedersen, D.M. (1965). The measurement of individual differences in perceived personality-trait relationships and their relation to certain determinants. *Journal of Social Psychology*, 65, 233-258.

Pedersen, D.M. (1969). Evaluation of self and others and some personality correlates. *Journal of Psychology*, 71, 225-244.

Perlmutter, H.V. (1956). Correlates of two types of xenophilic orientation. *Journal of Abnormal and Social Psychology*, 52, 130-135.

Peterson, D.R. (1965). Scope and generality of verbally defined personality factors. *Psychological Review*, 72, 48-59.

Pineo, P.C. (1961). Disenchantment in the later years of marriage. *Marriage and Family Living*, 23, 3-11.

Pineo, P.C. (1969). Development patterns in marriage. *Family Coordinator*, 18, 135-140.

Pinter, R., & Fortano, G. (1944). Some measures of dominance in college women. *Journal of Social Psychology*, 19, 303-315.

Podell, J.E., & Amster, H. (1966). Evaluative concept of a person as a function of the number of stimulus traits. *Journal of Personality and Social Psychology*, 4, 333-336.

Pollis, N.P., & Doyle, D.C. (1972). Sex role, status, and perceived competence among first-graders. *Perceptual and Motor Skills*, 34, 235-238.

Powell, G.E. (1977). Psychoticism and social deviancy in children. *Advances in Behaviour Research and Therapy*, 1, 27-56.

Powell, G.E., & Stewart, R.A. (1978). The relationship of age, sex and personality to social attitudes in children aged 8-15 years. *British Journal of Social and Clinical Psychology*, 17, in press.

Powell, G.E., Stewart, R.A. & Tutton, S.J. (1973). The development of person perception. Presented at the London Conference of the British Psychological Society, December, 1973.

Powell, G.E., Stewart, R.A. & Tutton, S.J. (1974). The development of person perception: A grid study. *Bulletin of the British Psychological Society*, 27, 149. (Abstract.)

Powell, G.E., Tutton, S.J. & Stewart, R.A. (1974). The differential stereotyping of similar physiques. *British Journal of Social and Clinical Psychology*, 13, 421-423.

Pyron, B. (1965). Accuracy of interpersonal perception as a function of consistency of information. *Journal of Personality and Social Psychology*, 1, 111-117.

Raw, M. (1976). Persuading people to stop smoking. *Behaviour Research and Therapy*, 14, 97-101.

Reece, M.M. (1964). Masculinity and femininity: A factor analytic study. *Psychological Reports*, 14, 123-139.

Reich, J.W. (1968). Stimulus complexity mediation of categorization behavior. *Perceptual and Motor Skills,* 27, 723-732.

Reitz, W.E., & Jackson, D.N. (1964). Affect and stereoscopic resolution. *Journal of Abnormal and Social Psychology*, 69, 212-215.

Rist, R.C. (1970). Student social class and teacher expectations: the self-fulfilling prophecy in getto education. *Harvard Education Review*, 40, 411-451.

Rodin, M.J. (1972). Informativeness of trait descriptions. *Journal of Personality and Social Psychology*, 21, 341-344.

Rodgers, E.M., & Havens, A.E. (1960). Prestige rating and mate selection on a college campus. *Marriage and Family Living*, 22, 55-59.

Rokeach, M. (1961). Belief versus race as determinants of social distance: Comments on Triandis' paper. *Journal of Abnormal and Social Psychology*, 62, 187-188.

Rokeach, M., Smith, P.W. & Evans, R.I. (1960). Two kinds of prejudice or one? In Rokeach, M. (Ed.), *The open and closed mind*. New York: Basic Books. Pp. 132-168.

Rosenberg, S., & Jones, R. (1972). A method for investigating and representing a person's implicit theory of personality: Theodore Dreiser's view of people. *Journal of Personality and Social Psychology*, 22, 372-386.

Rosenberg, S., Nelson, C. & Vivekananthan, P.S. (1968). A multidimensional approach to the structure of personality impressions. *Journal of Personality and Social Psychology*, 9, 283-294.

Rosenberg, S., Olshan, K. (1970). Evaluative and descriptive aspects in personality perception. *Journal of Personality and Social Psychology*, 16, 616-626.

Rosenberg, S., & Sedlak, A. (1972). Structural representation of perceived personality trait relationships. In Romney, A.K., Shepard, R.N. & Nerlove, S.B. (Eds.), *Multidimensional scaling: Theory and applications in the behavioral Sciences: Applications*. Vol. 2. New York: Seminar Press.

Rosenkrantz, P.S., Vogel, S.R., Bee, H., Broverman, I.K. & Broverman, D.M. (1968). Sex-role stereotypes and self-concepts in college students. *Journal of Consulting and Clinical Psychology*, 32, 287-295.

Rosnow, R.L., Wainer, H. & Arms, R.L. (1969). Anderson's personality-trait words rated by men and women as a function of stimulus sex. *Psychological Reports*, 24, 787-790.

Ryle, A. (1975). *Frames and cages*. London: Sussex University Press.

Sager, E.B., & Ferguson, L.W. (1970). Person perception as a function of perceiver's position on a cold-warm dimension. *Psychological Record*, 20, 321-325.

Sailor, P.J. (1971). Perception of line in clothing. *Perceptual and Motor Skills,* 33, 987-990.

Salzman, L. (1967). Psychology of the female: a new look. *Archives of General Psychiatry*, 17, 195-203.

Sandstrom, C.I. (1953). Sex differences in localization and orientation. *Acta Psychologica*, 9, 82-96.

Sappenfield, B.R. (1969). Stereotypical perception of a personality trait in fraternity members. *Perceptual and Motor Skills,*29, 460-462.

Sappenfield, B.R., Kaplan, B.B. & Balogh, B. (1966). Perceptual correlates of stereotypical masculinity-femininity. *Journal of Personality and Social Psychology*, 4, 585-590.

Sarbin, T.R. (1942). A contribution to the study of actuarial and

individual methods of prediction. *American Journal of Sociology*, 48, 593-602.
Sarbin, T.R., & Berdie, R.F. (1940). Relation of measured interests to the Allport-Vernon Study of Values. *Journal of Applied Psychology*, 24, 287-296.
Sarbin, T.R., Taft, R. & Bailey, D.E. (1960). *Clinical inference and cognitive theory*. New York: Holt, Rinehart & Winston.
Schell, R.E., & Silber, J.W. (1968). Sex-role discrimination among young children. *Perceptual and Motor Skills*, 27, 379-389.
Schonbuch, S.S., & Schell, R.E. (1967). Judgments of body appearance by fat and skinny male college students. *Perceptual and Motor Skills*, 24, 999-1002.
Schonfeld, W.A. (1950). Inadequate masculine physique as a factor in personality development of adolescent boys. *Psychosomatic Medicine*, 12, 49-54.
Scodel, A. (1957). Heterosexual somatic preference and fantasy dependency. *Journal of Consulting Psychology*, 21, 371-374.
Sechrest, L., & Jackson, D.N. (1961). Social intelligence and accuracy of interpersonal predictions. *Journal of Personality*, 29, 167-182.
Secord, P.F., & Backman, C.W. (1964). *Social psychology*, New York: McGraw-Hill.
Secord, P.F., & Jourard, S.M. (1956). Mother-concepts and judgments of young women's faces. *Journal of Abnormal and Social Psychology*, 52, 246-250.
Selcer, R.J., & Hilton, I.R. (1972). Cultural differences in the acquisition of sex-roles. Proceedings of the 80th Annual Convention of the American Psychological Association.
Sharma, K.I., & Sinha, S.N. (1968). A note on cross-cultural comparison of occupational ratings. *Journal of Social Psychology*, 75, 283-284.
Shaw, M.E., & Wagner, P.J. (1975). Role selection in the service of self-presentation. *Memory and Cognition*, 3, 481-484.
Sheldon, W.H. (1940). *The varieties of human physique*. New York: Harper.
Sheldon, W.H. (1942). *The varieties of temperament*. New York: Harper.
Sheldon, W.H. (1954). *Atlas of men*. New York: Gramercy.
Sheldon, W.H. (1963). *The varieties of human physique*. New York: Hafner. (Reissued.)
Sherriffs, A.C., & McKee, J.P. (1957). Qualitative aspects of beliefs about men and women. *Journal of Personality*, 25, 451-464.

Shoben, E.J. (1949). The assessment of parental attitudes in relation to child adjustment. *Genetic Psychology Monographs*, 39, 101-148.
Shor, R.E. (1957). Effect of preinformation upon human characteristics attributed to animated geometric figures. *Journal of Abnormal and Social Psychology*, 54, 124-126.
Shrauger, S., & Altrocchi, J. (1964). The personality of the perceiver as a factor in person perception. *Psychological Bulletin*, 62, 289-308.
Sieber, J.E., & Lanzetta, J.T. (1964). Conflict and conceptual structure as determinants of decision making behavior. *Journal of Personality*, 32, 622-641.
Sieber, J.E., & Lanzetta, J.T. (1966). Some determinants of individual differences in predecision information-processing behavior. *Journal of Personality and Social Psychology*, 4, 561-571.
Siegel, S. (1954). Certain determinants and correlates of authoritarianism. *Genetic Psychology Monographs*, 49, 187-229.
Siegel, S. (1956). *Nonparametric statistics*. New York: McGraw-Hill.
Sigall, H., & Aronson, E. (1969). Liking for an evaluator as a function of her physical attractiveness and nature of the evaluations. *Journal of Experimental Social Psychology*, 5, 93-100.
Sigall, H., & Landy, D. (1973). Radiating beauty: The effects of having a physically attractive partner on person perception. *Journal of Personality and Social Psychology*, 28, 218-224.
Sigall, H., & Ostrov, N. (1975). Beautiful but dangerous: Effects of offender attractiveness and nature of crime on juridic judgment. *Journal of Personality and Social Psychology*, 31, 410-414.
Signell, K. (1966). Cognitive complexity in person perception and nation perception: A developmental approach. *Journal of Personality*, 34, 517-537.
Sistrunk, F., & McDavid, J.W. (1971). Sex variable in conforming behavior. *Journal of Personality and Social Psychology*, 17, 200-207.
Slater, P. (1965). The test-restest reliability of some methods of multiple comparisons. *British Journal of Mathematical and Statistical Psychology*, 18, 227-242.
Slater, P. (1967). *Notes on INGRID '67*. Institute of Psychiatry, London.
Slater, P. (1969). Theory and technique of the repertory grid. *British Journal of Psychiatry*, 115, 1287-1296.
Slater, P. (1972). The measurement of consistency in repertory grids. *British Journal of Psychiatry*, 121, 45-51.
Slater, P. (1976). *Explorations of intrapersonal space*. London: Wiley.
Sleet, D.A. (1969). Physique and social image. *Perceptual and Motor*

Skills, 28, 295-299.

Slovic, P. (1966). Cue-consistency and cue-utilization in judgment. *American Journal of Psychology*, 79, 427-434.

Soskin, W.F. (1959). Influence of four types of data on diagnostic conceptualization in psychological testing. *Journal of Abnormal and Social Psychology*, 58, 69-78.

Sparrow, N.H., & Ross, J. (1964). The duel nature of extraversion: A replication. *Australian Journal of Psychology*, 16, 214-218.

Spinetta, J.J., Rigler, D. & Karon, M. (1974). Personal space as a measure of a dying child's sense of isolation. *Journal of Consulting and Clinical Psychology*, 42, 751-756.

Staffieri, J.R. (1967). A study of social stereotype of body image in children. *Journal of Personality and Social Psychology*, 7, 101-104.

Staffieri, J.R. (1972). Body build and behavioral expectancies in young females. *Developmental Psychology*, 6, 125-127.

Steele, R.E., Powell, G.E. & Stewart, R.A. (1973). Physique and personality: The problem of discrimination within somatypes. Paper read at Western Psychological Association, April, 1973, Anaheim, California.

Stelmachers, Z.T., & McHugh, R. (1964). Contribution of stereotyped and individualized information to predictive accuracy. *Journal of Consulting Psychology*, 28, 234-242.

Stewart, R.A., Powell, G.E., Rankin, H.J. & Tutton, S.J. (1975). Concordance coefficient (*W*), correction for the inequality of interval in the underlying *rhos*, *Perceptual and Motor Skills*, 40, 459-462.

Stewart, R.A., Powell, G.E. & Tutton, S.J. (1974). Subjective factors in social stereotyping and impression formation. *Perceptual and Motor Skills*, 39, 867-871.

Stewart, R.A., Steele, R.E. & Miller, A.R. (1970). Individual and sex differences in the perception of female physiques. Paper read at Western Psychological Association, Los Angeles, April, 1970.

Stewart, R.A., Tutton, S.J. & Steele, R.E. (1973). Stereotyping and personality: I. Sex differences in perception of female physiques. *Perceptual and Motor Skills,* 36, 811-814.

Stolz, H.R., & Stolz, L.M. (1951). *Somatic development in adolescent boys*. New York: Macmillan.

Stroebe, W., Inske, C.A., Thompson, V.D. & Layton, B.D. (1971). Effects of physical attractiveness, attitude similarity, and sex on various aspects of interpersonal attraction. *Journal of Personality and Social Psychology*, 18, 79-91.

Strongman, K.T., & Hart, C.J. (1968). Stereotyped reactions to body build. *Psychological Reports*, 23, 1175-1178.

Stuckert, R.P. (1963). Role perception and marital satisfaction. A configurational approach. *Marriage and Family Living*, 25, 415-419.

Suchman, J.R. (1956). Social sensitivity in the small task-oriented group. *Journal of Abnormal and Social Psychology*, 52, 75-83.

Suedfeld, P., Bochner, S. & Matas, C. (1971). Petitioner's attire and petition signing by peace demonstrators: A field experiment. *Journal of Applied Social Psychology*, 1, 278-283.

Suedfeld, P., Bochner, S. & Wnek, D. (1972). Helper-sufferer similarity and a specific request for help: bystander intervention during a peace demonstration. *Journal of Applied Social Psychology*, 2, 17-23.

Sweeney, E.J. (1953). Sex differences in problem solving. Stanford University Department of Psychology Technical Report, No. 1, 1953.

Taft, R. (1955). The ability to judge people. *Psychological Bulletin,* 52, 1-23.

Taft, R. (1959). Multiple methods of personality assessment. *Psychological Bulletin,* 56, 333-352.

Taft, R. (1966). Accuracy of empathic judgments of acquaintances and strangers. *Journal of Personality and Social Psychology*, 5, 600-604.

Tagiuri, R. (1969). Person perception. In Lindzey, G., & Aronson, E. (Eds.), *The handbook of social psychology*. (2nd ed.) Vol. 3. Reading, Mass.: Addison-Wesley. Pp. 395-449.

Tagiuri, R., Blake, R.R. & Bruner, J.S. (1953). Some determinants of the perception of positive and negative feelings in others. *Journal of Abnormal and Social Psychology*, 48, 585-592.

Tagiuri, R., & Petrullo, L. (1958). *Person perception and interpersonal behavior*. Stanford: Stanford University Press.

Tanaka, Y., & Osgood, C.E. (1965). Cross-culture, cross-concept, and cross-subject generality of affective meaning systems. *Journal of Personality and Social Psychology*, 2, 143-153.

Taylor, A.J.W. (1968). A search among Borstal girls for the psychological and social significance of their tattoos. *British Journal of Criminology*, 8 170-185.

Taylor, W.L. (1964). Correcting the average rank correlation coefficient for ties in the rankings. *Journal of the American Statistical Association*, 59, 872-876.

Taylor, W.L., & Fong, C. (1963). Some contributions to average rank correlation methods and to the distribution of the average rank correlation coefficient. *Journal of the American Statistical*

Asociation, 58, 756-769.
Tesser, A., & Brodie, M.A. (1971). A note on the evaluation of a 'computer date.' *Psychonomic Science*, 23, 300.
Thorndike, E.I. (1920). A constant error in psychological rating. *Journal of Applied Psychology*, 4, 25-29.
Tipton, R.M., & Browning, S. (1972). The influence of age and obesity on helping behaviour. *British Journal of Social and Clinical Psychology*, 11, 404-406.
Todd, F.J., & Rappoport, L. (1964). A cognitive structure approach to person perception: A comparison of two models. *Journal of Abnormal and Social Psychology*, 68, 469-478.
Tolor, A. (1975). Effects of procedural variations in measuring interpersonal distance by means of representational space. *Psychological Repots*, 36, 475-491.
Triandis, H.C., & Davis, E.E. (1965). Race and belief as determinants of behavioral intentions. *Journal of Personality and Social Psychology*, 2, 715-725.
Triandis, H.C., & Fishbein, M. (1963). Cognitive interaction in person perception. *Journal of Abnormal and Social Psychology*, 67, 446-453.
Triandis, H.C., & Osgood, C.E. (1958). A comparative factorial analysis of semantic structures in monolingual Greek and American college students. *Journal of Abnormal and Social Psychology*, 57, 187-196.
Tripodi, T., & Bieri, J. (1963). Cognitive complexity as a function of own and provided constructs. *Psychological Reports*, 13, 26,.
Tripodi, T., & Bieri, J. (1964). Information transmission in clinical judgments as a function of stimulus dimensionality and cognitive complexity. *Journal of Personality*, 32, 119-137.
Tutton, S.J. (1973). *Generalized grid technique*. Institute of Psychiatry, London.
Tutton, S.J., Stewart, R.A., Powell, G.E. & Rankin, H.J. (1974). An examination of sex-role stereotyping through physique perception. *Bulletin of the British Psychological Society*, 27, 186. (Abstract.)
Tzeng, O.C. (1975). Differentiation of affective and denotative meaning systems and their influence in personality ratings. *Journal of Personality and Social Psychology*, 32, 978-988.

Vannoy, J.S. (1965). Generality of cognitive complexity-simplicity as a personality construct. *Journal of Personality and Social Psychology*, 2, 385-396.
Vernon, M.D. (1955). The functions of schemata in perceiving.

Psychological Review, 62, 180-192.
Vernon, P.E. (1964). *Personality assessment*. London: Methuen.
Vogel, S.R., Broverman, I.K., Broverman, D.M., Clarkson, F.E. & Rosenkrantz, P.S. (1970). Maternal employment and perception of sex-roles among college students. *Developmental Psychology*, 3, 384-391.
Vogel, S.R., Rosenkrantz, P.S., Broverman, I.K., Broverman, D.M. & Clarkson, F.E. (1975). Sex-role self-concept and life style plans of young women. *Journal of Consulting and Clinical Psychology*, 43, 427.
Vroegh, K., Jenkin, N., Black, N. & Hendrick, M. (1967). Discriminant analysis of preschool masculinity and femininity. *Multivariate Behavioral Research*, 2, 299-313.

Wahler, H.J. (1958). Social desirability and self-ratings of intakes, patients in treatment, and controls. *Journal of Consulting Psychology*, 22, 357-363.
Walker, R.N. (1962). Body build and behavior in young children: I. Body build and nursery school teachers' ratings. *Monograph of the Society for Research in Child Development*, 27, No. 3 (Serial No. 84).
Wallach, M.A., & Caron, A.J. (1959). Attribute criteriality and sex-linked conservatism as determinants of psychological similarity. *Journal of Abnormal and Social Psychology*, 59, 43-50.
Walster, E., Aronson, V., Abrahams, D. & Rottman, L. (1966). Importance of physical attractiveness in dating behavior. *Journal of Personality and Social Psychology*, 5, 508-516.
Ward, C.D. (1967). Own height, sex, and liking in the judgement of heights of others. *Journal of Personality*, 35, 381-401.
Ware, R., & Harvey, O.J. (1967). A cognitive determinant of impression formation. *Journal of Personality and Social Psychology*, 5, 38-44.
Warr, P. (1974). Combining three items of personal information. *British Journal of Psychology*, 65, 1-5.
Warr, P., & Jackson, P. (1975). The importance of extremity. *Journal of Personality and Social Psychology*, 32, 278-282.
Warr, P.B., & Knapper, C. (1968). *The perception of people and events*. New York: Wiley.
Warr, P.B., & Smith, J.S. (1970). Combining information about people: Comparisons between six models. *Journal of Personality and Social Psychology*, 16, 55-65.
Watts, F.N., Powell, G.E. & Austin, S.V. (1973). The modification of

abnormal beliefs. *British Journal of Medical Psychology*, 46, 359-363.

Wells, W.D., & Siegel, B. (1961). Stereotyped somatotypes *Psychological Reports*, 8, 77-78.

Werner, H. (1957). *Comparative psychology of mental development.* New York: International Universities Press.

West, D.J., & Farrington, D.P. (1973). *Who becomes delinquent*? London: Heinemann.

Westbrook, M. (1974). Sex differences in the perception of emotion. *Australian Journal of Psychology*, 26, 139-146.

Whitfield, J.W. (1954). The distribution of the differences in total rank value for two particular objects in *m* rankings of *n* objects. *British Journal of Statistical Psychology*, 7, 45-49.

Whorf, B.L. (1956). *Language, thought, and reality: Selected writings of Benjamin Lee Whorf.* Edited by Carroll, J.B. Cambridge, Mass.: MIT Press.

Wiggins, J.S., Wiggins, N. & Conger, J.C. (1968). Correlates of heterosexual somatic preference. *Journal of Personality and Social Psychology*, 10, 82-90.

Wiggins, N., Hoffman, P.J. & Taber, T. (1969). Types of judges and cue utilization in judgments of intelligence. *Journal of Personality and Social Psychology*, 12, 52-59.

Wiggins, N., & Wiggins, J.S. (1969). A typological analysis of male preferences for female body types. *Multivariate Behavioral Research*, 4, 89-102.

Wiley, M.G. (1973). Sex roles in games. *Sociometry*, 36, 526-541.

Willemsen, E., & Reynolds, B. (1973). Sex differences in adults' judgments of the horizontal. *Developmental Psychology*, 8, 309.

Williams, E. (1971). The effect of varying the elements in the Bannister-Fransella Grid Test of Thought Disorder. *British Journal of Psychiatry*, 119, 207-212.

Wilson, G.D., & Brazendale, J. (1976). Reported in Wilson, G.D., & Nias, D.K.B., *Love's mysteries: The psychology of sexual attraction.* London: Open Books.

Wilson, G.D., Nias, D.K.B. & Insel, P.M. (1972). *Manual for the Children's Scale of Social Attitudes*. London: Children's Studies, Ltd.

Wilson, P.R. (1968). Perceptual distortion of height as a function of ascribed academic status. *Journal of Social Psychology*, 74, 97-102.

Winer, B.J. (1962). *Statistical principles in experimental design.* New York: McGraw-Hill.

Wish, M., Deutsch, M. & Kaplan, S.J. (1976). Perceived dimensions of interpersonal relations. *Journal of Personality and Social*

Psychology, 33, 409-420.
Wishner, J. (1960). Reanalysis of "impressions of personality." *Psychological Review*, 67, 96-112.
Wolfgang, A. (1968). Exploration of limits of information processing in concept identification as a function of sex and background-relevant information. *Perceptual and Motor Skills*, 27, 1035-1038.
Woodworth, R.S., & Schlosberg, H. (1954). *Experimental psychology*. Revised edition. New York: Holt, Rinehart & Wilson.

Yarrow, M.R., & Campbell, J.D. (1963). Person perception in children. *Merrill-Palmer Quarterly*, 9, 57-72.

Zuckerman, M., Ribback, B.B., Monashkin, I. & Norton, J.A. (1958). Normative data and factor analysis of the Parental Attitude Research Instrument. *Journal of Consulting Psychology*, 22, 165-171.
Zimring, F.M. (1971). Cognitive simplicity-complexity: Evidence for disparate processes. *Journal of Personality*, 39, 1-9.

Appendix I

Targets Represented By Differences in Body Build

(reduced in size by 20 per cent)

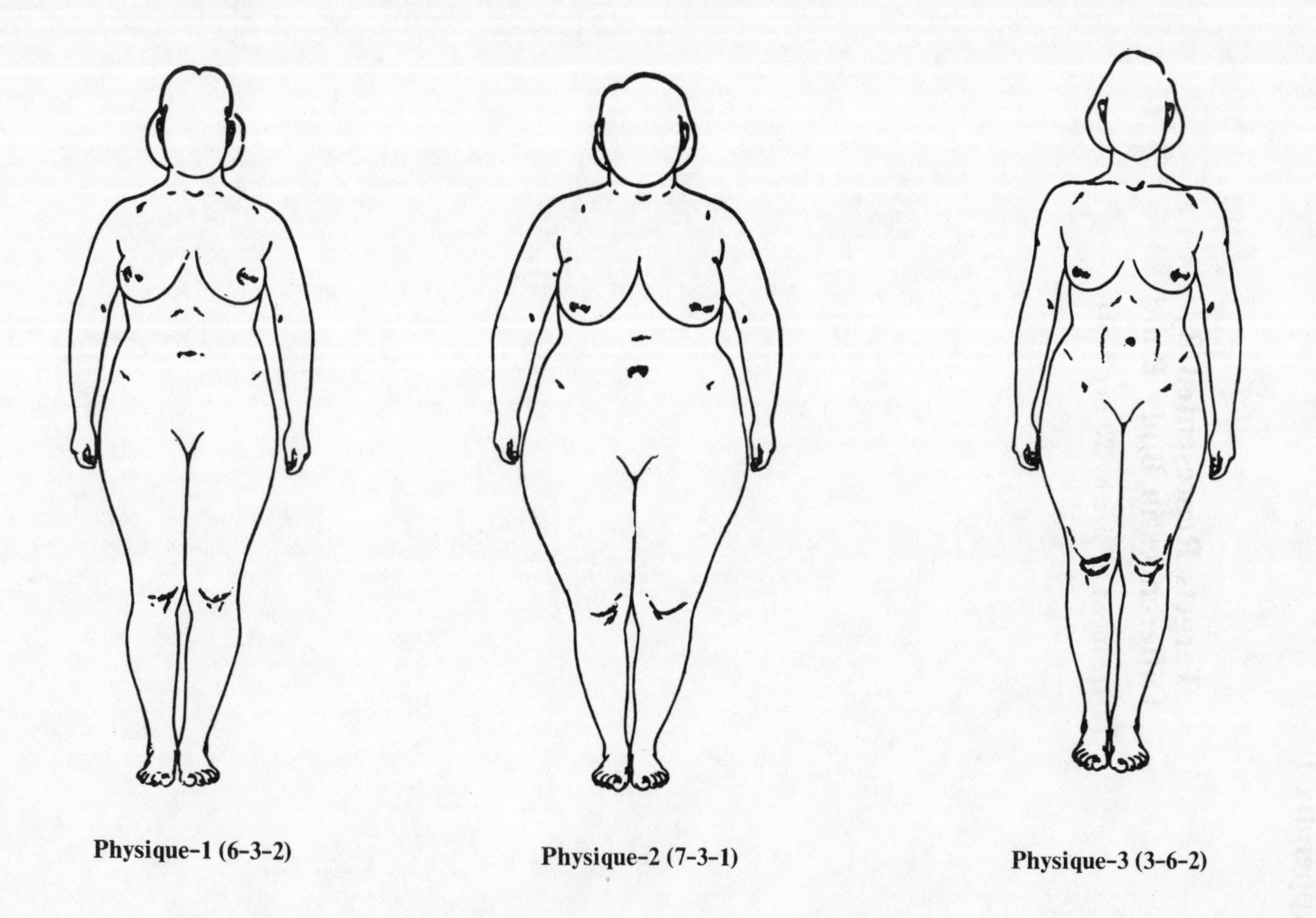

Physique–1 (6–3–2)

Physique–2 (7–3–1)

Physique–3 (3–6–2)

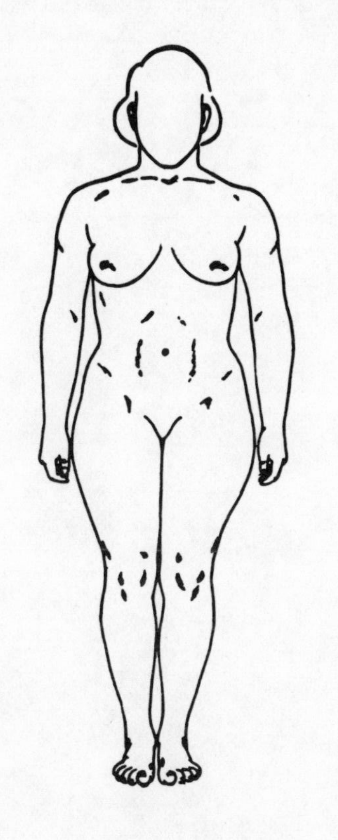

Physique - 4 (1-7-1)

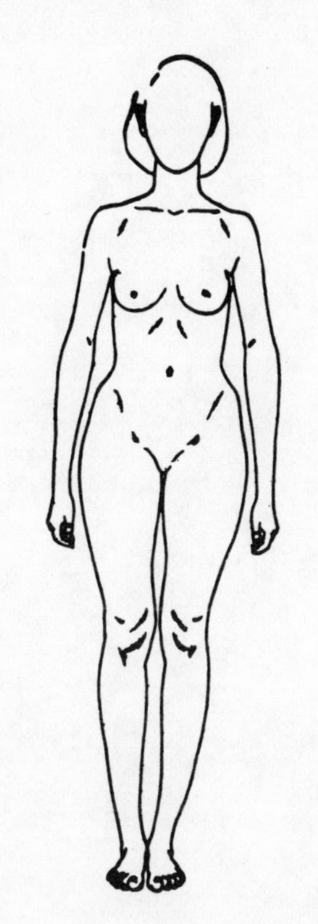

Physique-5 (1-2-7)

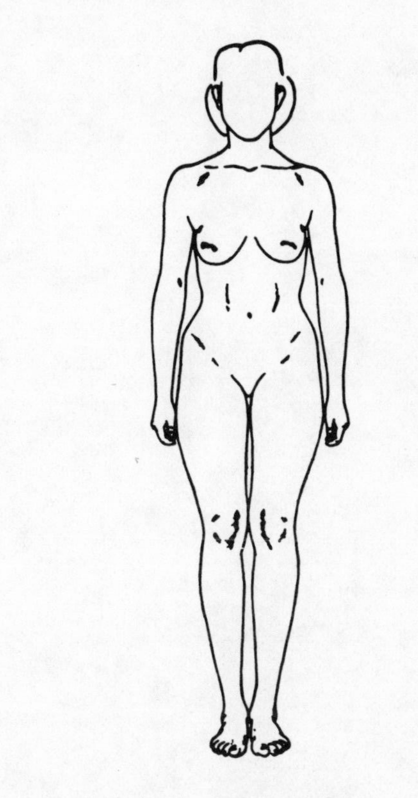

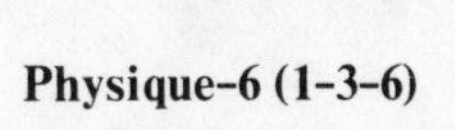

Physique-6 (1-3-6)

Appendix II

Targets Represented By Differences in Dress

(reduced in size by 15 per cent)

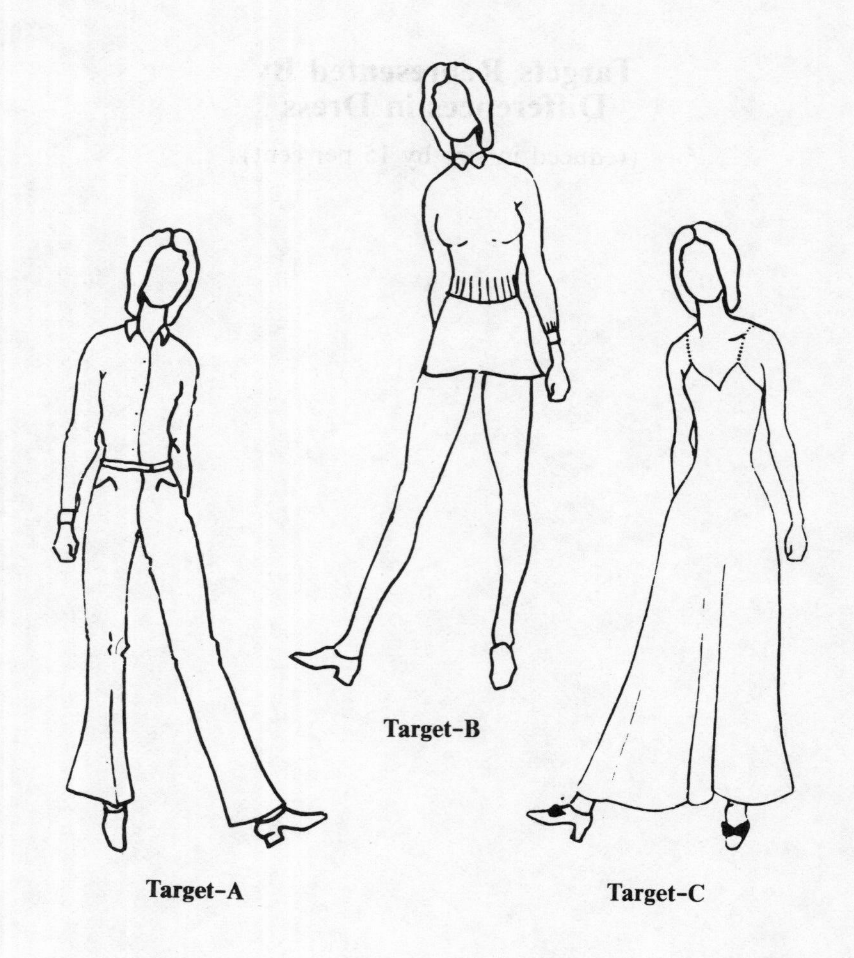
Target-A
Target-B
Target-C

Target-E
Target-D
Target-F

Appendix III

The Measurement of concordance in data based on ranking[1]

III-1 Kendall's Coefficient of Concordance (W)

When wishing to ascertain if a set of *m* judges have employed a similar criterion in ranking *n* stimuli or target-persons, it is most usual to turn to the *Coefficient of Concordance* (*W*), a statistic specifically developed by Kendall (1948) to deal with this type of problem. In order to outline this procedure, a hypothetical example is presented in Table III-1, illustrating how five target-person might be ranked for Attractiveness by three judges.

In his approach to this problem, Kendall suggested that it would be useful to describe concordance or degree of agreement by computing the mean of the intercorrelations (as Spearman *rhos*, r_Ss) between all possible pairs of judges. In the present example, three judges give rise to three intercorrelations — viz 0.90 for 1 and 2, 0.80 for 1 and 3, and 0.90 for 2 and 3 — yielding a mean intercorrelation (mean-r_S) of 0.867 indicating a moderate degree of agreement between the judges. By way of interpretation, we would conclude that the three judges had employed similar criteria in evaluating Attractiveness, thus evidencing a *social-stereotype* for this quality.

While this procedure does provide an index of concordance which is much less ambiguous than other statistics, such as the X^2 (which differs according to sample size), the required computations become extremely tedious as the number of judges is increased, with the number of comparisons being equal to $m(m - 1)/2$, or 4,950 individual r_Ss in the case of 100 judges. To eliminate this difficulty, Kendall devised a method of computing mean-r_S indirectly from sums of ranks (R_j). To use this approach, it is first necessary to compute W according to the following:

$$W = \frac{12\,\Sigma(R_j - MR)^2}{m^2\,(n^3 - \mathrm{n})} \qquad \text{(III-1)}$$

where R_j is the sum of ranks for each target, MR is the mean of the R_js, m is the number of subjects or judges, and n is the number of targets. After

1. The problem of measuring concordance in graded or parametric data is not often encountered, but the statistical basis of this problem has been quite thoroughly worked out (e.g., Edwards, 1954, pp. 412-415; Haggard, 1958; Winer, 1962, pp. 124-132, 136-138) and apart from its treatment in Section 6.6.2 above will not be considered further here.

obtaining W, the mean-r_S can be obtained through the following formula:

$$\text{Mean-}r_s = (mW - 1)/(m - 1) \qquad \text{(III-2)}$$

where the quantities have the same meaning as in formula III-1. It is worth noting that for large sample sizes, W is approximately equal to mean-r_S and the step involving formula III-2 can, for all practical purposes, be omitted. Siegel (1956) should be consulted for more detailed examples of computations, while the various procedures for testing the significance of W are treated most fully in Edwards (1954, pp. 402-415) or Maxwell (1961, pp. 119-121).

Table III-1

Ranking of five target persons (I-V) by three judges (artificial data), accompanied by the more important computational entities (R_j, M_r, T_r) and four equivalent statistics (W, $Mean\text{-}\bar{r}_S$, ρ_{av}, $\bar{r}_{iM}$) for assessing concordance

	Targets					
	I	II	III	IV	V	
First Judge	1	3	2	4	5	
Second Judge	1	3	2	5	4	
Third Judge	1	2	3	5	4	
						Sum
Sum of Ranks (R_j)	3.00	8.00	7.00	14.00	13.00	45.00
Mean Rank (M_r)	1.00	2.67	2.33	4.67	4.33	15.00
True Rank (T_r)	1	3	2	5	4	15.00
(T_r x M_r)*	1.00	8.01	4.66	23.35	17.32	54.34
(M_r^2)**	1.00	7.13	5.43	21.81	18.75	54.12

Four equivalent measures of Concordance — Based on the above data

$W = 0.911$ Mean $-r_S = 0.867$† $\rho_{av} = 0.933$ $\bar{r}_{iM} = 0.955$

* Used in computing ρ_{av}. ** Used in computing W and $\bar{r}_{iM}$.

† Based on a transformation of W (see text).

In our investigations of W, we were able to obtain an equivalent form of formula III-1 which allows W to be computed directly from mean rankings (M_rs) rather than sums of ranks. The equivalent expression is as follows:

$$W = \frac{\frac{1}{n}\,\Sigma M_r^2 - GM^2}{\frac{1}{12}(n^2 - 1)} \qquad \text{(III-3)}$$

where M_r is the mean rank of each target, GM is the Grand Mean (which is equal to $(n + 1)/2$), and n is, again, the number of targets or stimuli.

This formula confers two immediate advantages over that shown in III-1. First, by not requiring a term to represent the number of subjects (m), it is computationally less complex than its predecessor (and is more convenient for programming). Second, since most journal articles and computer programmes present data as means rather than sums, the latter formulation is much more efficient than III-1 should one need to compute Ws on data from these sources. Apart from these two considerations, the formula shown in III-3 does, because of its simplicity, provide a clear demonstration of the relationship of W to a more lately developed statistic. This hitherto unsuspected relationship, discussed in Section III-4, serves to greatly increase the utility of W, by allowing one to test whether two Ws are significantly different from one another without resorting to some very laborious nonparametric procedures (see Section 3.6.2).

Bearing in mind that mean-r_s and W are in most circumstances numerically equivalent, we will discuss some of the more important features of W. As a statistic, W can assume values ranging from 0 to 1 — with 0 indicating *maximum disagreement* among judges, and 1 occurring only when the ranks assigned by each judge are *exact replicas* of those assigned by the remaining judges. Amplifying upon this point, it should be borne in mind that W refers explicitly to the *similarity between judges*, while other comparable statistics, such as the one to be discussed in Section III-2 below, approaches the problem of consensus in terms of *similarity of the judges to the group criterion*. As can be anticipated, the latter approach does, when applied to the same data as W, yield a numerically larger index of concordance — a condition which arises because markedly dissimilar judges are always more similar to a common mean than they are to one another.

Kendall (1948, p. 89) has pointed out that W is subject to confounding when the subjects from which it is derived are composed of two (or more) samples with incompatible criteria. In this case, each of the constituent groups may exhibit a large degree of consensus, but because of the dissimilarity between the various criteria the over-all W is much smaller than that which could be obtained from any one of the constituent groups in isolation. While this problem has been discussed in detail in Chapter 2, it is important to recognise that this type of confounding makes the interpretation of small or even non-significant Ws very problematical, with Kendall going so far as to suggest that they should not be interpreted until the raw data upon which they are based has been examined against such contingencies. W is not, however, alone in this failing, since it is quite clear that all measures of consensus which rely upon agreement with a single criterion — including those to be discussed below — are open to this type of confounding. On the other hand, a large value of W has quite clear implications, and consequently W has proved to be a very useful measure of concordance in many varied circumstances.

Apart from confounding, one of the greatest drawbacks to W has been the lack of a convenient means of ascertaining if observed Ws differ significantly from one another. As mentioned above, such comparisons can be carried out by means of nonparametric procedures, but this approach is tedious, and to a certain extent arbitrary, since various non-parametric tests (e.g., Mann-Whitney vs. Kolmogorov-Smirnov) are liable to provide results which occasionally show appreciable differences. Moreover, the nonparametric procedures require access to the raw data, making it extremely awkward to compare Ws which have been prepared or published by others. It was primarily for these reasons that we set out to investigate the alternatives to W considered below.

III-2 Consensus as an expression of the average similarity of judges' rankings to a criterion ranking

Starting with Lyerly (1952), there have been a number of investigations into the relationship of the rankings of m judges to a *criterion ranking*, a single ranking in which the stimuli or targets are ordered in accordance with some principle, such as expert judgement (Cureton, 1958, 1965; Taylor & Fong, 1963; Taylor, 1964; Whitfield, 1953, 1954). As a result of these investigations, it has been shown that the average Spearman *rho* correlation (ρ_{av}) between a single criterion ranking and the rankings of m individual judges can, in a slight modification of Taylor and Fong (1963, p.759, eq. 5), be written as follows:

$$\rho_{av} = 1 - \frac{2(2n+1)}{n-1} + \frac{12\,\Sigma M_r C_r}{n^3 - n} \qquad \text{(III-4)}$$

Here, n is again the number of targets or stimuli, M_r is the mean ranking ascribed by the judges, and C_r is the criterion ranking, as provided by a single expert, for example. By employing such a procedure, it could be ascertained to what extent the judgements of a group of m lay persons agreed with that of a single expert on, say, fine paintings.

To measure concordance by means of ρ_{av}, it is necessary to obtain the criterion ranking from the mean rankings of the individual targets — by rank-ordering the targets (or stimuli) on the basis of their mean ranks. In so far as this procedure yields the most representative ranking, the resulting order is, in some contexts, referred to as the 'true ranking' (Kendall, 1948, p. 87; Siegel, 1956, p. 238). The relationship between the mean ranks and the true ranks can be seen quite clearly in Table III-1.

After determining which are the true ranks, ρ_{av} can be computed according to the following formula:

$$\rho_{av} = \frac{\frac{1}{n}\Sigma M_r T_r - GM^2}{\frac{1}{12}(n^2 - 1)} \qquad \text{(III-5)}$$

which is numerically equivalent to III-4, but considerably more compact and consistent with the body of formulae presented here. In III-5, n represents the number of targets, M_r corresponds to mean rank, T_r to true rank (which has been substituted for the C_r appearing in III-4), and GM is, again, the grand mean of the ranks (equal to $(n+1)/2$).

In respect to the hypothetical example shown in Table III-1, it can be shown by using either III-4 or -5 that the ρ_{av} is equal to 0.934. Since the correlations between the rankings of the individual judges and the true ranking are, respectively, 0.90, 1.00, and 0.90 (and yield an arithmetic mean of 0.933), it is obvious that the value of ρ_{av} is the same whether obtained by summing individual r_ss or by means of the appropriate formula. In looking back as Section III-1, it is readily apparent that ρ_{av} is somewhat larger than the mean-r_s (0.867), or its corresponding W (0.911), derived from these data. For reasons which will emerge most clearly from Section III-4 below, this difference becomes progressively greater for smaller values of ρ_{av} and mean-r_s, but is, at the same time, shown to be trivial in its consequences.

Turning to the statistical and psychological implications of ρ_{av}, it is well to remember that this statistic corresponds to the *average correlation*, in terms of Spearman's *rho*, between a *single true rank* — which is the most representative ordering of the targets with respect to the trait in question — and each of *the subjects' individual rankings*.

Consequently, ρ_{av} is based on only m correlations (i.e., one per judge) rather than $m(m - 1)/2$ as in the case of W. In common with W, ρ_{av} can assume any value between 0 and 1 — where 0 indicates that the judges' individual rankings are maximally dissimilar from the true ranking (and each other as well), while 1 signifies that each judge's ranking is an exact replica of the true ranking (and consequently identical with one another as well). From this relationship, it can be seen that W and ρ_{av} not only resemble one another in terms of formulae (cf. III-3 and III-5), but also in their implications for consensus — being, as we shall see, almost exact equivalents. Irrespective of this near equivalence, it is shown in the following Section that ρ_{av} does, indeed, have several distinct advantages over W and mean-r_s in a variety of applications.

III-3 Comparing ρ_{av}s: Testing for differences in concordance between independent groups

In 1969, Miller and his colleagues (Miller, et al., 1969) found it necessary to compare the degree of concordance with which four different diagnostic groups stereotyped body-build. They solved this problem by using the various true rankings to compute a squared deviation score for each subject, and, in turn, introduced these individual deviation scores into a multiple-group nonparametric test to ascertain if any of the four groups differed in respect to concordance. A similar approach was adopted by Granger (1957, pp. 38-40), excepting that he substituted an analysis of variance for the nonparametric test. Subsequently, we (Stewart, et al., 1973, 1974) were able to show that the individual deviation scores correspond with r_ss, and that the over-all process does, in essence, test whether any of the groups concerned differ significantly with respect to their ρ_{av}s. An example of this nonparametric testing of differences between ρ_{av}s is shown in detail in Section 3.6.3 above.

Contrasting W with ρ_{av}, with requires $m(m-1)/2$ *rhos* rather than m in the case of the latter, it is clear that the problem of significance testing cannot be solved in such a simple manner as the above. The problem with W is further complicated by the great interdependence which arises when the data from m subjects gives rise to $m(m - 1)/2$ correlations. This is, then, one of the great disadvantages of W — that its constituent parts (i.e., r_ss) are not amenable to a further analysis or meaningful partitioning, even if it were practicable to obtain them. On the other hand, we will show, in Section III-4 below, that there is a test which can be applied directly to Ws derived from independent groups to determine if the differences between them are significant.

The nonparametric testing of ρ_{av} is, as mentioned above, not entirely satisfactory — it is excessively tedious for large samples, and the likelihood of finding or not finding differences occasionally varies according to which of the several available nonparametric tests happens to be employed. Consequently, it is of more than passing importance that Hartley (1953; Bendig, 1956, p. 77) has shown that conventional z' statistics (Edwards, 1950, p. 136) can be used to test whether two ρ_{av}s from independent groups differ significantly from one another. Using this approach, the two ρ_{av}s are first transformed to z's (according to Fisher), and then entered into the following formula:

$$z = \frac{z'_1 - z'_2}{\sqrt{\dfrac{1}{m_1\,(n-3)} + \dfrac{1}{m_2\,(n-3)}}} \qquad \text{(III-6)}$$

where z'_1 and z'_2 represent the transformed ρ_{av}s, m_1 and m_2 refer, respectively, to the number of subjects in groups 1 and 2, n is the number of targets, and z corresponds to a *standard score* or *relative deviate*. Thus if the obtained z exceeds the conventional limits for a 1- or 2-tailed test (i.e., is in excess of 1.64 or 1.96), then it may be concluded that the two groups differ with respect to consensus, as expressed in the ρ_{av} statistic.

It is worthwhile to mention, here, that the procedure exemplified by formula III-6 is also suitable for comparing those intercorrelations which have been obtained by averaging a number of correlations — i.e., where each subject contributes one correlation towards the average of their group, as described in Section 3.9.1. In addition, it is clear from the comments of Hartley (1953) and others (Edwards, 1950, p. 136; McNemar, 1969, p. 158) that this procedure is applicable irrespective of whether the means are based on *rho*s or product moment correlations. Accordingly, formula III-6 was employed to test for sex-differences in both Chapters 3 and 5, and could be applied to the correlations appearing in Chapters 7 and 8 as well.

While the test outlined here is satisfactory in most respects, the need to obtain true rankings does introduce some undesirable complications. Recalling that the true rankings are based on the mean rankings, the greatest difficulty arises when there is a tie in the means. Considering that ties are not permitted in the criterion ranking (Cureton, 1958, 1965) — or the true ranking as it is referred to here — it is necessary to assign true ranks to the offending targets in a more or less arbitrary manner whenever ties are encountered. Kendall (1948) has suggested that the stimulus with the greater variance should receive the more neutral true rank in the case of ties, but even this option is sufficiently arbitrary to leave doubts.

The prohibition against ties in the criterion rank or true rank also leads to a considerable increase in programming complexity when data are analyzed by means of computer. True rankings can, as an alternative, be obtained manually and input along with the data, but this is a retrograde and surprisingly time consuming task.

Because of these difficulties, we decided to consider a third avenue to the measurement of consensus — by a direct substitution of mean rankings (M_rs) for true rankings (T_rs) in the computation of an average correlation comparable in kind to that of the ρ_{av} discussed above. The results of this endeavour are treated in the sections which follow.

III-4 The $\bar{r}_{iM}$ statistic — A measure of concordance based on the substitution of mean-rankings for true rankings in the computation of average correlations

As a first step it was necessary to derive a formula of minimal complexity for finding the average correlation when each individual ranking is correlated with the mean rankings ($M_r s$) obtained from the group as a whole. This process is the exact equivalent of computing ρav, with the sole exception of substituting mean ranks for true ranks (T_rs). It can be shown by means of straightforward algebra that the new statistic — designated as r_{iM} — can be calculated with the aid of the following formula,

$$\bar{r}_{iM} = \sqrt{\frac{\frac{1}{n}\ \Sigma M_r^2 - GM^2}{\frac{1}{12}\ (n^2 - 1)}} \qquad \text{(III-7)}$$

where M_r corresponds to the mean ranks ascribed to the targets, n the number of targets, and GM is again the grand mean, as described on p. 307 above. An example of this statistic is shown in Table III-1.

Having found a convenient means of computing r_{iM}, the next task was to ascertain if it could be substituted for the computationally more difficult ρ_{av} statistic. As a first step a Monte Carlo procedure — providing 500 pseudo random samples for each combination of parameters (i.e. sample size versus number of stimuli) — was employed to investigate the behaviour of ρ_{av} and r_{iM} under null expectations. In carrying out this investigation, data were collected for sample sizes of 25, 50, 75 and 100 under conditions of 3, 4, 5 and 6 stimuli, resulting in the generation of

8,000 pairs of ρ_{av}s and r_{iM}s. For all conditions the correlations between these two statistics were very large, being 0.994 on average. Turning to the coefficients themselves, it was found that riM was, on average, 0.01 larger than ρ_{av}, so for example that data yielding a ρ_{av} of 0.180 would be expected to provide a $\bar{r}_{iM}$ of, say, 0.181. Clearly, there is a close correspondence between these two statistics when the majority of test pairs are small and nonsignificant.

To get a picture of the performance of these two statistics under more realistic conditions — i.e. when the majority of coefficients were significantly greater than zero — we simply reanalized all the data contained in the present studies plus those available from a later study of somewhat greater scope (Powell, 1977; Powell & Stewart, 1978). In all, 614 supplementary comparisons were obtained by this means, with all but a few of the constituents being significantly greater than zero. The results of this supplementary analyses were remarkably similar to those obtained from the Monte Carlo study, yielding a correlation of 0.992 between the two statistics, and a mean difference of 0.022 in favour of $\bar{r}_{iM}$.

Against this background, it seems reasonable to treat $\bar{r}_{iM}$ as a viable alternative to the computationally more cumbersome ρ_{av} statistic, at least within the range of parameters considered here. Of equal importance, the closeness of this relationship implies that the z test for differences between independent groups, as suggested by Hartley (1953 — see p. 311 above for details), is also appropriate to the new statistic. This latter point is particularly germane here, for as we shall see below it provides an immediate solution to the problem of testing whether Ws from independent groups differ significantly from one another.

The relationship of $\bar{r}_{iM}$ to W and its implications for comparisons among independent Ws. Looking first at the relationship between W and $\bar{r}_{iM}$, it is patently obvious from equations III-3, representing W, and III-7, for $\bar{r}_{iM}$, that the latter statistic is equivalent to the square root of W. In other words, the mean correlation *between subjects* (e.g. W) is, for larger samples, equal to the *square* of the mean correlation *between subjects and criterion* (e.g. $\bar{r}_{iM}$), where the criterion is represented by the mean rankings of targets. Consequently, one can use W to derive $\bar{r}_{iM}$ and with slightly less accuracy, ρ_{av} as well.

Turning to the problem of comparing Ws from independent groups, the invariant and explicit relationship between W and $\bar{r}_{iM}$ implies that what is true of W is also true of the latter statistic — that the finding of a significant difference between $\bar{r}_{iM}$s implies that the corresponding Ws are also significantly different. This being the case, it is only necessary to take the square roots of Ws, transforming them into r_{iM}s, to enable them to be compared in the z procedure outlined by Hartley (1953; Bendig, 1956) and ascertain if they differ significantly from one another (see p. 311 for details).

By way of caution, however, it is necessary to point out that experience with a variety of correlation coefficients of the type being considered here has suggested to us that the use of Hartley's procedure — e.g. the application of z'/ procedures to ranked data — may error strongly on the side of conservatism. It can be suggested, for example, that the nonparametric procedures outlined in Chapter 3 (pp. 83-8) may be considerably more powerful than the z'/transformation detailed here. This matter will not be truely settled until the non-null sampling distribution of W is accurately known — this being a problem which has, however, been pending for some 40 odd years now. We are actively investigating the relationship between r_{iM} and W, and hope the identity found here will facilitate a solution to the problem of the non-null sampling distribution of this otherwise useful statistic.

Index